The development of the family and marriage in Europe

Studies in Literacy, Family, Culture and the State

Works by Jack Goody

LITERACY

Literacy in Traditional Societies (edited, 1968)
The Domestication of the Savage Mind (1977)
The Logic of Writing and the Organization of Society (1986)
The Interface between the Written and the Oral (1987)

FAMILY

Production and Reproduction: A Comparative Study of The Domestic Domain (1977)
The Development of the Family and Marriage in Europe (1983)

CULTURE

Cooking, Cuisine and Class: A Study in Comparative Sociology (1982)

THE STATE

Technology, Tradition and the State in Africa (1971)

The Development of the Family and Marriage in Europe was first published in *Past and Present Publications*.

The development of the family and marriage in Europe

JACK GOODY

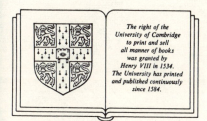

The right of the
University of Cambridge
to print and sell
all manner of books
was granted by
Henry VIII in 1534.
The University has printed
and published continuously
since 1584.

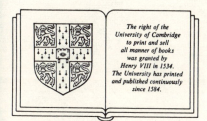

CAMBRIDGE UNIVERSITY PRESS

Cambridge

New York   Port Chester

Melbourne   Sydney

Published by the Press Syndicate of the University of Cambridge
The Pitt Building, Trumpington Street, Cambridge CB2 1RP
40 West 20th Street, New York, NY 10011, USA
10 Stamford Road, Oakleigh, Melbourne 3166, Australia

First published 1983
Reprinted 1984 1985 1986 1988 1990

Printed in Great Britain at the
University Press, Cambridge

Library of Congress catalogue card number: 82–23465

British Library Cataloguing in Publication Data
Goody, Jack
The development of the family and marriage in Europe.
1. Family–Europe
I. Title
306.8'5'094   HQ611

ISBN 0 521 24739 X hard covers
ISBN 0 521 28925 4 paperback

CS

Durum est ab aliquo filiis ac propinquis parum relinqui: multo est durius in aeternitate torqueri. (Salvian, *Ad eccl.* III. 51)

It is hard to leave but a little to sons and near ones; it is much worse to be tortured throughout eternity.

Contents

Figures

Maps

Tables

Preface

There are some undertakings which, while they cannot hope to be fully scholarly in the professional sense, may be illuminated by a particular background of experience and thought, of theory and practice. My own curiosity about how European patterns of kinship, marriage and family came to develop as they did owed something to reading medieval drama, Scottish history, the works of Marc Bloch and George Homans on France and England, and the 'comparative sociology' of the nineteenth-century legal historians and jurists. In trying to make my knowledge somewhat more extensive and up-to-date, I am deeply in debt to a number of scholars on whose generosity and friendship I have presumed. The value of my links with *Past and Present* and with the École des Hautes Études en Sciences Sociales in Paris are apparent. Clemens Heller and La Maison des Sciences de l'Homme have always provided the right combination of interest and disinterest. And it was due to a timely invitation from Pierre Bourdieu that I was able to undertake a final revision over Easter 1982. Keith Hopkins, Keith Thomas, Edward Miller and Patrick Wormald read through substantial portions of the first draft, corrected many errors of fact and made many suggestions. Diane Owen Hughes read the second Appendix and her comments caused me to rethink and reformulate. Chris Dyer offered suggestions and emendations for Chapter 6. Peter Linehan, John Bossy, Keith Wrightson, David Sabean, Robert Pollock and Bob Ombres supplied me with important references. Other colleagues at Cambridge and London, the late Munia Postan, John Hajnal, Alan Macfarlane, Peter Laslett, Tony Wrigley, Richard Smith, have stimulated my interest in various ways. If parts of my argument appear to challenge the trend of some of their more general assumptions (and I have left implicit rather than explicit the implications for theory, hypothesis and for practice), this should not be viewed as confrontation, but as an attempt to suggest the advantages of refocussing the historical eye, of restating the problem from a different perspective.

On the anthropological side I owe a measure of thanks to those who did not consider that I was wasting my time by plunging into such deep waters; members of a series of seminars beginning at Nanterre (1979), Aix-en-Provence, Harvard, Berkeley, Santa Cruz, London, and especially at Stanford where, as a conjugal visitor to the Center of Advanced Studies in the Behavioral Sciences from December to April 1979–80, I found the right combination of intellectual stimulus, access to libraries and freedom to write. My thanks are due to Dan Sperber, Ernest Gellner, S. J. Tambiah, Gene Hammel, Lokki Pandey and Sylvia Yanagisako for arranging these sessions, as well as to Terry Turner for a less formal occasion and to the late Tom (L. A.) Fallers for a passing conversation. In Cambridge, Martha Mundy and Paul Sant Cassia helped sustain my interest and widen my knowledge.

In preparing the manuscript, I am most grateful to Norman Buck of the Library of St John's College for constant help over the years, to Cathie Roth, Jane Moon and Penny Clarke, for assistance with research, and to Anne Robson and Lucia Szeto for the labour of typing various versions. Patricia Williams and Sue Allen-Mills were, as always, the most helpful of editors.

In the final stages I was most grateful to C. R. Whittaker for reading the opening chapters and for making corrections and suggestions. Unfortunately I was at this point unable to follow up his doubts that A.D. 321 saw the beginning of the Church's right to receive inheritances. But he sees the extent of the donations of Constantine as crucial in the transformation of the Church, much of whose success depended upon its *elimonia*, its charity.

My approach to the material that follows may not always satisfy all the conventions of historical scholarship. I have not in every case used the 'standard' editions of works; sometimes because I did not always know what these were, and sometimes because I work in a peripatetic fashion and use what is available wherever I am. Also there are topics on which I should have read more and in more languages. But one has to compromise with the realities of the allocation of time and the desire to develop a line of argument in a field one can never, in an academic sense, make one's own.

JACK GOODY

1. *Perspectives*

For the last hundred and fifty years the study of the European family and marriage has been dominated by the growing preoccupation of scholars about their links with the great events that took place in the West at the outset of the modern period. What was the relationship of the family with the Reformation outside and inside the Catholic Church, with the growth of capitalism and the coming of industrial society? The question has world-wide implications. For the problem of 'the rise of the West', which gripped the intellectual imagination of Marx, Weber, and countless others, is closely linked with 'the uniqueness of the West'. What precisely did happen to marriage and the family at this period? What aspects of the pre-existing family might have assisted these changes? What features resulted from the new forms of socio-economic organisation?

Clearly the separation of production from the domestic group, the growth of non-familial education, the dispersal of kin, had important implications for the household. Demographically, the improvement in mortality and the control of fertility led to a sharp rise, followed by a drop, in the rates of population growth, a demographic transition that resulted in fewer and longer-lived children, and, according to some, in a radical change in our attitudes towards them.

Some of these developments, such as the demographic transition for example, clearly follow, even if they do not necessarily follow from, the vast socio-economic changes that have occurred in the West beginning in the sixteenth century. But were there earlier aspects of family, kinship and marriage that actually encouraged the mobility, the saving, the 'bilaterality', the 'love', the 'individualism' that is seen as characteristic of the modern world? Were these aspects peculiar to Europe, to Western Europe, to north-west Europe, or even to England? Some contemporary historians have seen features such as conjugal affection as following after, or developing

1

concurrently with, the rise of the West. Others see late marriage for men and women, the close elementary family, 'individualism', as being unique features of the European scene at an earlier period, which positively assisted the socio-economic transformations in that continent.

Here is not the place to examine these various arguments in detail. What I try to do in this essay is to approach the problem from quite a different perspective, different in both time and space. As for time, most of the historians, sociologists and economists who have tackled these questions have done so from the standpoint of contemporary concerns, looking from the present backwards to try and account for the rise of capitalism, for the advent of the Industrial Revolution or for those special features which they regard as unique to their own society. None of us can entirely divest ourselves of our cultural clothing, nor is such nudity always becoming. But one area where we need to exercise particular caution, indeed restraint, is in the study of the family itself, especially when examining the 'affective' aspects of the fundamental relations between its members, which we have all experienced from various angles. Assumptions based on an ethnocentric version of ameliorative evolutionism have to be worked over with special care. Looking back at the 'Bad Old Days' (the phrase used by Shorter in his history of the modern family) to see how things have 'improved' (neglecting on the way the higher incidence of divorce, suicide and mental breakdown) is not the most detached approach. Moreover, even to think of making an assessment of this (or any other) kind, we need to be quite sure of what we mean by concepts like love and lineage, individualism and patriarchy, not to speak of the more technical terms, because otherwise we are unable to assess similarity or difference, either before or after the rise of the West, or even when comparing the West as against the Rest.

Chronologically, the studies of these authors may begin in 1500 or 1800; conceptually, their orientation is backwards from today. The difficulty with this backward look is that it tends to overvalue the present – in either a positive or a negative way. The concerns of the present, one's own present, stand in the way of understanding the past, especially when one is offering, or more usually implying, some kind of causal or functional link between family and society. They lead to the adoption, as so often throughout the social sciences, or, indeed, in the folk concepts of everyday discourse (which are not so very different), of a dichotomous approach that draws a sharp line between we and they, between modern and traditional, capitalist and pre-capitalist. But this array of binary categories has limited value when the problem is to try and analyse differences and similarities in patterns of family, kin and marriage over the longer term and the wider range. Everything 'traditional' gets lumped together in one undifferentiated mass, as is the case with Weber's concepts of 'authority' or with many notions of peasantry. Such dichotomies, rooted in the present day, inevitably tend to overstress the special, unique features of the 'modern'. A recognition of this deep-rooted bias should lead one to query hypotheses that appear to privilege the West, not simply in its technological achievement but in its spiritual and moral claims both before and after the sixteenth century. Was Protestantism quite such a unique theological and ethical force in economic affairs? Were capitalist social relations characteristic only of the West? Was the world of 'traditional authority', of Islam, Buddhism and Hinduism, of the 'Asiatic mode of production', really so different, then and now, as our categories and theories assume? Was it not these same 'static', 'traditional', 'despotic' societies that in the fifteenth century and before were intellectually, commercially and culturally 'modern', in contrast to a relatively backward Europe?

These questions highlight issues of great intellectual and historical importance. I raise them because my analysis of the structure and development of certain features of the European family focusses on a much earlier period than is often granted. I raise them to justify an approach to European institutions and attitudes that starts from the beginning of the present era, from the Mediterranean and Middle Eastern roots of the ideology which has been so pervasive over the last two thousand years, in domestic as well as in theological matters, in politics as in production. But in addition to a temporal and conceptual perspective on the family that tackles 'la longue durée' from the other end, I have tried to look at these European institutions and attitudes from the standpoint not only of our own past but from a comparative perspective that starts elsewhere. Hence the approach again differs from that of historians who seek to contrast their findings on the family with an undifferentiated traditional, pre-industrial, non-European, or 'anthropological' world.

My own starting point, at least in terms of field research, lay elsewhere, in West Africa. The research was concerned with domestic groups – their structure and sentiments, the role of the lineage, marriage arrangements – the whole area of what Morgan called consanguinity and affinity, what anthropologists now refer to as kinship and sociologists as the family; it is a field that covers the spheres of interest of Freud in the psychology of relationships, of Marx in the economics of production, and of demographers in the statistics of household composition. It was a subject that continued to be a central focus of my empirical research and theoretical problems, and it was mainly rooted in the African experience.

This research suggested that some general features of 'African Systems of Kinship and Marriage' (to use the title of a seminal collection of essays) stood out in contrast to those reported for the major societies of the settled areas of Asia, the Middle East and North Africa – for, like the distinguished editors of the series on African systems of politics, religion and kinship, I use the term Africa as a convenient 'shorthand' for Black or sub-Saharan Africa. It seemed that we needed to seek an explanation for these differences and similarities, an explanation which was not simply phrased in terms of African or Eurasian predispositions, whether cultural or genetic, but in the specific links of these features with other aspects of the social system, and particularly with the 'modes of production', the concerns of livelihood. The results of this enquiry were embodied in an earlier book, *Production and Reproduction: a comparative study of the domestic domain* (1976) where I tried first to predict, then test, the distribution of monogamy and polygyny, of dowry and bridewealth, of in-marriage and out-marriage, of adoption and terminologies for kin, which seemed to be linked to attitudes and sentiments within the domestic group on the one hand, and, on the other, to interests of a socio-economic kind.

This enquiry went part of the way to resolving, for me at least, some of the problems raised in comparing Black Africa with the major societies of Asia and Europe. But from the later Roman Empire onwards, the situation in Europe raised further queries, for family and marriage differed in certain important ways from the more general pattern of the major Eurasian societies, from what existed earlier in Rome and other parts of southern Europe, and from what continued to exist on the other, North African, shore of the Mediterranean. That was the problem. How was it that after about A.D. 300 certain general features of European patterns of kinship and marriage came to take a different shape from those of ancient Rome, Greece, Israel and Egypt, and from those of the societies of the Mediterranean shores of the Middle East and North Africa that succeeded them? This was not true of all the variables I had earlier discussed – for example, monogamy and the dowry – but it did apply to some important aspects of the domestic domain which have influenced the course of social life until very recent times, and which continue to do so even today. The ones with which I shall be most concerned will be spelled out in the course of the next two chapters; others, perhaps not less important, will be discussed in the concluding chapters.

2. *Two sides to the Mediterranean*

From the vantage point of a broad, geopolitical approach to history, the unity of the Mediterranean world is an obvious fact of life. The French historian, Fernand Braudel, has stressed how the lives of its inhabitants from different countries were influenced by the problems and advantages posed by their common frontier on the inland sea, especially their shared experiences of changes in climate and in population, and their joint involvement in trade and warfare. But there was also diversity, consisting not simply of small differences but of broad oppositions. A recent historical study of the Spanish-African frontier insists that 'the separation of the Mediterranean world into different, well-defined cultural spheres is the main theme of its sixteenth-century history' (Hess 1978: 3); Latin Christian culture had always been opposed to Turko-Muslim civilisation throughout the Middle Ages, but now the opposition increased as the Crescent was surrounded by the Cross with its superiority of ship and gun.

The question of whether the emphasis should be placed on diversity or unity impinges very directly on the spheres of family, kinship and marriage. To some writers, especially from a northern viewpoint, the systems that obtain on the European and African shores now and in the past, seem to differ very radically. Yet others, stimulated not only by the works of Braudel but by the growing interest in 'Mediterranean studies', have been impressed by the common features in the daily life of the inhabitants of the two shores of the sea. The former emphasise the part played by descent groups, by close marriage and by polygyny among the Arabs in contrast with the societies of Europe to the north; the latter stress the common role of dowry, perceive bilateral elements in the schema of unilineal descent and point to the notions of honour and shame that mark the whole of the Mediterranean world.

The unitarian view is expressed very clearly by Solinas writing of the contemporary Mediterranean family in a volume edited by Braudel: 'Among many Mediterranean peoples there is a remarkable continuity in the way of living and in conceptions of life in its moral, social, economic and biological aspects; sexual love, jealousy, respect towards the elders, filial love, feelings about death and beyond, all imply the same idea of the family' (1977: II,92). Stated in these terms the similarities should not be taken too seriously. There are few parts of the world in which this array of features could not be found and declarations of such a kind, which abound in the writings of Western historians of the family, must be judged for what they are, ethnocentric expressions of ignorance of the wider world. Looked at in a more precise and technical manner – and it is not easy to be precise unless we are technical, as many of the arguments about the European past bring out – there are some powerful similarities in daily life to be discerned when we set the Circum-Mediterranean area as a whole against the background of, say, Africa south of the Sahara (which I shall often call Africa for short). This contrast is specially marked if we raise our eyes beyond the striking features of the nomadic Bedouin tribes and focus upon the settled elements of the Middle East, the region which was the *fons et origo* of the early civilisation that eventually spread out to overwhelm a backward Europe.

These differences in forms of inheritance and marriage payment are related to differences in the systems of production, which in that earlier work (1976b) I saw as characterising the major societies of the Eurasian continent in contrast to those of Black Africa. In this context, the settled societies of the Middle East and North Africa formed part of the general Eurasian constellation. In that study I did not intend to elaborate a monolithic single-factor theory, nor yet one that failed to allow for counter-examples; to establish a positive association is already an achievement. Nevertheless, it was clear that after the end of the Roman Empire there were important differences in the domestic domain between the two sides of the Mediterranean that have since persisted over a long period. With regard to some of these features, the European shore runs counter to the general theory I proposed. Other areas, too, diverge with regard to close marriage for example, but we cannot simply leave aside the whole continent of Europe as a partial and unexplained exception, especially when evidence exists that in classical times Europe did not differ in these particular ways, and when the systems of marriage and the family in that continent have been linked to the great socio-economic changes that took place there in modern times. It is a critical case, so we need to explore these differences and their historical development not only in order to elaborate the theory we have earlier proposed but also to try to throw further light on the question of the uniqueness of the West.

First we need to establish what these differences are by taking up the contrast between the two sides of the Mediterranean – Europe on the one hand, North Africa on the other – during the medieval and early modern periods.

A number of caveats need to be entered before beginning this enterprise. First, I will concentrate upon a particular set of features of marriage, family and kinship that arise partly out of my previous studies but mainly out of the accounts of early European writers themselves; I am concerned only indirectly with that important set of factors analysed by demographic historians under the heading of 'the European marriage pattern'. Second, even when European features are examined in a comparative way by historians of the Mediterranean, the terms of the discussion need clarifying. And third, it has to be remembered that we are dealing with regions that vary regionally and hierarchically.

'European marriage patterns' were the subject of an article by Hajnal (1965) in which he draws a contrast between Western Europe and the totality of 'non-European', 'traditional' or 'developing' countries (including Eastern Europe). The main features of this pattern were delayed marriage for both women and men, and a high degree of celibacy, features that were linked demographically with relatively low crude rates of births (below 40 per thousand) and, less certainly, of deaths. Since women marry later than in other societies, there are more young adult females in the labour force who are able to accumulate wealth of their own. When they eventually marry and have children, they are more mature, a fact that suggests a particular set of relations between husbands and wives, and between parents and children, which may be associated with the existence of separate dwellings and smaller holdings for married couples.

The notion of the uniqueness of a late marriage for women and of frequent celibacy for both sexes may require some modification in view of the evidence from twentieth-century Tibet and from Roman Egypt, even if this is less substantial than one would like. In Egypt Hopkins writes of a ten-year post-pubertal delay for women

(1980: 333) while in a survey earlier this century among the Khams of eastern Tibet, there were numerous unmarried women and nearly 40 per cent of households had no married couple (Carrasco 1959: 69). The failure to achieve uniqueness would not make the facts any the less important to explain; it would tend to reduce the claims that this demographic regime is linked by a causal nexus with the rise of the West, that is, of Western Europe.

While Hajnal suggested that these patterns emerged in the late sixteenth century and were possibly to be linked with the development of capitalism and Protestantism, other writers have seen these same features as present in a yet earlier period, but characterising the north-west rather than the whole of Western Europe.[1] Some take the view that England was unique in these and other important respects, and Macfarlane has recently seen this singularity as including the presence of a strongly 'individualistic' streak, which he tentatively derives from its roots in the German woods (1978: 206). Those who find these features present before the sixteenth century see them as predisposing factors in the rise of capitalism.

I want to look at a different set of inter-related characteristics, which are not identical with those that have occupied the attention of demographic writers, historians of the modern family or sociologists of modernisation. This is partly because of the different direction of my approach but also because some of the features they have dealt with, such as the emergence of the nuclear family, love and individualism, seem to require a great deal of reconsideration and reformulation. The factors with which I am concerned are certainly linked with some of those variables; yet these factors are not ones that supposedly distinguish medieval from modern Europe nor yet pre-industrial (undeveloped) from industrial (developed) societies. On the contrary, the significant change seems to have occurred towards the end of the Roman Empire. In trying to specify how they differed, I am also attempting to explain why they differed and to analyse the process that led to the shattering of the unity of Circum-

---

[1] Hajnal himself thought that medieval villagers did not follow a 'European marriage pattern'; Razi has given support to this idea, finding that in the pre-plague period in the village of Halesowen in the West Midlands of England, marriages took place between the ages of 18 and 22 (1980: 63; also Dyer 1980: 234); however the basis of the calculations has been criticised by Smith (1979: 112), who, like Macfarlane, leans towards the view that the late marriage of women is early and English. See also Smith's valuable comments (1981) on Herlihy and Klapisch-Zuber (1978).

Mediterranean patterns. As a starting point it is useful to turn to one of the main meeting-grounds between the two sides of the Mediterranean in the medieval period, namely, the Spanish 'frontier', internal as well as external, between the Islamic and the Christian worlds.

'EASTERN AND WESTERN STRUCTURES'

Of a number of very interesting contributions to the social history of medieval Spain, the most relevant is the account by Guichard (1977) of the encounter between what he calls 'Eastern' and 'Western' social structures as the result of the Arab invasion of the country in the eighth century. The background to his enquiry is the way in which the contact between the Christian West and the Muslim East has been viewed in the setting of Spanish history. Earlier historians regarded the 'Arab' conquest (711–1031) as constituting a hiatus in time, a devastating invasion that reduced the local population to servitude. Subsequent writers pointed out that most of the people stayed where they were, continuing the same practices as before, and that the invaders themselves adapted to these local traditions. Guichard contends that neither approach, devastation or absorption, is satisfactory, and that the Eastern and Western structures continued actively to oppose one another until the final withdrawal of the Moors from Spain to North Africa. Each group, conquerors and conquered, retained their separate ways of organising the domestic domain, ways that linked them with Europe on the one hand and the Middle East on the other.

What were the major features of these two systems? Guichard (1977: 19) presents a tentative model on the basis of six characteristics (see Table 1): (1) system of 'filiation' or descent; (2) the conjugal pair; (3) kin groups; (4) matrimonial alliances; (5) the position of women; and (6) notions of honour.

These characteristics, phrased in a variety of ways, have often been adduced in drawing contrasts between the social systems of Europe and the Middle East over the last thirteen hundred years. There is undoubtedly a difference of emphasis, in some features more than others, and to this we will return. However, if we look at these features from the standpoint not of Europe, or North Africa, but of Africa south of the Sahara, the differences in emphasis do, I suggest, seem rather slight. The same is broadly true of marriage

Table 1. *Western and Eastern structures* (according to Guichard 1977: 19)

		Oriental structure	Occidental structure
1	System of descent (*filiation*)	Strictly patrilineal (only kinship in the paternal line counts)	Clearly bilineal (great importance given to the maternal family and to marriages (*alliances*)
2	Conjugal pair	has little strength because of patrilineality (*agnatisme*), polygyny and ease of divorce	The basic cell of social organisation because of bilineality (*cognatisme*), the tradition of monogamy, and the weakness of more extended kin groups.
3	Kin groups	Derived from the segmentary tribal system. The basis is the agnatic lineage (*lignée*), a group clearly defined in time and space in relation to an ancestor, bound together by *'asibiyya* (solidarity) and having a great influence at all social levels.	In the aristocracy alone, the ascending kindred (*parentèle bilatérale*), which does not exist in itself but only in relation to each individual, therefore having no continuity in time, nor cohesion in space.
4	Matrimonial alliances	The agnatic group has strongly endogamous tendencies. Preferred marriage is with the father's brother's daughter. To give a wife to another lineage (*lignage*) is dishonourable and the wife-takers are superior to the wife-givers.	Tendency towards exogamy. Endogamy is also found but for economic rather than social reasons. Marriage alliances are valued; women circulate, bringing goods and honour; the wife-givers tend to be superior to the wife-takers.
5	Position of women	Strict separation of the sexes and exclusion of women from the public sphere.	No rigid separation of the sexes; in the Germanic tradition, women appear to be able to play a public role and to have some political authority.

Table 1. (*cont.*)

	Oriental structure	Occidental structure
6 Notion of honour	Arising from being rather than having; feminine honour is passive, masculine honour, active.	Honour is tied to the possession of a title, a rank or riches; it can therefore be handed on and circulated in the social system.

transactions. The so-called brideprice payments among the Arabs, as is the case with the payments listed in the earliest European version of the 'barbarian' laws, were largely directed to the bride, not to her kin (though they may pass through her father) and thus constitute a form of what I have called 'indirect dowry'. I need to substantiate these points before examining what seem to me more significant differences and this makes it necessary to refer to some technical and definitional arguments about the nature of these features in a wider comparative perspective. These arguments are elaborated in Appendices 1 and 2. So that the chronological and thematic course of my essay does not become too interrupted, I refer yet a further discussion to Appendix 3, in which I broach the question, touched upon by Guichard, Macfarlane and others, of the bilateral nature of European institutions and the claim that this is revealed in the terms that were used to address and refer to kinsfolk. Here, as elsewhere, 'bilaterality' is a slippery concept to deal with but I would argue that it is implicit not only in all European systems but in all Circum-Mediterranean ones as well.

KIN GROUPS AND GROUPINGS: SUCCESSION, INHERITANCE AND DESCENT

The major focus of Guichard's attention is on 'the system of descent' and 'kin groups' (items 1 and 3) which, as his remarks imply, can well be considered together.[2] The presence of strong patrilineal groups in North Africa is also seen as directly linked to the weak

---

[2] In Table 1 I have translated the French term 'filiation' by the English 'descent'. In English anthropological usage the two terms have been distinguished, descent referring to eligibility to membership of a kin group (following Rivers) and hence to its genealogical framework. Some writers have confined the usage to unilineal

nature of the conjugal bond, to the prevalence of polygyny, the ease of divorce, and more generally to the low position of women, which Guichard considers under different heads (2, 4, 5 and 6). Here I want to take a closer look at the difference that is said to exist on the level of descent and filiation, partly with a view to shifting attention elsewhere. In so doing I shall refer to the African situation, now and in the past, because in this way one can place the European and North African material on kin groups in a more satisfactory perspective than has been provided by much earlier comparative work.

Here I return to my third caveat. In considering either the history of North Africa or developments in the European past, we have to be clear whether we are dealing with tribal or with settled regions (not to speak of differences between the classes within those areas). The role of kin groups and the nature of 'filiation' differed radically in each, a point that has been well documented by Peters (1976) for the recent past. In the settled areas Islamic law and practice allocate a dowry to women and permit them to inherit the conjugal property of their parents, though they may not enforce this claim, leaving their share in the hands of their brothers in return for other, less material, benefits (Mundy 1979). In those farming and urban areas, the extensive agnatic lineages so characteristic of the tribal peoples (where the written norms of Islamic law received a different weight-

descent groups (to clans or lineages), although others, taking the term more literally, have applied it to 'descending kindreds' and similar groupings that are recruited and organised around both paternal and maternal filiation. In English the term 'filiation' refers to parent-child links that are necessarily 'bilateral' in virtually all societies.

Since these links with kin are used across a wide variety of contexts of social action (eligibility to kin groups, succession to office, transmission of property, all kinds of behaviour between kin) we cannot oppose societies as 'patrilineal' versus 'bilateral', unless we restrict the usage to the presence or absence of particular features, e.g. patrilineal descent groups. In these varied contexts, links to and through males or females are always given a differential stress; to describe these differences I would myself avoid the terms 'patrilineal' and 'matrilineal', using paternal and maternal for the immediate links of filiation, masculine and feminine for those *to* males and females, and agnatic and uterine for those *through* males or females. These usages are not standard; but the distinctions to which they refer (not necessarily the terms) are essential (indeed are minimal) if we are to understand the variety of human organisations and the way they have changed over time. A significant number of problems in the analysis of family and kinship could be cleared away by more careful distinctions, definitions and usages. Many existing controversies and hypotheses are generated by ambiguities inherent in terms like 'patriarchal' and by the tendency to deal crudely in the presence or absence of qualities (affection, etc.) when it is more subtle ways of discrimination that are required.

Map 1 Europe: mountains and plains

Land over 1000 m
Coniferous forests
Marshland areas
Land suitable for agriculture

Plateaus
Deserts
Poor land

ing) are less significant than bilateral ties. As Ibn Khaldun long ago pointed out, the solidarity of the lineage was radically modified in the urban setting; while some importance was still attached to carrying the same patronymic (the same 'surname'), any groupings that emerged were very different both from the segmentary lineages of the pastoral tribes and the kin groups of the farming population.

Europe itself was differentiated in a similar way until very recent times. In presenting his picture of the early modern period, Braudel has drawn a broad contrast between the civilisation of the plains and, on the one hand, the hill zones, and, on the other, the cleared forests of northern Europe. In the forest and on the hill, as later in America, all one needed was a pick and an axe to make the land productive. But in the Mediterranean plains, rich and powerful landowners were instrumental in the organisation of production, the optimum level of which could be achieved only by a disciplined social order. Egypt and Mesopotamia were never farmed by independent peasants. In Spain, travelling from the dry to the irrigated zones meant leaving behind a 'relatively free peasant to find a peasant slave' (1972 [1966]: 75), inherited from the Muslims with the irrigation system during their long occupation from the eighth to the fifteenth centuries. The plains, argues Braudel, were 'the property of the nobleman', in Spain, in Portugal, in Italy, as in the irrigated lands of the Moroccan Sous, where, once again, the gap between rich and poor was much greater than in the hill areas.[3] It was the same in the great plains of the Balkans, in Bulgaria, Rumelia and in Thrace, where the Turkish regime of large estates and serf-villages took strong root, as it never succeeded in doing in the mountains. Of course there were exceptions. In some plains, such as the early Roman Campagna, the lands of Roussillon in southern France, or in much of Provence, there were small and medium-sized farms; after 1486, Catalonia was a land of prosperous peasantry. Nevertheless, Braudel maintains, a general contrast is found. The difference had an important influence on the organisation of kin groups. For it was in the hill areas, the areas of freedom from the imposition of State and landlord, that clans played a significant role.

So in Europe, as in the Middle East, the settled agriculturalists tended to be more bilateral, while clan organisations, giving a

---

[3] On the difference between the French nobility of the highlands and lowlands, see Le Roy Ladurie 1978: 14ff,97.

greater emphasis to branching agnatic kinship, were found in the less accessible regions, not only among pastoralists but also among those involved in a predatory economy, though the two occupations were not always distinct. Indeed, the presence of such groups may have enabled the tribal systems of the Basques and Cantabri to meet the challenge of the Muslim invaders from North Africa more effectively than the inhabitants of the plains, since their similar segmentary organisation prepared them for the continual warfare that true resistance required (Glick 1979: 142).[4]

Although such differences existed in the organisation of kin groups and groupings, the contrast must not be drawn too dramatically. No kinship system is entirely agnatic; even where we find patrilineal clans or lineages (which should not be confused with the *lignages* of medieval scholarship, see Appendix 1), that is, large ramifying descent groups organised on a unilineal basis by means of recruitment through the father, kinship relations are almost invariably bilateral since ties also exist with and through the other parent, ties that are often of political and social importance. The same is true of matrilineal clans. The kind of rigid exclusion that is often posited by Guichard and other writers is rarely found, even when unilineal criteria are used by groups, and recognised by the actors, as a means of recruitment and organisation. For though descent groups are unilineal, kinship is everywhere bilateral.

In the period of the classical civilisations, forms of clan organisation appear to have existed right round the Mediterranean, as it still does among the pastoral peoples of North Africa and some hill tribes of the Balkans, and in very residual forms in Ireland and Scotland. In the early medieval period, the existence of patrilineal clans among the peripheral Celtic peoples is well attested (Patterson 1979). But there is also evidence of such groups among other Indo-European peoples. In

---

[4] The usage of the term 'segmentary' in the social sciences is drawn from Durkheim's analysis of the division of labour. It was employed by him with reference to the Kabyles of North Africa and subsequently in Montagne's study of the Berbers (1930); the concept was greatly elaborated in Evans-Pritchard's classic account of the Nuer (1940) and has since been widely used in social anthropology to characterise the process of association and opposition of nested social groups at different levels of inclusiveness. The word has been used for a certain type of non-centralised (or acephalous) polity, such as that of the typical Bedouin tribe, in which this process forms the basis of the political system; but I have argued elsewhere (1957) that such a usage is better avoided since, while the process is of great importance to 'tribes without rulers', it is in no sense confined to them.

reviewing the literature on Europe, Anderson remarks that although it is difficult to define the exact nature of the Celtic *clann*, the Greek *genos* and the German *Sippe*, we do find patrilineal, exogamous clans – of the type of the *gotra* of modern India – in the *fis* of Albania and the *plemé* of Montenegro, as late as the early part of this century (1963: 3–4). In the Eastern Mediterranean there is much earlier evidence of clans among the Ancient Hebrews, the Ottoman Turks, the Ancient Greeks, and the Romans – all civilisations that we know from the written word – although in general the importance of these groups appears to have been limited; they were certainly not exogamous, indeed their members were often encouraged to marry in rather than out. In the settled areas of Mediterranean Europe they disappeared altogether in the post-Roman period, even in their residual forms. But in North Africa a clan organisation was re-established, or reinforced, as a result of the seventh-century invasions of the Arabs, who had a strong tradition of nomadic pastoralism. This invasion entailed not only the substitution of a more diffusely organised Islam for the highly centralised Christianity of the Roman Church, but also the re-introduction of 'oriental' structures of kinship and marriage, that helped to set the northern shores of the inland sea apart from the southern littoral. I say re-introduction because Guichard (1977: 342) observes that the process of Romanisation, beginning with the defeat of the Carthaginians in the Second Punic War (201 B.C.), had led to the disappearance of the *gentilitates* in Spain.[5] Clearly it is difficult to know what kind of *gens* this had been, but the notion that Rome, and Roman Christianity, did away with clan organisation is in itself significant. Did the same occur in North Africa under Christianity? What happened when the Germanic peoples and other barbarian tribes over-ran the Roman Empire and occupied the Balkans, Italy, North Africa and Spain, and became converts to Christianity? Their laws reveal little emphasis on unilineal structures of any kind.

---

[5] Glick assumes that the *gens* of the Hispano-Romans was 'patrilineal and agnatic', in contrast to 'the matrilineal systems of the Cantabi and Basques' (1979: 142). Both are contrasted with the bilateral systems of later Europeans. As I explain in Appendix 1, by patrilineal systems of descent I mean the reckoning of membership to, or organisation of, a unilineal descent group, that is, a clan or lineage. Agnatic I use in a more general sense for relations through males. All systems are bilateral in one sense; but the word may also be used for societies where unilineal descent groups are absent. Bilateral societies may be given different values of agnatic or uterine emphasis depending on the context of interaction.

The difficulties in reaching an understanding of the social organisation of these early European peoples are many. For in the virtual
absence of any indigenous writing before their conversion we see
them only through Roman eyes, or else after contact with Rome, with
Christianity, and with the developed economy of the Mediterranean,
which transformed their societies in very radical ways. Among the
Germanic peoples, the evidence of the Anglo-Saxons, those post-
Roman settlers in a peripheral Roman colony, is in some ways the
clearest. At the dynastic level at least, they operated by means of an
agnatic genealogy by which local rulers traced their roots back to the
god Woden, and even to Adam (Stenton 1971: 19; Sisam 1953: 305
and Bede's *History*); starting from this apical ancestor, the calculus
appeared to spread out in the way that distinguishes the branching
genealogy of a lineage from the lineal pedigree possessed by every
royal house. However, at the local level of social organisation, we find
bilateral groupings (specific personal and descending kindreds, not
merely the universal bilateral reckoning of kinship) were significant
in matters, for example, of inheritance and feud; given the diffuse
nature of the authority structure of the kingdom, the protection given
to individuals by such groupings of kin was a factor of great significance,[6] for in weakly centralised states, justice is more often obtained
through organised self-help.

Whatever the situation may have been earlier, the Anglo-Saxon
England we learn about from literature and records was marked by
the absence of patrilineal clans – and hence of patrilineal descent, in
the technical sense of eligibility for such groups, the criteria by
which they are recruited or organised.[7] Kin groupings (or ranges)
were bilateral; that is, they were neither recruited nor organised on a
patrilineal or a matrilineal basis. Responsibility for vengeance
spread out through maternal and paternal kin.[8] Nevertheless, given

[6] For a recent and very thorough discussion of early medieval genealogies, see
Dumville 1977.
[7] On this topic see Philpotts 1913, Gluckman 1955, Lancaster 1958, Black-Michaud
1975, and other writers.
[8] In medieval Castile responsibility for violence was also a 'bilateral' affair (which
Glick regards as 'Germanic'); vengeance for the murder of a relative was not a
crime if the avenger had the same great-great-grandfather as the original victim
(Glick 1979: 142). Gradually responsibilities shifted away from kin. Kinship solidarities, especially in the shape of the 'extended family', diminished in the high
Middle Ages as public authorities ensured personal security; as the Church promoted the 'Peace of God'; as guilds and military orders replaced other ties; and as

that post-marital residence was usually virilocal, that is, women went to live with their husbands who in turn often resided with or near their fathers, and given that offices were by and large transmitted between men, the system of kinship had a definite bias in favour of the agnatic line. In another context, however, the 'bilateral' emphasis of the system received further underpinning in the way that property was devolved between the generations. Both men and women had claims on the funds established at the marriage of their parents, either in the form of an endowment at marriage or by way of inheritance at their death.

MARRIAGE TRANSACTIONS AND INHERITANCE TRANSFERS

A bride could receive transfers not only from her own but also from her husband's parents. The latter transfers I call 'indirect dowry', although many authors use the term 'brideprice' – misleadingly in my opinion since brideprice (now usually known as 'bridewealth' in order to avoid the implications of 'bridepurchase') is already employed for a very different kind of payment found in many sub-Saharan African societies. This problem is examined in greater detail in Appendix 2.

As a marital transfer or assign, dowry was characteristic of the major societies of the ancient Mediterranean, and probably of most, if not all, systems of clanship in Europe. The very fact that women as well as men are given these rights in money, goods or land means that the notion, and especially the practice, of clanship differed in certain important respects from the sub-Saharan African model. First, in Europe and the Mediterranean women acquired property from males as well as from females, at marriage, through inheritance, or both; this was so virtually from the earliest times of which we have knowledge. Under a bridewealth system of the African kind, women are the subjects of transfers of property between males at marriage, not the recipients of those goods; their inheritance is from other females rather than from fathers, brothers or husbands.

---

as urbanisation and colonisation fragmented kinship bonds. 'Feudal relations, involving the dependency of unrelated persons, were . . . substitutions for bonds formerly maintained within the kindred circle' (p. 143). I argue that the actions and ideas of the Church played a significant part in this process, but these important socio-political factors were also at work.

Second, through direct dowry or inheritance women take property out of their family of birth and possibly, if such groups are also 'out-marrying', out of the clan altogether. If such transfers include land (or livestock in pastoral societies), the movement to a woman's family of marriage raises important problems for the clan or its segments. Since resources are split up as the result of the out-marriage of daughters – whether this division occurs in practice at betrothal, in the course of the marriage or at the death of the parents – under this system of marital assigns even the elementary family has to re-organise its holdings at every new union. Dispersal of the means of production, that is, land or cattle, clearly has a more radical effect than the transfer of other forms of wealth. But even when a woman receives cash or valuables, the effort of raising such funds within the family may affect the productive capacity of the holding, and in the extreme case lead to the accumulation of debts or to the sale of resources. All transfers of valued goods to women necessitate some degree of internal re-organisation, although probably less when rights in property of a mobile kind are devolved from parents or alternatively from the groom's family (that is, where we find an indirect dowry). While such re-organisation occurs regardless of whether the woman is endowed by her parents or by her affines, an indirect dowry leaves the family holdings relatively intact, since the bride joins her husband's family at marriage, receives her endowment from them, so that an adjustment of the funds may be required only if the marriage is dissolved by divorce. Under such a system lands allocated to the bride remain 'under the same management', while movables, though they may change hands, remain within the same household. However, indirect and direct dowry is rarely, if ever, a strict alternative; where women are endowed by their husbands, they usually receive a 'portion' from their parents as well, even if not until the deaths of the latter.

The fact that from the earliest historical period some of these European societies had patrilineal clans while others were organised on the basis of bilateral kindreds had, in some ways, less importance than that both were marked by what I have called diverging devolution; that is, with both types of kin grouping, some form of dowry or inheritance was allocated to women. So that even where some kind of patrilineal clan did exist, in the earlier Mediterranean for example, it differed in major respects from the type which is found in sub-Saharan Africa, and epitomised in Evans-Pritchard's study of the Nuer (1940) and in Fortes's work on the Tallensi (1949). In Ancient Israel women received a share of the inheritance as well as benefiting from marriage transfers. In this respect their clan system was closer to the bilateral organisation of the ancient Anglo-Saxons than to the unilineal organisation of recent Africa.[9] While the genealogical structures of contemporary African and earlier Mediterranean clans are often similar in form, the latter groups were distinguished by the fact that the clan's own patrimony was distributed not only to its own daughters, but also to its daughters-in-law at their marriages. This is so today among the Arabs. Despite the oft-quoted passages of Islamic law restricting a woman's share of the inheritance to only half that of a man's, a bride often receives property, first, as dowry, then later as inheritance, and possibly in both forms. In other words, the system of devolution, by which rights are transferred to the heir over the life-span of the holder, whether at birth, marriage or at the holder's death, is essentially 'bilateral' ('bilineal') or, as I have called it in an attempt to separate the transmission of goods from the transmission of membership of a kin group or of rights to office, 'diverging'. Hence 'diverging devolution' is the transmission of property to heirs of both sexes.

BILATERALITY IN KIN TERMS AND THE FAMILY

In considering these questions, the bilateral or patrilineal organisation of kin groups or groupings is often merged, and hence often confused, with related features of kinship and marriage, such as the nature of domestic authority ('patriarchal', 'matriarchal', etc.) or the allocation and control of property to and by women. We have seen that in Europe devolution was in a sense already bilateral. So, too, in parts of Europe was succession, since women as well as men had claims to high office if they were daughters of kings. Early on, in England, Ireland, France, Italy and Germany, they exercised important rights over the control of property. In Appendix 1 I discuss the structure of kin groups at some length, to make the point that it is not bilaterality, in contrast to patrilineal descent or filiation, that

[9] Much, if not all, of what we know of Anglo-Saxon law and practice dates from the Christian period. Was the bilateral organisation so evident in earlier times? Was there less emphasis placed upon the role of women? Was the society more 'patrilineal' as the dynastic structure might hesitatingly suggest? These are questions that do not readily admit of any answer.

differentiates later Europe from the earlier Mediterranean and from many Asian societies, at least, not as that opposition is usually expressed. With the passage of time all forms of extensive kin grouping came to assume lesser importance, whether these were the bilateral kindreds of the Anglo-Saxons, the similar but possibly looser groupings of early medieval France or the agnatically based *fine* of Ireland and the clans of the Scottish highlands. The contraction of these wider ties was accompanied, however, by a definite move towards a mode of referring to and addressing kinsfolk that was definitely more 'bilateral' in form. A kinship terminology that grouped together the siblings of both parents, placing each in the same category of 'uncle' and 'aunt' (though the holders of these roles were not interchangeable in all spheres of activity), developed first in Vernacular Latin in the late Roman Empire, then spread throughout the Romance languages, reaching England with the Norman Conquest (see Appendix 3). But even in this case the germs of change were already in existence; the earlier terminology included bilateral components, consistent perhaps with the fact that structures of kinship and clanship were necessarily modified by the practice of diverging devolution – as well, of course, as by changes in production, by more elaborate stratification and by the increasing dominance of the State in matters of law and war, tax and administration, all of which inevitably had an impact on the domestic domain and on the wider groupings of kin.

Medieval Spain provides an interesting example of the process of change. In the Islamic areas the tendency was for the clan to be replaced as the main focus of local organisation by relations of a client-patron type as a result of pressures from the dual forces of sedentarisation and urbanisation. In Christian Spain 'the dissolution of the extended family' is seen as 'a significant and central social process of the high middle ages' (Glick 1979: 137). Glick regards this movement as being complicated by a growth of 'agnaticism', of what other medievalists refer to as 'lineage', but through a process that *limits* rather than extends the establishment of significant relations between more distant kin. While there was 'a general drift away from the typical bilateral, cognate structures of primitive Germanic society, towards an agnatic patrilineal structure', there was an oscillating movement, varying with class, that left room for cognate relations as well as for 'agnaticism' and that led to the weakening of the extended family 'in the face of a socio-economic context that favoured the stem or nuclear family' (1979: 140–1). The terms which derive from Guichard require further clarification if they are to be understood comparatively; the question of increasing 'agnaticism' is one to which I will later return. Here I confine my comments to drawing attention to the antiquity of the process in which the 'extended family' is seen as giving way to the 'nuclear family', a process which, while not identical to the stressing of bilateral features, is certainly consistent with those changes. It is also consistent with a greater stress on the conjugal pair and their relationships, as well as on the role of the individual. Here there were undoubtedly some differences in the teachings of the Christian and Islamic traditions, as Glick observes: 'Islam provided a framework which legitimated tribal values and gave them religious significance; Christianity tended to work in the opposite direction, toward the development of inter-personal, rather than inter-group bonds' (1979: 141–2). Dumont (1981), too, has elaborated the thesis that Christianity gave birth to modern individualism. Certainly the ideologies of these two Middle Eastern religions had their origins in different socio-economic situations which had some important consequences for the authorised notions of kinship, marriage and the family. But beneath the ideological umbrellas of the written creed, members of these two faiths have, over the last fifteen hundred years, changed their domestic practices in important ways. Even initially the forms of 'succession, inheritance and descent' were not so different when contrasted with the patrilineal societies of Africa today, especially in the settled areas of the Islamic world which displayed distinct 'bilateral' tendencies, though these were less marked in the nomadic lineages.

The same general comment should be made for marriage transactions. Although the point is not included in Guichard's comparison, it is sometimes claimed that Islamic societies were, or are, marked by brideprice rather than dowry, while the opposite obtained in Europe, where dowry came to replace an earlier system of brideprice. Certainly there are differences between the marriage transactions of the nomadic pastoralists of North Africa and the inhabitants of medieval Europe, whether peasants, nobles or bourgeoisie – for such transfers were certainly class specific. But the same holds of the settled areas of Islam and once again the contrast is much less than with the peoples of sub-Saharan Africa, whether farmers or pastoralists. The elaboration of this point requires a clarification of the technical terms and actual transactions, which I have tried to provide in Appendix 2.

If we set aside these aspects of kinship, marriage and the family, which Guichard and others have used to distinguish occidental and oriental structures, that is to say, the nature of kin groups, marriage transactions, etc., what were the central features that came to differentiate the two shores of the Mediterranean? Let me leave on one side for the time being the important demographic variables discussed by Hajnal and others, partly because they need to be related to social action. I open up the discussion by turning first to the other distinguishing features of East and West in Guichard's table, namely the nature of the 'conjugal couple' (2), the position of women (5), notions of honour (6) and matrimonial alliance (4).

THE CONJUGAL COUPLE

Guichard sees the strength of this bond as being inversely related to agnaticism, to extended kin groups, to polygny, and to the ease of divorce. I have already touched upon the first two aspects of conjugal relationships in discussing descent groups, marriage transactions and inheritance. The two latter I prefer to treat in the context of item (5), the position of women. There is however another important aspect of conjugal relations which has been the special concern of historians of the Christian Church (Brooke 1978), namely, the consensual nature of marriage, how far the inauguration and continuation of a union depended upon the choice of the couple or of the parents (or possibly of the wider social system). Some students of the English family have seen such consensus (perhaps 'love' itself) as being characteristic of that country, even in late medieval times, while others see it as a feature of the modern affective family that is thought to have developed there in the last two centuries. Reviewing the discussions of this problem as they affect the medieval period, R. M. Smith has recently written of the need to look at the larger question, the extent to which the Church's doctrine was 'more compatible with the social structure that existed in England . . .' (1979: 98). Than where? Northern France? The consent of the couple does of course take on a different meaning depending upon the age of the individual and the social context in which it is elicited; the older the bride and groom, the more likely consensus will emerge as a requirement. But the requirement was not limited to countries of a particular demographic structure or historical destiny; it was a characteristic of the Christian Church as a whole, in principle from earliest times, and was in no way peculiar to the English. Indeed, the English Protestants re-established the requirement of parental agreement in the sixteenth century although it was absent in Catholic doctrine, even though laymen often insisted on their veto. For the Church, the consensus of the couple, as distinct from that of the parents, was an essential condition of entering a union, in contrast to the 'arranged marriages' on which parents, especially the nobility, often insisted. But the penetration of the Church into the domestic domain was not only in the establishment of a union, where it demanded to lay down the conditions, and later the forms of celebration, of marriage, for its dissolution was also brought under its wing, making divorce virtually impossible. So, while consensus (love, affection . . .) was considered essential to the establishment of a marriage, it was no longer necessary for its maintenance. The contrast with Islamic societies is dramatic; their rates of divorce appear always to have been high and the history of the 'modernisation' of Western patterns has been marked by the effort to catch up, and in some cases surpass, the easy dissolution of Arab marriage, with the 'freedom' it gave, above all to men, but in some cases to women as well, more often perhaps in polygynous than in monogamous societies.

The stress on the conjugal couple of husband and wife as the basis of domestic organisation is certainly not unique to Europe, but the emphasis on it has in some ways increased as wider kinship ties have been shed. The process has been a long one. According to Patlagean, the shift from consanguinity to conjugality as a central principle of social relationships had already taken place in fifth-century Byzantium; Duby looks upon consensus and its consequences as being one of the features of the ecclesiastical model of medieval marriage in eleventh-century France; others attribute the increasing stress on conjugality and the elementary family to the influence of reformist groups such as the Cathars in south-western France of the thirteenth century,[10] or, in a more enduring way, to the teachings of the Protestants and to the subsequent changes that occurred in Catholic ideology (Flandrin 1979: 110–11).[11] Undoubtedly there has been a general move away from the solidarity of kin groups to

[10] See Nelli (1969: 88) on 'L'émancipation de la femme' under the Cathars.
[11] 'While the strengthening of the framework of the family was a deliberate intention on the part of the Protestants in their struggle against the clericalisation of the Church and the paganism of the traditional ceremonies, this policy rather imposed itself, less evidently, on the leaders of the Catholic reforms' (Flandrin 1979: 111).

the independence of the conjugal couple, and even of its constituent members as individuals. In recent times the process has been more marked in the Western than the Islamic world. But it is less easy to make such assertions for an earlier period. One is never entirely sure whether different authors are not picking up different aspects of a complex, multi-faceted situation, involving conflicts of interest between husbands and wives, sons and daughters, Church and laity, as well as the overwhelming shift to non-domestic production and non-familial education that took place in the course of the nineteenth century. For all these changes in conjugal relations have taken place over a long period of time and have been influenced by many factors. In her account of the relationship between husband and wife in rural France of the nineteenth century, Segalen sees these linked to recent changes in modes of agricultural exploitation and the related transformation in residential arrangements (1980: 143).[12] And apart from the nature of the productive system, the influence of the Church was of prime importance. She also implies (1980: 7ff) that it is important to be precise about what aspect of the husband-wife tie one is discussing if one is to make any adequate assessment of these changes. Some historical accounts of the rise of the modern family read as if the authors thought that conjugality, marital affection, and attachment to children were inventions of bourgeois capitalism. While we must be equally cautious about Engels' contrary view of the middle-class family of Victorian times, such statements display a surprising disregard of the wider human perspective, that of world history and human culture. And at the same time they place too much credence on the restricted evidence of particular documentary sources and upon vague analytic concepts of an all-embracing kind. For these changes have been long-term, difficult to measure, and, in some respects, very uneven.

THE POSITION OF WOMEN

Of nothing is this truer than the many attempts to assess, in comparative or historical terms, the related problem of the changes in the position of women, Guichard's item (5). That position clearly differed in the various regions of Europe, as in the rest of the world; for

[12] See in particular the section entitled 'solidarité du couple au sein de l'exploitation' (Segalen 1980: 143, as well as p. 60ff).

example, in Africa between matrilineal and patrilineal societies, in Europe between northern and southern France (Flandrin 1979: 74ff; Segalen 1980: 181ff). And it obviously differed over time. But it is profoundly difficult to establish a composite measure that will sum- marise the whole span of relationships between men and women, and the extent, and especially the meaning, of differences between societies have been greatly exaggerated if only for this reason.

At first sight the difference between the polygyny typical of the Arabs and the monogamy which characterises Europe is very strik- ing. But partly because of the influence of the devolution of property on conjugal ties, the difference in marital relations between the two areas, while significant, is less than the dramatic contrast between monogamy and polygyny would suggest. Under the system of div- erging devolution wives require an endowment, whether at marriage or by inheritance, whether from parents or affines, and this fact alone places some restriction on their accumulation, except in the harems of the rich and powerful. Low rates of polygyny in North Africa and the Middle East, apparently a feature of earlier as of more recent times, meant that most men and women had only one spouse at any one moment (Goody 1973: 176), so conjugal relations were less rarely diffused by a plurality of spouses than is often supposed. In the Turkish city of Bursa in the seventeenth century, only 1 per cent of men whose details are entered in the lists of estates had more than one wife compared with some 33 per cent in Africa in the recent past (Gerber 1980: 232).

The Islamic world has often been looked upon as a purgatory for women, in implicit contrast to Christian Europe, a continent in which some see pre-industrial England as the particular paradise for the female sex (Macfarlane 1978). Once again the comparison is more complex than might be thought. What criteria are to be used and what types of evidence advanced? It has been claimed that the view of women expressed in the poetry of medieval Andalusia is very different from the main thrust of the Islamic tradition of the same period, providing evidence of the influence of marriages made between the Muslim conquerors and the women of the indigenous Christian population of Spain. Guichard denies that the conquerors came without women; and though they also married Spanish women, they usually sought brides from their own groups, still hold- ing the same 'endogamous' ideals as other Arabs, those ideals char- acteristic of what Tillion (1966) has called 'the republic of cousins'.

The dichotomy between the poetry and tradition reflect a situation that existed elsewhere in the Islamic world, where there were two major categories of women. Free women were normally 'matériellement et moralement recluses' (Guichard 1977: 169). But the slave singers, the *djawârî*, whose honour was not affected by exposure (that is, by non-veiling or even by nudity) and who were often well-educated for the purpose of pleasing their masters, engaged in very different types of behaviour. It was to such women that love-poetry was directed, not only in Spain but elsewhere in the Islamic world.[13] The *djawârî* were an essential element in 'la vie "courtoise" andalouse' (p. 174) where they played a role rather similar to the *geisha* of pre-war Japan and the *hetairai* of Ancient Greece.

The reference to the ancient world of the Middle East reminds one of the very favourable position of women that Hopkins (1980), and before him Hobhouse in *Morals in Evolution* (1915), identified in Egypt at the beginning of the first millennium A.D. In practice the Islamic world was often very different from its traditional image and the image of its tradition. Even in the warrior empire of the Turks, women played a vigorous role both in public and in private life. In the central Anatolian city of Kayseri in the seventeenth century they appeared freely before court, sued other citizens (even members of their own families), and were sued in their turn. They were owners of property and made frequent transactions, no less than 40 per cent of all those recorded for the first quarter of the century (Jennings 1975). In contemporary Bursa, the Ottoman capital before the fall of Constantinople in 1453, they were directly involved in litigation over the inheritance and ownership of land, horses, shops and other property, which they even sold to members of their own families. They acted as shop-keepers, merchants, money lenders, investors, artisans and producers of textiles. The value of their estates compared poorly with the businessmen of Bursa but very favourably with poor males and even with male artisans. As Gerber (1980) remarks, modern Western society displays no greater equality: the position of women in seventeenth-century Turkey refutes any notion of 'the large patriarchal family' and its accompanying domination of social life by men.

---

[13] See Ibn Hazm, *The Ring of the Dove*, who claims an oriental model in the work of Ibn Dāwūd of Ispahan (d. A.D. 909), *The Book of the Flower* (Guichard 1977: 173). Interestingly, the Arab-Andalusian poetry, of Ibn Quzmann (1095–1159) for example, has been held to be a source of the love songs of the Troubadours of Occitania (Lafont 1971: 62).

THE NOTION OF HONOUR

Under this heading Guichard draws a contrast between the Occident where honour is a question of being and the Orient where it is having (having, for example, a title); and in the former, the honour of males is active, that of women passive. Honour attached to whole persons and honour attached to roles or titles (if I may so express Guichard's distinction in another way) are surely features of most of the societies under consideration, though there may well be differences of emphasis associated with the incidence of feud, acts of vengeance and other forms of aggressive activity (since honour once acquired, has to be defended). And it was defended as vigorously in early medieval Ireland (Patterson 1981) as it was in the Mediterranean.

However, the notion of honour associated with women does seem to have differed, connected as it is with their roles (including their particular, differentiated roles, in the fields and in the house) as well as with their age at marriage. When women marry early, the custody of their honour tends to pass from their natal to their affinal kin, from brothers to brothers-in-law (who may also be paternal cousins under Muslim practice). Initially at any rate young brides are more passive vessels. Breaches of faith or honour tend to be more deeply felt when they concern a virgin of sixteen or a young bride than for women who remain unmarried until their mid-twenties and who, at least in rural circles, may have undergone the pleasures and dangers of 'bundling', *la fréquentation* or similar forms of courting (Flandrin 1975). The virginity of older brides is less likely to be such an issue; and even pregnancy may constitute no bar to marriage, possibly an advantage, for certainly it was quite widespread (Hair 1966; 1970; Laslett 1977).

The age of marriage for women differs not only between the Occident and the Orient but between northern and southern Europe. Commenting upon the situation in nineteenth-century France, Segalen remarks that despite the greater difficulties in carrying out a comparative study for this period than for the sixteenth century, for which Yver (1966) had made an interesting attempt on the basis of the custumals, it is possible to see, as other authors have done (e.g. Flandrin 1979: 74–92), certain persisting differences between north and south. One of these differences relates to concepts of honour. In northern France in the sixteenth century the weakening of the ties of *lignage* (meaning here a complex household) was accompanied by a strengthening of conjugal bonds (Segalen 1980: 181), one feature of which was quarrels about male and female authority. In the south, on the other hand, the supremacy of the lignage was maintained in such a way that it influenced social relationships down to the nineteenth century. Under such a regime, the conjugal pair was incorporated in the larger unit, male authority was supported by the kin group and a woman's independent role in the household was minimal.

While well aware of the analytic problems, Segalen employs proverbs to examine the differences between north and south during this period. In the south, these oral forms insist upon the restricted movement of women, upon their beauty and its concomitant dangers, upon the sadness of a love match, upon the antagonisms between in-laws, and upon male supremacy. Referring to Blok's work in Sicily (1974), Segalen notes how women in Mediterranean Europe are forbidden from working in the fields, since this activity would be seen as endangering a man's honour (1980: 182). By and large this picture holds for Provence, Gascony and Languedoc, but in the Basque country, where the heir to a holding is the eldest child irrespective of sex, we find the 'strong woman' rather than the subjected one.[14] In the north, men and women work together outside the house, and in Brittany and Lorraine both participate in village affairs. The role of women in the house is closely linked to the greater role they have in the fields, which is in turn related to differences in the concepts of honour.[15]

---

[14] It should be added that in the south 'la femme soumise' is also favoured in some significant respects over her northern equivalent.

[15] In the rural societies of Northern Europe a woman's activities were sometimes as closely linked to the house as in the south. I know of no general survey of sex roles in European agriculture but Patterson (1981) makes the point for pre-Norman Ireland. For more recent times, in the nineteenth-century Oxfordshire village of Lark Rise 'any work outside the home was considered unwomanly' (Thompson 1973: 114); even the vegetable garden and allotment were forbidden, her regular outside tasks being confined to the flowers and herbs. Later on the women of the village even managed to shift the fetching of water from the well to their husbands. But in other respects practice did not always tally with aspiration. In earlier days Sally had minded her father's cow and geese and even in the latter years of the century 'a few women still did field work, not with the men, or even in the same field, but at their own special tasks . . . Formerly, it was said, there had been a large gang of field women, lawless, slatternly creatures, some of whom had thought nothing of having four or five children out of wedlock' (p. 58). It was their reputation that had given most country-women a distaste for 'goin' afield', but changes in the division of labour were not only due to the 'embourgeoisement' of the countryside but also to the fact that the villagers of Lark Rise had lost their land and it was the men who were employed as labourers, while the girls went into service in the towns.

MATRIMONIAL ALLIANCES

While there is much to be learnt from a detailed discussion of all
these points, I want to suggest that, with one major exception, they
are not ones that most significantly differentiate the north and the
south of the Mediterranean, and indeed in some cases the features
are found distributed very widely in human societies. This to my
mind is the case with the argument about the elementary family,
which is found, if not everywhere, then very generally, like love and
individualism, though certainly with important variations. The central differences that developed between the two shores of the
Mediterranean lie elsewhere. One, the fourth of Guichard's variables, has to do with marriages which are permitted, prohibited or
encouraged; 'endogamy' versus 'exogamy', in-marriage versus out-
marriage. As Duby (1981) has recently insisted, this problem was of
overwhelming concern in medieval Europe. The extent to which that
very critical feature of Hajnal's 'European marriage pattern',
namely late marriage, is linked to the projection of marriages outside the circles of consanguinity, affinity and even friendship (in so
far as this was linked to spiritual kinship), and in the absence of any
organising preferences, is a point that I shall touch upon later.

Regarding the direction of marriages, the oriental or Arab system
is characteristically endogamous (or in-marrying), while the occidental or European one is exogamous (or out-marrying). In my
earlier study (1976b) I tried to show that diverging devolution is
positively linked with the tendency to in-marriage, and that it is
especially closely associated with an emphasis on marriage with the
father's brother's daughter, the *bint al-'amm* of the Arabic-speaking
world, which means that the bride is a member of the same patrilineal clan as the groom. Arab clans and lineages are sometimes
described as endogamous. Strictly speaking, the designation is in-
correct since the technical term refers to the obligation to marry a
member of the same group which we find, for example, in Indian
castes; endogamy is the opposite of exogamy, the obligation to
marry out, found so frequently in Africa. Among the Arabs marriage is permitted outside as well as inside the lineage or clan. But,
like other Mediterranean peoples, they encouraged, sometimes even
enforced, marriage between close members of the same kin group,
the same patrilineal clan.

There are many reasons that could account for such a system

which, as Tillion, Guichard and others have pointed out, runs quite contrary to the exchangist 'logic' of marriage which is found so often in simpler societies. One reason, however, stands out in the minds of the actors themselves, although it has not always been taken sufficiently seriously by ethnographers. 'The simplest explanation', writes Guichard, 'often provided by the Arabs themselves, is economic; by marrying their sons with their cousins german, the members of the elementary kinship group prevent part of the patrimony – the inheritance of the girls – from leaving the clan' (1977: 34). But, he goes on to say, the explanation is only valid when the Koranic law on the inheritance of property by daughters is practised. Despite this restriction, and despite the further objection of Murphy and Kasdan (1959) that a woman from outside may bring in the equivalent of one from inside (an objection that certainly misses the point as far as land is concerned), the explanation has some force. Ideological factors to do with the work of women and the maintenance of internal solidarity are also involved; so too is the force of custom once established and then considered to be blessed by God. But looking at the distribution of in-marriage more widely, the availability of one's own women as possible wives does appear to be positively associated with the fact that they and their offspring are carriers, potentially at least, of one's own property.

In these Arab societies not all marriages are internal. There is no *rule* of endogamy. Rather there is a tendency to in-marriage that can be expressed in quantitative as well as in normative terms, and which varies between societies and within strata. It is a tendency that does not exclude, as Bourdieu (1977) has perceptively pointed out, the use of other matrimonial strategies, such as out-marriage to establish or maintain a political alliance. But it encourages close unions of a kind that run contrary not only to exchangist principles – general or restricted, implicit or explicit – but also to many ideas of and theories about 'incest', what is 'unchaste' in terms of sexual unions.

Europe, on the other hand, came to reject the 'logic' of close marriages, at least at the level of kinship, for classes remained in-marrying. By so doing, that continent differentiated itself not only from the present practices of the Arab world but also from the ancient civilisations of the Mediterranean. The reasons behind the prohibition of close marriage are central to my enquiry, though I will also be concerned with other related aspects of family and kinship. Today close marriages continue to distinguish the Asiatic and African shores of the Mediterranean, running from the Bosphorus to the Maghreb, from the European one running from Turkey to Spain. While Protestant areas have abandoned their formal opposition to cousin marriage and the Catholic areas modified theirs in 1917 to exclude only first cousins, for the Orthodox Church such unions are still forbidden. These prohibitions have existed for some fifteen hundred years. But before that, in Ancient Greece and Rome, another pattern prevailed, the pattern that seems more fitting to the preservation of the status of men and women by means of diverging devolution in a complex productive system where classes or estates were economically differentiated one from another. Indeed there is some suggestion that in-marriages were frequent in Western Europe before its conversion to Christianity. Why and when did this radical change occur? With what other features of the family was the change associated?

3. Change in the German lands

The encounter of Western and Eastern structures in Spain, between the Muslims from North Africa and the inhabitants of the kingdom of the Visigoths, with its fusion of Roman, Christian and German elements, took place in the eighth century. From the beginning of that same century we get a vivid picture of the impact of the Christian missions from Rome on a more northern society, that of the Anglo-Saxon kingdoms of England, a picture that reveals some interesting features of the earlier patterns of behaviour in western Europe and of the kind of changes that were taking place at the time.

When attempting to reconstruct the patterns of marriage and the family in pre-colonial African societies, at least in the coastal areas where they have changed most, the absence of indigenous documents leads one to turn to the writings of outsiders, that is, of travellers and traders, of administrators and missionaries. Missionary accounts often have a particular interest because, since Christian practice is linked to specific patterns of the domestic life, the upholders of the new faith often discuss the difficulties with which they are faced in this sphere, thus revealing some critical aspects of the system they are attempting to change.

Such was the case in England during the Anglo-Saxon period. In what Wormald (1978: 39) has labelled that 'instant best-seller', *The Ecclesiastical History of the English Church and People*, the Northumbrian monk, Bede, tells of some of the problems involved in converting the pagan English. He explains how after Augustine, the first archbishop of Canterbury, arrived in 597, he sent messengers back to Pope Gregory at Rome seeking advice on certain current questions, including ones relating to marriage.

Bede's *Ecclesiastical History* was not, of course, simply a repository of information. It was read in England wherever Latin was known and its influence was enormous, moulding the minds of, for example, Alfred, Dunstan and Aldwin, as well as later monastic writers (Knowles 1940: 24). Before discussing the content of this particular section of the *Ecclesiastical History*, known as *Libellus Responsionum*, two caveats need to be entered. First, the questions posed by Augustine, 'the first bishop and apostle of the English', to Pope Gregory, and the answers of the latter to his subordinate, have been criticised as lacking authenticity in that they did not stem from Augustine and Gregory at all. Second, the content of one of the passages was already being queried in the eighth century. In 735, the year of Bede's death, Boniface, the apostle of Germany and organiser of the Frankish Church, wrote to Nothelm, the newly consecrated archbishop of Canterbury, and expressed his surprise on hearing that Gregory had stated that 'marriages between Christians related in the third degree were lawful' (Tangl 1916: 57). Less than ten years later, Pope Zachary reported having heard 'what is spread abroad through the lands of the Germans', that Gregory had allowed marriages within the fourth degree, which were not in fact permissible (*dum usque se generationem cognoverit*). 'Nevertheless we are prepared to believe that he allowed this because they were as yet uncivilized (*rudi*) and were being invited to the faith' (*Monumenta Germaniae Historica, Legum* III, *Concilia* II.I, 19–21; Meyvaert 1971: 16).

Despite these queries the Letter of Gregory provides us with some very valuable evidence. Manuscripts giving the same series of questions and answers existed in forms quite independently of Bede. The 'entire tradition of this substantially Gregorian text or an important branch of it' may have originated in north Italy in the late seventh century (Bullough 1969: 12). In its separate manifestation the document is preserved in more than 130 versions which were distributed very widely, in northern Italy, Gaul, Switzerland, Germany, Denmark, as well as in England (Meyvaert 1971). In other words the text circulated throughout the German lands, where it was apparently used as a point of reference and where its terms were seen as a concession to the practices of the local inhabitants. In this way it helped to impose a common code over customary practices that differed in similar ways from these new laws, and no doubt also among themselves. It is the implications of its extraordinarily wide distribution that make the document so important.

Four of the nine questions on which Augustine asked advice from the Pope had to do with sex and marriage (I. 27). The two last

concerned the purity of men and women, which raised, among other
things, the problem of whether a man might receive communion
after a sexual illusion in a dream; sexuality and spirituality were
incompatible. The fourth of the nine questions asked whether two
brothers (*germani fratres*) could marry two sisters, to which the
answer was affirmative; 'there is nothing in the sacred writings on
this point which seems to forbid it' (Bede 1969: 83). Augustine's fifth
question was more complicated and more revealing: 'Within what
degree may the faithful marry their kindred;[1] and is it lawful for a
man to marry a step-mother or a sister-in-law?' (p. 85).[2]

Pope Gregory's reply clearly indicates the change that Christianity
had brought to Rome and presumably to the other countries of
western Europe. 'A certain secular law in the Roman State allows
that the son and daughter of a brother and sister, or of two brothers
or two sisters may be married.[3] But we have learned from experience
that the offspring of such marriages cannot thrive. Sacred law forbids
a man to uncover the nakedness of his kindred. Hence it is necessary
that the faithful should only marry relations three or four times
removed, while those twice removed must not marry in any case, as
we have said' (p. 85). He goes on to condemn marriage to the step-
mother and to the sister-in-law for the same reason, declaring that it
was for denouncing this sin that John the Baptist was beheaded.

Since a special dispensation had to be given to those who had
contracted such unions before conversion, it is clear that the practices of close marriage (presumably to cross-cousins, and possibly,
as in Rome, to parallel cousins, at least to the father's brother's
daughter) and of marriage to the widow of the brother or father
(though not one's own mother) must have been common in English,
and indeed German, society. But they are now forbidden, the arguments against them being framed partly in physical terms (the likelihood of infertility) and partly in religious ones (on grounds of incest

[1] *Usque ad quotam generationem fideles debeant cum propinquissibi coniugio copulari.*
     Literally, 'To what generation should the faithful marry those near to them.'
[2] The words *nouercis* and *cognatis* have been translated as *steapmodrum* and *broðor-
     wiifum* in the Anglo-Saxon version.
[3] The literal translation of the Anglo-Saxon text runs: 'which allows brother and
     sister, or the children of two brothers or the son and daughter of two sisters to be
     joined in marriage', a rendering that is closer to the original Latin. It is not clear
     why modern writers have interpreted 'brother and sister' as 'the children of
     brother and sister' (i.e. cross-cousins) except that it makes more logical sense to
     include all first cousins.

– 'uncovering the nakedness of one's kin' – a formula derived from the Old Testament).

Bede also comments upon several other aspects of marriage and the family; marriage is encouraged between Church members (pp. 173–5) and divorce is disapproved of. The Church's attitude to divorce was laid out very clearly at the Synod of Hertford in A.D. 673. Chapter 10 of the Council's decision read: 'That lawful wedlock alone is permissible; incest is forbidden; and no man may leave his lawful wife except, as the gospel provides, for fornication. And if a man puts away his own wife who is joined to him in lawful marriage, he may not take another if he wishes to be a good Christian. He must either remain as he is, or else be reconciled to his wife' (Bede IV. 5).

Finally, Bede enjoins a long *post-partum* sex taboo, though this should not lead to the fostering of young children by wet nurses. 'Her husband should not approach his bedfellow until her infant is weaned.[4] But an evil custom has arisen among married people that women scorn to suckle the children they have borne, but hand them over to other women to be suckled; and this presumably has arisen solely as a result of incontinence because, as they will not be continent they are unwilling to suckle their infants' (1969: 91). The passage brings out an interesting relation between the use of wet nurses and the avoidance of the *post-partum* prohibition on sex, though one presumes that, as in later England, their use was more common among the rich than among the poor.

The comment on wet-nursing runs quite contrary to Tacitus' remarks on the German family in the first century. For he claimed that 'every mother feeds her child at the breast and does not depute the task to maids and nurses' (*Germania* XX). But here, as in the previous section (XIX), Tacitus is clearly acting as a moralist, using the *supposed* practices of the tribes to criticise the *actual* ways of the Romans. Among the Germans, chastity is impregnable, adultery rare (they do not know clandestine love letters), single marriages universal, contraception and infanticide unknown. ('To restrict the number of children or to put to death any born after the heir is

---

[4] This practice persisted into much later periods. At the beginning of the twelfth century, Ivo of Chartres noted that a woman could not lawfully make love while pregnant or while feeding her child (Duby 1978: 42). In the sixteenth century Hay (1967 [c. 1534]: 193) counsels that a father should not have intercourse with a nursing mother. Indeed, marital intercourse should also be avoided on a day when the Eucharist is to be received (p. xxxiv).

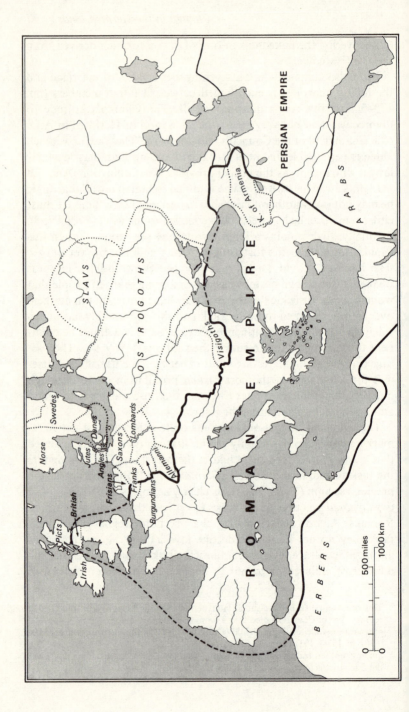

PERSIAN EMPIRE

ARABS

K. of Armenia

SLAVS

OSTROGOTHS

Visigoths

R O M A N   E M P I R E

Swedes

Norse

Jutes

Danes

Angles

Saxons

Lombards

Frisians

British

Franks

Alemanni

Picts

Burgundians

Irish

BERBERS

500 miles

1000 km

considered criminal'.) Marriages are not made early, for 'the young men are slow to mate, and their powers, therefore, are never exhausted. The girls, too, are not hurried into marriage'. Was the 'European pattern' of late marriage (Hajnal 1965) already in evidence or was this too a figment of Tacitus' moralising?

If we look at the society from which these Christian missionaries came, that of Rome, we find that in the domestic domain the earlier legal and customary system conformed to patterns that were widespread throughout the Mediterranean and Middle East and that permitted, indeed encouraged, the practices of, firstly, marriage to close kin; secondly, marriage to close affines or the widows of close kin (possibly by inheritance, of which the levirate was the extreme form); thirdly, the transfer of children by adoption; and, finally, concubinage, a form of secondary union.

The first two practices are explicitly condemned by Pope Gregory; the latter were also discouraged by the Christian Church in early assemblies. In other words, key features of the kinship system have undergone a sudden change from the former 'Mediterranean pattern' to a new 'European one', or, in Guichard's terms, from the oriental to the occidental. Why should such a change have occurred? Gregory relies upon Holy Scripture to support his injunctions, yet all the procedures he condemns are to be found recorded in the Old Testament – they were the common currency of the Mediterranean world. The support cited from the New Testament is distinctly ambiguous and hardly seems to refer to these customs at all. As Patlagean remarks, 'The extension of the prohibitions on marriage is *an original feature* of medieval Christian law, as compared with its Biblical or Roman origins, even compared to the Justinian version of Roman Law' (1966: 59, my italics).

It was not only Roman and Biblical law that had nothing to say against most forms of close marriage. In the other regions to which Christianity later spread, the earlier presence of close marriage was yet more marked. In Ancient Greece, unions were permitted with half sisters; in Egypt at this time with full sisters.[5] Yet marriage to

[5] The Roman rules on 'incest', restricted as they were, ran into obvious difficulties in some parts of that widespread empire; Egypt was a major problem since the society countenanced very close marriage. At times Christian Emperors imposed the death penalty, although in the final state of the law, the punishment decreed was the confiscation of one's property. In Osroene and other parts of Mesopotamia Justinian considered the frequency of 'incest' to be so high that he threatened the parties with death.

any close kin was forbidden by the Church and its proscriptions were given legal sanction by Christian monarchs. In Anglo-Saxon England the punishment for breaking these rules was very heavy, namely slavery (that is, according to the late text, Edward and Guthrum, 4, Whitelock *et al.* 1981), with the man passing into the ownership of the king and the woman into that of the bishop (Whitelock 1930: 111; 1981: I, 307). Eventually these extensive prohibitions, which varied in extent over time, were relaxed as a result of the Protestant Reformation. But even so, the reduced range of prohibited degrees were prominently displayed in the Anglican churches and in the Book of Common Prayer; marriage to the widow or widower of close kin (or to the siblings of a dead spouse) was still forbidden, despite the absence of any scriptural authority for either. Indeed, in Ancient Israel marriage to the dead brother's wife was an obligation under the practice of the levirate, which also appears to have obtained among the Assyrians, the Hittites, and the Hurrians, as well as in Israel at the time of Christ (Matthew 22: 23–7). No scriptural text queries the institution. Yet its prohibition became a feature of the law of the Church. St Basil condemned leviratic marriage, despite the Mosaic precedent, because it was not custom (Letters CLX; Godefroy 1927: 2112), but when such a prohibition came into being, and where, is unknown. It is true that such marriages were not found in all the major Eurasian societies. In China and India, at least at the upper levels of society, widows were not supposed to remarry; they lived as post-marital celibates, continuity being provided where necessary not by the levirate but by adoption and other strategies. Nevertheless the levirate was certainly an important institution in Ancient Israel and, in different forms, of Ancient Mediterranean society more widely.

Just as close marriage and unions with widows of kinsfolk were forbidden, so too were adoption and concubinage. Bede does not condemn the first, which was very common under Roman law, although the objections are very clear in the earlier writings of Salvian. He rather directs his attention to another way in which children are separated from their parents, namely, wet-nursing, a practice that pertains to upbringing rather than to heirship and therefore, unlike adoption, implies no change of kinship status. Although this practice was also condemned by the Church, it continued for very much longer, in England until the end of the nineteenth century when it retreated before the spread of feeding bottles and baby formulae. At roughly the same time adoption, after a gap of some fifteen hundred years, was reintroduced into Western society.

Concubinage continued to exist in the Christian world for several centuries, often in priestly circles as an alternative to full marriage. But as a quasi-formal status it was eventually repressed, both among priests and laity. The priesthood was in principle celibate, and those married laymen who took on additional partners had their children defined as illegitimate, as non-heirs. Indeed just as a man could not acquire a second wife, since polygyny was forbidden, so too it was hard to change one for another since divorce became difficult, and subsequent remarriage impossible, as marriage came increasingly under the aegis of the Church, at least as far as its establishment and dissolution were concerned.

Divorce had been permitted under Roman law, though the grounds laid down varied according to the imperial edict. Justinian permitted a woman to divorce her husband for a number of reasons including bringing a concubine into the house. The Greeks likewise allowed both husband and wife to demand divorce. Among the Ancient Hebrews there was no prohibition and even after rabbinical control was instituted in the eleventh century A.D., a man could still divorce his wife for childlessness. (Once again China and India employed different strategies of heirship.) But Christianity decreed otherwise, and in this case the change goes back to the words of Christ himself (Matthew 19: 3–9): 'What therefore God has joined together let no man put asunder.' Divorce became virtually impossible in Europe until Luther declared marriage a 'worldly thing' and allowed dissolution at least for adultery. The Church of England, on the other hand, inherited Roman canon law unchanged in this respect. While marriage was no longer a sacrament, it was still Holy Matrimony, and hence indissoluble – except for a brief period of fifty years after the Reformation and then again after 1857 when jurisdiction over matrimonial causes was taken away from the ecclesiastical courts. During the intervening period divorce was hard and remarriage impossible, creating the problem not so much of setting aside a spouse, since this could be done informally, but dissolving the marriage legally and then being in a position to remarry.

The same conflict of the (Roman) Church with local custom took place in the Celtic lands. The 'Ancient Laws of Ireland' provide the most detailed evidence we have of family law in pre-Christian Europe, for although composed after the conversion of the country, many earlier practices appear to have continued. Women received a substantial dowry, marriage (for men at least) appears to have been late – those aspects were not threatened; but concubinage, divorce, adoption and fostering were permitted, and close marriage not forbidden (Patterson 1981) – indeed an heiress (*banchomarmba*) was obliged to marry a close agnate, as in Ancient Greece.

Such practices were not to the Church's liking. The group of sixth-century canons from Ireland forbade the 'Irish practice of divorce and remarriage', as well as, by implication, the practice of concubinage (Hughes 1966: 31), and the prohibition on concubinage, as we shall see, changed the whole conception of who was a 'legitimate' person.

The existence of this conflict in Ireland, in England, and apparently in the rest of Europe, raises an obvious but fundamental question. Why should the Christian Church institute a whole set of new patterns of behaviour in the sphere of kinship and marriage, when these ran contrary to the customs of the inhabitants they had come to convert, contrary to the Roman heritage upon which they drew, and contrary to the teaching of their sacred texts?

It might be held that control of marriage was in itself one way of breaking down the earlier, 'pagan', religion. Since religion was embedded in the domestic domain, conversion implied the control of family life. The acquisition of property that resulted from conversion could be seen as a means of taking over the gods of the land, of conquering the 'White Goddess'. The rejection of adoption attacked the worship of the ancestors, since the provision of an heir and the provision of a worshipper were inextricably woven together (Goody 1962a: 221ff; Cicero, *De Legibus* II. 19). Some such considerations were doubtless present. Nevertheless the particular constellation of practices condemned in Bede, and the continuing attacks against them, require a more precise explanation. For the religious implications of these changes need to be looked at in terms of their wider consequences and the profound effects they had on the social system.

Let me begin by observing that one aspect of all the rejected practices (which in itself in no way exhausts their implications for social life) has to do with the inheritance of familial property, with the provision of an heir, and with the maintenance of status in a stratified society. These are elements of what I have elsewhere (1962a and 1976b) called 'strategies of heirship', as these mechanisms operate in a society based on a relatively advanced agriculture. Take in-marriage, especially in the form of marriage to close kin. What Tillion has called 'this Mediterranean desire not to exchange, to "keep all the girls of the family for the boys of the family" ', is a pattern so patently different from the exchangist, exogamic structures of which Lévi-Strauss and others have written (Lévi-Strauss 1949; Tillion 1966: 37). The practice is related, at least in part, to the desire to maintain the property of women within the family. This is not to deny other implications of, say, marriage to the father's brother's daughter, either in a particular culture or across the gamut of societies in which it is found. I would, in any case, doubt whether a general explanation, either in a specific instance or overall, can be satisfactory, as Bourdieu (1977) has also remarked. But we have here a practice that is found throughout the early Mediterranean cultures. In Ancient Greece, a man was obliged to marry the daughter of his father's brother (FBD) if she were an epiklerate, that is, an heiress who had no brothers; otherwise the property would be dispersed. As the elders of Israel similarly knew, having considered the case of the daughters of Zelophehad, 'c'est l'héritage féminin qui détruit la tribu' – or rather the corporate lineage (Tillion 1966: 26; Goody 1972: 121). Tillion goes on to explain the reasons: 'If the daughter inherits the half-share that is allocated to her under Koranic law, she will transmit this portion of the patrimony to her children, that is, to strangers. To avoid this danger, the people of the Maghreb have combined the two available methods of defence: disinheriting all daughters (that is to say, violating Koranic law) and systematically marrying them to kinsfolk in the paternal line' (1966: 27). The most extreme example of this desire to reject exchange comes from Egypt, where the Roman census records of the first three centuries A.D. show a remarkably high percentage of brother-sister marriages among the indigenous population (Middleton 1962; Hopkins 1980). So strong is the pressure to retain women that even the intragenerational taboo on 'incest' within the nuclear family disappears. In Ptolemaic Egypt (with its very tight relation between land and people) there existed an actual 'preference' for brother-sister marriage, at least at the statistical level.

Marriage between kin serves to reinforce 'family' ties. These particular forms also prevent female heiresses from removing property from the 'family', and thus combat the problem of the absence of sons. They do nothing to eliminate the dangers of heirlessness in general. Any 'direct' system of inheritance (one in which children are the primary beneficiaries of parental wealth and status) has to contend with the fact that approximately 20 per cent of couples will have only girls and a further 20 per cent will have no children at all (Goody and Harrison 1976; Wrigley 1978); the figures will be higher if there are high rates of sterility, homosexuality or contraception. These forms of close marriage would take care of the absence of sons; other strategies, adoption, polygyny, divorce and remarriage can be used to provide a solution to childlessness. But prohibit close marriage, discourage adoption, condemn polygyny, concubinage, divorce and remarriage, and 40 per cent of families will be left with no immediate male heirs.

If these forms of acquiring spouses and heirs were so central, their interdiction must have created enormous problems for the Church and for the society. The Church of course successfully influenced local life in many radical ways. Since one could not celebrate mass without the bread and the wine, the country had to accept either a change in agricultural practice or else a lively import-export trade in those commodities. Dress too was controlled. In fifth-century Ireland, St Patrick drew a distinction between the habits of the 'Romans', that is Christians, and those of barbarians. In a later canon clerics were told they must conform to civilised Roman practice in three ways: by wearing a tunic, by shaving their heads, and by seeing their wives go veiled. And an early Welsh synod required that no Catholic (*catholicus*) should let his hair grow *more barbarorum* (Hughes 1966: 47–8).

But as far as the family and marriage were concerned, the wishes of the Church did not always prevail and resistance was often prolonged. The difference between 'local custom' and ecclesiastical law is nowhere stronger than in Ireland, even as late as the Norman period. It was then, during the late eleventh and early twelfth centuries, that English (or Norman) influence came to play a dominant role in reshaping the Irish Church. The archbishops of Canterbury, Lanfranc and Anselm, both protested against the Irish customs of marriage and divorce. From the seventh century Irish Church legislators had recognised only four degrees of kinship within which marriage was prohibited (and the law tracts fewer), whereas the papacy acknowledged seven. Divorce and remarriage were allowed by local custom, which was stigmatised by Lanfranc as a 'law of fornication'. 'Native law', comments Hughes (1966: 260), 'triumphed over the stricter provisions of the church, to the disgust of the Anglo-Norman prelates, who were used to very different customs.'

In theory, this state of affairs was altered by the first of the reforming synods, held at Cashel in 1101. However this conclave did not introduce the full requirements of the Roman Church, and, although it did forbid a man to marry his step-mother (or step-grandmother), or his sister or daughter, his brother's wife, or any woman of similarly near kinship, it said nothing of the 'Irish practices of concubinage and divorce'. Even so, the legislation seems to have had little effect on social life, for some time later Pope Alexander III was told that the Irish 'marry their step-mothers and are not ashamed to have children by them; that a man may live with his brother's wife while the brother is still alive; and that one man may live in concubinage with two sisters; and that many of them, putting away the mother, will marry the daughters' (Sheehy 1962: I,21; Hughes 1966: 265).

The continuing resistance of the population to these measures makes it more difficult to understand why the Church should place so much importance on introducing and enforcing rules, most of which had no scriptural backing. There is a sense in which the establishment of any set of rules, particularly ones that were difficult to observe, promoted its position, and increased its control of a people's destinies. The nineteenth-century historian, Hallam, said of marriage prohibitions: 'they served a more important purpose by rendering it necessary for the princes of Europe, who seldom could marry into one another's houses without transgressing the canonical limits, to keep on good terms with the court of Rome' (1868: 456). Similar considerations held for the bulk of the population with regard to the local Church. By insinuating itself into the very fabric of domestic life, of heirship and marriage, the Church gained great control over the grass roots of the society itself. Not only was royalty in its thrall, but the peasants too. Religion entered into the basic units of production and reproduction. The whole world was sinning and paying for it.

Important as this argument is, it takes no account of the specific nature of the prohibitions, many of which affected the strategies of heirship that a family could pursue. If they inhibited the possibilities of a family retaining its property, then they would also facilitate its alienation. As is made clear by Bede's account of the processes of conversion, one of the most profound changes that accompanied the introduction of Christianity was the enormous shift of property from private ownership to the hands of the Church, which rapidly became the largest landowner in England (as in most other European countries), a position it has retained to this day. The acquisition of this huge estate involved the transfer of rights in land and other goods either *inter vivos* or else at death. The Church encouraged forms of tenure, such as copyhold and bookland, that made these transfers possible. Aside from the question of how far the introduction of these written procedures challenged the validity of oral transactions, they constituted ways of alienating property that were introduced by the Church largely for its own benefit. It was the same with the written will. 'The written will, no less than the land-book, was an exotic in England. Ecclesiastical in origin, it was not only developed under clerical influence for the material benefit of Anglo-Saxon churches and convents, but it was ultimately brought in a later age within the scope of the jurisdiction of ecclesiastical courts' (Hazeltine 1930: xii). Indeed, these testaments date from about the period of the great build-up of Church lands, the earliest that have been preserved dating from the first half of the ninth century (Whitelock 1930: xli).

If the Church introduced and encouraged procedures for acquiring land and other property for itself, did it also discourage, at least in consequence if not always in intention, those practices that might provide a family heir for the property of a dead man or woman? If so, this would provide some explanation for the dramatic shift from close to distant marriage, as well as for the abandonment of adoption, widow inheritance, concubinage, divorce and remarriage, and other strategies of heirship available to the Romans, to the Anglo-Saxons, the Irish, as well as to the rest of the Mediterranean and probably to most of Europe. Did the interests of the Church effectively determine some of the important characteristics of English and European kinship up to the Reformation, and, in some respects at least, to the present century?

We cannot, of course, disregard the influence of the Pauline tradition about sexuality and marriage, nor the character of early Christianity as a religion of the oppressed, nor yet the function of the Church as a guardian of the poor, the orphans and the widows. But these considerations do not run counter to a view of the role of the Church as an accumulator of property, for property it had to have in order to look after the faithful and to provide a home for those who had set aside, either in prospect or in retrospect, the possibility of marriage. Monasticism meant not only the rejection of marriage by a certain proportion of the population, but also the accumulation of property, in land and in buildings, to support, in a modicum of comfort, those who had undertaken the vow of chastity (or the vocation of priesthood). Such rejection also occurred without as well as within the physical buildings of the Church. Apart from individual hermits, laymen too 'chose' celibacy, some for reasons of religious or personal conviction, others because marriage was difficult from the economic standpoint. In thirteenth-century England as in twentieth-century Ireland, the marriage of men and women might be delayed or postponed in order to prevent the dispersal of family property (Homans 1941; Arensburg and Kimball 1940). The two sets of considerations are closely intertwined. And, as we have seen, high rates of celibacy are characteristic of Hajnal's 'European marriage pattern'.

I have sketched out some of the ways in which early Christian missionaries tried to change the practices of the German lands, which of course included the lands where the Romance languages are now spoken and where Celtic was formerly the tongue. The specific practices to which the missionaries objected represented ways of conducting one's domestic life that were more like those of earlier Mediterranean cultures, and hence more like Eurasian systems in general, than was the case in later Europe. These practices had one thing in common. They can all be seen as strategies which an individual (sometimes a couple) might adopt in order to produce an heir and continue the line, some of which were described by Maine as 'legal fictions'. In the following chapter I want to enquire in more detail into the origins of these new injunctions of the missionising Church, especially those which applied to cousins and widows, adoptees and concubines, and how they differed from both Roman law and Biblical custom.

4. *Cousins and widows, adoptees and concubines*

Towards the middle of the first millennium A.D., changes were taking place in the kinship systems of Europe that involved a break with earlier practices and made their mark for centuries to come. These changes appear to have been connected with the advent of Christianity, but they were derived neither from the sacred books, with their Israelite and Palestinian background, nor yet from the Graeco-Roman world from which its exponents came. Both these worlds adhered to 'Mediterranean' practices; Christianity introduced a new element.

As we saw in the previous chapter, some of the emergent features of European kinship are embodied in the Letter of Pope Gregory to Augustine. Others are referred to elsewhere in Bede and in the works of various writers of the period. They included the difficulties placed in the way of divorce, which increased still further with the ecclesiastical reforms of the eleventh century (Bouchard 1981); the encouragement of spiritual kinship (godkinship) in preference to consanguinity; the insistence on the *consent* of the parties, and the *affection* of the partners, in any marriage. I will concentrate first of all on those four features that emerged from Augustine's encounter with the Anglo-Saxons – cousin marriage, marriage to affines, adoption and concubinage. Let me begin with the history of prohibited unions, since this is one of the most politically visible features of the development of Christian marriage and one that became particularly prominent in England at the time of the Reformation.

During the Reformation, the discussion centred upon what was and what was not God's law, a matter of deep and continuing concern to Henry VIII as well as to the Protestants he reluctantly followed. The Biblical prohibitions on intercourse and marriage are listed at some length in Leviticus 18: 6ff, and repeated in Leviticus 20. One problem is that it is not always clear when the injunction concerns intercourse, when marriage, when it concerns widows and when not. In the King James' version, verse 6 runs, 'None of you shall approach to any that is near kin to him, to uncover their nakedness: I am the Lord.' The rest of the chapter sets limits on legitimate sexual intercourse, including the forbidding of bestiality, homosexuality and intercourse with unclean women. The prohibitions on intercourse (and hence marriage) with female kin relate to direct descendants of the first and second generations (including a son's wife) and direct ascendants in the first generation (i.e. the mother), together with father's wife, father's brother's wife, father's sister and mother's sisters.[1] But in his own generation a man is only prohibited from marrying his full sister and his half-sister ('the daughter of thy father, or daughter of thy mother, whether she be born at home, or born abroad'). There are also prohibitions arising from the relationship to one's wife, for her direct descendants (daughter, son's daughter, daughter's daughter) are forbidden as well. The reference to not taking a wife's sister (Leviticus 18: 18) 'to vex her . . . in her life time' may refer to a later period than that of the Patriarchs (Strype 1711: App. 32), for otherwise it is impossible to reconcile with the example of Jacob's unions, his marriage to two sisters, both of them daughters of his mother's brother. Equally, the prohibition of 'uncovering' the brother's wife clearly does not apply after his death, since there is an explicit obligation, at least in the case of a childless brother, to marry his widow.

What is clear is that there is simply no warrant in Holy Writ for the ban on cousin marriage. Unlike canon law, the prohibitions in Leviticus have a certain agnatic twist; it is the wives of members of the same agnatic line (father, father's brother, brother, son) who are mentioned, though this would appear to mean as widows, since adultery was in any case condemned – unless this was an attempt to draw attention to the heinousness of the offence; in any case the wives of other relatives are not included in the lists. As for female kinsfolk, the daughters of collateral kin are not excluded as partners, neither in the form of 'oblique marriage' to nieces, nor in the

---

[1] The Vulgate terminology of the prohibited relationships are listed in the following verses of Leviticus 18: (8) uxor patris; (9) sororis tuae ex patre, sive ex matre, quae domi vel foris genita est; (10) filiae filii tui vel neptis ex filia; (11) filiae uxoris patris tui, quam peperit patri tuo, et est soror tua; (12) soror patris; (13) soror matris; (14) patrui . . . nec accedes ad uxorem eius, quae tibi affinitate coniungitur; (15) nurus tuae; (16) uxoris fratris tui; (17) uxor tuae et filiae eius. Filiam filii eius, et filiam filiae illius; (18) sororem uxoris tuae in pellicatum illius non accipies, nec revelabis turpitudinem eius adhuc illa vivente.

form of cousin marriage. However, this did not prevent ecclesiastics and laymen alike from claiming that the source of the later ban on marriage to cousins of a wide degree lay in the Bible. Pope Gregory justified the prohibition not only 'because the offspring . . . cannot thrive', but because 'sacred law forbids a man to uncover the nakedness of his kindred' (*cognationis*) (Bede 1969: 85). This general statement from Leviticus could be used to forbid all unions between kin, yet marriages to relatives of certain kinds were clearly permitted and often encouraged in the Scriptures. The same verse is seen by Meyrick (1880: 1726) as the possible grounds for the prohibition of marriage to the wife's sister, while in a recent book the distinguished historian, Georges Duby, also appears to accept that source as the basis for later restrictions on marriage (1978: 17). But by no stretch of the imagination can the medieval or modern system of marriage prohibitions in Europe be legitimised by the Mosaic model. The same is true of Roman law.

In his reply to Augustine, Gregory relies on sacred law for his rejection of cousin marriage, which he claims was allowed by the Roman State. There is some difference of opinion among scholars on the question of whether marriage between first cousins was permitted at the very earliest stage in Roman history, so that the matter needs to be looked at in some detail. There are three main references that have been used as evidence to suggest that such unions were prohibited. First there is the description by Tacitus of Vitellius' defence of a marriage with the brother's daughter, that is the union of the Emperor Claudius with Agrippina, who were already thought to be having sexual intercourse (*Ann.* XII. 5).[2] Vitellius tries to obtain a reversal of the prohibition on this marriage by claiming that

[2] In his description of the arrangements for the marriage of Claudius to his niece, Agrippina, Tacitus shows Vitellius attempting to overcome the resistance to this incestuous union, for they had not dared to celebrate the marriage:
necdum celebrare solemnia nuptiarum audebant, nullo examplo deductae in domum patrui fratris filiae: quin et incestum ac, si sperneretur ne in malum publicum erumperet, metuebatur . . . (*Ann.* XII. 5).
Vitellius enters the Curia and makes a speech directed towards obtaining a mandate to change the practice:
At enim nova nobis in fratrum filias coniuga, sed aliis gentibus solemnia, neque lege ulla prohibita; et sobrinarum diu ignorata tempore addito percrebruisse . . . (*Ann.* XII. 6).
A textual problem arises with the term *sobrinarum*; it is suggested that perhaps a word (*consobrinarumque*) has been omitted, or that the author is using *sobrini* in a wide sense (an unlikely conjecture). In any case, the marriage was not to the daughter of a parent's sibling ('cousin' in modern English) but to a brother's

aliis gentibus, other peoples, allowed it. In the course of his argument he maintained that although 'cousin marriage' was for a long
time unknown to us, it has now become very frequent. The Latin
word used here is *sobrinarum* which usually appears to mean second
cousin, while *consobrini* refers to first cousin,[3] although there is one
reference to *sobrini* as the children of two sisters and *consobrini*, the
children of a brother and a sister (*Donati Commentum Hecyrae*: 459).

However, the status of this evidence seems dubious since it is
introduced into a court case where Vitellius is trying to change the
law in favour of a powerful client. Suggestions that a similar prohibition over the years had been relaxed would therefore have provided
a valuable precedent for allowing the oblique union of uncle and
niece.

One editor of Tacitus, Furneaux, claims (1841: 233) that all such
close marriages were prohibited until the enactment of the permis-
sory plebiscite referred to by Plutarch (*Quaestiones Romanae* VI) in
a discussion of the *ius osculi*, the kiss that women were permitted to
bestow on relatives of the sixth degree: '. . . men did not anciently
marry their kinswomen, just as to this day they do not marry their
sisters or aunts; cousin marriage was permitted at a recent date for
the following reason. There was a man of slender means but excellent character, who stood higher than any other statesman in the
favour of the people. His cousin was an heiress, and he was found
to be married to her and to be enjoying her fortune. In consequence
he was impeached; but the people quashed the proceedings and

daughter; it was, in other words, an oblique marriage, the kind of marriage that
was common in the states of southern India and that most nearly approximates to
a brother-sister union. However, objections to this marriage often took the form of
a desire to protect a 'ward', a close kinswoman of junior generation, a problem
that arises in many societies, especially where property is at stake.

  The prohibition on the oblique marriage between uncle/aunt and niece/nephew
is still a feature of the Church of England's Table of Kindred and Affinity, and was
prohibited in Islam, as well as by the Jewish sect of Karaites in medieval Cairo
(Goitein 1978: 26). But it was regarded as natural in the Talmud and is still
practised by Jews, even modern ones, both of European and Oriental extraction.
In Cairo however, the Rabbinite Jews appear to have avoided marriages with the
sister's daughter, since they were condemned as licentious unions by the Karaites
with whom they intermarried.

[3] The attempt of Patlagean (1977: 118–27) to establish an earlier distinction between
cross and parallel cousins does not seem to hold water. There is little evidence for
cross-cousin terms in the oldest Sanskrit sources (Anderson 1963: 4; Trautmann
1981).

released him from the charge by decreeing that marriage between cousins or more distant relations should be legal, although marriage of nearer kin remained prohibited' (Rose 1924: 121–2). As with the earlier example from Tacitus, this pronouncement seems to be a case of special pleading, providing little evidence of an actual plebiscite. It is a type of statement common in 'mythical charters', which indicates perhaps that such marriages require some measure of justification, since there is often an ambivalence about cousin marriages even where they are encouraged (Goody, J. and E., 1969). But it provides no solid evidence of any recent change. In any case the motive force behind the 'new' law is interesting; marriage to the cousin heiress prevented the dispersion of family property, as well as uniting in the marital couple all that had been split by the taboo on brother-sister unions at the generation of their parents.

Livy provides two other references to possible prohibitions on cousins. In one the patrician Celius, or Cloelius, is said to have been the first to marry a woman within the seventh degree, contrary to the old custom (*primus adversus veterem morem intra septimum cognationis gradum duxit uxorem*) (*Hermes* IV. 372). This fragmentary text offers no adequate supporting evidence for the assertion and even the name of the patrician himself is uncertain. The other reference occurs in the *History* (XLII. 34. 3) and is even less convincing. Here Livy gives an account of an old soldier in 171 B.C. who declares, 'When I first came of age, my father gave me the daughter of his brother to wife.' Livy's meaning is clear but the editor writes of the possibility of this union being a rustic irregularity. There seem no grounds at all for this suggestion, given that such marriages to the father's brother's daughter were also practised by the aristocracy. In one of the Philippic orations (II. 99) Cicero rages against Antony, accusing him of shameful behaviour towards his father-in-law who was also his uncle (*patruus*, father's brother), referring to his second wife, Antonia, as *soror* (sister) rather than *consobrina* (cousin, a term that some have derived from the word for sister). But Cicero's disapproval is not directed at the marriage as such; it is reserved for Antony's behaviour towards a man who was his father-in-law as well as his father's brother, and towards a woman who was both wife and cousin. The same incident is described in Plutarch's *Life of Antony* (Loeb transl. p. 157), where again no disapproval is expressed of cousin marriage itself, just an acknowledgement of its difficulties. The author notes that 'Antony took the matter much to heart, drove his wife from his house'. As in the case of Brutus' marriage to Porcia, daughter of his uncle, Cato, Plutarch makes no comment on the legality of the marriage (Loeb *Life of Brutus* XIII, p. 153).

There is therefore no reason to suggest that the preferred marriage of the Arab world, which Guichard identifies as a defining feature of the oriental or eastern structure, was forbidden in the Roman world, any more than it was in Ancient Greece, where it was actually prescribed for an heiress, an epiklerate, or in Ancient Israel where it was permitted in the levitical rules, or in the Palestine of Jesus Christ, who was himself, according to one legend, the offspring of just such a marriage (Huth 1875: 33–4). Certainly, as the writings of Livy show, by the year 171 B.C. there was no question of any disapprobation of it (Liv. XLII. 34).

That continued to be the case in early Christianity. The closeness of permitted marriages is well illustrated by the genealogy of the first Christian emperor, Constantine the Great, whose son, Constantius, married the daughter of Julius Constantius, that is, married the Emperor's half-brother's daughter. Constantine's own daughter, Helen, married the son of Julius Constantius, Julian, while another daughter, Constantia, first married the son of another of the Emperor's half-brothers, Flavius Dalmatius, and afterwards another of Julius' sons, making a total of four marriages to father's brother's sons (or daughters).

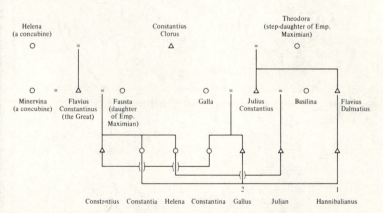

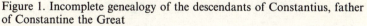

Figure 1. Incomplete genealogy of the descendants of Constantius, father of Constantine the Great

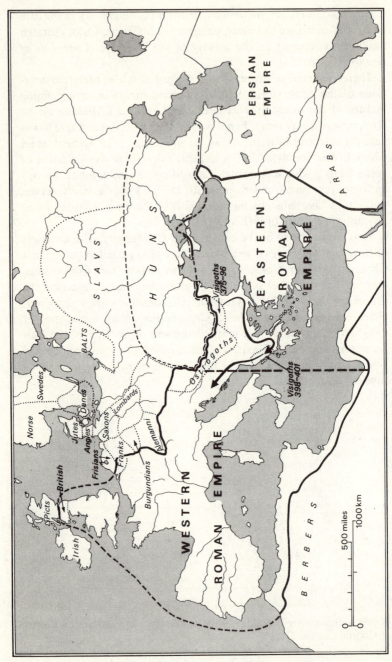

Map 3. The Western and Eastern Empires A.D. 406

It was by means of these marriages between paternal cousins that Constantine endeavoured to consolidate his dynasty, and at the same time the newly established faith itself. Despite these strenuous efforts his death saw a change of direction under the weight of pagan protest. His brother's son, Julian, whose mother had bequeathed large estates to the Church, succeeded in 361, twenty-four years after Constantine died, and turned back to the old gods. When he was proclaimed Augustus, he accused his uncle 'of having wrought the destruction of the law and custom by his revolutionary actions' (Vogt 1963: 52).

It was after the reconversion of the Roman Empire to Christianity that the issue of marriage to close kin was raised. The Emperor Theodosius I condemned unions between cousins in a law made in 384 or 385. It was still possible to effect such a marriage by imperial dispensation, a means of avoiding its own prescriptions that the Church was not slow to use. Indeed, the early history of such prohibitions was very chequered. In A.D. 405, some twenty years after his father's introduction of the prohibition, Arcadius (A.D. 378–408) legalised cousin marriages once again for the Eastern empire based on Constantinople.

While Arcadius legalised cousin marriage in the East, under his younger brother, Honorius, who was the western Roman emperor from 393 to 423 when Rome was captured by the Goths (and who married his dead wife's sister), such marriages were permitted only if the parties obtained an imperial rescript of dispensation and it was not until later that under civil legislation they became freely permissible once again. Some years later, in about 428, St Augustine recalled that cousin marriages had earlier been allowed by the civil authorities but were now prohibited, though he did not regard them as forbidden by divine law. What remained forbidden under the Roman law of this period were 'oblique marriages', both between senior women and junior men and vice versa (i.e. aunt and nephew, uncle and niece, including great-uncle). It was precisely this type of marriage that Claudius had entered into with Agrippina and that had subsequently been made a capital offence by Constantius and Constans (337–50) who declared it an abomination and punishable by death (Corbett 1930: 49; Biondi 1954: III,94). Arcadius substituted for the death penalty the loss of the ability to make bequests to strangers as well as introducing certain disadvantages as to property.

The subsequent prohibitions on marriage in the secular law are very clearly stated in the *Institutes* of Justinian (A.D. 533) where cousin marriage is recognised as perfectly legitimate. The section on marriage (Book I. Tit. X. 4) declared: 'Again, the children of two brothers or two sisters or of a brother and sister can intermarry' (Thomas 1975: 30). Other close marriages were permitted and there is no mention of the ban on a union with the sibling of a deceased spouse, though this partnership had been forbidden by the sons of Constantine (p. 32).

But while the secular authorities pursued this unsteady course, the Church refused to make any about-turn. As the letter of Pope Gregory to the first Archbishop of Canterbury declares, a difference emerged between the secular and ecclesiastical law of marriage and the family, with the latter coming to dominate the scene. Whereas no such prohibition had existed, in Israel, Rome or Christianity before the end of the fourth century A.D., the matter now became of prime significance, for the Church rather than for the State. Indeed, not content with the prohibition on first cousins, the ban was then extended, increasing the span of 'co-sanguinity', variously described as *cognatio carnalis*, *parentela*, *progenies*, *proximatas*, 'the union which exists between two or more persons and which derives from their common blood, from their common origin'.[4] In the sixth century the ban was extended to the third canonical degree, that is, to second cousins, the offspring of a common great-grandparent 'in imitation of Roman law which limited inheritance to the sixth degree of kinship' (Oesterlé 1949: 233), calculated in the Roman manner, that is, the third degree reckoned by the German or canonical method, which became dominant in the medieval period. Later the prohibition was pushed out still further to the fourth and then, in the eleventh century, to the seventh canonical degree, when the latter method was used to recalculate the earlier prohibitions. Not only were these enormously extended prohibitions attached to blood or consanguineal ties, but they were assigned to affinal and spiritual kinship as well, producing a vast range of people, often resident in the same locality, that were forbidden to marry.

What were the grounds for these extensive prohibitions on con-

---

[4] *Dictionaire de Droit Canonique* (1949) p. 232. Nearly every council in the sixth century dealt with the subject of incest, that is, with the prohibited degrees (Galy 1901: 370).

sanguineous marriages? The *Dictionnaire de Droit Canonique* (1949) gives three general reasons that have been proposed:

1. The moral reason, that marriage would threaten the respect and shame due to near ones.
2. The social reason, that distant marriages enlarge the range of social relations. This common 'anthropological' notion was put forward by those great theologians, St Augustine and St Thomas Aquinas, who recognised that out-marriage multiplied the ties of kinship and thus prevented villages from becoming 'closed communities', that is, solidary ones.
3. The physiological reason, that the fertility of the mother or the health of the children might be endangered.

The statement of Thomas Aquinas, which appeared in his *Summa Theologica* and was highly influential during the Middle Ages, raised a number of possible objections to consanguineous marriage. First, 'incest' is objectionable because of the 'natural and instinctive' feelings of honour towards our parents and close kin (1 above). Second, because of the very availability of such partners, intercourse between them would lead to lust, to over-indulgence. Third, such unions would 'prevent people widening their circle of friends' (2 above). And fourth, to add sexuality to the natural affection between kin would be to encourage libidinousness (2a2ae. 154. 9).[5] It was this last consideration, which must be linked to the second, that was later taken up by Montaigne in a curious passage: 'there is a danger that the affection that one has for such a woman may be immoderate; for if marital affection exists there entire and perfect, as it should do, and one overburdens this further with the affection that one owes to one's kinsfolk, there is no doubt that this addition will transport such a husband beyond the bounds of reason' (Flandrin 1979: 164).

[5] In Thomas Gilby's translation of the *Summa*, the passage reads as follows:
 article 9. is incest a determinate species of lust?
 THE NINTH POINT:[†] [†cf IV Sent, 41, 4 i & ii. De malo XV, 3] I. It would seem not. For incest takes its name[a] [a in-castus] from defiling chastity. And in general chastity is opposite to all kinds of lust. Therefore incest would seem to be lustfulness in general, not one special kind.
  2. Again, Gratian declares, 'Incest is intercourse between a man and woman related by consanguinity or affinity.'[1] [1 Gratian, Decretum II, 36, I, append. 2] Now affinity differs from consanguinity. In consequence incest is not one but several kinds of lechery.
  3. Besides, what does not of itself imply ugliness does not constitute a special kind of vice. To lie with relatives, whether by blood or by spiritual ties, is not ugly in itself, else it would never have been lawful. And so incest is not a determinate species of lechery.

ON THE OTHER HAND the species of lechery vary according to the condition of the woman who is abused. Incest tells of a special condition, namely that she is kin or related by spiritual affinity. Incest, therefore, is a determinate species of lust.

REPLY: We have pointed out that a special kind of lust is discerned where the proper exercise of sexuality is especially contravened.[2] [2 art.I & 6] This is the case with intercourse between relatives by blood and affinity. And for three reasons.

First, because of natural and instinctive feelings of honour towards our parents, which extend to our kindred descended from a common close ancestor; so that, as Valerius Maximus relates, in ancient times it was not felt right for a son to bathe with his father lest they should see one another naked.[3] [3 Factorum et dict] mirab. II, I] For evidently, as we have noticed, a certain delicacy is required in matters of sex, a respect which is the opposite of shamelessness.[4] [4 2a2æ. 142,4; 15],4] It sets up a certain reticence and a sense of impropriety about exposure. And so it is written, 'She is thy mother, thou shalt not uncover her nakedness.'[5] [5 Leviticus 18, 7] And similar sentiments extend also to other relatives.

The second reason is that blood relations have to live closely together. Were they not debarred from sexual intercourse the opportunities presented would make it too easy, and their spirits would be enervated by lust. And so the Old Law especially directed its prohibition to those who dwell together within the family.

The third reason is that incest would prevent people widening their circle of friends. When a man takes a wife from another family he is joined in special friendship with her relations; they are to him as his own. And so Augustine writes, 'The demands of charity are fulfilled by people coming together in the bonds that the various ties of friendship require, so that they may live together in a profitable and becoming amity; nor should one man have many relationships restricted to one other, but each single should go to many singly.'[6] [6 De civit. Dei XV] 16. PL 41, 458]

A fourth reason may be added from Aristotle:[7] [7 Politics II, I.1] 62a37. Lect. 3] since a man has natural affection for his own kin, were this to be charged with sexuality, it would be set ablaze and rage in libidinousness against chastity.

For these reasons it is manifest that incest is a special kind of lust.[a] [a There are other property reasons for legislation about marriage within the forbidden degrees of kindred.]

Hence: 1. Intercourse between persons closely related to one another is so much the worse for chastity because, as we have noted, of the occasions offered and the excessive heat of desire. Such lust is called incest by antonomasia.

2. Relationship by affinity is occasioned by the relationship of consanguinity, and because one is for the other, a similar unseemliness is present.

3. There is something indecent and repugnant to natural reason in the sex intercourse of relations, particularly when it is between parents and children, who are directly and immediately related, and where there is a natural bond of honour. Aristotle tells of a stallion who covered his dam by mistake and from terror plunged over a precipice.[1b] [1 De animalibis IX] 47.631a21] [b Modern eugenics and cattle-breeding have changed old conceptions.] And even certain other animals show a natural respect for those who have begotten them.

The same unseemliness is not present when the parties are not related to one another directly, but through their parents. This varies according to customs and laws, whether human or divine, for, as we have noted, intercourse being directed to the common good is subject to law.[2] [2 art. 2] Augustine writes, 'The union of brothers and sisters goes back to olden times, when necessity compelled it; all the same so much the more damnable did it later become when religion forbade it.'[3] [3 De civit. Dei XV] 16. PL 47,457]

More unequivocally spiritual reasons have also been given for this radical extension of the prohibited degrees. The American historian, Howard, writes that the early Fathers of the Church 'dreaded the sins of the flesh through which the sacramental nature of marriage might be defiled' (1904: I, 352). And giving his comment a more specific context, he goes on to add: 'and they may have felt a reaction against the freedom of the German custom touching the marriage of blood kindred'. The freedom of the Germans was no greater than that of the Romans, the Greeks or the Jews. And, in spite of Montaigne, it is difficult to see why marriage to close kin would be more overwhelming and less spiritual; recent research suggests the opposite. In any case, we have to remember that the prohibitions on marriage not only covered consanguines, but were applied in the same manner and to the same extent to affines, that is, to the kin of one's partner (even in the absence of marriage), and to spiritual kin, that is, to sponsors at the ceremonies of baptism and confirmation, the numbers of whom proliferated in the later Middle Ages.

As the author of the *Encyclopaedia* article admits, we do not know all the reasons that prompted the early Christian legislators; the reasons offered are all very much *post factum*. The negative reasons may, in fact, have been more important than the positive. The *Encyclopaedia* sees the motivations for close marriage as being 'either the desire to maintain patrimony intact within the family, or the sentiment of caste which seeks to exclude those of inferior rank, or the difficulty of marrying outside the family circle, or finally local or national customs' (Osterlé 1949: 240). Dauvillier (1970: 369) and many others have remarked that the in-marrying practices of the Greeks were associated with the desire to avoid the break-up of the family's patrimony. It follows that the encouragement of out-marriage in a system that allocates property to women, especially as heiresses, would promote the dispersal of estates and weaken the corporations of kin based upon them. At the very least, such prohibitions enabled the Church to exercise a large measure of control in the domestic domain, as was also the case when they took over the protection of widows and orphans. But they could also loosen the bonds of kinship and prevent the consolidation of estates where there were no male heirs.

WIDOWS

At about the same time as marriage was prohibited to first cousins, the Church also, in A.D. 393, forbade unions with the wife of a dead brother and the sister of a dead wife, thus making impossible not only the levirate and the sororate, that is the inheritance of such women (or men) as spouses but also the weaker form of permitted marriage to such affines. Marriage to the dead brother's wife was an important institution of the Ancient Mediterranean world, especially in Israel where it took the form of the levirate. Under this intense form of the institution, a man was obliged to marry the widow of a brother who had died without issue; it was the duty of the survivor to produce offspring on behalf of the dead man and so provide him with an heir to his name, his line and his property.

The term 'levirate' is derived from the apparently rarely used term in Latin, *levir*, for brother-in-law. It implied an obligation, which was legal in Judaism, customary in Islam (Goitein 1978: 210), but non-existent in Rome. While marriage to the dead brother's widow was not forbidden in Roman law, such unions were not common. As a feature of Islamic law, they were permitted by the Muslim inhabitants of North Africa and Europe, in Spain and in the Balkans. In addition they were practised by certain Finno-Ugrian speakers. The inheritance of the widow by the dead husband's brother is also reported for the Dukagini or Mirdite tribe, which was the largest in Albania and wholly Catholic. As elsewhere the Church made strenuous efforts to suppress this marriage by inheritance, which also applied to the wives of uncles and cousins if they were living in the same house. But its attempts met with little success (Durham 1928: 202–4).

From the end of the fourth century, the Church had tried to forbid such marriages, in both the intense and the non-intense forms. Ironically, however, it is possible that while Christ was himself the product of cousin marriage (FBD), his earthly father may have been born of a leviratic union; for two twin brothers, Jacob and Heli, had in turn married the same woman, Jacob having raised seed to the name of his dead brother (Scarisbrick 1968: 169). The immediate progenitors of Christ thus practised the very marriages later forbidden to Christians. Christ himself clearly accepted the levirate as legitimate. The Gospel of Matthew relates how certain Sadducees came to him posing a question. If two brothers had successively married the same woman, which one could claim her after the Resurrection? 'Master, Moses said, If a man die, having no children, his brother shall marry his wife, and raise up seed unto his brother' (Matthew 22: 24). The reply had to do with the afterlife, not with unions on earth; for the institution itself was not subject to disapproval. Of course, a man was forbidden to have intercourse with or marry his brother's wife when the brother was still alive (or with his wife's sister when she was still living). But after his brother died he had a duty towards the widow, which included sex and marriage. How then could Christian theologians claim scriptural authority, except on the general but vague grounds perceived in Leviticus? The Biblical reference used by Pope Gregory to justify the prohibition on marriage to a sibling's widow, was the passage in the Gospel of Mark where John the Baptist is said to have been murdered following his condemnation of Herod's marriage to Herodias, 'his brother Philip's wife'. But in this case the condemnation obviously referred to the wife of a living brother, not of a dead one.

The specific prohibitions on marriage to the siblings of a dead spouse seem to start not with the brother's widow but with the wife's sister. Canon 61 of the Spanish Provincial Council of Elvira in 305, the first of the series of major councils of the Church, which was to be followed by several others around 314, leading to the first General Council of Nicaea in 325, made possible by the support of Constantine, prohibits the marriage of a widower with the sister of his first wife. 'Si quis post obitum uxoris suae sororem ejus duxerit et ipsa fuerit fidelis quinquennium a communione placuit abstineri . . .' The same council prohibited marriages and intercourse with Jews, 'pagans' and heretics, while other canons forbade participation in pagan festivals and recognised the clergy as a special class with peculiar privileges and responsibilities; one of the priest's duties was that of celibacy (canon 33), the first of such injunctions to be made.

In A.D. 314 the Eastern Provincial Council of Ancyra took up the complicated case of a man who slept with the sister of his betrothed (*sponsa*). The girl gave birth to a child and then killed herself. The two survivors, then man and wife, were excluded from the body of the faithful for ten years (canon 25, Lambert 1868: 99; Bruns 1839: I,70). In this case, however, we are dealing not with a ban on marrying the affine of a dead spouse, but with a prohibition on intercourse with the sister of a man's present (or future) wife, a sin that parallels Herod's marriage to his living brother's wife.

Something closer to the levirate, or rather marriage to the siblings of dead affines, appears to be discussed in the second canon of the Council of Neo-Caesarea (*c.* 314–325), which reads, 'if a woman marry two brothers let her be excommunicated till death' (Lambert 1868: 101). It is not clear whether the first husband had to be dead at the time of the woman's second marriage. In any case the punishment is severe, more so than in the equivalent case of a man marrying two sisters. In Ireland the *Responsa* of the Second Synod, attributed to St Patrick, held at the earliest in the seventh century (Hughes 1966), states that a man cannot marry his brother's wife. There is no longer the dilemma as to whether we are dealing with the relationship before or after his death. 'Audi decreta sinodi: Superstas frater thorum defuncti fratris non ascendat, Domino dicente: *Erunt duo in carne una* (Eph. 5,31); ergo uxor fratris tui soror tua est.' 'Hear the decree of the synod: "A surviving brother shall not enter the bed of a dead brother." For the Lord saith: They shall be two in one flesh; therefore the wife of thy brother is thy sister' (Bieler 1963: 194–5).

But the most specific statement of the general ban as it developed in the early centuries appears in one of the decisions of the Roman Synod of *c.* 402 (*Espistola ad Gallos episcopos*, canon 9). The judgement refers specifically to the Biblical evidence about the marriage of Herod to his brother's wife and to the union of Jacob with two (living) sisters in soral polygyny, though of course neither case provides an instance of the prohibition on marriage to the widows of close kin. That particular prohibition became part of the wider ban on marrying close affines that continued right down to the present century; but it was an innovation of the Christian Church of the fourth century.

Let us now look at the question of marriage to affines from the standpoint of the widow. If levirate, widow inheritance or remarriage to a husband's sibling are prohibited, the following possibilities are open to her:

1. Unless all remarriage is forbidden, as among higher groups in traditional India or China, she can remarry an outsider, although this solution is often available only for the young or for the rich.
2. She can return to her own natal family and depend upon her kin (as among the Gonja of Ghana, see E. Goody 1974).
3. She can maintain herself independently, with the help of her children and her dower.
4. Finally, she can depend upon the State or upon some charitable institution outside the family.

While it is clear that the marriage to the brother's widow was not forbidden in the Christian community of Palestine during Biblical times, and that younger widows were expected to remarry (I Timothy 5: 11–15), nevertheless older women had to be taken care of. The Acts describe how, when the number of disciples multiplied, 'there arose a murmuring of the Grecians against the Hebrews because their widows were neglected in the daily ministration' (6: 1). As a result of these ethnic problems, new arrangements were made for the administration of the sect, including the care of its needy widows. These arrangements did not exclude a measure of family responsibility. The continuing obligation of a family to look after its own widows is made very clear. 'If any man or woman that believeth have widows, let them relieve them, and let not the church be charged; that it may relieve them that are widows indeed' (I Timothy 5: 16). Presumably the Church was responsible for those not looked after by their children or by their dead husband's brother. Previously such kinsfolk would have taken charge of most if not all of the widowed members of the Israelite community. Until the development of large scale, extra-familial welfare institutions, widows and orphans in most societies were supported by natal kin or, through some form of 'remarriage', even among the elderly, by affinal kin. This latter solution was partly excluded by the early aversion to the remarriage of widows, including the outright condemnation of the levirate and of all marriages to affines, that became a feature of the Christian Church. It should be remembered that among the Jews the levirate came into play when a dead man had no children. It was therefore selective from two angles: first it applied to women who were still capable of childbearing, and second it did not operate where sons had already been born. Widows with or without offspring, kin or affines needed looking after, and in the time of Timothy this was often because their adhesion to Christianity had led to a break with their own families. The Church did not wish widows and orphans to return to a pagan background; they were widows of the sectarian family, who repudiated, or were repudiated by, their natal or affinal kin.[6]

---

[6] The concern with widows rather than widowers relates to the age difference between spouses, the generally lower mortality of women, the greater likelihood of widowers remarrying, or having another wife, and the fact that in a society where marriage is predominantly virilocal, a man lives with kin, a woman with affines.

Such widows were not only cared for, but were organised to care for others. The early Christians established an order of widows, those who had renounced the possibility of remarriage. It was these women who were charged with the care of orphans, saints and other widowed members of the sect. In Jerusalem property was pooled so that provision could be made for the care of priests. The sectarian community had to look after its members, particularly the weak, and in order to do so, it had to receive donations from its supporters, donations which are at once gifts to God (and hence a direct means to grace) as well as gifts to his Church on earth (Dauvillier 1970: 357–8).

During the late Roman and early medieval periods, rich widows made an important contribution to the Church, which was more likely to benefit if they remained chaste and unmarried. The close relation between the fate of widows and the property of the Church is illustrated by the story of Clotild, the Christian queen of the Franks. In 511, at the death of her husband Clovis, the conqueror of the Gallo-Romans, she went to the church of St Martin in Tours where 'she remained all the days of her life, distinguished for her great modesty and kindliness' (Dalton 1927: II,81). 'To the churches, the monasteries, and other sacred places she gave the lands needful for their welfare . . .' (p. 103).

In most human populations, women usually enjoy greater longevity than men; in early medieval Europe a man's expectation of life was further reduced by the likelihood of his succumbing to violence. This was probably the case in early medieval German society where both the contributions to the Church and the position of women were affected, at least among the leading families, by the 'surprising number of matrons who outlived their husbands'. Elsewhere this is often due to their earlier age at marriage which means a greater number of widows or a greater number of spinsters than when the differential marriage age is small. In eleventh-century Germany wives were not always much younger than their husbands, though according to Leyser brides of thirteen or even twelve 'were not in the least unusual' (1979: 52,54). Despite suggestions of female infanticide in the Parisian basin during the ninth century, early medieval European women usually appear to have lived longer than men; certainly this was so among the ruling families, whether aristocratic or bourgeois, and violence seems to have been a major cause of the earlier demise of men.

The result of this greater longevity of women, combined with the system of dowry and dower, meant that despite the preference given to men in the devolution of property, much land accumulated in female hands (Leyser 1979: 58). In general it can be said that custom treated women better than the *Lex Saxonum*, the written code of the law on transmission. Their ability to accumulate property meant that women, especially widows or spinsters, had more to leave to the Church. It was not uncommon for a single woman to live in the household of a clerical kinsman, in which case her funds might go to enrich his see, to enlarge existing foundations or to help to set up new ones. Or women might give their lands in return for *precariae* and for rents in money and kind for their sustenance.

However, the position of a wealthy widow in medieval Germany was always precarious and her best security probably lay in the foundation of a religious house through which she was protected from the importunity of her *co-heredes* (Leyser 1979: 63).[7] A considerable number of nunneries were founded by the Franks and Anglo-Saxons after their conversion; in Saxony, the same happened three centuries later, but the underlying social conditions, suggests Leyser, were similar: 'Marriages were costly [under a dowry system, JRG] and the presence of many unbetrothed girls in the houses of Anglo-Saxon, Frankish and Old Saxon nobles threatened their peace. Infanticide was not unknown even among the aristocracy. Unmarried girls were exposed to the incestuous advances of their own kin' (1979: 64). Outside the family, the danger for such girls came from strangers and unequals, especially slaves. Leyser considers that religious houses offered an escape from a life of 'unending promiscuity' for single women whose state arose not only from the differences in mortality but also from the differences in age of marriage. If women begin their marriage careers earlier than men, they end them sooner, unless remarriage is a real possibility. The more remarriage, the more spinsters (or never-marrieds). In the case of both widows and spinsters, dangers proliferate; they tend to be vulnerable in terms of sexuality and property. Retirement into a

---

[7] The concern with property inherited by women is clearly demonstrated in early Irish canon law of the eighth century. When a woman inherited family land she gained only a life interest, having to give legal guarantees that she would not alienate the land, which had later to be restored to the kin. Female heirs, it was declared, 'should give sureties and guarantees not to transfer the inheritance to strangers' (Hughes 1966: 128–9).

religious house kept them within their own class but placed them in a protected sphere of social activity. On entering the nunnery a woman added her portion to the endowment of the house where she could live comfortably under royal protection.

The lavish endowment of nunneries 'distorted the pattern of land-holding' (Leyser 1979: 70), causing the Saxon nobility to lose control of their possessions. In the eleventh century, Saxon princes became less tolerant of wealthy widows disposing of great inheritances. 'Instead they forced them to remarry and used their possessions to build up those competitive territorial lordships . . .' (1979: 71). So the attempt of the aristocracy to protect their women ran up against contradictions, and the new measures limited but did not stop the transfer of wealth for religious ends. The works and prayers of those women was seen as securing the welfare of the menfolk in this world and the next, but that welfare was maintained only at the expense of a substantial transfer of property from lay to clerical hands.

In canon law the concern with the treatment of the widow was closely allied to the problem of the disposition of the property of the wife when a marriage was brought to an end (Sheehan 1963a: 111). In the course of time various customs and institutions were developed to protect her. As a *miserabilis persona* she was entitled to the special protection of God and king. She was also free to choose her future state, either widowhood or remarriage, and canon law gave some consideration to the testamentary capacity of married women, that is, the power to bequeath property to kinsfolk or to the Church.

The common law of England, taking shape in the last years of the twelfth century, influenced the position of women and property in two ways, first by insisting that any plea of land be held before the secular rather than the ecclesiastical courts, and second, by limiting the proprietary capacity of a married woman. While she retained ownership of her lands, a woman's movable property, her chattels, fell not under the *control* of the husband, as in some of the community systems of Europe, but under his *ownership*. On the other hand, he could not legally dispose of her dower – the property which she would take over on his death. Moreover, when separation or death occurred, both canon and common law agreed that a married woman was entitled to the return of the property she had brought into the marriage.

A conflict arose in the matter of wills. Since a woman as wife

could own no chattels, she could not make a will. However, Glanvill, author of the first English legal treatise (*c.* 1187), considered it
to be fitting that a husband permit his wife to bequeath that part of
his property that would fall to her if she survived him. This concession, Sheehan points out, clearly corresponded to the desires of the
majority of the population, since many women, wives as well as
widows, did in fact make wills. However, despite the Church's insistence, following Roman law, that all adults had the right of bequest,
the common law continued to stress the incapacity of women in this
respect and refused to enforce the testament of one who was married.
From the Church's point of view, on the other hand, the testament
was associated with donations in alms, the importance of which had
been emphasised by Christian teaching since the beginning, to the
extent that in some areas of the West the will became known as the
eleemosyna. The notion of alms, and the bishops' right of supervision
of the delivery of legacies in alms, led the Church to support an
opposite position in relation both to a woman's testamentary freedom and to the disposition of a husband's movable property
(Sheehan 1963a: 112,119,124).

In the early Middle Ages it was men who, with their resort to armed
might, were the plunderers of Church property, though some among
them did contribute to its increase. Women, and especially widows,
were more positively involved with the Church, as givers rather than
as receivers. From the beginning, Harnack claimed, 'Christianity was
laid hold of by women in particular, and also the percentage of
Christian women, especially among the upper classes, was larger than
that of Christian men' (1908: II,73, quoted Gager 1975: 108). In
general, women were greater allies of the Church and greater potential contributors to its material welfare.[8] Hence their freedom as
testators and controllers of their own property was, like continued
widowhood and spinsterhood, clearly in the Church's interest.

[8] On the role of women in Western Europe in the early Middle Ages, see especially
Herlihy 1962. Women exercised considerable control over property even within
marriage in the late Roman and Germanic codes, although the most conservative
of the latter, the Lombard, was more restrictive in respect to a widow's rights,
possibly reflecting 'old German practice'. Especially in Spain and southern France
women held land and were widely admitted to feudal fiefs from the tenth century.
They are recorded as principal donors, sellers and otherwise alienators of property
in the charters, and 'in most instances' it is churches that are receiving their land,
perhaps illustrating 'their higher sense of piety and greater generosity' towards
those bodies (1962: 108).

Except to close affines, the remarriage of widows and widowers was not absolutely forbidden as was the remarriage of divorced persons; but little encouragement was given by the Church to any form of second union.

ADOPTEES

There are several widespread institutions that involve shifting children between domestic groups. The first is wet-nursing, which is essentially a service institution, and may consist in bringing in a servant rather than sending out an infant ('baby-farming'). The second is fostering, which is often reciprocal between kin though it too may have a service component, for it is a practice that is related to the in-house nursing (nannying) of older children, to servanthood, and to apprenticeship (E. Goody 1982). The third is adoption, a practice associated with the problem of heirship (Goody 1976b).

The Christian Church objected to the first of these but failed to put a stop to the practice; the second only in a general sense did it discourage, but the third it effectively prevented for fifteen hundred years. Both wet-nursing and fostering were fundamental features of Anglo-Saxon and Viking life (Foote and Wilson 1980). The latter took ecclesiastical forms. Bede tells how his family entrusted him to Abbot Benedict, of noble origin and founder of the monastery at Wearmouth and Jarrow, where the Abbot devoted his life to the study of the Scriptures. When Benedict journeyed to Rome, his companion, Wilfred, was detained by the Bishop of Lyons, who offered him his young niece as a wife and desired to 'adopt' the Englishman as a son (V. 19), an offer that resembled the practice of the living-in son-in-law. Fostering itself was also widespread in the Celtic areas. 'Noble and freeborn boys and girls were sent away from home to be fostered in another household during childhood and adolescence . . .' Such arrangements were ordered by special laws as well as by the payment of fosterage fees (Hughes 1966: 6,154). As a result the emphasis in some domestic situations fell on rearing rather than on birth; at an Anglo-Saxon marriage it was necessary to know 'to whom belongs the remuneration for rearing' the bride (Whitelock 1979: 467). Certain payments were made to the foster-parent rather than the social or physiological parent, devaluing, or perhaps diffusing, paternity or maternity in favour of extra-familial relations. Given the widespread nature of these practices, it is not surprising that, despite the Church's condemnation of such non-parental relations, fostering and especially wet-nursing should have continued so long to be an intrinsic part of the domestic scene, not only in England (McLaren 1978; 1979) but also in France and Germany right through until the present century (Sussman 1975; 1977a; 1977b). One authority estimated that in eighteenth-century Hamburg there were 4,000–5,000 wet-nurses out of a total population of 90,000 (Lindemann 1981: 385); in contemporary Paris a special *bureau de nourrices* was set up by royal edict to supervise the farming out of infants to the countryside.

Over the centuries, churchmen and other moralists continued to protest against wet-nursing. Others, anyhow in the eighteenth century, saw it as necessary if wives were to act as sexual partners to their husbands within two years after childbirth, since, as in many societies, intercourse was seen to corrupt the milk-supply (Flandrin 1979: 206). Concern about this practice, incompatible with the 'child-centred family', did not begin with Rousseau, but had already been a feature of earlier Catholic and Protestant admonitions. Thomas Becon, chaplain to Archbishop Cranmer, was adamant on the duty of a mother to nurse her own children:

> Thirdly, it is the duty of a good and natural mother not to put forth her children to other women to be nourished, fostered, and brought up with strange milk, except very necessity compel her; but to nurse them herself, yea, and that with her own milk. For to what end hath God given her milk in her breast, but that she with the same milk should nourish and bring up her children? If God hath created nothing in vain, then hath he not given that milk into the mother's breast without cause; verily to nourish and to bring up her infants. Those mothers therefore, which, either of niceness or for ease, put out their children from them to other, when they themselves have abundance of milk, and might well bring them up, if they would take the pain; as they be but half mothers indeed, so likewise do they greatly offend God, and corrupt the nature of the infants. They offend God, in that they resist his ordinance and workmanship by putting away their milk, and by the refusing the labour of nursing their children, which God as a penance hath laid upon them. They corrupt also the nature of the infants, in that they be fostered and brought up not of their mothers, but of strange women; not with the natural, but unnatural milk. And by this means it many times comes to pass, that children, being brought

forth of gentle and godly parents, prove churlish and wicked, and utterly estranged from the nature and good disposition of the parents. For children, by drinking in strange milk, drink in also strange manners and another nature. Therefore, as it is the duty of a good and natural mother to nurse her child herself, yea, and that with her own milk; so likewise is it the part of a true father to provide that his wife, having abundance of milk, do not refuse the labour of fostering her infant, according to the work and commandment of God, knowing that in so doing she shall greatly please God, and satisfy the office of a true and natural mother. (1844: 347–8)

However, such injunctions did little to stop wet-nursing, for which the demand and the supply continued to be so strong. In Tudor England, Hurstfield remarks, the employment of a wet-nurse was widespread among the middle and upper classes (1958: 63). He was commenting upon the case of Charles Framlingham of Shelley, Suffolk, who was taken off by a servant within a fortnight after his birth 'to be nursed'. In this instance, the infant was sent away from his parents' house, a practice that no doubt encouraged the widespread belief in the changeling, not so much the substitution of fairy children but of one child for another. At no time does the practice seem to have been confined to the rich, though doubtless it was more common among them. Nor was it a function of the Christian situation since it was found in Arabia in the time of Mahomet and very recently in Turkey. In a different form, it is found in Africa. The suckling of children by co-wives is reported for the Tallensi of northern Ghana (Fortes 1949) where it represents status equality rather than inequality. Even in stratified societies in West Africa this reciprocity exists, as in the legend of Silamaka, son of a Fulani chief, and Poullori, son of a slave, who were born the same day, and who were carried around and nursed by each other's mother (Vieillard 1931: 146).

Neither in medieval nor in later Europe was wet-nursing confined only to the rich. In south-western France of the thirteenth century, when Raymonde Arsen decided to accept the offer of employment from her first cousin, Raymond Belot of Montaillou, an offer made when an only sister was about to depart, she had first to finish her annual contract with the town family where she was working. She then went off to fetch her illegitimate daughter who had been put out to nurse at Saint-Victor. On her way to Montaillou, she again put her daughter out to nurse before taking up her new post (Le Roy Ladurie 1978).

Wet-nursing continued to be of the greatest importance in France, among the poor as well as among the rich (Flandrin 1979: 203ff). In the eighteenth century, children, except for eldest sons, were frequently sent from town to country to be nursed, even by poor silk-weavers. As a result the fertility of urban couples was greater, since sexual intercourse was recommenced more quickly and the contraceptive effects of lactation were avoided. On the other hand, the mortality of the children may have been higher under 'mercenary wet-nursing', though not as high as has often been assumed (Lindemann 1981: 391). Flandrin sees maternal nursing and 'the simple joys of family life' as becoming fashionable in the mid-eighteenth century, partly as the result of Catholic moralists and later the *philosophes* (1979: 238). He also argues that the position of the Catholics was qualified by their desire to prevent a husband being 'incontinent' while his wife was breastfeeding the baby – an argument strikingly similar to that of Bede (who argued the opposite, *for* continence and the retention of children). Another factor was the early development in eighteenth-century France of the 'Malthusian' family that limited the number of children. With the transformation of marriage into a 'courtly relationship' at the end of the seventeenth century, the wife could then insist upon birth control by coitus interruptus (p. 226), a form of contraception that had been characteristic of medieval courtly love (p. 223). But whatever the change in attitudes and practices, wet-nursing remained a widespread feature of family life in France, England and Germany until late in the nineteenth century.

It is surprising to find wet-nursing criticised by churchmen as early as the eighth century, yet persisting in practice for the next thousand years. Similarly, the use of coitus interruptus was a feature of lay practice as distinct from ecclesiastical advocation throughout this period; it was, for example, widely accepted by the Cathars of the twelfth century, since it was an aspect of the emancipation of women and of contempt for this world. Indeed, according to Nelli, 'contraceptive practices were fairly widespread throughout the middle ages in many different forms, mechanical, chemical and magical' (1969: 62).

Adoption had a very different history from either wet-nursing or fostering. It was essentially a legal act, with many practical implications but which required a formal enactment. The ancient law books of Rome, India and Mesopotamia are full of statutes and commentaries on the subject, although there is little trace of it in the Bible, possibly because of the importance of the levirate as an alternative 'strategy of heirship'.[9] For the two institutions of the levirate and adoption tend to be inversely distributed, the one involving the acquisition of a spouse with a view to reproduction (in the Biblical case), the other the direct acquisition of a 'fictional' heir. The levirate and other formal methods of widow (or spouse) inheritance pose problems for societies that reject plural marriage, since they may entail taking on a second wife or partner; such societies may well prefer to take on a ready-made heir by adoption.

Two possible instances of adoption are found in the Old Testament. Mordecai took his uncle's child, Esther, 'for his own daughter' because she had neither father nor mother (Esther 2: 7 and 15), while Pharaoh's daughter put Moses out to a nurse (presumably farmed to a wet-nurse) and when he returned made him her son (Exodus 2: 10). But adoption was found more frequently among the Greeks and formed a very important part of Roman law, so it might have been expected, *ipso facto*, to have entered into the legal practices of Western Europe.

Given its dominant position in Roman law, its disappearance was remarkably abrupt. The nature of the secular law on adoption was 'drastically reformed in the post-classical period' (Schultz 1951: 148). On the one hand, the adrogation of women (in simple terms, their adoption as adults) was now permitted; and women were now able to adopt, since under Justinian's law *adoptio* did not necessarily create *patria potestas*. On the other, there had to be a gap in age of eighteen years between the adopter and adoptee, while adrogation, carried out by imperial prescript, was as a rule refused where the adopter was less than 60 years old.

These changes have been ascribed to the ethical influence of Christianity (Biondi 1954: 59–68). The inclusion of women emphasises the increasingly 'bilateral' tendencies in the patterns of kinship. At the same time, the act of adoption itself appears to have become more difficult, a prelude to its virtual disappearance from the early

---

[9] *Catholicisme Hier-Aujourd'hui-Demain*, I: 152–3, art. Adoption, Paris, 1948. As for Ancient India, adoption is seen as an alternative strategy of heirship. It is suggested by Kharve (1953) that in Ancient India the earlier preference was for the levirate, followed by a shift to adoption. In Rome the levirate was virtually absent but adoption very much to the fore. Whereas in Islam, as in Israel, the opposite is true (Goitein 1978: 248), though forms of fostering, *rabib*, are mentioned in the Geniza documents.

legislative codes of the German, Celtic and Romanised peoples in the West. Despite their heavy debt to Rome, there is no mention of adoption in the Visigothic Codes of Spain. The sale, donation or pledging of children was forbidden, although children were frequently given by their parents 'for upbringing by others', and the law recognised a contribution (*pretio*) of one *solidus* a year under this arrangement (King 1972: 239). But within a relatively short period, adoption itself had virtually disappeared from the West. The Merovingian practice of *affatomie*, recognised in the laws of the Ripuarian Franks, resembled the testamentary adoption of the Romans; it was a kind of irrevocable testament that could be entered into only where there were no children (Galy 1901: 312–21), a sure sign of its role as a 'strategy of heirship'.[10] Anglo-Saxon codes knew nothing similar (Goffin 1901). Only the early Irish tracts give any substantial evidence of its continuance, at least in the pre-Norman period.

The change was radical. There is no entry for adoption in the whole thirteen volumes of Sir William Holdsworth's *The History of English Law* (1909 etc.). Its absence from the legal systems of Europe was striking and long-lasting. The first law on adoption in the United Kingdom was introduced in 1926; previously the act was unknown in common law. In France it was only reintroduced in 1892, for the Merovingian practice did not long continue. The history is similar in most Western nations, although in the United States, the possibility of adoption was available somewhat earlier, first in Massachusetts in 1851 and then in other states.

What were the consequences of the disappearance of the practice of adoption? In his analysis of inheritance among the great landowners of fifteenth-century Europe, Cooper remarks upon the problems it created for continuity (1977: 302). A partial way out existed in 'the creation of artificial agnatic kinship by the recruitment of new families to Genoese *alberghi* who adopted the name and arms of the albergo' (p. 302). Another possibility lay in the recognition of bastards as legitimate children. This happened from time to time; indeed the fifteenth century in France has been called a bastardocracy, 'the golden age for bastards of the great nobility',

---

[10] The best-known example was political, the adoption by the childless King Gontran of his nephew, later King Childebert II. For other references to adoption in the early codes, see Lex Romana Raetica Curiensis, V. 1. 2ff,22. V. IX (*Monumenta Germaniae Historica, Legum* V. 352ff, 408ff).

but the practice was quite contrary to the Church's insistence on marriage as the instrument of legitimation.[11]

Another 'kind of adoption', as Cooper calls it, was found in Castille from the sixteenth century, where there existed the practice of *mayorazgos* (a sort of entail), which tended to prefer female heirs in the direct line before remoter males. Such a practice is simply a recognition of a daughter as heiress in the absence of sons and it gave rise to problems concomitant with such recognition, namely the oblique marriages between uncle and niece, whereby protector took the protected as wife, and to the custom – also found in English and French settlements – of making the husband of an heiress take the name and arms of her family. Note that this form of oblique marriage was precisely the one that raised objections in Rome and that was clearly prohibited by the Christian Church. Moreover the forms of 'adoption' employed were obviously not adoption in the strict sense and could not be enforced (Cooper 1977: 303).

It was the Church's attitude to the practice that was important, since it came to dominate the enforcement of family law. As we have seen, in the early Christian Church, the widows, who might formerly have been looked after by their husband's family, looked after the orphans, who might earlier have been adopted, usually by kin. Instead of guardianship by kin, the early Church made arrangements to look after its own, who were thus protected from being assigned to non-members of the sect at the death of their parents or of their spouses. The faithful had to be looked after by the faithful; otherwise there was a danger of apostasy. Later on godparents were called upon to play their part on a practical level, but institutional care was also required. When Christianity became the dominant religion, these particular objections to adoption were less significant since while there were many backsliders, there were few 'pagans'. However, the Church still had the duty of looking after the poor as well as after itself, and for this purpose resources were needed. The discontinuity of families encouraged bequests for charitable ends, so that the two considerations fed into one another.

There was also a shift in the concept of adoption to a spiritual plane. In Christian theology, adoption often referred to baptism or was used metaphorically in other ways; in Galatians we read: 'But

---

[11] The case of William the Conqueror was exceptional: here a bastard did succeed, with difficulty, in following his father as Duke of Normandy.

when the fulness of the time was come, God sent forth his Son, made of a woman, made under the law, to redeem them that were under the law, that we might receive the adoption of sons' (4: 4–5). By baptism we became adopted sons of God; it was no longer something that men carried out with respect to other men. Typical of this general transformation of usage is the fact that in the eighth and ninth centuries, the Latin word 'adoption' was used to refer to the relationship between Christ (or the saints) and earthly rulers (Ullmann 1969: 79).

But adoption was to some extent replaced by godparenthood; spiritual kinship was preferred to fictional kinship, and indeed to the wider ties of kinship itself. The relationship between the two, adoption and godparenthood, is made explicit in a text of Gratian, the twelfth-century author of the basic compendium of canon law: 'A godchild could not be less closely related to its godfather than an adopted child to its adoptive father. The act of the godfather was likened to an act of adoption before God' (Gratian, Sec. I and V, c.XXX, qu. 3). Even though adoption was in theory a barrier to marriage in canon law, the fact was of little practical importance in the Middle Ages because it was 'extremely rare'. For canon law took no account of local customs recognising only full legal adoption as defined in Roman law, and this was virtually non-existent (Mortimer 1940: 128).

Why and how this change took place will be discussed in the next chapter. But the results are clear enough. The way that the Church could profit is clear from the nature of an Anglo-Saxon settlement in which a husband and wife leave their land and property to each other and to their future children (Thorpe 1865: 462; Robertson 1939: 45). If there is no child, the land is to go to Archbishop Wulfred 'for their souls'. A man could not adopt a son and heir when he had none of his own. He was therefore more likely to leave his possessions for charitable purposes, as is the case with childless individuals today. The Church could only benefit by excluding 'fictional' heirs.

CONCUBINES

The last feature condemned by Gregory was concubinage. The term refers to two kinds of partner, one who has not been married according to the full rules of the game, or one who has been taken in addition to, and on a different basis from, a wife in the full sense. In both cases the difference concerns the status of the partner and the legal nature of the union. For the woman is usually one who has been married without dowry. In Ancient Greece the most essential difference between wife and concubine, consisted in 'the former having a dowry and the latter none' (Robinson 1827: 452).

The status of the mother does not necessarily determine the status of her offsprings as heirs of the father. In later Rome such children were certainly allowed to inherit; and one of the functions of concubinage in traditional China and in Ancient Israel was to provide an heir when the full, legitimate wife, married with dowry, had failed to produce one. In this respect concubinage served a similar role to polygyny in those societies where an extra wife, of full status, could be taken on to provide an heir. But where the dowry exists, plural marriage involves an allocation of property to women, as wives or daughters, which may weaken the estate and weaken the position of the first wife.[12]

Once again, the change introduced by the Church was striking. The change in concepts of concubinage has been well analysed for the Anglo-Saxons by Margaret Clunies Ross (forthcoming).[13] As in many other societies of the Eurasian continent, concubinage (which some authors call 'polygyny') existed alongside monogamy. In the earliest period of our records a concubine was a member of a man's household and her children could inherit from him if he so wished; in this respect early Germanic law distinguished them from his children by a slave. It was this crucial distinction between freeborn and slave-born that the Church changed into one between legitimate and illegitimate children, a reclassification, 'no doubt often fiercely resisted', that can be 'considered as no less than a social revolution'. While neither lay nor ecclesiastical concubinage came to a sudden end, continuing down to the Norman period (Searle 1981: 161), the Church gradually removed the traditional privileges of the concubine and her offspring; in later Anglo-Saxon times such children were classified as illegitimate and 'thus debarred from the inheritance of family property'. 'Thus it can be seen that the implications

[12] On the role of concubinage as a 'strategy of heirship' in the major Eurasian societies, see Goody 1976b.

[13] See the unpublished paper by Margaret Clunies Ross entitled '"Concubinage" in Anglo-Saxon England', to which I am much indebted.

of the Church's reforms . . . were far-reaching, extending beyond the institution of concubinage itself to the autonomy of the kin-group to determine its heirs' (Clunies Ross n.d.).

And so, under Christianity, the concubine became the mistress and her children bastards. The 'legitimate' status of offspring was of course critical for heirship. The fact that in *King Lear* Edmund had not been begotten between the wedded sheets whereas Edgar had, made all the difference to their personalities and to their life-chances. The estates of 'illegitimate' offspring, as the astounding history of the Mackays brings out (see pp. 216–19), were open to confiscation by the Church or State. The redefinition of marriage changed the whole notion of the legitimacy of a person's progeny, leading to a split between sex and marriage, as well as between 'filiation' and parenthood.

The objection of the Church to concubinage has usually been seen in moral and ethical terms, arising out of the Church's view of sexuality as basically sinful. Even so, it cannot be accidental that it set aside one way in which an individual or kin-group determined its heirs.[14] The 'morality' of the family that we have inherited has to be seen against the background of the accepted practices in earlier societies and the way in which these were set aside or encouraged by the Church. One possible reason for the suppression of secular con-cubinage (ecclesiastical concubinage was attacked for other reasons) may have been its very ability to create 'fictional' or additional heirs, the existence of which might prevent a couple from donating its wealth for religious purposes.

Clerical concubinage was a function of the celibacy of priests. Like other major features of Christian teaching about marriage and the family, this doctrine was not fixed, even in principle, until the fourth century. According to the Apostolic Constitutions of the late third century, members of the higher grades of the Church, bishops, priests and deacons, must be men of only one wife who could not marry after ordination. But members of the lower grades could

Searle argues that in Norman England the growing definition of marriage as monogamous (i.e. the process we have described in relation to lay concubinage) was important not only to the Church but also to the seignorial world 'who welcomed and encouraged clerical aid in reducing the 'pool' of legitimate claim-ants, and thereby reducing the dangers and violence of succession-disputes'. 'The baronage soon went beyond the Church in England, and denied legitimacy even to "mantle children" whom the Church accepted' (1981: 169), that is, children born to parents who married after their birth.

marry at any time, providing the wife was not a concubine, slave, widow or divorcee. Despite the occasional blast against the ties of family and marriage, by Christ as well as by Paul, asceticism is not specifically advocated in the New Testament, although the idea of abstinence and withdrawal, especially on the part of priests, was certainly an important element in the intellectual climate of the first few centuries.

St Augustine's debate with the Manichaean bishop, Faustus, recalls the alternative and more ascetic traditions of the Middle East, influenced in this case not only by the dualism of the Magi, but also by Buddhist and, more generally, Indian views concerning the rejection of meat and the avoidance of sex, which appear to have promoted the doctrine of a sacerdotal class, devoted to abstinence and separated from the masses.[15] But there is no acknowledgement of this trend in the first General Council of the Church held at Nicaea in 325, a widely drawn assembly that was made possible by the Emperor Constantine who placed the governmental machinery of posts at the service of the prelates. It was not until about the year 385 that the Pope issued the first definite command, imposing celibacy as an absolute rule. Once again it was shortly after the time Christianity became an established Church that it chose the path of celibacy for its priesthood.[16]

The reasons have to do partly with the gains made by the ascetic tendency and partly with the establishment of monastic orders who took the vow of celibacy. The belief that celibacy was a higher state than marriage was not an intrinsic feature of the early Church, although it marked the beliefs and practices of other sects such as the Essenes. Nevertheless the rise of monasticism and the establishment of a Christian society promoted this belief from the middle of the fourth century; 'the intensified worldliness of the new fashionable Church would naturally foster the growth of the ascetic ideal. The command, "Love not the world" (I John 2: 13), had to find

---

[15] Abstinence from meat seems to have been connected with the refusal to eat the produce of generation rather than with a concern for life itself; the Cathars, for example, consumed fish, just as Catholics did on Fridays. However, the important treatise on abstinence from flesh by the Neoplatonic philosopher, Porphyry, rehearses a whole range of arguments, directed against a recent convert to Christianity (Wynne-Tyson 1965).

[16] The Eastern Church itself nearly imposed celibacy on its clergy in the fourth century.

some new interpretation when the world was no longer a professedly heathen world, but a community of nominal Christians' (Foley 1915: 436). While the teaching of the earlier Gnostics and similar sects was firmly condemned, the idea of the superiority of the single state became widely diffused in the Middle Ages, especially in the Western Church which partially diverged from the Eastern in this respect. By the third General Council of Constantinople (A.D. 680) the marriage of clerics after their ordination was forbidden, but except in the case of bishops, existing conjugal relations did not have to be broken off. This remains the position of the Eastern Church today, where bishops are recruited from monasteries while the parish clergy are drawn from the ranks of the married. In the West it was only with the Reformation that the marriage of priests was vindicated doctrinally. In Luther's eyes, all monastic vows were essentially sinful (*de Votis monasticis* 1521).

On one level the adoption of clerical celibacy can be seen as part of the gains of the ascetic and monastic trends, though the prohibition of the marriage of priests only led, in many cases, to their taking concubines. Asceticism was an aspect of the monastic tradition, less so of the priestly one. Yet it also continued to be a subdominant theme in the wider tradition of Christian thought and practice, and at one level merged with the more general reaction to the worldly life of some clergy, an important aspect of later anticlericalism, just as it had been of earlier monasticism. Inside the early Church, men like Origen (*c.* 185–*c.* 254) were against marriage. Outside the Church, there was the whole Gnostic tradition in which everything of this world was alien to God. Manichaeism developed the idea of an absolute cosmic dualism between soul and matter, a doctrine which survived centuries of persecution in the East and returned through Bulgaria and Lombardy to southern France at the close of the twelfth century in the form of the teachings of the Cathars or Albigensians.[17] For them the dualistic doctrine by which the world was irremediably evil was accompanied by an ascetic

---

[17] The teaching of the Bogomils returned in spirit if not by direct contact to the earlier dualistic doctrines. On the discussion of the origin of the 'medieval Manichee', see Moore 1977 and Runciman 1947. Mani considered himself the founder of a universal religion, which was persecuted both by Christianity and Zoroastrianism. Supported by merchants, written largely in Aramaic, the religion spread as far as the T'ang Empire of China (Brown 1972: 94ff).

attitude towards food and sex. 'No necessity was regarded as justifying the use of meat, or even of eggs and cheese, or in fact of anything which had its origin in animal propagation. Marriage was an abomination and a mortal sin, which could not be intensified by adultery or other excesses' (Lea 1867: 370).[18] Catholic priests, on the other hand, failed to separate themselves from their concubines, and even their wives, for many centuries.[19] Matters changed with the ecclesiastical reforms of the eleventh century, directed as they were against the preponderance of familial and proprietary, of dynastic and political interests that interfered with the ecclesiastical tasks of the Church. In 1072 the Council of Rouen forbade any minister who married to receive or dispose of any of the Church's revenue. It was only after 1073 with the actual accession to the papacy of Archdeacon Hildebrand, who had spent a short period of his life in a monastery like most of the reformist leaders (Brooke 1964: 250), that the celibacy of the priesthood became widely accepted; the earlier papal efforts at reform, inspired by the teachings of the Italian hermit-monk, Peter Damian (1007–1072), had done little to achieve this end. But Gregory VII, as Hildebrand became, was determined to establish the priesthood as a hierarchical autocracy. To this end, the priest had to be a man set apart, superior to human frailties. Besides, Gregory had himself come from humble beginnings and the opportunity to rise in the Church would have been closed had the marriage of priests led to the hereditary transmission of benefices, creating a 'separate caste of individual proprietors . . . lazily luxuriating on the proceeds of former popular beneficence' (Lea 1867: 236).[20]

---

[18] The great American historian of the Church, Henry C. Lea, also wrote works on mortmain, superstition and force, indulgences and a number of similar topics. He was defended against attack by G. G. Coulton in his *Sectarian History*, Taunton, 1937. See also Bossy 1975: 22 and Moore 1977: xi for more recent approval.

[19] 'Though Ethelred's and Cnut's orders repeatedly state that the priest has no right to marry, clerical marriage was not uncommon throughout the Anglo-Saxon period' (Whitelock 1941: 15). In Scotland there seem to have been similar difficulties with clerical celibacy and close marriage, including marriage to the widows of near kin (Duncan 1975: 122,129–30), as we learn from Turgot's attempt to reform the Church during his short episcopate (1109–1115). On marriage to the step-mother and the deceased brother's wife in the eleventh century, see p. 122; on Irish 'polygyny' see Ó Corráin 1972: 38. It was the famous German-Jewish Talmudist, Gershon ben Judah (960–1028), known as 'Light of the Exile', who banned polygyny among the Ashkenazi (Patai 1981: 51).

[20] '. . . as possession of property and hereditary transmission of benefices would have necessarily followed on the permission to marry, an ecclesiastical caste, combining

The reason behind Gregory's enforcement of clerical celibacy is clear. According to Lea, similar reasons lay behind the earlier pressure in that direction. Attention has already been drawn to the ascetic undercurrent in the early centuries. This movement had been reinforced by the fact that when the Church became established, a new class of men found their way into its ranks; increasing laxity gave rise to a call for asceticism. But yet another factor probably played its part: 'The church was daily receiving vast accessions of property from the pious zeal of its wealthy members, the death-bed repentance of despairing sinners, and the munificence of emperors and prefects, while the efforts to procure the inalienability of its possessions dates from an early period. Its acquisitions, both real and personal, were of course exposed to much greater risk of dilapidation when the ecclesiastics in charge of its widely scattered riches had families for whose provision a natural parental anxiety might be expected to over-ride the sense of duty in discharging the trust confided to them. The simplest mode of averting the danger might therefore seem to be to relieve the churchman of the cases of paternity, and, by cutting asunder all the ties of the family and kindred, to bind him completely and forever to the church and to that alone. This motive . . . was openly acknowledged in later times, and it no doubt served as an argument of weight in the minds of those who urged and secured the adoption of the canon' (Lea 1867: 64–5). In support of this contention, Lea refers to the problems created by the great influx of pious legacies which gave rise to the law of Valentinian (*Cod. Theod.* XVI, Tit. II. 2.20) of A.D. 370 forbidding testamentary provisions made under priestly influence, a law repeated in A.D. 390 with additional provisions. While the ban on lay concubinage augmented the patrimony of the Church, the celibacy of the priesthood kept that wealth from being dispersed into lay hands.

By the time Bede was writing, indeed by the fourth century, the Christian Church had taken up specific, though not necessarily uni-

temporal and spiritual power in the most dangerous excess, would have repeated in Europe the distinctions between the Brahmin and Soudra of India' (Lea 1867: 237). Indeed this danger was already in the air, for 'By the overruling tendency of the age, all possessions previously held by laymen on precarious tenure were rapidly becoming hereditary' (p. 149): the decay of royal power would have meant the rise of an independent hereditary caste.

form, positions with regard to these four major aspects of marriage and the family; the close marriages, unions with affines and the fate of the widow, adoption, and concubinage. The positions ran contrary to those of earlier Mediterranean practice and apparently to those of the German and Celtic lands. They continued to run contrary to the ways of the Middle East in medieval times, as revealed in the wealth of material that has survived from the community of Jews in Cairo (Goitein 1978), as well as to the contemporary practices of the Islamic world.[21]

These new forms of social action did not derive from the models of Hebrew or Roman law. Nor did they clearly result from the teaching or practice of early Christianity. How then did these changes actually arise?

[21] I have earlier (p. 51) noted some of the possibilities of close marriage in the Jewish community of medieval Cairo when commenting upon oblique marriage. It was also the case that marriage between first cousins was 'extremely common', the marriage with the father's brother's daughter being twice as frequent as that with the mother's brother's daughter. Cousin marriage was also widespread among the Christian Copts of Egypt. Goitein (1978) notes that such marriages were used to unite properties, though he regards the main reason for such unions as connected with the belief that members of the 'extended family' would be more considerate one of another, especially of young wives. Such marriages may also be encouraged by the levirate, or by the inheritance of a widow. For if she were to bring her children to live with her husband's brother, her daughter might become the bride of one of her protector's sons (in Arabic the word for bride and father's brother's daughter is the same).

In the case of a brother who died without leaving children, the levirate was compulsory in Judaism and customary under Islam. Adoption, as we have seen, was rare. Given the discussion of the difficulties in marrying those with whom one has been reared (Wolf and Huang 1980, Hopkins 1980, Shepher 1971), a problem that is raised by the marriage of the widow's children, it is interesting to read Goitein's account of the woman who took a little girl into her house, probably at the beginning of the Crusading period when many female prisoners had to be ransomed and cared for. She already had three girls and two boys but took on an orphan to acquire religious merit. After four or five years when the girl matured, one of the boys asked her to marry him. But the marriage only lasted a few weeks and she refused to return to her husband 'even if he pours gold pieces upon my head'. All pressure failed to reverse her decision and eventually the girl was driven out of the house by her foster-siblings (1978: 248).

5. *From sect to Church*

The far-reaching changes in family structure that occurred in Europe were not due to the influence of Roman or Jewish law and custom. Nor were they the ones sometimes seen as peculiarly Christian. Many of the features that apologists associate with Christianity were already present, at least in embryo, in the contemporary patterns of marriage and the family in the Middle East, for example, those which stressed the conjugal family and the position of women as heirs. But there were also important changes, including those recorded by the Venerable Bede, which were not embodied in the teaching and practice of early Christianity. These new features did not emerge until the fourth century after Christ, by which time the Church had become established and an orthodox Christianity had arisen. This orthodoxy, by corollary, necessarily entailed the rise of heresy; for orthodoxy, according to Brown, was not a dogma but 'an ecclesiastical vested interest' (1972: 243),[1] an interest that accompanied the development of the Church as an organisation with buildings, land, personnel and legitimacy. These features did not have much to do with the attitudes and doctrines examined in the accounts of ecclesiastical historians, except in the stress that they placed on the conjugal family (even in opposition to wider ties of kinship), on consensual unions (even in opposition to parental wishes), and on the role of women as holders of property.

Dauvillier is not untypical of historians of canon law in maintaining that, 'As far as marriage was concerned Christianity introduced quite new ideas which turn the laws and customs of antiquity upside down: the sacred character of Christian marriage which nevertheless remained an inferior state than celibacy consecrated to God; freedom to choose between celibacy and marriage . . .' as well as chastity;

---

[1] Brown's comment is based upon Gottfrid Arnold's study, *Impartial Historical Examination of Churches and Heretics*, published in 1699.

fidelity of both husband and wife; and indissolubility (1970: 25). In fact marriage seems to have continued very much as before until the fourth century when the regulations that were introduced moved in a rather different direction than Dauvillier suggests. For the features he selects do not seem peculiar to Christianity, which was not the only force in the Mediterranean world to see chastity and fidelity as important; nor the only doctrine to value celibacy and abstinence as paths to holiness. And while divorce was possible in Rome and Israel, it was never as easy as it was to become in the Islamic world, or had been in earlier Egypt (Hopkins 1980: 335).

The thrust of the fourth-century decrees and legislation lay in another direction, one that changed the patterns of marriage in the whole area under Christian domination, but which had little or no relation to the doctrines of the faith, much less to its scriptures. In the main these patterns can hardly be regarded as an *ethical* advance on the rules and customs of earlier societies; some might wish to argue against concubinage on universal ethical principles, but the same can hardly be done for the marriage of cousins or the adoption of children. Their one common feature was the control they gave over strategies of heirship, and in particular the control over close marriages, those between consanguineal, affinal and spiritual kin.

The evidence for the attitudes of the early (pre-fourth-century) Church towards marriage and the family rests on three main written sources, namely the recorded teachings of Jesus, the Pauline epistles and the ante-Nicene Patristic literature. The first source comprises the narratives of the life of Christ by the four evangelists as presented in the New Testament. From these, and specifically from their accounts of the 'Holy Family', it is clear that Palestinian kinship centred on the elementary family, in the sense that the household consisted of parents and children, sometimes giving shelter to an aged relative. There is no evidence of any 'joint family' as the term is often understood. 'The patriarchal family, which Genesis attributes to the Hebrews of the 2nd millennium, seems to have completely disappeared' (Gaudemet 1962: 62). Whether or not we can agree with this statement in all its particulars, Christianity clearly invented neither the conjugal family nor the simple household.[2]

---

[2] Along with other anthropologists, I have argued that in one or other of its definitions the elementary family is found in the vast majority of human societies; and in the vast majority of societies households are relatively small (1972: 124).

Scriptural sources have also been held to stress the indissolubility of marriage, except in the case of adultery (Matthew 19:9 '*nisi forni-cationis causa*'), insisting upon the reciprocal fidelity of the spouses and the importance of widows and children (Gaudemet 1962: 62). But this 'strengthening of the family' was carried out in the process of strengthening the sect, which, as will become apparent, led to very different results, very contradictory doctrines.

The Pauline epistles are explicit in seeing marriage and the family as only one of the possible conditions of mankind. Here we find stress placed upon the superiority of virginity, of the asexuality of widows, and of sexual continence in general. Although Paul did not condemn marriage (which served as the basis for the analogy of the union between Christ and his Church), relations within the family were subject to the over-riding demands of religion. The obedience of children to parents had to be 'in the Lord'.

The Fathers of the Church writing before the fourth century have little to say on the subject of marriage and the family, which become topics of importance in the Patristic literature only after the conversion of the Empire and the establishment of the Church. These authorities of the fourth and fifth centuries display the same divisions as the earlier sources. All were concerned only with 'la famille étroite', the elementary family (Gaudemet 1962: 65), which was itself compared to the Church by Saint John Chrysostom (*c.* 347–407). St Augustine (354–430) defended the institution of the family against various sects, Gnostic, Montanist and Manichaean, which, in the name of the ascetic ideal, condemned marriage and led the world to its ruin (*Contra Faustum Manichaeum* XIX. 29). On the other hand there were Catholics such as Priscillian (d. 385), who shared that same view of marriage, organising themselves into bands of *spiritales* and *abstinentes* like the Cathari of the twelfth century, and all these writers acknowledged the superiority of the celibate state.

St Augustine was the strongest defender of marriage – monogamous marriage as in Rome and following the Roman prohibitions. The Church also preserved the forms and customs of Roman marriage, including the dowry. But relations between husband and wife, and between parents and children were little different in 'pagan' circles, although Christians did object to abortion, to the exposure of the new-born and to the sale of children by unredeemed debtors, all of which had been Roman practices and which could be seen as reducing the number of the faithful.

During this early period there were few changes in Roman law that can unambiguously be put down to the influence of Christian doctrine, since other members of society also made similar recommendations for reform. One such reform of late antiquity was the abolishing of the power of the father over the life and death of his offspring. Such a right exists in many societies but is largely notional, a vague sanction on the behaviour of the junior generation. Nevertheless its abolition can be considered as a possible index of the relaxation of parental authority.

It is suggested by Gaudemet that the legal prohibitions on marriage to affines which were established in the second half of the fourth century (between 355 and 415) may have been influenced by the ideas put forward at the Synod of Elvira held in Spain in 305. He also claims that penalties on those who broke off a betrothal as well as the measures designed to protect the children of the *premier lit*, of the first marriage, may both have been influenced by Christianity, though such sanctions and measures existed (and still do) elsewhere, and have a more general link with dowry systems (Goody 1976b). The evidence is sparse and the influence of the Church was even less certain on a range of legislation which, while consistent with Christian ideals, had also been advocated by non-Christian contemporaries and could be considered as part of the emergent corpus of written law. Into this category fell not only the legislation that controlled the abuse of paternal authority but also that which provided for the welfare of children; as early as the beginning of the second century A.D., the Emperor Trajan organised a foundation for feeding poor children. Even the idea of the consensual nature of marriage was to be found in Roman law. Formerly thought to be a feature of the later Roman Empire, developing under the influence of Patristic doctrine, it is now clear that in classical law, and in the pagan period itself, 'marriage was held to be a purely consensual act' (Gaudemet 1957b: 531); *consensus facit nuptias*. Nor was the agreement of the spouses absent even earlier in Egypt (Hopkins 1980); while it is still a requirement, and here I speak from my own experience in Africa, in those systems of marriage where parental or societal regulation is much more strongly in evidence. Neither in practice nor in law, concludes Gaudemet, did Christianity have much influence on the family life of imperial Rome.

The argument is correct enough regarding those features of marriage, such as the consensus of the partners, the focus on the conjugal family, restrictions on parental authority, which apologists have attributed to the ethical nature of Christian doctrine; at any rate the Church seems to have had little decisive influence on Roman law at this stage. But in other ways the coming of Christianity had very significant, and to some extent very conflicting, results.

Let us look in greater detail at the teachings of Christ on the subject of marriage and the family, and then at the implications for the domestic domain of the growth of the Church as an established and endowed corporation. The Church began as a sect, first within, then breaking away from Judaism, a process that, initially at least, meant not the recognition but the denial of family ties. This aspect of the sectarian message of the Gospels is very clearly set out in the New Testament:

'I came not to send peace, but a sword.

For I am come to set a man at variance against his father, and the daughter against her mother, and the daughter in law against her mother in law.

And a man's foes shall be they of his own household.

He that loveth father or mother more than me is not worthy of me: and he that loveth son or daughter more than me is not worthy of me.' (Matthew 10: 34–7)

Nine chapters later the message is repeated:

'And every one that hath forsaken houses, or brethren, or sisters, or father, or mother, or wife, or children, or lands, for my name's sake, shall receive an hundredfold, and shall inherit everlasting life.' (Matthew 19: 29)[3]

One's 'kin' were no longer one's family but the members of the sect:

'Who is my mother? and who are my brethren?

And he stretched forth his hand toward his disciples, and said, "Behold my mother and my brethren!"

For whosoever shall do the will of my Father which is in heaven, the same is my brother, and sister, and mother.' (Matthew 12: 48–50)[4]

These are the words of the millenarian prophet to the primitive community of the faithful, words that set aside family ties, minimise

[3] On the importance of this text, see Angenendt 1972: 130ff.

[4] This incident is repeated in Mark and Luke but no other Evangelist puts the general situation quite as strongly as Matthew. However Luke's words are unambiguous: 'if any one come to me and does not hate his father and mother and wife and children . . . he cannot be my disciple' (Luke 14: 26).

the distinctions between the sexes, play down status differences, and point perhaps to the ownership of property in common (Gager 1975: 34]).[5] But with the establishment of the Church, the recruits were no longer mainly the 'disinherited poor' of Palestine struggling against Roman occupation, but the propertied classes of the Empire itself. The nature of the conflict between Church and family took on a very different character.

While I have selected those texts from the New Testament that unambiguously place the family in opposition to the Church, or rather the sect, others have claimed that Holy Writ also provided the model for a patriarchal or even monarchical family. Referring to the Old as well as to the New Testament, Flandrin points not only to the Fifth Commandment (the Fourth in Catholic eyes), 'Honour thy father and thy mother, that thy days may be long', but also to the passage from the Epistle to the Ephesians in which Paul establishes the authority of the father over wife, children and servants, as well as his duty of love and correction towards them. More than this, Flandrin sees patriarchal authority as not only an intrinsic part of the world in which Christianity emerged, but as one of the conditions for the development of monotheistic religion. At the same time, the new creed is credited with an original contribution in insisting upon the reciprocity of duties between the father and the family; the authority of the father and of God legitimised not only each other but all authorities that were seen as representative of God on earth.

The nature of family structures in early Palestine seems ill-described by the word 'patriarchal', if only because the term is imprecise enough to comprehend most types of domestic arrangement; neither patriarchality nor the reciprocity of rights and duties are in any way singular to the Christian past. Indeed, the major texts of the New Testament tend to diminish the importance of kinship and of family relations for the reasons I have suggested (p. 46). Did the influence of the Church help to abolish the father's powers of life and death over the children, even though such powers were largely nominal or symbolic? As Pagels has argued in her examination of the Gnostic documents of Nag Hammadi (1980), the insistence on

---

[5] Some early Christian sects gave more prominence to the role of women than others; the Montanists had important prophetesses and in Marcionism, where marriage was prohibited, women shared in a wide range of cultic roles (Gager 1975: 35).

authority was not so much a feature of early Christianity as of the later, dominant, Catholic branch; the triumphant Church became concerned with authority when it had achieved a commanding position. On becoming the universal Church, its fight was not to detach members from their ancestral religions, and hence from their families, a fight that the words of the Gospel so vividly express, but a struggle to retain the faith of those who had acquired their religion in the bosom of those families, a struggle against heresy and apostasy. On the other hand, the established Church had a yet greater need to maintain itself by attracting alms and legacies, forms of 'endowment' that were often alienations of property from other members of the family.

In certain ways the effects of conversion on the family in the time of Constantine were devastating: 'In Graeco-Roman society the family was held together not merely by the interests of labour and reward; it was a community united by cult and celebrations. The stability of the house and the survival of the clan were guaranteed by the *sacra familiae* and *sacra gentilicia*. Even in the later empire, when in general spiritual ties became less stringent, family cults remained deeply rooted in the sanctity of tradition; they were the strongest supports of the ancestral religion which had largely become the concern of the family, particularly in senatorial circles' (Vogt 1963: 42). The author goes on to claim that Christianity, like Judaism, required a personal avowal of faith from its converts, a feature that we may regard as not so much an attribute of a particular religion as of the conversion process in general. For, as Christ foresaw, this demanded the break away from, and in a sense the destruction of, family ties.[6] 'We know for instance from the Acts of the martyrs Perpetua and Felicitas how often family ties were

---

[6] Following my source, I am using the term faith (like belief) in a loose way. In a paper (1982), 'Christians as believers', Ruel argues for a more exact usage as well as for a greater attention to the sociological particularity of Christian belief. In a comment to me he adds that conversion to Christianity was marked by the special ritual of baptism: 'there is a constant boundary-marking issue of whether you are in or out, with us or against us ... Moreover all this has implications for the structure of the Christian community (the 'brothers' in earliest times) who are admitted individually, who are clearly demarcated from others by their individual badge of belonging.' Although the particularity of Christianity supports my general thesis, I would nevertheless wish to suggest that Christian baptism represents an extreme case of the widespread procedures of entry that open the way not only to other world religions but also to some of the 'new cults' of transitional and traditional societies.

broken by the Christian mission throughout the empire; and the legend of St Martin tells us that he won his mother for the new faith while his father remained true to the tradition of his ancestors' (p. 42). The conversion of individuals to new beliefs meant weaning them away from cults that had been closely linked to the family, and involved a radical separation from those members who still continued in the old ways.[7]

The Gospels thus provide the scriptural basis for a rejection of family ties in favour of membership of the sectarian community. It is into this sectarian family that one should marry, or so Paul requires of widows: the wider obligation is implicit in the Pauline Epistles (I Corinthians 7: 12–16, II Corinthians 6: 17) and strongly recommended (sometimes insisted upon) by the Fathers (Gaudemet 1962: 524). No Christian could marry a Jew. Similar sentiments are expressed by many other sects and reform movements, in the present as well as in the past. Like Christianity, they have to take up an extreme position with regard to family life as the reproducer of culture, since they must attract individuals away from the beliefs of their fathers and forefathers. The despair of parents is the joy of the revolution. It is when the sects become established, when they are on the way to becoming Churches (to use the Weberian distinction), that they welcome doctrinal continuity in the family, ensured by the endogamy of the faithful. Then the routinisation of charisma, the establishment of the revolution, is, in one sense at least, complete.

In discussing what he calls the quest of Christians for legitimacy and consolidation, which occurred over the period from A.D. 30 to 312, Gager calls attention to a cluster of relevant factors; 'growing numbers, geographic expansion, the need for administrators of community resources, the decline of End-time enthusiasm, and the inevitable instinct to preserve the ideal and material interests of the community itself', together with the inherent weakness of the idea of apostolic authority (1975: 72). Throughout most of the first century, Christian communities defined themselves in opposition to the

---

[7] 'One feature of late Roman society – usually seen more clearly by the medievalist than by the classical scholar – is the slow emergence of a society ever more sharply contoured by religious belief. The heretic, the Jew, the pagan became second-class citizens. The bishop, the holy man, the monastic community rise in increasing prominence above the *saeculum*, the world of the average man. The community is ringed by the invisible frontier between the "saved" within the Christian fold and the "damned" outside it' (Brown 1972: 14, 303ff).

'world'; by the end of the third century, they had created their own 'world' (p. 82). Initially recruiting from the poor and illiterate, the unprivileged (p. 96), the religion later attracted wealthy believers who provided a new basis of financial support but at the same time forced upon the Church a revaluation of the ideology of poverty permanently enshrined in the Scriptures (p. 106). Doctrinally, the shift from 'folly' to 'wisdom' (I Corinthians 1: 21) meant a synthesis of Christian faith and of Greek philosophy, Hellenistic Christianity taking over from Hellenistic Judaism, using the Greek translation of the Jewish Bible already available for Greek-speaking synagogues (p. 127).

Early Christian communities used the synagogue as a model, adopting its liturgical calendar, its forms of worship, communal care of the sick and the elderly, and its system of financial contributions (Gager 1975: 128–9). For two hundred years they possessed no identifiable places of assembly, putting their emphasis upon the community of the faithful, which was especially important in the urban environment in which they first flourished.

The process of establishing the Church, with places of worship and as a charitable, ecclesiastical and residential organisation, required the accumulation of funds. Financial contributions provided part of the income needed. But once the missionary phase of the disciples had passed, a more permanent basis of operation entailed the acquisition of other forms of immovable property, land and buildings. The same process of accumulation is a familiar one in modern sects and communes, leading to contradictions in theory and conflicts among the members.[8] For, even when acquisition is carried out by the organisation rather than by individuals, it frequently runs counter to the tenets of the reforming ideology. In Christianity the Scriptures explicitly reject the accumulation of all wealth. Christ's instructions to his disciples ran as follows:

---

[8] For communes, see Abrams and McCulloch 1976, who contend that both continuity and conflict are related to the acquisition of property. For an example of sectarian acquisition, see the recent history of the much-praised rehabilitation (and later religious) organisation in California called Synanou. Started by C. E. Dederich in 1958, within a short time it had acquired 'thousands of acres of property, over 450 motor cycles, 275 buses, trucks, cars, airplanes, gliders and the nation's second largest advertising novelty company' (*San Francisco Chronicle*, 'This World', 6 Jan. 1980, p. 5). New members made over title to their property to the organisation.

'Heal the sick, cleanse the lepers, raise the dead, cast out devils: freely ye have received, freely give.

Provide neither gold, nor silver, nor brass in your purses.' (Matthew 10: 8–9)

And the instructions to his followers were equally unambiguous:

'If thou wilt be perfect, go and sell what thou hast, and give to the poor, and thou shalt have treasure in heaven: and come and follow me.' (Matthew 19: 21)

The contradiction between the reforming creed and the acquisitive society was an obvious source of conflict, and not simply in the early stages. A characteristic of written creeds is that they perpetuate the early beliefs of the sect even when it has become an institutionalised Church, thus providing within itself a continuing focus for potential opposition. Such statements cannot be wished away nor erased by the passage of time, as is the case in an oral society. The devastating demands of the revolutionary formulation can be re-interpreted in an allegorical fashion or be reformulated for 'modern' use. But there is always the possibility that, approaching the text without the mediation of the priesthood, someone will take the words literally and demand that the Church give up its possessions, or that the family be subordinated to other ends. 'If thou wilt be *perfect*' in the way that the Church could no longer be, but in the way the Cathars (or at least their elect) thought was possible.

In this way the writings that embody the 'charismatic pedigree' may themselves 'become a recurrent focus of change and conflict' (Gager 1975: 75). The very fact that the sectarian sayings of early Christians were preserved in sacred writings made them available as potential models for the behaviour of future generations, even though their teachings ran contrary to the accepted practices of Church and country. Sometimes the sayings were revived by a new sect attempting to combat the teachings of the dominant Church. Sometimes an individual might use their authority for his own personal ends.[9]

The Christian Church did not at first own any landed property; those who had lands and houses sold them to give the money to the

---

[9] There was a mixture of both elements in Raimon Roussel's attempt to persuade Beatrice de Planissoles to flee with him to join the Cathars in Lombardy. When she was hesitant, wondering how she could leave behind her husband and children, he urged her on by reminding her that the Lord had said a person should leave father, mother, sons and daughters to follow Him (Nelli 1969: 261–2).

Church (Acts 4: 34). The revolution of the fourth century began with the conversion of Constantine and his victory at the Battle of Milvian Bridge in 312. The Christians were ready to take over the Roman Empire and to ensure the impossibility of a return to earlier conditions of inferiority and persecution' (Momigliano 1963: 80). At this time Christianity was still largely an urban religion, despite the fact that the basic economic activity of the region was agricultural. Then in the fourth century it penetrated into the upper classes and the large number of conversions from that group gave its members a dominant position (Jones 1963: 21; see also Gibbon 1898: III,194). It was these propertied classes who were now to pass on some of their immovable property to the Church.

The edict of Constantine of A.D. 313 declared that Christians were known to possess property that did not belong to any individual, and from this time on immovable property was given to the Church in abundance. In some cases the donor gave the property absolutely; in others he reserved some rights of usufruct for himself or a near relative. But in general, Church property was freer than that of others; for example it was not subject to the statute of limitations. Again, legacies to the Church often received special treatment as under the Lex Falcidia.

It was in A.D. 321 that Constantine decreed that a dying man might bequeath property to the Church even orally. This 'freedom' for the individual encouraged a person to disinherit his kin in favour of God; indeed all religious bequests were a kind of alienation from kin and problems soon began to emerge. As a result of abuses that arose from excessive zeal in making ecclesiastical bequests, a reaction set in later that century. St Augustine would not allow the Church to accept a legacy from a man who had disinherited his son (*Sermo* 355: 4). This action was approved by St Jerome (*Epist.* CXXVII, To Principia) who applauded one Marcella for surrendering her own wishes to those of her mother and bequeathing her property to relatives rather than to the Church. On the other hand, he advised the widow Furia to leave her money to the Church in spite of the opposition of her father (*Epist.* LIV): 'To whom then are you to leave your great riches? To Christ who cannot die. Whom shall you make your heir? The same who is already your Lord. Your father will be sorry but Christ will be glad; your family will grieve but the angels will rejoice with you. Let your father do what he likes with what is his own. You are not his to whom you have been born, but his to whom you have been born again, and who has purchased you at a great price with his own blood' (Wace and Schaff 1893: 103). It is not simply that the sect replaces kin, but that Christians are adopted or purchased by God; physiological or natural kinship is less important than spiritual to those who are 'born again', and it is to their 'adopted' Father that they should leave their wealth. The implications are dramatic.

The reaction to this testamentary freedom took a variety of forms, some of which placed restrictions on the priesthood. A law of Emperor Valentinian III in A.D. 455 forbade clerics to receive legacies from virgins and other religious persons (*Cod. Theod.* XVI. 2. 20), while already in A.D. 390 the Emperor Theodosius had prevented deaconesses from making bequests to the Church, though they could offer gifts in their lifetime (XVI. 2. 27).

The reaction took on a more general character. St Augustine advised those with sons to include Christ as one more heir and give the Church an equal share with the rest (*Sermo* 86: 11–14; *Enarratio in Psalmos* 38: 12; Bruck 1956: 84–8). Thus some protection was given to children against the desire of their own parents to alienate familial property either for religious grace or for personal revenge. But kin beyond the elementary family had a thinner time. In A.D. 590 the first Council of Seville (c. 1) was asked by the deacons to annul certain manumissions of slaves owned by ecclesiastical bodies, since the alienation of Church property was forbidden by the canons. The freed men were allowed to remain free but under *ius ecclesiae*, which meant that they could leave their property to their sons but to no-one else.[10] The direct line only had rights, collaterals were excluded. Such a restriction was part of a more general tendency in ecclesiastical legislation. In the case of the restriction of inheritance to sons, the property would revert to the Church in some 40 per cent of the cases, which, as we have seen (p. 44) is the rough proportion of families who, under this type of demographic condition, would be without direct male heirs at the death of the parents (Goody and Harrison 1976).

In earlier Mediterranean societies the state of heirlessness could be remedied by the use of one of the widespread strategies of heir-

---

[10] See also Herlihy, who notes that the enormously extended servile tenures of Carolingian times were protected in the sense that they were heritable, but typically only in the direct line (1961: 91–2).

ship current in the region, namely, adoption, concubinage, plural marriage, widow remarriage (including the levirate). It does not seem accidental that the Church appears to have condemned the very practices that would have deprived it of property. For the accumulation of property was essential so that it could assume responsibility for the maintenance of those orphans and widows who, under the pre-existing arrangements, would have been cared for by their kin. If a widow was to remarry rather than enter a nunnery, then the property would come under the control of the new partnership. If an individual or a couple adopted a child, they provided themselves with an heir for their goods. So too, in a less direct fashion, does a man who takes a second wife or a concubine if his first wife is barren. Is it by chance that the Church forbade such strategies of continuity, that it set limits to the efficacy of kinship ties outside the elementary family in matters of property? Even within the immediate conjugal family, while the Church often protected relationships, it could also threaten them. The widowed daughter was encouraged by St Jerome to leave money to the Church against her father's wishes. Such a policy was not only destructive of the idea of 'family property', it also encouraged filial disobedience. Or to phrase the trend in another way, it promoted 'freedom' and 'individualism' at the same time as strengthening the independence of women.[11]

The initial permission given to the Church to acquire inheritances led to problems which resulted in attempts of the State to limit some of the effects. It was a continuing problem. In a later period such restrictions took the form of mortmain. In the English sense of the term, the law of mortmain is one that limits the acquisition of property by permanent corporations, especially landed property vested in organisations of a religious character. Such restrictions arose for two main reasons. First, there was the desire to prevent property from being withdrawn for ever from the general pool of transferable goods, that is, from being grasped by the 'dead hand' of an artificial legal personality who would seize it and not let it go. Second, there was the wish to diminish fraudulent or extortionate pressures from religious advisers. These problems arose largely as a result of the freedom given to Christians. Only under special conditions did Roman law allow of such transactions: 'we are not permit-

---

[11] On the Christian contribution to the growth of individualism, see Dumont 1981.

ted to appoint the gods as our heirs . . .' wrote Ulpian *c*. A.D. 200 (Rules XXII. 6). A *collegium*, a corporate body consisting of at least three persons, could not receive an inheritance unless it was specially privileged. As we have seen, the Christian Church fell into this category only after Constantine's Edict of Milan (A.D. 313) which restored to the Church the property taken in recent persecutions and formally recognised its right to own land. It was in A.D. 321 that the Emperor enlarged the Church's power to inherit. Within fifty years the first restrictive law was established by the Emperor Valentinian I in A.D. 370. Trained as a soldier, the son of Gratian, who had held the military commands of Africa and Britain, Valentinian was elected in A.D. 364. Choosing his brother Valens (who adopted the Arian faith) as his co-ruler, he allocated him the Eastern Empire. His attempt 'to restrain the wealth and avarice of the clergy' was held by Gibbon to be the model for future regulations in the later Middle Ages, such as those introduced by the Emperor Frederick II, by Edward I of England and by various other Christian princes of the time. His measure safeguarded the property of widows and wards from alienation to ecclesiastical persons, though the later rulers were more concerned to protect royal and feudal interests than those of the weak (Miller 1952: 123–6).

The attraction of the priest to the riches of those without heirs was not without precedent in the secular sphere. In Rome, 'the childless old man and woman ("orbus", "orba") and their courtiers ("captatores"), who were after their money, were a joke and a scandal . . . in the early Empire. Calvia Crispinilla, a disreputable old noblewoman at Nero's court, survived his fall and enjoyed great influence from her wealth and childlessness' (Mattingley 1948: 154). Acquisition by flattery occurs in many societies with significant differences in wealth, and we might regard the ecclesiastical version as a 'sublimated' form which channels those resources not only to religious purposes but to wider social ends.

From one angle the appearance of the monastic way of life in fourth-century Egypt was a reaffirmation of the ascetic tradition, stressing celibacy as a spiritual alternative to marriage. It was equally devoted to poverty and represented both a movement of reaction against the concentration of power in a priestly hierarchy and the accommodation to the norms of the surrounding society. It was a deliberate attempt to recover the radical enthusiasm of early Christianity as preserved in the written Scriptures. In his life of St

Antony, Athanasius reports that the great hermit entered upon
the ascetic life after reading the command of Jesus, 'Go and sell
what thou hast, and give to the poor' (Matthew 19: 21; Gager
1975: 74).

The effects of the growth of the monastery as an alternative focus
of ecclesiastical power had other important influences on marriage
and the family, apart from providing a high-status model for the
celibate life. The convent became a refuge for widows and daughters; the monastery, like the Church, attracted and sometimes protected family funds. The means it used affected the family very
intimately in ways that were vividly proclaimed by Edward Gibbon.
'The influence of the monastic orders', he claimed, 'acted most forcibly on the infirm minds of children and females' (1898: IV,63).
'They insinuated themselves into noble and opulent families; and
the specious arts of flattery and seduction were employed to secure
those proselytes who might bestow wealth or dignity on the monastic profession. The indignant father bewailed the loss, perhaps, of an
only son; the credulous maid was betrayed by vanity to violate the
laws of nature; and the matron aspired to imaginary perfection, by
renouncing the virtues of domestic life' (p. 63). As he goes on to
remark, 'Time continually increased, and accidents could seldom
diminish, the estates of the popular monasteries . . .' (p. 69).

The accumulation of property by priests and monks was not
simply a way of lining their own pockets. For the Church needed
revenue not only to support the clergy and maintain the buildings
but to provide charity for the poor. Support for the poor, the Christian poor, was an important feature of early Christianity but by the
third century it had become a major enterprise requiring full-time
administration. Eusebius quotes Bishop Cornelius (*c.* A.D. 250) as
claiming that the Roman Church alone supported some 1,500 widows and poor members of the Church (Eusebius, *Ecclesiastical History* VI. 43). Such philanthropy was later not confined to Church
members alone. Julian the Apostate complained that 'Galileans support not only their own poor but ours as well', indicating that the
wider social aspect of their teaching was, *pace* Troeltsch, a significant aspect of early Christianity that no doubt helped the rapid
recruitment to the faith (Gager 1975: 131).

At first these charitable gifts were voluntary offerings (Jones
1964: II, 894), the Biblical custom of regular first fruits or tithes
(one-tenth) being a later revival. When the Church began to acquire

its own property in the third century, though by questionable title, this consisted at first of places of worship and burial grounds. After the end of the Great Persecutions and the toleration edict of his uncle, Galerius, the Roman Emperor Maximinus Daia (308–314) turned against the Christians, instigated by the pagan priests, and restored any houses or lands which had been in the ownership of the Christians (Eusebius, *Ecclesiastical History* IX. 10).

From the time of Constantine the property of the Church grew rapidly and steadily. The Emperor himself gave large gifts of land and houses. Vast properties were received from members of the Roman nobility as well as many small bequests from more humble people. 'It seems to have become almost common form', writes Jones, 'for every will to contain a bequest to the Church' (1964: II, 895), and he cites the example of a civil servant who bequeathed half his house.

Some of this property came from individuals or couples without offspring. Some came from the priesthood itself. By a law of A.D. 434 the estate of any cleric who died intestate without heirs passed to his church. Childless bishops often made their church their heir. An African Council of 409 anathematised any bishop who left his property to outsiders other than his kin, rather than to his church.

When the first rules were elaborated, clergy were permitted to marry. Hence the maintenance of a distinction between Church and personal property was a constant problem, since the latter normally went to a man's heir. Those without heirs often left their wealth to the Church, which made efforts to limit the extent of possible inheritors (Jones 1964: II, 896). The Church was also concerned to see that its own property was not alienated to the kin of clergy, or indeed under any other circumstance; an imperial law against such alienation was issued by Leo in 470 for the Church of Constantinople, banning all sales, gifts or exchange.

Most of the new wealth came from the members the Church recruited after its establishment at the beginning of the fourth century. 'The Christians of Rome were possessed of a very considerable wealth', wrote Gibbon, '... many among their proselytes had sold their lands and houses to increase the public riches of the sect, at the expense, indeed, of their unfortunate children, who found themselves beggars because their parents had been saints' (1880: II, 132). This tension between the interests of the senior generation using its earthly possessions to secure heavenly benefits and those of the junior generation more concerned with the production of material goods, was to mark much of European history, until a more secularised environment brought young and old together in a more single-minded concentration on the things of this world. But it was not solely by beggaring the children that the Church acquired land so rapidly. This was also achieved by discouraging those procedures that provided heirs to childless persons and by reducing the rights and duties of kin in favour of the sect and later of the Church.

The alienation of property to the Church at death was intimately connected with the development of the testament. The German tribes had recognised donations which, as Tacitus remarked, were buried or burned with the dead. Among the Anglo-Saxons as elsewhere the growth of Christianity led to a change in notions of life and death, in particular to the gradual abandonment of the idea that property should be buried with the dead (Sheehan 1963b: 7; Leeds 1936). The original notion that a proportion of a person's property needed to be devoted to his welfare in the other world was easily converted to the later view of this proportion as the 'share of the soul' (*Seelteil*), frequently a third, over which the owner had full right of devise, and which the Fathers of the early Church proposed should be used as alms for penitential purposes (Sheehan 1963b: 6ff).

There were two traditions concerning the amount of alms one should leave for charity, the proportion of one's estate to be given away. St Jerome (*c.* 342–420) and St Augustine followed St Gregory of Nyssa (*c.* 331–395) in advising that the poor should be given a child's part. On the other hand, Salvian and Peter Chrysologus recalled the words of St Basil, brother of St Gregory and founder of the monastic rule of the Eastern Church (*c.*330–379), and of St John Chrysostom (*c.*347–407) which pressed the rich to give all (Lagarrigue 1971: 38).

In drawing a connection between the Church's modification of the accepted strategies of heirship and its wish to encourage bequests from the faithful, I have relied on deductive arguments, although the advice of Jerome to the widow Furia gives some idea of the pressures placed upon the congregation to leave property to the Church rather than to family and kin. However, there is one remarkable contemporary text which makes the point very forcibly, especially with regard to adoption. Salvian, the fifth-century Christian writer who became a priest at Marseilles, apparently came from a well-to-do family, but in later life he divested himself of all his property in favour of the Church. In his work *Ad ecclesiam*, also known as *Contra avaritiam*, the author commended the giving of alms to the Church, even encouraging parents to leave their wealth to that body rather than to their offspring, on the plea that it is better for the children to suffer in this world than that the parents should be damned in the next (III. 4). Salvian's injunctions were more extreme than those of other writers, but there is little doubt that it was by bequests, left not simply by the few but by the many (Lesne 1910: 23) that the Church in Gaul built up its wealth so rapidly between the fifth and eighth centuries. Nor is there much doubt from the evidence of amendments in legislation, of the tone of Salvian's writings, and of the disputes to which the process gave rise, that considerable conflict was stirred up between the generations. The Church's doctrine was in favour of alienation, especially from the heirless and from women. It encouraged heirlessness by disallowing the use of collaterals, adopted sons and other means to plug the succession gap. No longer, as in Cicero's time, could a man's fictional heir keep alive the worship of the family; oblations placed this responsibility in the hands of the Church. The take-over of the worship of the ancestors was also a take-over of their inheritance.

In fifth-century Gaul the great expansion of Church property was brought about by bequests that were offered to the dead to refresh their souls (Lesne 1910: 14,25–6). The giving of alms destroyed sin, and Salvian insisted that the dying should make a legacy to the Church for this end, especially as those goods a man possessed were only his temporary possessions. So he castigated those who leave their property to relatives or to strangers and neglect the Church. A father should not love even his own children more than his Lord, and therefore he should leave the same share of his property to God as to his own children. If he had no children, then it is inexcusable to leave his property to others, even to an adopted son (*Ad. eccles.* III. 2). In this way the Church would rapidly accumulate property in Gaul. Like bishops and clerics, laymen without children often made a saint their heir (Lesne 1910: 161). But such donations were not only made by the childless. Others too used the Roman formulae of disinheritance to leave property to a saint. And women, more particularly the widows and daughters of kings, bequeathed part or all of their dower to religious establishments (p. 100).

Salvian's anger was directed above all against those who, without children of their own, adopted those of others, whom he described as the 'offspring of perjury' (*Ad. eccles.* III. 2; O'Sullivan 1947: 322). He continued: 'In this way some very wretched and most unholy people, who are not bound by the bonds of children, nevertheless provide for themselves chains with which to bind the unfortunate necks of their own souls. When there is no crisis at all within the home, they summon one outside the home. Although the causes of danger are lacking they rush headlong, as if into voluntary death.' Adoption was firmly condemned exactly because it was a strategy of heirship, feeding the avaricious kinsmen instead of saving one's soul by giving alms to the poor or to God, which usually, but not always, went to the Church (Lagarrigue 1971: 34). That corporation did not give all the revenue it received in this way to the poor. At roughly the same period Pope Gelasius I (d. 496) recognised a quadripartite division of gifts to the Church between the bishop, the poor, the clerics and the ecclesiastical buildings (Gaudemet 1957a: 310). The poor were entitled only to a quarter of the offerings often made in their name.

Salvian's work, composed right at the beginning of the great build-up of the wealth of the Church in Gaul during the fifth to eighth centuries, forms a critical text on the sin of creating heirs. Strategies of family heirship were condemned as ways of circumventing the wishes of God, of neglecting the possibility of saving one's soul and of encouraging the 'avarice' of members of one's family. There is a straightforward declaration of the conflict of interests between Church and kin, between spiritual and familial concerns. If wealth was to be passed on between kin, then it should be kept within the restricted, elementary family. Fictional heirs, heirs who were not 'of the body', 'natural' kin of the parents, were not admitted. Thus the text provides an explanation of why adoption, so prevalent in Rome and so much in keeping with the contemporary type of productive system (Goody 1976b, chapter 6), was virtually abandoned in Europe for the next 1,500 years. It also provides some suggestion as to why the Church should have insisted on 'natural' kinship, on 'blood' relationships, on 'consanguinity'. Natural kinship was created by the union (*copulatio*) of men and women, that is, by a physical act. Increasingly attention came to focus on the sexual element of marriage, so that in the early Middle Ages 'formal consummation made a marriage' (Hughes 1978: 275–6), although consensus was also required.

It is my argument that the radical change in the ideology of marriage which occurred from the fourth century A.D. had a mixed effect on Western Europe. On the one hand, the views expressed by Salvian had an important consequence, not only in turning the Church into a property-owning organisation of immense power within a relatively short period, not only in changing the formal structure of many aspects of kinship and marriage, but in influencing the character of the ties between the generations as well as the structure of property relations. Can the extent to which land was bought and sold *among kin* in medieval England (e.g. Razi 1981) be seen as a way of compensating for the absence of other mechanisms of continuity in face of the strictures against 'avarice'? Clearly, and this is my complementary point, the stated policy of the Church met with resistance and underwent modification. The immediate family took its share of inheritance as well as giving the Church its portion. Dispensations made it possible to get round the restrictions on close marriage. The restricted bonds of consanguinity were supplemented by other ties.

Changing the rules had many consequences. But the accumulation that it made possible embodied the whole shift from sect to Church, the routinisation of the charisma, the adoption of orthodoxy, the loss of the millennarian character, now to be abandoned to 'heresies'.

6. *Church, land and family in the West*

The Christian Church began as a loosely organised body within the Empire. With the conversion of Constantine, a radical change took place. As emperor, he removed the restrictions that had lain upon the Church and bestowed privileges and authority upon its priesthood, at the same time as becoming its moderator. 'This created, once and for all', declared Knowles, 'the problem of Church and State' (1970: 10). This problem arose partly because the Church became a property-holding corporation, capable of acquiring land by gift, by inheritance or by purchase. As Hughes points out for the early Irish Church, as it gained property and privileges and assumed responsibilities, it had necessarily to take an interest in material wealth (1966: 167). This interest involved an adjustment to and in both secular and ecclesiastical law.

THE ACCUMULATION OF WEALTH

Once permitted, the build-up of wealth was very rapid. In the East the Church's property grew enormously between the fourth and sixth centuries. In the West, during the early Merovingian period in Gaul, the process continued so swiftly that at the end of the sixth century Chilperic complained that all the wealth of the kingdom had been transferred to the churches. Some of the methods of accumulation were ingenious. In Spain even the property of a freed ecclesiastical slave who had married a person of free birth belonged to the Church, until the Visigothic king Wamba did away with this 'profitable convenience'. This massive transfer was not simply of income, not just of tithes or taxes, but consisted in a continuing change of title to land in favour of the Church as the result of the voluntary offerings of its members. As in the later Roman Empire, every known Anglo-Saxon will includes a bequest to the Church (Lancaster 1958: 362), not perhaps so surprising in view of their preservation in ecclesiastical

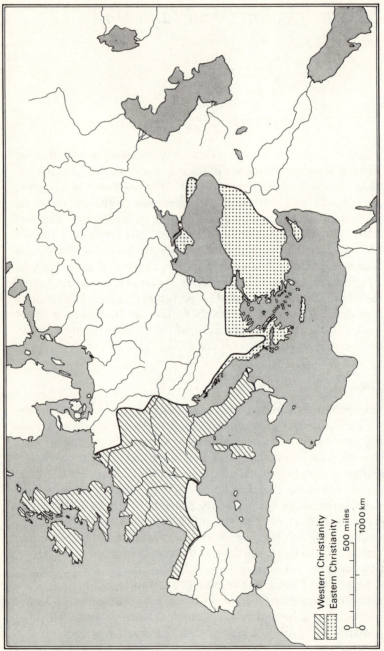

Map 4. Europe A.D. 737: the time of Bede and the Arab conquest

Western Christianity

Eastern Christianity

0   500 miles

0   1000 km

archives. As a result there was a shift in the ownership of the basic resources of production. It has been estimated that one third of the productive land in France was in ecclesiastical hands by the end of the seventh century. In the two following centuries the growth was again rapid. 'In German lands, in northern France, and in Italy the Church owns twice as much land in the ninth century as in the eighth. In southern France, too, between the first and second quarter of the ninth century, Church property increases from 21 to 40 per cent' (Herlihy 1961: 87).

In England the great build-up of Church lands occurred during the period A.D. 600–1100, that is, beginning with the arrival of St Augustine down to the Norman Conquest. Devotion and the new monastic orders of the sixth and tenth centuries played their part; so did royal patronage. Much was alienated in the ordinary course of seeking salvation, by gift and by bequest.

A characteristic example of the deed of gift was the one made in favour of the abbey of Gomerfontaine in 1207, outside the main period of accumulation:

'I, Hugh of Chaumont, with the consent of my wife Petronilla, of my sons John and James, and of my other sons, for the salvation of my soul, of the soul of my wife, the soul of my father Galon, and of my mother Matilda, for the salvation of the souls of my predecessors and of all my heirs, I make and concede in pure and perpetual alms the following donation . . .'

From the standpoint of the study of the family, the interest of the document lies in Hugh's seeking the consent of his wife and children (sons) for the donation, which is made for the salvation of their souls, as well as for the souls of his direct ascendants (or 'predecessors') and his immediate descendants (or 'heirs') (Evans 1969: 57). Joint salvation is restricted to conjugal and lineal kin, to the exclusion of collaterals.

The effects of such gifts on relations between kinsfolk are dramatically illustrated in a bequest (as distinct from a donation) which is referred to in the poem *Hervis de Metz* written in the time of King Philip-Augustus of France (1165–1223). It begins:

'Today when a man falls ill, and lies down to die, he does not think of his sons or his nephews or cousins; he summons the Black Monks of St Benedict, and gives them all his lands, his revenues, his ovens, and his mills. The men of this age are impoverished and the clerks are daily becoming richer.'

The Church increased its holdings and its income not only by 'voluntary' donations and bequests, not only by taxes and rents, but through a third charge – the tithe (*la dîme*), a tenth of a person's produce, which was levied primarily on the rural population. The tithe had a long prehistory in the ancient world and was revived in fourth-century Byzantium. Originally a voluntary payment in the West, it was made compulsory by Pepin in France and Aethelstan in England. When this happened donations to the Church took on the form of taxes to the State. Of Byzantium Patlagean remarks that 'Our study of the Christian gift has listed the motives, the expiation of sins and the expectation of divine protection, or thanks for blessings already received. But one also sees, during the same period, a tendency of the ecclesiastical organisation to acquire rights of a fiscal kind, comparable to those exercised by the political authorities' (1977: 273).

The accumulation of property or income on this scale meant the development of the Church into a quasi-state of its own, capable in certain circumstances of assuming governmental functions and always a potential competitor as well as a valued ally. In post-Norman England the Church was granted every kind of temporal right, including those due to a secular lord. There were also the financial rights peculiar to the Church; that is, the five customs which in the tenth and eleventh centuries were sanctioned by royal laws: tithe (one-tenth of young stock by Pentecost, one tenth of the fruits of the earth by All Saints), church-scot (first fruits due at the feast of St Martin, 11 November), plough-alms (a penny for each plough or ploughland, to be paid fifteen days after Easter), light-dues (half-a-penny's worth of wax three times a year) and soul-scot or mortuary, due when a Christian was buried (Barlow 1963: 161–2).

The considerable income of the Church stimulated further investment. In sixth-century Spain some landowners built churches as a commercial speculation, splitting the offerings of the congregation with the priest (Jones 1964: 901). The precious metals received as offerings in the late Saxon period were used to purchase, or repurchase, land and privileges. In the eleventh century the church of St Mary in Huntingdon passed through six owners in one generation (Barlow 1963: 192–3), indicating speculation in real estate.

THE CONTINUATION OF LAY INTERESTS

Not all of the speculation was carried out by the Church itself, for until the reforms of the eleventh century, the transfer of lands to the Church did not necessarily entail their total estrangement from the donors, providing the latter belonged to a powerful family. In the early medieval period, the separation of lay and clergy was much less marked than after the reforms. The connection between a particular 'house' (*lignage*) and a particular monastery was often very close. In many Italian foundations of the eighth and ninth centuries, that is, of the Lombard and Carolingian periods, a direct tie existed between the founder's family and the monastery. The abbot was either the founder himself or else a member of the same kin group, and the relation continued into the subsequent generations.

The early British Church provided further examples of the 'hereditary monastery', the church belonging by right to the family of the founding saint or patron. In Ireland families built churches on their own lands and 'the donors of land retained a powerful interest in their property' (Hughes 1966: 77), sons often following fathers as abbots (p. 164). Within the Church itself, a movement developed towards the separation of lay and clerical interests. But just as some monks were devoted to celibacy and poverty, so others were educated by the Church, 'sometimes having a voice in its government, but married, holding land and stock as clients of the church' (p. 142).

The continuing interest of donor families in ecclesiastical land grew out of the existing mode of land tenure, which made it difficult for an individual to alienate inherited as distinct from self-acquired property. When a layman in Ireland built a church or monastery on hereditary land, he had to obtain the consent of the *fine*, or wider kin group, and then to have the grant confirmed by the king who would liberate the land from certain dues. In the sixth century, 'as Christianity gathered force and the ascetic movement attracted admiration' (Hughes 1966: 76), the desire of the Irish aristocracy to found monasteries had to be reconciled with their obligations to family property. One solution was for the entire family to turn to the religious life, as in the example of the British saint, Samson, all of whose family lands were used to endow a monastery ('let all that is ours become wholly God's'). In other instances, the Church had to make some concession to the families who had alienated, or partly alienated, their property.

High ecclesiastical office also ran in families, as in the sixth-century instance of Gregory of Tours himself. All but five of his predecessors were connected to him by kinship; his father's brother was bishop of Auvergne and other kinsmen held bishoprics elsewhere. These were close-knit, noble families (Gregory was himself the issue of a father's brother's daughter's marriage) who retained power through the Church which not only provided for them as incumbents but also protected their family estates.

Similar kin lines were attached to the monasteries in England; just as laymen used the Church to protect their estates, so lines of clerics inherited ecclesiastical domains. 'Ecclesiastical dynasties were founded. And even churches granted by the king to priests who became bishops, or to bishops themselves, tended to become attached to, even if not absorbed in, the bishopric and to be "inherited" by their successors. In these features clerical were no different from lay estates' (Barlow 1963: 190). The Scottish Church was the same; ten or eleven of the first thirteen abbots of Iona were members of St Columba's branch of the Ui Neill dynasty. Churches and monasteries belonged to noble families who often provided the higher office-holders (Wormald 1978: 52ff). In the Anglo-Saxon case of the descendants of St Aetheldreda at Ely, three of her uterine relatives in succession became abbesses of the monastery she founded. After its refounding, one family, that of earldorman Brihtnoth of the East Saxons, himself killed at the Battle of Maldon in 991 fighting the Viking invaders, constituted the major patrons of the abbey for three generations.

There are difficulties in interpreting some of the gifts made by these nobles 'for many of them seem to have been encumbered with life interests and slow to come to fruition' (Miller 1951: 22).[1] While in the period after Gregory's reforms of the eleventh century the patrons no longer provided the abbesses, no longer 'owned' the church in quite the same way as before, the gifts clearly served family as well as ecclesiastical interests.

In the northern regions of Europe, churches were established outside the main religious centres, often by aristocratic landowners and thegns. No doubt such men were sometimes moved by the same

---

[1] For example, Thurstan, great-grandson of Brihtnoth, bequeathed property, some to the abbey of Ely, which had already been given to the abbey by his father. Did they buy it back, or not give it? (Whitelock 1930: 190).

motives as some of the landowners of Constantinople, urged on to help by John Chrysostom, because 'the priest would preach obedience to the peasants and prevent unrest' (Jones 1964: 901). What later became parishes were initially their private oratories whose priests they would appoint and support, a system of patronage that became known as 'advowson'.[2] In this way their endowment (*dotem*) remained outside the bishop's power of disposition and very much inside that of the family in question, who often appointed their own members to positions that were lucrative and privileged.[3]

One way in which the aristocracy and Church leaned on each other emerges from the history of the Cadolingi family, who were the counts of Pistoia from 923 to 1113. At the end of this long period 'the "*lignage*" became extinct through lack of male heirs, the only daughter having entered a convent' (Violante 1977: 96). There are two points to make. First, the fact that the *lignage* was extinguished in this fashion emphasises the great difference between the traditional lineages of North Africa and the *lignages* of medieval Europe (that is, the houses or lineal dynasties). In Europe there were no segmentary lineages and few mechanisms of substitution. Collaterals often did not inherit, no-one was adopted, there was no plural marriage to secure an heir. Henry VIII could of course try to meet the

[2] Some of the colleges of Cambridge University still maintain 'advowson' funds and act as electors of priests to those parishes. In the case of St John's College, Cambridge, ecclesiastical patronage increased during the late seventeenth and early eighteenth centuries, both by gift and by purchase. The advowsons constituted a kind of pension fund for Fellows who had to retire from College work when they got married or for other reasons. The situation changed with the Statutes of 1882, following on the Universities Tests Acts of 1871 which abolished the necessity for members of the University to subscribe to the articles of the Church of England. These statutes removed the obligation of Fellows to take Holy Orders as well as all restrictions on matrimony. A new Advowson Fund was then established with different ends in mind (Howard 1935: 81,138–9,220).

[3] In a personal communication Edward Miller notes that 'there is indeed a distinction to be made in the patronage of (a) bishoprics and monastic houses and (b) parochial churches. Largely as a result of the tenth-century 'reform' movement, kings acquired something like a monopoly of the first type of patronage (for example, under the policy of Otto I in Germany); but parochial patronage was apt to go with the lordship over land.' For the origins of this lay patronage, see Stenton 1971: 149–50; in early times it also applied to monasteries (pp. 162–5). So far as the lesser churches went, one version of the eleventh-century tract on wergelds and dignities includes a church among the requisite property rights of a ceorl who had prospered to thegn-right (Whitelock 1979: I, 432 and Fn. 3); and even in urban tenements in Winchester there were churches which may have originated as the private chapels of their lords (Biddle 1976: I,333,340).

problem by taking successive spouses, but divorce and concubinage were disapproved of, at least by the Church and by Christianity. Second, at the eighth generation of the 'house', the only daughter, Bertha, like her name-sake Bertha (who was her father's father's father's sister) of the fifth generation, entered a convent and, instead of becoming Count as she would have done had she been a male, became an abbess, presumably taking with her all the property.

The mechanisms and the problems behind the acquisition of the immense Church holdings are well illustrated by the history of the founding of Ely. A traditional twelfth-century account relates how St Aetheldreda, daughter of Anna, King of the East Angles, founded the monastery. 'She was married about the middle of the seventh century to Tonbert, chieftain of a people called the Southern Gyrwe; and it was from her husband, according to the Ely chronicle, that she received possession of the "Isle of Ely" as her "dower" ' (Miller 1951: 8–9). In earlier documents the dower would probably have been termed 'morning gift', that is, the provision for a wife's widowhood which a husband made on the morning after his wedding day, a gift over which she had full proprietary rights provided she did not remarry within a year of her husband's death. In Bede's seventh-century account of the foundation, no mention is made of the dower; he claims that St Aetheldreda wished to found a monastery there because she was descended from the royal house of the area. It was only after her second marriage that she was able to return to Ely and build the abbey over which she ruled till her death. She was succeeded first by her sister, then in turn by the latter's daughter and grand-daughter.

But the real basis of the medieval monastery at Ely was its re-founding by Bishop Aethelwold in 970, following which a large estate was built up with astonishing rapidity, first by the purchase, then by the gift, of land. After the death of King Edgar, from whom the charter had been obtained, there was, as elsewhere in eastern England, a reaction against the territorial growth of the new monasticism. The real problem was one of land-title. The 'old restrictive common law' of Anglo-Saxon times was a law 'which keeps land in families' (Miller 1951: 19). The protest was specifically against the alienation of land from families because of a forced bargain, or through sale at a low price at a time of financial embarrassment. But a wider issue was at stake. For 'if a man sold his lands to the church he was, in effect, disinheriting his family; and some of the controversies that arose after Edgar's death do seem to suggest that the right of a man to do so was not fully conceded in the custom of the time' (p. 19). In effect there was a conflict between the custom of the people and the law the Church was trying to impose, a conflict between the disinherited and the new acquisitors that was expressed in the two different ways of conveying land. 'On the one side the act of conveying the land might still be mainly oral and depend for its validity upon a series of traditional ceremonies carried out before witnesses. On the other side, there were also occasions when older procedure was supplemented at some stage or another by the transfer of a written instrument, a charter or a land-book' (Miller 1951: 19). Unlike 'bookland', 'folkland' did not require a written charter, which was an instrument bearing witness to an alienation.

In England the use of writing to record the transfer of land and the gift of privileges stemmed from the influence of the Church (Whitelock 1979: 375), the first authentic charters coming from the last quarter of the seventh century. One category of royal charter was the diploma, almost always in Latin, recording the creation or transfer of 'bookland' (the book being a title-deed), a term that 'probably describes land which was freed from payment of the king's farm and certain other royal dues, originally with the intention that it should be devoted to religious purposes, and which was held with the power to alienate it freely' (p. 376),[4] and which Barlow (1963: 17) describes as 'a tenure as absolute as Anglo-Saxon wit could contrive'. Whitelock sees the introduction of bookland as necessary under the existing system of tenure because of the difficulties of alienating land from the kindred. New arrangements had to be made before landowners could allot 'permanent endowments to religious bodies'. For such a charter, the agreement of councillors had to be obtained, since the act not only diminished royal revenues but 'probably ran counter to traditional rules of inheritance'. Before long the Church introduced the written record as 'a better security against the claims of the donor's descendants or of the later kings', though subsequently the grant of bookland was made to laymen without any intention that it was going to be devoted to religious uses. At this point we are sometimes told that a payment has been

[4] The significance of the Anglo-Saxon charter is a hotly debated topic (John 1960, 1966; Holt 1972; P. Wormald, personal communication). I am aware that I have accepted one of a number of possible views but I do not think another choice would drastically affect my general argument.

made for the grant, indicating that royal revenues might have been temporarily raised by disposing of the right to taxes.

In acquiring estates the Church in England depended heavily on the monarchy to make grants of land,[5] in the course of which it came to replace the local prince as a main landowner. But the complex process by which lands were detached from lay hands and won by the Church – for most of the estates came from the cultivated area and not from clearing new lands – often entailed an intermediary stage which involved the creation of well-endowed minster churches. These churches were founded by prominent families, remained family property and were inherited from generation to generation.[6] Charters that granted land to the Church did not always do so immediately, but promised an eventual reversion which might in the end never take place.

No anticlerical writer of a later generation could have condemned so powerfully the rapid build-up of 'the Church in the hands of laymen' as did Bede himself. In his letter to Egbert, Archbishop of York, written in 734, he requested the appointment of more bishops to look after the spiritual welfare of the Northumbrian population. A bishop requires a see, which means procuring 'a site among the monasteries' (Whitelock 1979: 804), an act that may lead to opposition from the abbot or the monks. But in 'innumerable cases' monasteries are such only in name, being dedicated instead to wanton living, vanity, over-indulgence of the belly and gluttony. The acquisition of property for the purpose has affected not only the Church but secular life as well.

'For – what indeed is disgraceful to tell – those who are totally ignorant of the monastic life have received under their control so

---

[5] For example, Bede describes how king Aethelbert not only built a church in honour of St Andrew at Rochester but 'later added lands and property for the maintenance of the bishop's household' (II. 3).

[6] 'Men in high secular positions . . . strove to consolidate their fortunes and their families in order to secure as much as possible for their direct descendants to the detriment of the wider kin' (Leyser 1979: 50). Such a concentration of material interest in the direct line of filiation does not necessarily prevent the recognition of wider kin for other purposes and Leyser remarks that the early medieval German aristocracy were characterised by 'large groups of kinsmen'. Sociologists and historians often place kinship and the family in some kind of structural and developmental opposition. But at the heart of any kinship system lies the organisation of domestic groups, usually based on some kind of conjugal family.

many places in the name of monasteries, as you yourself know better
than I, that there is a complete lack of places where the sons of nobles
or of veteran thegns can receive an estate' (p. 805). The result is that
for such youths, marriage is delayed and they either leave the country
to fight or engage in loose living, not even abstaining from virgins
consecrated to God. Others, even more reprehensively, 'give money
to kings, and under the pretext of founding monasteries buy lands on
which they may more freely devote themselves to lust, and in addition
cause them to be ascribed to them in hereditary right by royal edicts'.
For such acquisitions were obtained by 'charters drawn up in defence
of their covetous acts' (p. 809).

THE NATURE OF THE CHURCH'S RIGHTS

The eleventh-century reforms of Gregory VII put an end to the
more blatant hereditary interests held by laymen in Church property. In other ways, too, the nature of the rights which the Church
acquired in land varied over time. During the Merovingian rule in
France, the *dominium* exercised by the Church was generally of a
loose kind, 'a shadow ownership, no managerial prerogatives, and
only a small portion of the fruits which the quitrent provided' (Herlihy 1961: 91). In late Saxon England the growth of feudal obligations led to a decentralisation of estates; and tenants gained closer
control over their fiefs, which were virtually heritable; indeed in the
fourteenth and fifteenth centuries the tenants became independent
landowners (Dyer 1980: 49). In France however cartularies from the
Carolingian period (the eighth and ninth centuries) reveal that the
looseness of the Merovingian tenure gives way to an extension of the
Church's effective ownership and the growth of a new kind of property based upon it. 'As we watch ... the shadow of the saint falls
ever more widely across the fields of Europe in Carolingian times';
the lands were often exploited 'by the direct cultivation of the
monks, by labor dues imposed upon neighboring dependent cultivators, by slaves, or ... by "housed" slaves and those who held in
servile tenure' (p. 91). Under these conditions, alienation without
the lord's permission became impossible.[7]

---

[7] See also Duby 1974: 83–111 for a more recent comment on the growing power of
the lords in the early Middle Ages. Dyer remarks that while our evidence comes
from Church sources, the trends are assumed to have been the same in lay estates.

The rise of these great properties, specifically the ecclesiastical estates, did not take place without resistance. The capitularies provide evidence of many protests about the dispossession of the small landowners by the 'powerful'. Indeed some historians have seen 'the small independent farm, and the free peasant' as being 'all but erased from the German countryside' at this time.[8] Under such conditions one possibility open to the small landowner to counter the threat of an ecclesiastical take-over was to seek protection from a lay lord, which meant becoming a feudal tenant.[9]

RHYTHM OF ACQUISITION

Not only did the nature of the rights in land vary over time, so too did the tempo of acquisition and the proportion of land held. The change in rhythm is illustrated in ninth-century documents from England that show laymen anxious to protect their property from the hands of the Church; royal grants appear less generous than before, possibly because there was less royal land left in Kent where most of the charters come from.

In Italy documents transferring land become numerous from the second quarter of the eighth century and increase rapidly to the early eleventh century when their numbers diminish, particularly over the period 1051–1125. Herlihy remarks that this diminution appears to reflect 'a stabilization of land tenures' (1961: 83). The same process occurred in the Christian lands in Spain as well as in France, especially in northern France where the virtual disappearance of sales from the cartularies after 1000 results from the establishment of these great properties (p. 84).

The changing proportion of land held is illustrated by the case of the Bishopric of Worcester (Dyer 1980). The see, founded in 680,

[8] Herlihy 1961: 88, referring to G. L. von Maurer, *Geschichte der Fronhöfe, der Bauernhöfe und der Hofverfassung in Deutschland* (Erlangen 1862–3) and other sources.
[9] On the procedure of seeking a lord as a protector, see the legendary origin of the Courts of Guines where the foundress of the lignage of the seigneurs of Ardres converted her allod into a fief (i.e. to a dependent tenure) in order to avoid an unwelcome marriage being arranged by her 'cousin' (Duby 1978: 99). The lay lord also offered protection against ecclesiastical pressure. In Montaillou in the early fourteenth century the feudal and political lord, the Comte de Foix, protected 'his people' against the attempts of the Bishop to collect tithes of lambs, 'a recurrent source of rural conflict' (Le Roy Ladurie 1976).

rapidly built up large holdings of land, so that by the time of the Domesday Book in 1086 the Church was overlord of more than a quarter of the land of Worcestershire and of substantial areas beyond the county. Already by the 750s the basic geographical framework of the estate had been established, and it expanded up until the early ninth century, after which time the proportion of land held by the Church throughout Europe began to decline (Dyer 1980: 13).

DEPREDATION

There are many reasons for the changes in the tempo of acquisition and the proportion of land held by the Church. The proportion would be affected by an increase in the colonisation of land by laymen. The amount of land brought under cultivation in this way seems to have been one factor behind the drop in the percentage of Church lands in the tenth century in France, Spain and Italy. The kind of resistance encountered in the acquisition of land at Ely as well as in the establishment of direct farming on the continent might have affected the tempo. But the problem was different in scale. The enormous build-up of Church lands made them a target for enemies within or without, and the proportion of land held was a balance between what the Church acquired and what it lost by depredation. In the present instance the decline was due to the 'great secularisations of the tenth century' when attacks were made on ecclesiastical lands, especially on those of the monasteries, partly by the State, partly by freebooters such as the Normans, and partly by reprobate clerics who used the Church property for their own ends. It was the immense accumulation of wealth by the Church through benefactions that created the problem of stability: 'Sometimes uncontrolled despoilers, whether internal or external, solved the problem for a kingdom. Sometimes the Church itself scattered what it had received. Sometimes the king had to confiscate superfluous ecclesiastical wealth by the favourite medieval method of placing burdens on the land, such as military service, food rents, or taxation. The English church had been robbed from every quarter in the eighth and ninth centuries. The generosity of the tenth had not created serious disequilibrium in the kingdom as a whole' (Barlow 1963: 171). It is not surprising to find that 'histories of churches at this time ... consist largely of the story of their estates and movable property' (p. 171).

In Western Europe the Church suffered constant attacks during the period of the invasions. At the same time as it received great endowments from one source, it was raided by another. Some of the loss was the result of general destruction, such as the despoliation of Cahors, capital of Quercy, by the Franks in 574. Many of the Norman raids into that province, which began in 846, came from the opposite direction, up the great rivers leading to the Atlantic, and were directed at the riches of abbeys such as Moissac.[10] On the national level these raids contributed to the separation of northern and southern France, to the break-up of the Carolingian Empire and to the growth of the strong principalities that now confronted the royal domain.

When endemic warfare ceased with the effective establishment of feudal order in the eleventh century the Church and State were left with grave problems. In Germany the long wars had meant that families had to increase their military strengths and for this they required land. 'As long as their men were employed they could hope to maintain them out of the activity of war as such: plunder, foraging, ransoms and any other rewards that successful expeditions and raids might procure' (Leyser 1968: 47). The coming of peace threatened the Church because nobles who had lived on a war-footing for so long now had to be enfeoffed out of ecclesiastical estates. Many had provided so many fiefs to their vassals that they had now to extort land from other sources.

The external raids of the barbarians gave way to the internal competition of feudal lords. Writing of Quercy in the Middle Ages, Saint-Marty remarks that 'the great riches of the church never failed to excite the envy of the nobles' (1930: 32). At the end of the eleventh century, Pope Urban II excommunicated several of the local lords for seizing goods belonging to the abbey of Figeac, despite the abbey having ceded much land and property to another lord for its protection. The Church's attempts to put a stop to this violence included efforts to get the lords to swear the Peace of God (for example, in 1031) and at the end of the twelfth century to institute a

[10] The Norman occupation of Noirmoutier at the mouth of the Loire took place in 843. Wormald points out that, judging from Alcuin's correspondence, there were Vikings off the Aquitaine coast in 799. On spoilation and secularisation in early France, see Lesne 1922. On the depredations of the Irish Church by the Vikings, see Hughes (1966: 197ff); within 150 years they were domesticated by conversion (p. 230). On Scotland and England, see Wainwright (1962: 129).

force for the maintenance of order. This was recruited among the nobility and paid for by a special tax (*pezade*), the proceeds of which were kept in the Cathedral of Cahors and at Figeac.

Threats to Church property were no new thing. In the sixth century Gregory of Tours had described this type of pendulum movement as the struggle of 'good and evil: the heathen were raging fiercely; kings were growing more cruel; . . . the churches also were enriched by the faithful and plundered by traitors' (Brehaut 1916: 1). Men provided for the Church, but they also despoiled it. One such provider at that time was Theodebert, who 'ruled with justice, venerated the bishops, was liberal to the churches, relieved the poor, and distributed many benefits on all hands with piety and friendliest goodwill. He generously remitted to the churches in Auvergne all the tribute which they used to pay to the royal domain' (Dalton 1927: II,105). But it was the same leaders who plundered the Church, an act for which Sigiwald, Duke of Auvergne, was miraculously punished (p. 100). Others, like King Lothar 'ordained that all the churches in his kingdom should pay a third part of their revenues to his treasury' (p. 117), although elsewhere Church properties were freed from tax. Indeed Chilperic, whom Gregory cursed, is reported as saying 'See how poor our treasury always is! Look how the churches have drained our riches away! Of a verity, none ruleth at all, save only the bishops. Our royal office is lost and gone; it hath passed to the bishops in their cities' (p. 279). The centralised accumulation of great wealth was constantly under threat from plundering by enemies and freebooters, from taxation or sequestration by the State, or from depredations by its own bishops, who not only had property interests and heirs of their own, but who sometimes moved in and out of the Church – as was the case with Promotus (pp. 297–8). A major problem was to prevent the property the Church had accumulated from being taken over by its own priesthood. In the Visigothic kingdom, Wamba (d. 683) condemned as sacrilege any episcopal appropriation of the endowments of churches or monasteries (King 1972: 154–5). Every bishop, priest or deacon had to make a witnessed inventory of the possessions of the church he took over. Donations to the Church, unlike others, were held to be eternally irrevocable.

Another strategy was to try and set aside the provisions of a will that left money to the Church. Of one Charegisel, Gregory of Tours wrote that he was 'no less frivolous in his conduct than serious in his avarice; he rose from a most lowly origin and became powerful with the king by his flatteries. He was greedy for the wealth of others and tampered with wills; but his own end was such that death left the thwarter of other men's intentions no time to fulfil his own' (Dalton 1927: II,160–1). One editor of Gregory's text remarks that the 'idea of conveying property by will was foreign to the Franks and was not received into their law, which regarded the family rather than the individual. On the other hand conveying property by will was a regular practice among the Gallo-Roman population. The Church was often made a legatee, a practice in part due to the desire to have its interest involved in the carrying out of the will. Therefore in the conflicts that arose in regard to succession to property the interests of the church and of the state were naturally opposed' (Brehaut 1916: 268).

PRIMOGENITURE AND PARTIBILITY

Depredations of Church property continued to be a fact of life but the trend was restrained at the end of the tenth century with the advent of the reform movement that reached a climax under Pope Gregory VII (1073–84). The reformers were keenly aware of past secularisations and were interested in recovering what they could of the Church's pillaged patrimony (Herlihy 1961: 97). The reforms instigated at this time included the enforcement of the celibacy of the clergy and the wide extension of the prohibitions on marriage, the latter tending to weaken the control of property by kin, the former helping to retain in Church hands what had already been secured. The movement of ecclesiastical reform was not, of course, simply a matter of administrative change at the top. In Germany it looked towards the *humiles* and the poor for support, and 'aimed at bettering their religious situation in a church less exclusively aristocratic than in the past' (Leyser 1968: 45). In his chronicle for the year 1091, Bernold of Constance describes aristocratic converts changing their way of life, the conversion of whole villages, and peasant girls who renounced marriage (Moore 1977: 51; *Monumenta Germaniae Historica, Scriptores* V. 452–3).

The economic effects of the reform movement resulted indirectly in a reorganisation of the landed property of laymen and in changes in its transmission, dependent tenures being passed on more frequently to a single heir. In his analysis of the marriage and property

arrangements of this period, Duby writes of the aristocracy of
northern France as being dependent on the booty of war in the
eighth century and on 'the legalised pillage of Church property' in
the tenth and first half of the eleventh centuries, after which the
reforms put a stop to the depredations of the laity (1978: 8). The
change to feudal order led to marriage policies designed to protect
what one had, and specifically to an emerging principle of devolution based on primogeniture (p. 9).

The adoption of single-heir inheritance is of particular interest.
Primogeniture was not of course confined to England. It is an aspect, as I have argued elsewhere (1962a), of the wider problem of the
division or preservation of the unity of the property that faces all
societies where agricultural resources are restricted, and especially in
the context of a growth in population. Herlihy notes that this problem existed for the old-settled regions of Europe in the tenth century, and that it was countered 'by the emergence and maintenance
of more efficient productive units, not subject to continuous parti-
tionings among heirs, and of a more effective management that
created and sustained them' (1961: 97). The new managers came
widely to insist that 'dependent tenancies be passed on to only a
single heir, or are beginning to rely on "true" leases that contained
no provision for hereditary succession'.

In France Champeaux sees primogeniture as emerging among the
nobility in the twelfth century, at which time only the eldest son was
given the title of *heres* (1933: 256). According to Falletti
(1923: 23,29–31), it was at the end of this century that the question
of seniority (*ainesse*) took on a special importance. However, this
did not only apply to noble tenures; as a result of pressure from
landlords on their tenants the system also extended to the lower
orders. In Ely, the bishop had a strong interest in protecting the
integrity of the holdings of villeins because the services they provided were commensurate with the size of their plots. But the estates
of free and semi-free (*censuarii*) tenants, whether their tenure was
described as socage or customary, were often partible among the
sons. Such a custom might put these tenants 'clean outside the
common law', as Miller writes, quoting a contemporary document,
although it was enforced by the bishop's courts (1951: 130–2).
Sometimes this resulted in pairs of brothers holding land jointly.
The continual sub-division of land could create uneconomically-
sized tenements, which in turn stimulated the active market in land

that flourished among the rural population of Ely during the thirteenth century.[11]

In England, this movement towards unigeniture was also the outcome of changes in the method of agricultural exploitation. The late twelfth century was marked by the expansion of the revenues from estates. In Worcester this was partly achieved by acquiring new lands, 'by pious donations and purchase in the case of ecclesiastics and by marriage and politics, as well as purchase by the laity' (Dyer 1980: 51). Demesnes were taken into direct management, allowing their lords to enter the growing market for agricultural produce. At the same time there was an increase in income from rents, tenants provided labour on the demesne, and other components of the seigneurial revenues were expanded. In Worcester the grants of land for military services, a feature of the twelfth century, contrast with the acquisitive policies of the thirteenth, which provoked strong reaction on the part of those whose land or privileges were being acquired (p. 57). But the expansionary period was followed by a further series of setbacks at the end of the thirteenth century, leading to the leasing of demesnes and the expansion of cash rents by commuting labour services. In view of later arguments, it is interesting to note that tenants were still subjected to considerable restraints on their personal freedom; in particular, the lord's anxiety to protect the integrity of holdings inhibited the fragmentation of customary tenements. The earlier signs of partible inheritance, which distinguished free tenants, had disappeared by 1299 (p. 106).

The move towards primogeniture involved a reduction in the claims of kin. While the earlier system of tenure was in no sense communal, kin often held subsidiary rights in land which made alienation difficult, as was clear from the history of the alienation of property to the Church and the retention of family rights in ecclesiastical possessions. Partibility was an expression of these interests, that inhibited, for example, the consolidation of noble lands in early

[11] On partible holdings in Norfolk, see also Pollock and Maitland 1895: II,270; Homans 1941: 109ff,207; Miller 1951: 132; Scammell 1974: 524. For the possible relation between partible inheritance and the activity of the land market at a much later period, see Habakkuk 1955. The same point, linking an active land market to partible inheritance, cash dowries and taxation, has been made for Roman Egypt (Hopkins 1980: 342), implicitly questioning the arguments of those who see such a market as being tied to capitalism, to Europe or to England. On the relation between impartibility and landlordism, see Le Roy Ladurie (1976) and Goody (1976c: 2).

medieval Germany. The partition of estates among the heirs, a feature of Anglo-Saxon inheritance (Charles-Edwards 1972: 8), led to their fragmentation, especially as daughters often had substantial claims (Leyser 1968: 51). Land given as a marriage portion (p. 50) eventually came under the control of the widow if she survived (p. 51). The leading stratum of German society was thus beset with 'age-old' problems: 'partible inheritances, the striving for parity between brothers and the rapid flow of estates within families or between them through the claims of affinity by marriage' (p. 47). The continuing rights of kin in an estate both posed problems for the permanent alienation of land and inhibited its concentration. The perpetuation of an estate by inheritance came into conflict, as Leyser points out, 'with the time-honoured principle of division, of treating the *proprietas* of a family-group as a whole to which brothers, uncles, cousins, lay and clerk, had a claim. In tenth-century Saxony, women, even nuns, were not excluded, for although custom placed them behind the men, their better expectations of life – and here nuns excelled themselves – meant that large inheritances accumulated in their hands. Cohereditas, if it was not checked by a high rate of mortality, could lead to the progressive fragmentation of a great fortune' (1968: 37).[12]

However, the emphasis on parity, on which the solidarity of kin partly rested, was disrupted by the 'existence of commanding heights which could not easily be shared' (p. 40). Riches could alienate a man from his family. But the major resource that could not be shared was high office itself (Goody 1968), and the very existence of office, more particularly when combined with an estate, was a threat to the unity of the kin group. On the other hand, the achievements of a single relative brought honour to the rest. 'Socially the whole kin was meant to share the honour which fell to one of its members' (Leyser 1968: 39). It is misleading, therefore, to take the *Libri Memoriales*, the record of the religious association of nobles with the prayers of a monastic community, as defining the structure of aristocratic kin groups or ranges. For the extent of kin reckoning in constructing these memorials is certainly different from that obtaining in the sphere of inheritance, which as Leyser remarks, did not draw men

---

[12] 'Additional sons and occasionally all but one were placed in the Church', but 'from the ninth century onwards a grant of land was expected when placing a child in a house like Corvey, and the reformed abbeys of the eleventh did not reject such gifts either' (Leyser 1968: 37).

together but drove them apart, especially in the more successful and wealthier families (p. 36). When men became rich and powerful, they tended to look towards their immediate descendants as their successors. 'Fathers strove for their sons and felt the full bitterness of losing them prematurely. They did not relish leaving their *hereditas* to some distant kinsman but harsh circumstances like the short expectation of life forced them to face this prospect. Even so many preferred to found monasteries and nunneries with the whole of their fortune instead' (p. 34).

The effects of the concentration of wealth and office on kinship ties are described by Leyser in terms of the prevalence of 'agnatic tendencies', a statement that throws some light on the discussions about the growth of *lignages* in the Middle Ages. The so-called agnatic tendencies often turn out to mean a concentration upon an individual's own descendants, daughters as well as sons, to the exclusion of collaterals. Such a narrowing of the focus was clearly in the interests of the Church and was encouraged by the general move to set aside the powers of kin to restrict the alienation of land, a process intimately bound up with the Church's policies of acquisition.

For the problems involving the rights of kin came to the fore in any attempt to hand over the estate, in part or in full, to an outside body. 'The complexity of claims upon a given estate was at no time more manifest than when it was proposed to alienate it to the Church. In the tenth and early eleventh century it had always been difficult to protect proprietary foundations against the importunate resentment of heirs, the kindred of the donors . . . Men who wished to found monasteries had to square their kinsmen in all directions lest their plans should come to grief after their deaths' (Leyser 1968: 48–9). At this time the brothers Achalm, who had no direct heirs, decided to found the monastery of Zweifakten near the Danube in Northern Swabia. Some time later, two sons of one of their sisters came forward to demand a share in the property. One of the authors of the foundation's history, a monk, thought that custom allowed them no claim and that they had 'already received their due out of their mother's inheritance' (p. 49). But the surviving brother took a different line, allocating his nephews a castle and an estate already granted to the monastery. What we have here is not so much an example of the generalised rights of kin (*pace* Leyser), but of the continuing claims of offspring, in this case females, on the parental estates, a practice that is in some respects similar to the optative system of northern France in the sixteenth century, where the *enfants dotés* are not necessarily paid off when they receive their early portion on quitting the farm (Yver 1966; Le Roy Ladurie 1972; Goody 1976c); they may return to complete their claim at the death of the parents.

THE EROSION OF THE RIGHTS OF KIN

A considerable proportion of the immense possessions of the Church came from donations made by particular families, either in a person's lifetime or, more usually, in a testament. As was argued in Chapter 3, by setting itself against certain 'strategies of heirship' that would assist a family line to continue – namely adoption, cousin marriage, plural marriage or concubinage, unions with affines, or the remarriage of divorced persons, the Church brought about the further alienation of family holdings. Its teaching emphasised the elementary family as all-important, thus eroding the rights of collaterals and of wider kin groups. For example, under the form of bookland employed by the Anglo-Saxon Church, such an area or so many units of land were transferred from A to B by means of a simplified and absolutist form of written conveyance. But in many cases folkland was held under a more complicated tenure allowing an individual the right to repurchase land that had been sold or devised by a kinsman, a situation which was obviously disadvantageous to those attempting to build up large estates or to place land permanently in the hands of another corporation. While Anglo-Saxon records give no indication of 'communal tenure' at the level of the kin group, they sometimes suggest that some land was inalienable from that group, as is seen, for example, in the will of Wolfgeat of Donington (Lancaster 1958: 359). Such restrictions meant that 'land held by an individual is to go to another individual within a certain range of kin'. Despite Lancaster's reservations on the subject, this case suggests the existence of a kind of *retrait lignager*, which was also found in Ancient Israel, in early Scandinavian law and, until recently, in Norwegian *odelsrett* (Barnes 1957). Indeed, an English law made by Aethelred at the end of the tenth century prohibited the kindred from revoking a sale, a provision that would appear to indicate a pre-existing practice of this kind.

While the *retrait lignager*, the 'lineal repurchase right' of kin, did not last in England as long as it did in France, being abandoned in the common law of the thirteenth century, the heir continued to be 'in some degree compensated by the prohibition on the devise of land' (Holdsworth 1909: III,66). Whatever he did with land during his lifetime, a man 'could not prevent the heir from inheriting what he left at his death' (p. 67). It seems likely, according to Holdsworth, that something was felt to be due to the heir, so that at the level of custom, rather than at that of law or custumal, the reciprocal rights and obligations of kin inside and outside the household with regard to inherited land pursued a kind of half-life in the hidden economy of the domestic domain.

These reciprocal rights meant that attempts at outright sale or donation would produce conflict between collaterals, as well as between laymen and the Church; testamentary bequests to the Church were likely to bring about a further cleavage between the interests, attitudes and emotions of adjacent generations in the same household. It is in the interest of members of the senior generation to invest a portion of their wealth in salvation in the world to come; Argyle's curve (1958: 67–70) suggests that, at least in the twentieth century, religious belief comes to a peak among the aged, whose hopes and fears might be fanned by clerical advisers. On the other hand, the younger generation is likely to be more concerned with the production and possession of material goods and less with the affairs of the next world. The salvation of the elderly entails a sacrifice for the younger generation who lose access to that land or wealth which has been given away and for which the senior generation no longer has any earthly use. In extreme cases the young may lose all, a danger which was perceived by those early Byzantine emperors who stepped in to control religious bequests.

The fear that property would be alienated in favour of the Church but away from the children remained a continuing feature of European history. The Visigothic king Wamba (d. 683) placed restrictions on alienation by condemning the disposal of property to the detriment of children, probably with the Church specifically in mind; 'certainly', comments King, 'his new law must seriously have affected its accumulation of property' (1972: 68,fn. 1). In the course of his efforts to reconstruct Western society, Charlemagne asked his assembled bishops, in 811, whether renunciation of the world was consistent with augmenting their positions by exploiting the hope of heaven and the fear of hell, and by encouraging men to disinherit their heirs. Five years later his son, Louis the Pious, decreed that no cleric should receive donations from anyone whose children would be disinherited; the property must be restored and the culprit punished.

The alienation of the property that would otherwise have been inherited by the children, especially when alienation was effected at the approach of death, in sickness, under priestly pressure or in fear of the world to come, remained a constant source of conflict at all levels of society, until eventually Protestantism, progressive secularisation and socio-economic changes gradually put an end to the problem, or radically diminished its significance. Even after the Reformation the opportunity was open to leave one's property for a range of charitable purposes, but the pressures, sanctions and incentives were of a different kind, less liable to aggravate the tensions between adjacent generations, between parents and children.

THE EXTENT OF CHURCH HOLDINGS

The effects of the Gregorian movement for Church reform in the eleventh century, of the lower levels of violence and of the reorganisation of estates made themselves felt on family life in a number of ways. The same factors produced a partial recovery in the Church's powers of accumulating and retaining property, although the proportion of land held seems to have dropped in France, Spain and Italy in the twelfth century as the result of the increased amount being brought under cultivation through active colonisation by laymen. Such settlers paid a tithe or quitrent to the Church and by the late twelfth century this income may have come to rival direct ownership as its main source of economic support (Herlihy 1961: 99). Certainly in England the subsequent centuries saw a shift in the basis of the Church's wealth from bequests of land to other forms, largely because of the legislation on mortmain by which the state limited the powers of the Church to acquire land as distinct from other assets (see p. 129–33). As a result there was not the continuous rise in the percentage of land held by the Church that might have been expected – in the hypothetical absence of depredations of various forms. The proportion held by the Church at the time of the Reformation was not very different from what it had been five centuries earlier.

At the time of the Norman conquest, that massive property register of the new aristocracy, the Domesday Book, showed the total

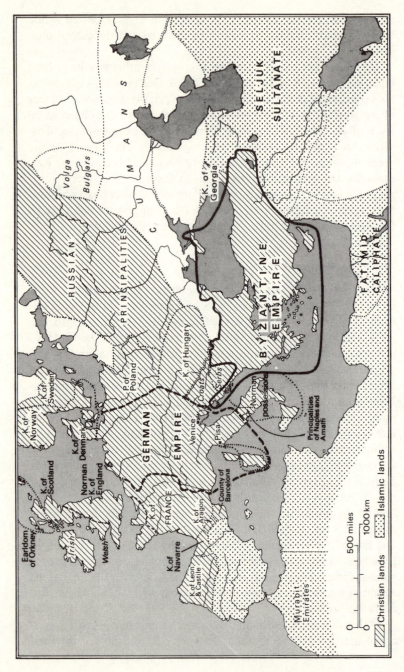

Earldom of Orkney

K. of Scotland

Irish

K. of England

Welsh

Norman Denmark

K. of Norway

K. of Sweden

K. of Denmark

RUSSIAN PRINCIPALITIES

C U M A N S

Volga Bulgars

GERMAN EMPIRE

P. of Poland

K. of Hungary

Venice

Croats

Serbs

Pisa

Norman possessions

BYZANTINE EMPIRE

SELJÚK SULTANATE

K. of Georgia

K. of France

K. of Navarre

K. of Aragon

County of Barcelona

K. of Leon & Castile

Murabit Emirates

Principalities of Naples and Amalfi

FATIMID CALIPHATE

0   500 miles
0   1000 km

▨ Christian lands   ⸬ Islamic lands

revenue from rural property as being around £73,000, a figure that excludes income from boroughs. This amount was divided in five main ways (Corbett 1926: 508):

For the Crown	£17,650
For the baronies (*c.* 170)	£30,350
For pre-conquest landowners	£4,000
For minor officials	£1,800
For the Church	£19,200 (26%)

Of the Church's share, £8,000 went to maintain the secular clergy and £9,200 for monks (plus £1,200 for nunneries), though these latter numbered only about one thousand.

The percentage of roughly a quarter of land rents going to the Church remained fairly constant after the conquest. William I insisted on reconfirming the grants of land to the Church; and while it suffered some losses, it also made some gains. Two hundred years later, in 1279, the Church's holdings in parts of six counties was 31 per cent, according to Kosminsky's calculations from the Hundred Rolls (1956: 108). Using the 1436 'income tax' records, Cooper very tentatively estimated that the Church owned about 20–25 per cent of the land in England generally, that is to say, some 4,000,000 notional acres (1967: 421). From the monumental valuation of 1535, immediately preceding the dissolution of the monasteries, not all of which has survived, the following figures give some idea of the extent of the Church's holdings:

Rutland	Church *c.* 33% of land (*c.* 10% for local monasteries)
	Crown *c.* 25%
Surrey (Southwark)	Church 48%
(rural)	Church 35%
Suffolk (Babergh)	Church 40% of revenues
Norfolk	Church 20%(+) of land.

The total revenue from Church lands was about £400,000 in 1535, while Crown lands yielded one tenth of that amount; in all the Church is estimated to have owned 20–30 per cent of real property (Hoskins 1976: 124).

It was the monastic component of these huge holdings of the country's land and wealth that was confiscated by Henry VIII. The Crown in turn sold the property to 'a select minority of eager subjects' (p. 134), mostly the gentry. The King himself retained an annual rent, at first making the grants subject to feudal service, with the possibility of wardship if the inheritance passed to a minor. It was this fear of wardship that seems to have been one factor behind the child marriages that took place among members of this class during the Tudor period (Furnivall 1897: xxxix–xl), providing a further example of the effects of changes in property ownership and distribution on family life.

PROPERTY AND AGE AT MARRIAGE

The marriage of wards received the special attention of moralists and reformers. 'Little infants in swaddling clowts', wrote Stubbes in his *Anatomy of Abuses* (1583), 'are often married by their ambicious Parents and frends, when they know neither good nor evill' (1877: 97). Indeed 'every saucy boy of x, xiiii, xvi or xx years of age' wanted 'to catch up a woman and marie her', installing her in a cottage before he has the means to support her. So his character, Philoponus, proposes a delay in marriage, possibly till the age of 24, in order to reduce the number of beggars. To Spudeus's objection that such a measure would create more bastards, he proposes that the punishments for sexual offences should be drastically increased (p. 98). The connection between late marriage and either bastardy or restraint, noted by later social historians (Flandrin 1979; Laslett 1977) and anthropologists (Tait 1961), was not lost on Tudor commentators. Some, such as Thomas Becon, chaplain to Archbishop Cranmer, maintained that 'untimely marriages' would enfeeble the body and produce weaklings (1884: 369).

The complaint about marriages between partners of ill-matched ages for reasons of property was not confined to feudal wards, to the 'Queen's wards' (Hurstfield 1958: 149). The desire for security led not only to the early marriages of wards but to the late marriages of widows with younger men. '"Body of our Lord" cried young Henry Kingston when he heard of the death of a man who left a wealthy, middle-aged widow, "I will go marry this olde widdow and pay my debts. Then when I have buried her will I marry a young wench and get children"' (Holles 1937: 215; Hurstfield 1958: 150). Becon complained of widows of four score years marrying boys of eighteen 1844: 366), and wrote that 'Some parents greatly abuse their authority while they sell their children for to be married for wordly gain and lucre . . .' (p. 372).

The early marriage of wards does nothing to counter the contention of Hajnal and others (e.g. Laslett 1977) that the mean age of marriage in Western Europe, at least since the Tudor period, was a late one. Such marriages with a high differential marriage age (DMA) in favour of males or of females, must always have been a small proportion of the total. In general, as Laslett notes, a significant feature of Western societies is the small age gap between the spouses, with a relatively high proportion of wives being older than their husbands, and this small age gap he links with 'marriage tending towards the companionate' (1977: 13). While 'companionate marriage' is difficult to define in a satisfactory manner, it does not seem to have been absent from earlier systems of marriage in the Mediterranean, and indeed elsewhere. The relatively small age gap between husband and wife is connected, though not in any absolute way, with monogamous marriage; or rather, widespread polygyny is linked with a high differential marriage age in favour of males, as a result of which women have a longer span of married life than men. The fact that a significant proportion of wives are older than their husbands, does seem 'peculiar' in a comparative perspective, and surely stems from the calculations of those such as Henry Kingston, which were related to the particular way in which property was allocated to women as well as to men (Goody 1976c), especially their right to a dower. In a few cases older brides are found among the brother-sister unions of Roman Egypt where women were also endowed (Hopkins 1980: 333); in China the situation was more pronounced (Wolf and Huang 1980: 41). As I have argued elsewhere (1976b), these forms of marriage are in turn associated with certain types of productive system and their property arrangements; the general match of age and property is not contradicted by a certain mismatching where age or security is weighed against property.

'THE DEAD HAND'

The acquisition of land by the Church set it up as a competitor to the State on two levels. First, it turned a religious institution into a powerful alternative in a political and economic sense. Second, it sometimes entailed a substantial loss of revenue for the government. Since Church lands were partly exempt from public burdens, it had more wealth available to reinvest in land, for which it could afford to pay more. In the case of the frankalmoign of the Cistercians, a form of spiritual tenure (or 'free alms') whereby a religious corporation held land free of feudal services, the State lost any obligations for military duties. When land was made over for ecclesiastical use, feudal lords often lost the right to reliefs, escheats, payments in respect of marriages, wardships and so on, since the land did not pass to an heir and so the lord was denied the opportunity of gaining these profits. As a result, State revenues dropped, or, alternatively, the burden on others had to be increased. So the acquisition of lands by the Church was a threat to the State as well as to others interested in maintaining or acquiring land, either by inheritance or by purchase.

The result was opposition and counter-action from the secular authorities. Already in the late sixth century the Merovingian king Chilperic (d. 584) was complaining of the general loss of revenue to the realm. A law of Chindasvind attempted to call a halt to this specific loss by making the new owner responsible for the liabilities of the alienator. In 811 Charlemagne protested to his bishops about these exemptions on both national and moral grounds, and his successor took the further step of legal action. Later on, in Spain, more drastic measures were taken to prevent the permanent alienation of land to the Church and in the tenth and eleventh centuries it was customary to regard bequests to the Church as limited to three years, after which they were reclaimed by the heirs. In an open struggle between Church and State, the councils of Leon (1020) and Coyanza (1050) decreed that such gifts were perpetual, while in 1106 Alfonso VI forbade all gifts of land to the Church, except in Toledo. Pressure on the State to limit the Church's acquisitions of land also came from below, especially from the parliaments in their role as representative institutions. The cortes of Najera prohibited land under royal jurisdiction from falling into mortmain, into the 'dead hand' of the Church. The State and monarchy were thus seen as potential or actual protectors against this massive alienation of land. For despite legislation, 'popular piety' and 'ecclesiastical greed' meant that it still continued. 'From this time [*c*. 1125],' wrote Lea, 'until the middle of the sixteenth century, with occasional intermissions, almost every assembly of the cortés of Castile petitioned the monarchs for their enforcement or adopted some plan to mitigate the evil, and every code of Spanish medieval law has provisions on the subject' (1900: 4).

Parallel legislation was introduced in other countries in Europe. In 1232 Frederick II revived a forgotten law in his Kingdom of the

Two Sicilies that forbad the alienation of land to clerics or clerical corporations by gift or by sale. About the same time similar restrictions took shape in Portugal, Flanders and France, though apparently somewhat later in Italy. The Saxon law, which prevailed in the north-east of Germany, allowed thirty years and a day for the heirs to reclaim property sold to the Church. In the south and west, however, no such restriction applied, with the result that at the outbreak of the Reformation, it is estimated that, according to Lea (1900: 6), more than half the land in Germany belonged to the Church.

In England a series of Mortmain Acts was passed with the aim of controlling such accumulation, especially in the Church sector; such control was in the interests of the nobility and provided the Crown with an income from licences. The statute of Edward I, *De Religiosis*, and the Statute of Westminster held that if any body politic, ecclesiastical or lay, sole or aggregate, should acquire land in such a way as it was subject to mortmain, then the feudal lord could take possession, and in default the land went to the king. A statute of Richard II extended this provision to all lands purchased for the use of guilds and fraternities. And when testamentary power over freehold lands was established under Henry VIII, such bodies were deliberately excluded. Land could not be devised to a corporation without royal permission; otherwise it reverted to the heir. The Church did, of course, try to get round such legislation in various ways, for the flow was already drying up beforehand (Raban 1974), demonstrating both the strength of its desire to extend its lands and the great concern that this caused its contemporaries; lay resentment had been vociferous for half a century before the statutes against mortmain and continued afterwards against the efforts to circumvent the legislation. The result of the long struggle was to drive accumulation into different channels; the Church was forced to take a greater interest in leasehold tenures and pious gifts were translated into cash or luxury goods.

The Statute of Mortmain had been anticipated in charters as early as 1220–5, when one John of Fountains included a proviso in a document forbidding alienation to a religious house. And the same kind of restriction was sometimes embodied in peasant charters, as when Geoffrey the clerk acquired a dwelling house at Sutton, with power to transfer it 'except to religion or Jewry' (Miller 1951: 130). In provisions of this kind one detects the worries of the rural population about the build-up of Church lands.

After this period the Church in England failed to increase its landed estate at the rate it had done previously. But this did not of course mean that wealth was no longer set aside by will and donation for religious purposes. That outspoken Elizabethan commentator, Philip Stubbes, remarked: 'The Papists also holde it to be a work of unspeakable merit, for a man or a woman . . . to give the greatest part of their goods and lands (the more, the more merite) to popish priestes, (though in the meane time, theyr wife, children, and whole families goe a begging all theyr lyfe long) . . . to the ende they may pray for them when they are dead . . .' In quoting this passage Furnivall (1882: xii) comments on the 'fifty earliest English wills' that 'the most surprizing and regrettable thing in these Wills is the amount of money shown to hav been wasted in vain prayers . . .' However, some contributions were devoted to helping poor girls get married, mending roads, and similar public ends.

The Mortmain Acts controlled gifts of land to religious houses, but movable wealth, used for song, prayer, buildings and other ends, continued to be devoted to the Church. As Holdsworth remarks, 'That the piety or the apprehensions of the dying evaded the spirit of these Acts by the establishment of these chantries no-one who reads any collection of wills of this period can doubt' (1909: III,429). We cannot be surprised at this development, partly of course because of the understandable wishes of the holders of the property. But partly too because, in England, wills concerning chattels lay exclusively in the hands of the ecclesiastical courts, not only for probate but for matters related to their making, revocation and interpretation (p. 419). Indeed it was the parson who often drew up a written will (p. 422). And if it was 'nuncupative' (that is, verbal), it was probably he who heard a man's final words at the time of the last rites, for many thought that a person should not make a will when in good health (p. 422). The frauds of those confessors 'who persuade dying penitents to impoverish their heirs' (Lea 1900: 5) was commented upon in similar terms by Philip V of Spain, who attempted to negotiate a statute of mortmain with the papacy in 1713.

The power of the Church over the dying was influenced by its role as a comforter of the sick and guardian of the bereaved, a role which was extended as the increase in ecclesiastical land-holding produced an increase in the amount of money that could be invested in the practical side of Church activities: in the building of places of worship, places of retreat, places of learning, as well as places for the treatment of the sick, the poor, the orphaned and the widowed. The increasing role of the Church was accompanied by a weakening of the efficacy of ties between kin.

CHURCH REFORM, FAMILY AND MARRIAGE

As we have seen, the Gregorian reforms of the eleventh century indirectly influenced the domestic domain in important ways. It is time to look more closely at the direct effects on marriage and the family.

The loss of Church lands was one factor behind the movement for ecclesiastical reform. In the West the Carolingian kings, especially in the person of Charlemagne, had provided a rival source of power to the papacy, and with the rise of feudal relations during the ninth and tenth centuries, there had developed 'the Church in the hands of laymen'. It was in the mid eleventh century, the period of the conquest of England by the Normans, that this trend was reversed with the reform of the papacy, the centralisation of Church government and the separation of the clergy as an estate (*ordo*) rigidly distinct from the laity, with extensive rights and privileges, with concomitant obligations and duties, and with jurisdiction over spiritual and quasi-spiritual matters. The eleventh century also saw the birth of new monastic orders, the spread of 'the regular life', the campaign of Damian and his allies against clerical marriage and 'immorality' in general, the attack on the lay ownership of churches and on the feudal control of elections. At the same time there was an extension of the Church's jurisdiction over marriage, an elaboration of the prohibited degrees, and a renewed emphasis on the consent of the partners.

These reforms included a prohibition which prevented lay persons from holding churches and monasteries, encouraging instead their transfer to ecclesiastical institutions and replacing ownership with patronage. One factor that had promoted the lineal continuity of property in land-owning circles was thus removed, for the concentration of possessions and the foundation of churches and monasteries had been one way of maintaining '*la cohésion familiale*' (Violante 1977: 101). Gifts and bequests had now to be outright.

Many of the reforms were directed internally at the clergy themselves. As the result of the council held at Westminster in 1102,

Archbishop Anselm laid down a series of canons that included the following rules:

(5) That no ... priest ... marry a wife, or retain one ...

(8) That the sons of priests be not made heirs to the church of their fathers.

(20) That monks and nuns be not godfathers or godmothers.

(21) That monks hold no land in farm.

(23) That faith in way of marriage, pledged secretly (*occulte*) and without witness, betwixt man and woman, be of no effect, if either party do deny it. (Fuller 1842: I,288–9; Whitelock *et al.* 1981: 674ff)[13]

The moves made against concubinage have already been reviewed in an earlier chapter; concubinage provided a physical continuity for both layman and priest each of which, after its own fashion, was inimical to the property interest of the Church. The only accepted union was marriage and that was indissoluble for laymen and illegal for clerics. The doctrines of the Church thus emphasised the distinction between legitimate and illegitimate partners. Those who, like the eleventh-century German nobles remarked on by Leyser (1968: 44), kept mistresses while remaining unmarried, jeopardised their patrimonies.

THE PROHIBITED DEGREES

In the complex matter of the prohibited degrees, the range was yet further extended. From the time of their establishment in the fourth century, the prohibitions on marriage to kin played a central part in the life of the Church. They enabled it not only to control its congregation, as would have been the case with any restrictions on 'customary' action, but also to profit from the sins of the delinquent by offering dispensations to the transgressors. Gratitude to the Church for providing both the definition and treatment of sin was expressed in the benefactions through which salvation could be achieved.

The prohibited degrees promulgated by the Church changed over time. Similarly, the sanctions for transgression meted out by the

[13] In addition, other regulations were more concerned with the suppression of non-Christian elements. No dead were to be buried outside the parish. Another regulation read. 'That none, out of a rash novelty, exhibit reverence of holiness to any bodies of the dead, fountains, or other things, without authority of the bishop'. See also Brett (1975) on the Church under Henry I.

Church varied in their severity. At the beginning of the tenth century, for example, the Church in France was imprecise about both the degrees and the punishments. A letter of Pope Leo VII (936–939) to the French and Germans referred to the possibility of dispensations for marriages beyond the second degree, recalling the 'tarifs de pénitence' of the Carolingian Church (Daudet 1933: 72). The French clergy do not appear to have dissolved incestuous marriages, let alone deprived the participants of the right of inheritance, a measure that was required by the Theodosian Code.[14] One of the most striking examples of their liberality – or subservience – was the marriage of Robert (the Pious) to Bertha, his cousin in the third degree, in 996, which was opposed by a lay council but which aroused no known reaction among the French clergy (Daudet 1933: 78; Duby 1978); although the Pope threatened them with excommunication, the status of the offender over-rode considerations of ecclesiastical morality and the threat was never put into effect. Nevertheless, such marriages gave rise to a moral problem with far-reaching practical implications. In general, as in the case of the papal legates at the English synod of 786, the Church insisted upon the illegitimacy of children born of adulterous or incestuous unions, who in their eyes could become neither priests nor kings. Whatever the outcome of particular cases, the existence of such judgements either reduced a man's opportunity to attain high office or increased the chance of dismissal of those who did so, whether by pressure from above or below. Even in the most relaxed periods, the Church's ideas of legitimacy, tied to the ban on concubinage, spelt danger for those with much to pass on.

The laxness of the tenth century was followed by the reforms of the eleventh. In 1059, Pope Nicholas II called a grand council at which the Gregorian reforms were given legislative force. An encyclical required that 'if anyone had taken a spouse within the seventh degree, he will be forced canonically by his bishop to send her away; if he refuses, he will be excommunicated'. The authority of the Church was re-established, even if it took twenty years for the French clergy to accept the new order. That order fixed the range of impediments as including the seventh degree.

---

[14] In 909 the reforms of the Council of Trosle recalled the secular law of the state which exiled the partners to such a marriage and confiscated their property, transferring the patrimony to their heirs (*Sacrorum Concilium*, 18, pp. 286–8).

What still remained open was the question of how the degrees should be calculated, a problem that was studied in depth during the pontificate of Alexander II. It was Peter Damian, in his *De Parentelae Gradibus* (*The Degrees of Consanguinity*) of 1063, who opted for the Germanico-canonical system of wider, inclusive computation, partly for a political reason, to refute the claims of the secular jurisdiction based on Roman law and sustained by the lawyers of Ravenna (Daudet 1933: 98–9).

Two types of system for reckoning degrees of consanguinity, the Roman and the Germanic, had been used by the Church at different times. The Roman system meant counting the number of acts of generation between ego and alter (Justinian, *Inst.* III,VI; *Digest* XXXVIII, VIII). For instance, I am related to my sister in the second degree, the first degree being from myself to my parent(s), the second from the parent to her. Uncle and niece are related in the third degree, i.e.:

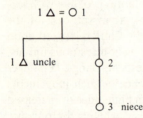

The Germanic system, on the other hand, was based upon the unity of the sibling group, the members of which were related in the first degree. It was this group that formed a generation, in contrast to the Roman system which made its calculations on the basis of acts of generation. While the former counted only the generations from the common ancestor, the latter computed the number of degrees by ascending from the base line to the common ancestor, then descending to the relative in question. At a relatively late period, at the time of the *Sachsenspiegel* in the thirteenth century, the Germanic calculus was represented by the human body, the head being the common ascendant, the shoulder the brother and sister, the elbow first cousins, and so on down to the nails, which stood for the seventh degree, at which point, as in Roman law, kinship stopped.

The formal shift from the Roman to the Germanic system occurred in the eleventh century, and was formulated in Alexander II's canon of 1076, which followed the thesis elaborated by Peter Damian. Pope Alexander II was the predecessor of Gregory, and worked with him and Damian on matters of reform. Roman law had reckoned seven degrees of kinship for the purpose of inheritance, a system which was linked by formalised analogy – a literate speciality, though not one confined to that mode – to the creation of the world in seven days (Isidore, *Etymologiae*).[15] It was this particular range that the Church eventually incorporated into its prohibited degrees; in effect one could no longer marry anyone from whom one could have formerly inherited, i.e. kinsfolk. The Church's concern was with restrictions on marriage (for inheritance from collaterals was discouraged). Since marriage was a union between two persons, at least two persons should be included in the same degree, that is, a generation. On these grounds Alexander accepted Damian's advocacy of the Germanic system. Whatever the reasons, its adoption meant *ipso facto* doubling the range of prohibited degrees (see Figure 2), the seventh degree in the Germanico-canonical method corresponding to the thirteenth or fourteenth of the Roman one (Esmein 1891: I,348–9).

The difference between the Roman and Germanic methods of computation created problems of a very substantial kind. Accusations of incest were frequently made against the imperial nobility of the eleventh and twelfth centuries. According to Champeaux, part of the problem arose from their continued use of the Roman methods of computing kin which reflected the attachment of the nobility to the legend of Troy and their putative descent from the *milites* of Julius Caesar (1933: 249). In fact, the in-marrying tendencies of the aristocracy had a more substantial basis than any legend of origin, since, as Duby has shown, they influenced the distribution of property and alliance. Nevertheless, the changes of the eleventh century were in part an attempt to set aside Roman law on which the computations of the seventh-century encyclopaedist, Isidore of Seville, had been based, or rather to bring it into line with popular modes of reckoning based on the 'Germanic' or 'fraternal' tradition of local kinship. It was an attempt to reduce the conflict between noble and commoner, between Church and people, between civil and ecclesiastical law, as well as among the scholiasts themselves.

---

[15] 'Ideo autem usque ad sextum generis gradum consanguinitas constitua est, ut sicut sex aetatibus mundi generatio et hominis status finitur, ita propinquitas generis tot gradibus terminaretur' (Isidore, *Etymologiae* I. IX, c. vi, 29).

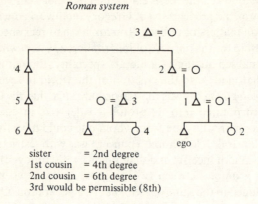

Roman system

sister   = 2nd degree
1st cousin   = 4th degree
2nd cousin   = 6th degree
3rd would be permissible (8th)

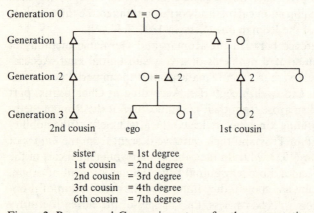

Germanic system

sister   = 1st degree
1st cousin   = 2nd degree
2nd cousin   = 3rd degree
3rd cousin   = 4th degree
6th cousin   = 7th degree

Figure 2. Roman and Germanic systems for the computation of kin

For a long time the question of the method of computation was a subject of dispute in the Church. Not only did the system of kinship out-marriage go against the earlier traditions of the Germanic peoples, not to mention the immediate interests of their descendants, but the Roman method of counting kin also appears to have run contrary to popular conceptions. While the first systematic evidence of the use of the human body, reckoning from the head to the nails, seems to be as late as the thirteenth century, the concept of 'articulations' (*geniculum, cnēow*, that is, of joints like the knee) appears

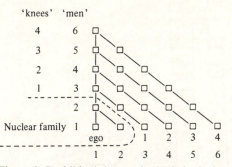

Figure 3. Prohibited degrees in Aethelred's laws (after Charles-Edwards 1972: 23)

much earlier as a mode of computation and the calculations implied in the laws of Aethelred have been represented in a manner that bears a greater resemblance to the later Germanic than to the Roman system (see Figure 3).

In Figure 3 the third articulation (knee), which is the fifth 'man', represents the fourth Germanico-canonical degree, which is the eighth Roman degree. Hence it corresponds to the 'popular' mode of calculation found in many areas of contemporary Europe and which is probably of long standing. The third articulation represents the third cousin in the current usage of much of Europe – in England, France and Spain. Champeaux (1933: 254) argues that it was at this third degree that popular calculations of specific kinship ties ceased in traditional Poland, in medieval Switzerland and elsewhere on the continent; and it was to this point that the Lateran Council of 1215 reduced the very extensive prohibitions of marriage which had been introduced some 140 years earlier.

Despite the attempts at clarification by Pope Alexander II, there continued to be many variations of procedure. In calculating relationships the canonical authors of the second half of the twelfth century distinguished between *truncus* (or *stips*) and *gradus*, that is, between 'trunk' and 'degree' (see Figures 4 and 5). The trunk was the point of departure for reckoning the degrees and there was considerable discussion as to whether one should take as the 'trunk' the brother, the father or the grandfather (Champeaux 1933: 242). The trunk comprised a group of which the blood was seen as identical, consisting sometimes of the siblings, sometimes the married

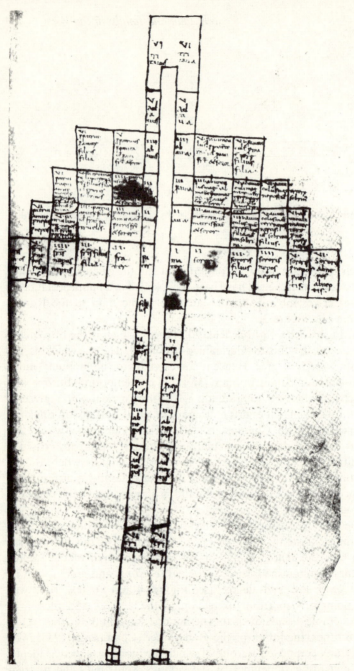

Figure 4. Early representation of degrees with no ego (*ipse*, *truncus*), from a ninth-century copy of an eighth-century manuscript of Isidore of Seville (Patlagean 1966: 66)

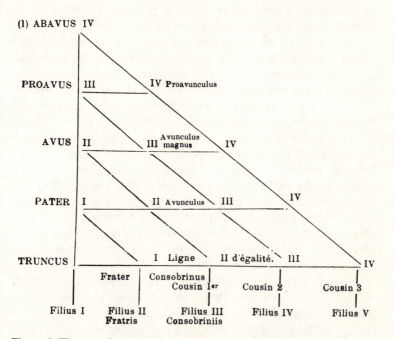

Figure 5. The use of *truncus* (from Champeaux 1933: 281)

couple, and sometimes even the individual whose relationships were being traced; in the latter case, the 'group' was his potential descendants. On this particular basis three types of reckoning can be distinguished, the calculation by the 'fraternal kinship of blood', by the matrimonial mode, and by the individual method, the two latter being considered 'canonical'.

While Damian and Alexander compromised with the local system, the Church was mainly interested, according to Champeaux, in eliminating the notion of 'fraternal kinship'. The charters are full of references to struggles by blood relations to get back charitable gifts made (wrongly in their view) by one of their own (p. 250). Such claims were connected with ideas of collateral inheritance within the *lignage des frères*, the group of blood and brotherhood, as well as with *le retrait et le bail lignager*, ideas which were all inimical to the permanent and undisputed alienation of property. The efforts of the Church, on the other hand, were directed to replacing the system of calculation based on siblings by one based on the unity of flesh (*unitas carnis*) established by marriage (or *copula*); that is, by one based upon the married couple and their children. This system tended to stress the direct line of descent, eliminating collaterals, especially by making use of the principle 'succession ne monte pas' in order to expropriate the *lignage* (p. 257). Finally, the third mode of calculation was adopted, introducing (or re-introducing from a manuscript of Isidore) the central notion of an *ipse*, that is, an *ego* (later the *truncus*), as a point of departure (see Figure 6). In other words, the *figura*, the visual representation of consanguinity, no longer consisted simply of the ordering of terms for relationships (*pater*, *mater*, *filius*, *filia*, etc.) but was based on an ego-oriented scheme that facilitated the computation of degrees and was in line, Champeaux maintains, with the increasing emphasis on individuality and consensus.

Certainly such ideas were becoming more frequently expressed, although, as we have seen, they were not foreign to earlier civilisations. While moral and ethical considerations are relevant to this change, perhaps a yet more important fact lay in the growth of both Church and State, in their bureaucratic and property-holding forms, which led to a weakening, often deliberate, of groups and ranges of kin. In the process the molecule of kinship became reduced to its constituent atoms, the individual whose consent – to marriage, to alienation and to many other activities – could not be challenged by recalcitrant or powerful relatives.

The extraordinary extension of the range of prohibited degrees arose partly out of the change in modes of reckoning. Their sheer extent made their application highly impractical. As Oesterlé remarks, 'Pushed to this degree, the canonical prohibitions could not be upheld, above all in a period where rural populations were tied to the land and where mobility was limited. One could hardly find any marriage the validity of which could not be challenged because of a violation of the tie of consanguinity' (1949: 236). Some authors such as Sheehan and Helmholz have questioned whether such violations were often used to set aside marriages in the Middle Ages, but this certainly occurred and attempts were made to counter the practice in the period immediately preceding the Reformation. The efforts of Cardinal Ximenes in 1497 to secure the registration of baptisms,

ISIDORI

STEMMA II

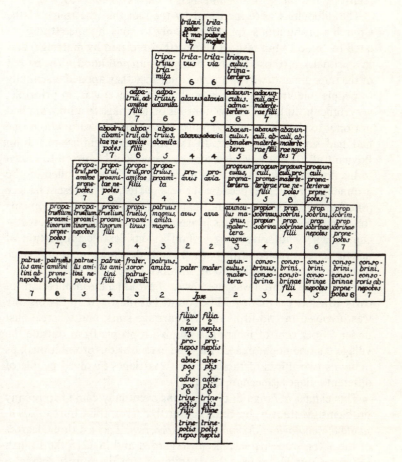

Figure 6. The introduction of an ego (*ipse*), from a manuscript of Isidore of Seville (*Etymologarium Sive Originum*, ed. W. M. Lindsay, Oxford, 1911, IX. vi. 29)

first in his own church and then throughout Western Europe, has been attributed to his desire 'to check the growing scandal of wholesale divorces, disguised as decrees of nullity, based upon the alleged spiritual affinity contracted at baptism between the baptised and his relatives, and the sponsors and their relatives' (Tate 1969: 43).

The difficulties were increased by the fact that the range of the Church's prohibitions applied not only to consanguines (those related by 'blood') but also to affines (those related by marriage) and to spiritual kin (those related through godparenthood). The extent of the impediments was enormous and since they applied essentially to people one knew, marriage at the village level was, in principle, very difficult. Indeed, the prohibitions on marriage to affines applied not only to the kin of one's spouse but to anyone with whom one had had sexual intercourse. In the fourteenth century one John Poynant of Ely even pleaded that he should not be forced to return to his first wife, with whom his marriage had been annulled on the grounds of impotence, because she was related to his present fiancée (Sheehan 1971: 261). After the abandonment of the feudal payments for marrying out of the lord's jurisdiction (Searle 1979; Faith, forthcoming), it is not surprising to find a considerable proportion of marriages contracted with partners outside the community, since distance reduced the likelihood of impediments; the contraction of an extra-village union was also a way of avoiding the implications of early attachments that could be counted as marriage. In Ely bigamy was involved in two-fifths of the marriage suits; and whereas just under 50 per cent of marriages were with people from outside the village (as one might expect with the extent of the prohibitions), as many as two thirds of the bigamous marriages involved people of different villages (Sheehan 1971: 251).

This extensive range of prohibitions eventually caused too many problems. Moreover, beyond the fourth degree, the Church *dispensando dissimulavit et dissimulando dispensavit*. The last three degrees of the seven were increasingly disregarded and in 1215 the Fourth Lateran Council reduced the prohibitions to the fourth degree, a diminution which was justified by analogy with the four humours – *quia quatuor sunt humores in corpore, quod constat ex quatuor elementis* (*Decr.* I. IV, Tit. xiv,c.3). Much later this was reduced to the second degree for Indians of South American origin in 1537, for Blacks in 1897, and then for the world at large in 1917.

The constant infringements of the extensive prohibitions have been seen as creating 'an extreme instability of the matrimonial tie' (Flandrin 1979: 24). In attempting to explain these 'unrealistic' extensions, Flandrin sees an analogy between the evolution of these impediments and the development of ties of 'lineage solidarity' which, he claims, having reached their zenith between the tenth and twelfth centuries, loosened in the thirteenth when 'the *lignage* became more narrowly based under the influence of the patrilinear tendencies which preceded the introduction of patronymic surnames, and when, paradoxically, the ties of lineal solidarity became weaker as regards both vengeance and rights to landed property . . .' (p. 25).

While Flandrin suggests that the extensions may have reflected the increased solidarity of the '*lignage*', Duby reverses the causal direction and sees the decrees of the Church as advancing family solidarity, strengthening 'lineage-consciousness' and leading to a burst of genealogical activity, some of it designed to serve particular ends (1978: 27). All the counting of ancestors involved in calculating the degrees was undoubtedly an important literate activity promoted by the desire to avoid 'incest', as was the later registration of baptisms. However, there is no general reason why out-marriage should necessarily be linked to the solidarity of the kin group, nor yet why the Church's interest should be the same as that of lay kin groups. Indeed the introduction of the prohibitions was partly directed against the solidarity of such groups, against the reinforcing of blood with marriage, and it is difficult to see that their extension in the eleventh century did anything to counter this pressure. In any case the contradictions between these two theses seem partly to be attributed to ambiguities in the use of the term *lignage* (Appendix 1).

The restrictions, even to the fourth degree, were constantly challenged by the laity. As the result of suggestions made at the Imperial Diet of Mainz in 1439, some fathers asked the Vatican Council to reduce the prohibitions to the second degree. In any case it is clear from the decrees of the Council of Trent of 1545–63 that it was easy enough to obtain a dispensation for a marriage in the third degree, given 'sufficient cause'. Dispensation was a recognised way around the extensive prohibitions and provided the Church with control over (and income from) even those marriages which went against its formal rules, rules that in the extreme form promulgated in the eleventh century appear to have been made only to be broken. As we have seen, the system gave the Church a powerful instrument of control capable of influencing the life of every family, as well as giving the rich a method of dispensing with unwanted wives. A more extreme view of its role as an ecclesiastical money-spinner, one which was associated with Luther and Henry VIII who saw it instituted 'for lucre's sake', was expressed by Huth in the following words: 'What more natural than when a set of greedy priests found that people were ready to pay a price to be allowed to marry, they should have made marriage yet more difficult, that they should increase the number of meshes in their net, and with it the amount of their revenues?' (1875: 78–9). Certainly the new rules did not emerge from below. The 'artificial' and literary nature of the calculation of canonical degrees, forced on the people from above, is indicated in the instructions of the Bishop of Troyes to his parish priests in 1374: 'The priests must teach their parishioners to reckon the degrees of relationship in the following manner . . .' (Flandrin 1979: 26). That such rules forced individuals to seek dispensations and hence increased Church revenues is true. But the reasons for the elaboration of the rules, particularly the eleventh-century version, were more complicated. Apart from those arising from the reform of the Church's organisation, others related more generally to long-standing attitudes towards kinship and marriage, which had important effects on the structure of kin groups and family lines that in turn influenced the process of accumulating property for religious ends.

THE VALIDITY OF MARRIAGE

Not only the rules for whom one could marry, but the ceremony of marriage itself became increasingly the affair of the Church. 'In England between the seventh and the twelfth centuries the ecclesiastical authority in matrimonial questions was slowly established' (Howard 1904: I,333). At first the Church appears only to have concerned itself with the nuptial mass but gradually it became involved both in the betrothal and in that *gifta* or handing over of the bride which was regarded as the essence of marriage. Finally, in the twelfth century, Peter Lombard's annunciation of the 'seven sacraments' proposed that marriage be included among them.

The law of the Church on the definition of a valid marriage varied over time and only became fixed in the course of the twelfth century. The older view, which was supported by Gratian and the school of

Bologna in about 1140, maintained that marriage was initiated by the consent of the parties (*desponsatio*), but was only made indissoluble by sexual union (Helmholz 1974: 26). The view expressed by Peter Lombard and the Masters of Paris about twenty years later distinguished between two kinds of *desponsatio*, one by words of present consent (*verba de presenti*), the other by words of future consent (*verba de futuro*). Consent alone, and not coitus, made a marriage valid, at least in terms of its 'present' form. With future consent, an indissoluble bond was created only by means of sexual relations.

This second view prevailed under Pope Alexander III (1159–81). But it created a problem for the courts in deciding if consent had been given and accepted, whether the words spoken established an indissoluble contract. No public ceremony was needed to make a marriage *valid*, but, in order to make it fully *licit*, certain procedures had to be followed:

After financial arrangements had been made by the families concerned, the betrothal took place. This consisted of a promise to marry (*per verba de futuro*) and often was expressed as a form of words before witnesses. Next the banns were read in the parish church. If no objection to the marriage resulted, or if objections had been dealt with in a satisfactory way, the couple publicly solemnised their union by an exchange of consent (*per verba de presenti*) at the church door. This would be seen as the moment when the sacrament was given by the couple to each other. The ceremonies before witnesses included the endowment of the bride, her delivery by her father to the husband, and various rituals, including a form of words and the giving of a ring. Finally, the bridal party entered the church for the nuptial mass. (Sheehan 1971: 237)

But while only this form of marriage was licit, other unions could be valid. The betrothal followed by intercourse became marriage, even without being solemnised in church. This being so, since men and women did not always get married *in facie ecclesiae*, some making their agreement at home, or in a field, a garden, or even in bed, problems often arose in proving to the satisfaction of the ecclesiastical judges that a marriage had taken place at all. Some 70 per cent of the marriages involved in cases heard in Ely between March 1374 and March 1382 took place in private surroundings. While it was doubtless the intention of most parties to follow the private with a public celebration, not in all cases did this occur. One result was the 'clandestine marriage', a form of union that has been seen as the continuation of older traditions of matrimony. The court records, Helmholz maintains, 'show the tenacity of the belief that people could regulate their own matrimonial affairs, without the assistance or interference of the Church' (1974: 31).

Ecclesiastical recognition of clandestine marriages is seen by some as arising from the consensual theory accepted by the Church and the freedoms that it encouraged (Sheehan 1971: 229). But the doctrine of consent was no invention of the eleventh-century reformers, nor yet of Christianity itself, though, as we have argued, sectarian and ecclesiastical support certainly encouraged the individualisation of choice in a number of social situations. Moreover, the acceptance of consent as the basis of marriage did not preclude any requirement that it be followed by a specific ritual. The explanation offered is based on the same universalistic 'ethical' interpretation of the Church's actions in the domestic domain that mark much of the work on the Patristic period, whose developmental presuppositions are singularly difficult to reconcile with the characteristics of marriage in Protestant cultures of a much later period, which were in many ways more severe, less 'modern', as far as consent was concerned. That is to say, the consent of the partners was subject to the consent of parents.

A better explanation of the Church's attitude to such marriages would seem to be based on the difficulties it experienced in imposing its will on the forms and patterns of marriage at all levels, whether that of the nobility as described by Duby, or in the more popular milieu of Ely. Only with the Council of Trent did the Catholic Church finally manage to impose its authority in this sphere by invalidating marriages that had not been performed in public before the parish priest, a notion that was later followed in Protestant circles. This resolution led to a vigorous attack on the traditional forms of extra-sacramental marriage. In Normandy in 1600, the *fiançailles* or betrothal still formed 'a binding contract, cemented by exchange of gifts or passage of money and preceding the church marriage by a considerable time: it was still widely considered, even by canon lawyers, to be entirely proper that the couple should share a bed in the meantime. A century later, with the disappearance of *fiançailles* as a distinct contract, Trent and the principle of parochial conformity had achieved one of its most important victories over kinship solidarity' (Bossy 1970: 57). But perhaps the victory was not as complete as one might suppose. The extent of premarital pregnancies, 'bundling' and, in England 'common law marriages', were signs of continuity with the past; even today in some Christian communities in the Caribbean and elsewhere, the wedding in church is seen as the climax rather than as the beginning of a marital career.

The Church had recognised the problems created by 'private' marriages long before the Council of Trent.[16] From late in the twelfth century local attempts were made to ensure that the priest made a public proclamation of a proposed marriage sufficiently far in advance to allow anyone to make an open objection to the union. The procedure became generalised under canon 51 of the Fourth Lateran Council when the priest was required to announce the marriage and to investigate the possibility of impediments. In England the announcement took the form of reading the banns on three Sundays. In fact this procedure appeared to have more effect on the enforcement of the prohibitions than on the publication of the marriage itself, since a marriage was perfectly valid even before the publicity occurred. In his study of a register of court cases from fourteenth-century Ely, Sheehan remarks that it was possible to get round the banns not only for 'the large group that avoided religious ceremonies entirely' (1971: 239), but even for many who wished to have the blessing of the Church; the latter simply went to a distant parish where people were not aware of any impediment to their marriage, sometimes returning after its solemnisation. Such measures operated even after they had been specifically prohibited in *Humana concupiscentia*, a canon emanating from a provincial council held in London in 1342.

When a marriage was discovered to have taken place outside the parish, the parties were liable to punishment. Nevertheless, it remained an important method of trying to get round the impediments, which while they had been 'relaxed' at the Fourth Lateran Council, were reinforced in other ways. If a couple did not wish to run the risk, it did not have to undergo a church wedding at all. In Ely such uncelebrated marriages were frequent at this time. Out of 101 unions mentioned in the register, 89 were of this 'irregular' kind. Of course it was precisely these marriages that were likely to come

---

[16] Secret marriages were common in Holland, Portugal and Italy. For examples of pre-Church marriage, see Coverdale 1575; Howard 1904: I,349, though these were not clandestine. People were exhorted not to delay marriage too long after the betrothal lest wicked men should talk (Coverdale 1575: 68–9).

before the court, for the large majority of disputes were not about divorce but were demands to recognise a marriage as valid; pleas of annulment were infrequent, as were references to parental consent. It would be wrong to imagine that either separation of spouses or control by kin were absent; but those kinds of issue were not often brought before the ecclesiastical courts.

Even in the form of annulment, divorce was very difficult in the Middle Ages. A marriage could be dissolved for precontract, which was a consideration in Henry VIII's divorce from Catherine of Aragon. Others certainly employed the prohibited degrees in a similar fashion. But in general the impediments arising from 'blood', marriage and 'spiritual' ties, which according to many commentators, offered an easy way out of marriage, formed the basis of relatively few disputes in the medieval English courts (Helmholz 1974: 77ff). When the Fourth Lateran Council reduced the prohibited degrees from seven to four in 1215, it also tightened up the proof necessary to establish these ties for legal purposes. While we know that the nobility treated these restrictions with little concern, obtaining dispensations when they were needed, surviving court records give little indication that the prohibited degrees presented any major problem for the bulk of the population. Helmholz argues that the actors accepted the rules, and sees evidence of this in the large percentage of marriages which were contracted outside the village (about 50 per cent). Evidence from elsewhere would suggest that, even if the ordinary people may have found dispensations hard to get, the courts also found it difficult to obtain proof that a breach of the prohibited degrees had taken place, particularly as the villagers themselves do not seem to have been keen on bearing witness against one another in such matters. In fact, we simply do not know the extent to which such marriages were overlooked within the community itself. The real hurdle for the courts, as Helmholz remarks in another context, 'was the persistent idea that people could regulate marriages for themselves' (1974: 5). Once again lay traditions stood opposed to Church regulations.

Thus from the eleventh century, when the spiritual and lay tribunals were separated by William the Conqueror, the Church in England gradually came to dominate marital affairs (Morris 1967). From the time of Glanvill the 'marriage law of England was the canon law' (Pollock and Maitland 1895: II,365–6). The same occurred in France where, at the end of the eleventh century, the Church finally won the exclusive jurisdiction over marriage that it had long claimed. 'Henceforth', writes Duby, 'matrimonial disputes became the chief business of the episcopal courts' (1978: 20).

THE CONSENT OF PARENTS AND THE CONSENT OF SPOUSES

This exclusive jurisdiction had important consequences, since the Church made no absolute requirement of parental consent, nor yet of an age of marriage (Howard 1904: I,338–9). The 'irregular' or clandestine marriages that resulted created problems for the civil law and led to the attempt of the temporal courts to make the acquisition of certain property rights depend upon the publicity given to the marriage. Indeed a public marriage could render children legitimate, and hence serve to legalise heirs, in spite of the existence of impediments to a marriage, in the case where one parent at least was ignorant of that hindrance.

The effect of the Church's doctrine on reducing familial authority is seen most clearly in the conflicts between the ecclesiastical and civil views on the necessity of parental consent. From the twelfth century the Church considered marriage as a sacrament, informally at least, which the partners administered to themselves by the exchange of consent, that is, the consent of the partners. While the Church agreed that disobedience to parents was a grave sin and that clandestine marriages were to be condemned, such unions were nonetheless valid. Their validity was confirmed by the Council of Trent, though it reaffirmed the condemnation of clandestine marriages, making the couple exchange their consent in the presence of a priest after the banns had been published.

Lay society, on the other hand, saw parental consent as essential and the French delegation to that Council were briefed to defend paternal authority. When they were defeated, the king refused to allow the Council's decrees to circulate in France; by the edict of February 1556, the children of families who contracted marriages without their parents' consent were disinherited and virtually outlawed (Flandrin 1979: 132), a position not dissimilar to that adopted by the Protestants whose rejection of the sacramental nature of marriage allowed for the re-establishment of parental authority. However, their positions differed in important ways, not only in how they were formulated but also in their consequences for the organisation of the household.[17]

In England it was with the Reformation that 'publication' became essential. In 1538 (or possibly earlier) parish registers of births, deaths and marriages were introduced. Luther urged the need for public espousals, regarding parental consent as essential, but publicity was not indispensable. A betrothal continued to be recognised as the initiation into marriage. Nor was it unusual for husband and wife to live together before the nuptials (Howard 1904: I,374) and 'bride-children' were given full rights as legitimate offspring. The Reformation changed the English form of marriage very little at first except in terms of the prohibited degrees which were supposedly reduced to the levitical prohibitions in 1540. It was not until the middle of the seventeenth century that the ideas of the early German Reformation relating to the temporal nature of marriage gained hold in England and only during the period of the Commonwealth, in 1653, did a civil marriage service become essential.

It is important to recognise that the notion of mutual consent, in contrast to that of parental authority, was intrinsic to the ecclesiastical model of medieval marriage and in this significant respect it ran directly up against the secular model. 'The Church', writes Duby, 'emphasized the union of two hearts in marriage and postulated that its validity rested more on the betrothal (*desponsatio*) than on the wedding, and especially on the consent (*consensus*) of the two individuals concerned' (1978: 16–17). This feature was firmly emphasised following the ecclesiastical reforms of the eleventh century, a period in which some historians have seen the development of dowry as having a particularly strong influence on the nature of the father-daughter relationship.[18] In about 1160 Peter Lombard in-

[17] The words here are virtually those of Flandrin (1979), but the overall conclusions differ somewhat in that I see certain aspects of Church policy as linked, at least implicitly, to its maintenance as a socio-economic organisation. Hence I place less importance on changes in doctrinal discussions. For example, Flandrin suggests it was the exclusive interest of the Church in individual problems that caused it to neglect social ones such as the redistribution of land (1979: 179). But given its status as the greatest land-owning body, the redistribution of land would have been a dangerous doctrine to espouse. In any case the position adopted towards individual problems certainly had social consequences.

[18] The evidence on this point does not seem altogether clear. In England there was of course some linguistic change. 'In post-conquest Latin texts the O.E. *morgengifu* is translated by *dos*, because there was nothing corresponding to the Anglo-Saxon gift after the Conquest. The *morgengifu*, however, was a gift by the husband to the bride, and the true *dos* was a gift by the bride's guardian' (Whitelock 1930: 144). But the two types of gift, as I have argued, are not exclusive and husbands still

sisted that a father could not force a daughter to marry against her will, although customary and statute law often deprived her of a dowry if she married against his wishes. The Church's insistence on a consensual definition of marriage, on 'what we might call love' (Duby 1978: 21), continued until the Council of Trent, running counter to the lay emphasis on the control of marriage (Hughes 1978: 284).[19] So too did its requirement that marriage be based on *dilectio*, that is, on 'affection' or 'pleasure' – the word *amor* in medieval Latin meant 'virile desire', 'concupiscence' (Duby 1978: 36,59); its legitimate expression required consent.

THE CHILD-ORIENTED FAMILY

The Church thus favoured a family which was bound by affective ties and created by mutual consent. Despite the thread of monastic and clerical celibacy running through the Christian tradition, it also favoured a 'child-oriented' family, which authors like Ariès, Shorter and Stone, have seen as basic to recent developments in domestic life, while others have considered it crucial in accounting for the demographic transition (Caldwell 1976). But the 'child-oriented' family was also intrinsic to the religious ideology of the Christian Church from a very early period. Byzantine paintings of the Madonna and Child are found from the mid sixth century, possibly

endowed their wives at marriage ('With all my worldly goods I thee endow'); the *morgengifu* like the dower was conditional, for a widow lost it if she remarried within a year (Whitelock 1930: 111). There was no universal shift from indirect to direct dowry, at least from the time of the first Codes, and the change of *emphasis* between one and the other is difficult to measure.

The complexities are increased by the difference of terminology between canonists, and Sheehan precedes his discussion of the influence of canon law on women's property rights with the following definition: '"dowry" will be used for the gift (sic) to the husband on the part of the wife. It will correspond to the marriage portion (*maritagium*) of the English law courts and writers and to *dos* as commonly employed by the canonists and civilians. The word "dower" will be used for the husband's endowment of his wife. It will correspond to the *dos* of the English writers and to the *donatio propter nuptias* of the canonists and civilians' (1963a: 109).

[19] Love was of course no monopoly of Europe. Hopkins sees Egyptian brother-sister marriages in these terms; Brough has made excellent translations of Hindu love poems and we are aware of the same sentiments among the Chinese, Japanese, and Jews: 'I do not attempt to prove the obvious', writes Goitein of tenth-century Cairo, 'namely, that love was present in the Geniza world just as in our own' (1978: 165).

earlier. These pictures are somewhat stylised in composition, the mother and child often looking straight ahead and usually away from one another. A similar stance is evident in paintings of the early Tuscan schools of the fourteenth century, although mother and child are often closer in a physical sense, holding hands or with the Child clutching a piece of the Madonna's garment. In the paintings of Rimini, Emilia and Siena we find pictures of the Madonna suckling the Child, a representation that must have stood as a perpetual reproach to those mothers, not only from the richer households, who had their children breast-fed by others, a practice that the Church had tried to stop as far back as the eighth century. Yet in many families the 'nurse' continued to be not only the one who looked after the child but the one who 'nourished' it as well; 'caring' was 'feeding'. It was the Church that would have it otherwise and that provided another model of mother-child relations.

In the Late Gothic of the fifteenth century and in the Early and High Renaissance of the early sixteenth, the suckling Madonna was less frequently portrayed. In the majority of paintings, Madonna and Child continue to look away from one another (or 'towards the world'). In those cases where one of them is turned towards the other, the direction of gaze varies slightly over this period; earlier the Child is more frequently looking upwards at his mother, later it is the Madonna looking down at the Child.

The iconography of Madonna and Child displays only limited changes over time.[20] Part of the overall change is no doubt due to developments of technique, in part due to fashions internal to painting and in part to the demands of patrons. Such paintings do not provide much by way of evidence about the nature of family life, except to remind us that positive sentiments of attachment between mother and child were not an invention of modern man, that Christ was suckled at the breast of a Virgin mother and that the Child was the most important member of the Holy Family, indeed its *raison d'être*. There could hardly be a more child-oriented model than the journey and adoration of the Magi, with its annual re-enactment at Christmas.

The Church's insistence on consent and affection, as well as on the

[20] The survey of paintings, in which I was helped by Penny Clarke, was extensive but not exhaustive; it does not seem worth presenting the results in tabular form.

freedom of the testament, meant taking 'a stand against the power
of the heads of households in matters of marriage, against the lay
conception of misalliance, and, indeed, against male supremacy, for
it asserted the equality of the sexes in concluding the marriage pact
and in the accomplishment of the duties thereby implied' (Duby
1978: 17). Duby describes these effects as 'unintentional'. The result
was to encourage the love match rather than the arranged marriage,
the freedom of the testator rather than inheritance between kin. But
these features, sometimes seen as definitive of the 'Western family'
(and sometimes only of the English variety), are surely intrinsic to
the whole process whereby the Church established its position as a
power in the land, a spiritual power certainly, but also a worldly
one, the owner of property, the largest landowner, a position it
obtained by gaining control of the system of marriage, gift and
inheritance. Such factors are associated with the guidelines supposedly laid down by Pope Gregory for the German lands as well as
with those Guichard sees as characteristic of 'Western structures'. In
essence they owe little to the later transformations of feudalism,
mercantile capitalism, industrial society, Hollywood or the Germanic tradition.

If we want to characterise these trends, they would be in the
direction of the elementary family as we know it, a concentration on
the small group of lineal descendants, with women and children as
important members, each with their own individual rights, depending upon sex and age. As Violante remarks, 'The ecclesiastical reforms begun in the eleventh century favoured the trend towards the
strengthening of the family by widening the range of degrees of
kinship between whom marriages were forbidden and increasing the
severity with which the canonical rules were applied. All this made it
more difficult, in effect, to restrain by means of kinship marriages,
the dispersion of patrimonial property and the maintenance of the
family community as well as the community of goods' (1977: 117).
Why the Church should interfere in the domestic domain in this way
is the question with which we are concerned. But the answer does
not rest upon the reforms of the eleventh century alone. Violante
remarks that in the later Middle Ages the tendency towards *la
famille naturelle* of parents and children or even towards *la famille
conjugale* grew stronger. Yet this same tendency can be discerned
not only under earlier Christianity, indeed at the very birth of Christianity itself, but elsewhere in the Near East. Patlagean observes

how in fifth-century Byzantium consanguineal ties tended to be replaced by conjugal ones. It was a tendency embedded at a very general level in the nature of social life in the Mediterranean world. But, more specifically, it was associated with the emergence of the new Christian sect and with the subsequent transformation of this body into a Church by means of the vast accumulation of property alienated from the hands of kinsfolk.

7. Reformation and reform

The Renaissance in Europe saw a dramatic change in the position of the Church, both culturally and economically. In the world of art the great princes of Italy, the merchants, bankers, warriors and landowners, became the dominant supporters. Drawing their wealth from the increased trade of the Mediterranean accompanied by a growth and diversification of productive activity, they took over much of the role previously played by the Church. The shift of patronage was linked to a change in content, the religious themes of medieval art being supplemented, in many ways replaced, by the portraits of Piero della Francesca, the classical subjects of Botticelli and the detailed landscapes of the Flemish painters whose new use of oils changed the tonality of expression. The process of secularisation affecting the graphic arts was a symptom of a wider process of demythification, rationalisation and reform, which had been stimulated by changes in ways of communicating, of exchanging and of producing.[1]

But the tradition of reform had more popular and long-standing roots, and at this level protests against the acquisition of property by the Church formed a continuing refrain in European life. Some would regard the eleventh century as signalling the origin of European dissent, at least in terms of 'popular heresy' (Moore 1973: 3), though others would insist that it was contained in the womb of Christianity, manifested itself in the early schisms and was well in evidence by the eighth century (Russell 1965). From the twelfth century, Arnold of Brescia, the Waldenses, Marsilius of Padua, the Wycliffites, were all condemning the greed of the Church and arguing for a greater emphasis on matters spiritual. The Church had to defend its position and its possessions not only against internal schism of this

---

[1] On the process of secularisation in Italy, see Larner, who thinks that the stress on merchant culture has been overplayed at the expense of the political environment (1971: 352–3).

kind, but also against the possibility of confiscation by the State or other external power – a possibility that sometimes became a grim reality, especially when combined with reforming zeal.

The Waldenses, founded at Lyon in 1173 by a rich merchant called Valdes, took seriously, that is, literally, Christ's injunction to sell one's possessions and give to the poor. Although Valdes first gained papal approval for a way of poverty, as St Francis did somewhat later, the group was subsequently excommunicated, after which it began to call itself the Poor in Spirit, declaring that the only true Church was the congregation of believers (i.e. not the organisation), that confession should be made direct to God (i.e. without the mediation of priests) and that indulgences were worthless.

Such movements of reform, designated as heresies by the orthodox, were not only concerned with questions of the accumulation of Church property, even though money was seen as the root of much evil, nor only with spiritual affairs. They also promoted alternative modes or styles of life, which necessarily bore on matters to do with the family and domestic organisation. Some of these, for example, the attitudes to marriage among the Western heresies of the period 1020–30, took forms not altogether unlike the practices encouraged by 'local custom'. Or rather they took two forms, reliving earlier polarities. One was the denial that salvation was possible through marriage or through sexual generation, a heresy which was vigorously expressed by the Cathars and which implied a confounding or identification of the lay and ecclesiastical orders (Taviani 1977: 1080). The other was a rejection of the restrictions on marriage laid down in the ecclesiastical rules. The clerks of Orleans and the laity of Arras scorned the rules of marriage, at least those of legitimate marriage which included a blessing that was contingent on an enquiry into any kinship relation – consanguineal, affinal and spiritual – which might serve as an impediment. Those who objected to or rejected the orthodox form of marriage desired that 'chacun prenne qui il veut comme il le veut', 'who he wants how he wants', and hence were inevitably accused of debauchery and incest (p. 1077).

The Cathars (or Albigenses) were one of the major groups involved in promoting an alternative style of life and flourished in southern France and northern Italy in the twelfth and thirteenth centuries. They professed a kind of neo-Manichean dualism. Two principles, one good and one evil, governed the world, and the material world was evil. These views may have derived in part from Bogomil missionaries from the Balkans and partly from crusading activity in the Near East which brought the Western world in contact with the Paulicians. Both of these influences linked them with dualistic thought at the time of Christ. But at the same time these notions represented a more general undercurrent of a puritanical and anticlerical kind that formed a continuing theme in European society with its well-endowed, well-established Church.

This movement of Christian reform, this heresy, considered that the world belonged to Satan. Salvation meant the rejection of the world, meant becoming one of the Perfect who rejected the flesh of animals and all intercourse with the other sex. Indeed it was because of generation that the flesh of animals was forbidden, for the Perfect were allowed to eat fish. And it was their opposition to procreation that had them tarred as 'Bougres' or 'Buggers', from the Bulgarian association of the Bogomils whose descendants they were believed to be.

Things of the world were held of little importance by them. Marriage was not a sacrament; concubinage was just as admissible, perhaps, as among the ancient Manicheans, even preferred since it did not involve the pretence of sacrament, rested on mutual acceptance, and had a greater chance of remaining a sterile union (Nelli 1969: 58). Given the insistence on mutual consent and the absence of a formal marriage ceremony, the position of the woman was probably easier than under either the ecclesiastical or the lay models described by Duby. Divorce was possible, though often enough this worked to a woman's disadvantage; 'love' was in, not only among the nobles as in the troubadour culture, but for all the believers, most of whom were urban in origin.

The absence of a formal ceremony was not so much a reaction against the Catholic prohibitions on marriage as against marriage itself. The fact that the world was defined as evil gave a totally different meaning to sin. All sexual intercourse was sinful and not rendered less so by marriage. For such a union to be established among the Cathars of second rank, the 'Believers', mutual consent and the vow of fidelity were demanded. So the emphasis lay on love between man and woman, already a strong element in the teachings of the Church and one which was given much stress in the internal reforms of the eleventh century.

More directly opposed to the Church's teaching was the discouragement of procreation and the advocacy of contraception. The freedoms accorded to women included the liberty not to have children (Nelli 1969: 62). Since all sins of the flesh were equal, it was in principle no worse to sleep with a sister or mother than with any other woman. But as Nelli remarks, 'they might have weakened the incest taboos had not these been so strongly embedded in their consciences and in family ties' (p. 18). For in practice no such liberty obtained and even first cousins were avoided. On the other hand the very extensive range of prohibited degrees which was imposed by the Catholic Church, but which was also set aside by those monetary payments which the Cathars rejected, was not observed: 'pour la cousine "seconde", comme dit le proverbe: "On peut y aller!" ' (*A cosina segonda tot lo li afonsa*) (p. 60–1).

Such extreme asceticism was only possible in a Church of the elect. The Cathars became a popular sect by separating the faithful into two bodies, the 'perfect' and the 'believers'. It was the former who had to maintain the highest moral standards, while the rest practised a kind of delegated asceticism.

To the inhabitants of the mercantile centres in southern France and northern Italy the Cathars offered more than salvation in the world to come. The new doctrine appealed to a widespread undercurrent of anti-clericalism, the causes for which were many. For the merchant, the Church's ban on usury restricted the development of trade, of mercantile capitalism. The Cathars did not recognise usury as a sin and encouraged the investment of money for their own profit; not by accident it might seem, since many of their adherents were artisans (particularly weavers) and merchants.

To the inhabitants of the countryside, the Cathars offered relief from the tithe and the *carnalages* (a payment on butchered livestock) to which there were constant objections. But like any other sect they had to acquire funds for their own maintenance and so they encouraged those who had received the final rites, the *Consolamentum*, to make a bequest to their Church, of money if they were rich, of a bed or clothes if they were poor (Nelli 1969: 74). Nevertheless their exactions were less institutionalised, the ideology of poverty more in evidence, their leaders closer to the perfect life which led to salvation, than those of the Catholic Church appeared to be, while the doctrine of transmigration meant that even the 'believers' would have future opportunities to throw off the sins of this world. The Cathars were reformers who stimulated both change (such as that generated by St Francis) and opposition (such as that of the Dominicans) from within the Church.[2] At the same time, they freed the domestic domain, as well as that of mercantile capitalism, from some of the important constraints of orthodox religion. Their impact on family life resembled that of the early Christians. One of the effects of sectarian conversion is vividly brought out in the complaint of Raimon V of Toulouse in 1177 that Catharism 'has thrown discord into all the families, dividing husband and wife, son and father, daughter-in-law and mother-in-law . . .' (quoted by Lindsay 1976: 95). They also accumulated property for their sect while rejecting individual ownership. They provided security for aging widows and homes for unmarried daughters (p. 97). The sectarian resemblances stand out firmly.

The Cathars' radical attack on the rules and doctrines of the Church on marriage and the family was broadly based. Others raised more specific objections. In 1065, not long before the pronouncement of Pope Alexander II and when the controversy over the Roman and Germanic modes of kinship reckoning was at its height, two councils in Rome solemnly anathematised the 'heresy of the incestuous', their pronouncements being directed at persons who were questioning the current method of calculating degrees of consanguinity and who favoured a more lenient approach (Russell 1965: 143; Mansi 1903: XIX, 1037–40).[3] To be lenient was to follow the custom of the people rather than the law of the Church; in the previous century, the Italian pastor, Atto of Vercelli, had protested that people of all strata were marrying uncanonically (Murray 1978: 15), that is, they were adhering to another set of norms.

In England, as in Ireland, popular resistance to the marriage rules had been felt as early as Anglo-Saxon times. Lancaster comments

---

[2] A parallel movement took place among Ashkenazi Jews in the twelfth century. 'The Pious (Haside) of Germany' lived a life of asceticism, reliance on God, abstention from pleasures and sexual temptations, and concentration on religious learning (Patai 1981: 51).

[3] 'Haeresim Nicolaitorum, qui clericorum incontinentium conjugia pertinaciter defendebant, per Damianum confutavit & eradicavit. Incestuosorum vero haeresim, quae auctoritate Justiniani imperatoris asserebat, eadem ratione qua in successionibus numerandos esse gradus consanguinitatis, non tantum per epistolam Petri Damiani, verum etiam duobus pluribusque Romae habitis conciliis impugnavit. Contra novos haereticos hoc tempore emergentes, qui docebant episcopatus a principibus laicis absque crimine simoniae licite emi posse, quosque Petrus Damiani scriptis suis graviter insectatus est, decretum edidit, quo omnis beneficii ecclesiastici venditionem & emptionem interdixit' (Mansi XIX,940).

that the frequency of defections from ecclesiastical rulings on marriage with near kin was a constant cause of complaint during this period. In 874 Pope John VIII wrote to the King of Mercia saying that fornication was rife and that men 'presume to marry women of their own kindred'. Some sixteen years later the Archbishop of Rheims wrote to King Alfred in the same vein. Sermons and legislation continued to condemn and prohibit the widespread 'incest' (Lancaster 1958: 240).

The same complaints were made about unions with the widows of close kin. Marriage to the father's widow (stepmother) is mentioned at least twice in the Anglo-Saxon records. The pagan king Eadbald of Kent made just such a marriage and Bede comments that he was 'guilty of such fornication . . . unheard of even among the heathen' according to the Apostle Paul (II. 5). In 858 Aethelbald married the widow of his father, King Aethelwulf, in a union which Lancaster describes as 'the Germanic practice' (1958: 241). In this comment she follows Bede who saw Eadbald as starting a general reversion to older custom. 'His immorality was an incentive to those who, either out of fear or favour to the King his father, had submitted to the discipline of faith and chastity, to revert to their former uncleanliness'. When Eadbald was converted to Christianity, he 'gave up his unlawful wife' (II. 6). Bede's comment that this marriage was unknown even among the heathen seems to contradict the general tenor of the rest of his remarks and may represent a way of heightening the condemnation.

Resistance to formal marriage continued to manifest itself in England as elsewhere in movements such as that of the Cathars, but it was not only a matter of asceticism or dualism. Neither were the practices of contraception and abortion, of which medieval writers were well aware. They represented a more popular, earthy philosophy. In Worcester in the fifteenth century a number of cases of abortion came before the Church court, and this was but the tip of the iceberg. In one case Agnes Consall was accused of administering to an unmarried girl 'certain medicines with herbs to destroy the child in her womb' (Dyer 1980: 233).

In England the undercurrent of opposition to the Church's rules and ideas on marriage was crystallised in the teaching of the Lollards, whose thoughts were often guided by the works of Wycliff, initiator of the translation of the Bible into English. The Lollards' view of marriage tended to follow the puritanical doctrines of the

Waldensians rather than the dualistic beliefs of the Cathars. In their writings and in reports of their trials we find specific comments upon the rules as well as more general remarks upon marriage itself. In a late fourteenth- or early fifteenth-century work attributed to Wycliff and entitled *An Apology for Lollard Doctrine*, we find a firm statement of opposition to the extensive restrictions on the marriage of cousins; it reads: 'marriage made in the third and fourth degree, although contrary to the ordinance of the Church, is rate and stable' (xl), that is, while marriage to second cousins ought to be avoided, it was nevertheless valid. The prohibition on the marriage of cousins was a law of the Church, and since marriage was not a sacrament in the eyes of the Lollards – a point that was critical to early Protestant reformers – the contravention of such rules was no sin.

Many of the Lollards held views of an even more radical kind. Reports of the Norwich heresy trials of sixty men and women between the years 1428 and 1431 show that among these believers 'the consent . . . of the two partners (together with the agreement of their friends) was regarded as sufficient for marriage' (Tanner 1977: 12). A church service was unnecessary and one defendant even wanted marriage itself abolished for a period of time, apparently reflecting the same trend as the libertarian doctrines of the Anabaptists which in Reformation times led to the establishment of polygynous communes in Münster and elsewhere.

Anabaptist was the name given to a number of sects on the radical wing of Protestantism who disapproved of infant baptism and rejected membership of a State or inclusive Church. The sects were persecuted by both Catholics and Protestants alike and it was to escape these persistent attacks that a group of members under John of Leyden went to settle in Münster in Westphalia, gaining control of the city in 1534 and setting up a 'communist state'. Women outnumbered men four to one, so John allowed polygyny to be practised, himself taking on sixteen wives, a perquisite deriving in the end from women's greater bent towards religion. In the following year, the combined forces of Lutheran and Catholic princes forced the group to surrender and its leaders were executed. Other Anabaptist communities continued the tradition in various parts of Europe. The Hutterites of North America (Peters 1965; Hostetler and Huntington 1967) are one of the three surviving groups, the others being the Mennonites and the Swiss Anabaptists, which include the Old Order Amish (Hostetler 1963). Family life in the contemporary Hutterite colonies

is very strict by present-day standards, with strong parental authority, male dominance and marriage within the Church, though not to
first cousins (Hostetler and Huntington 1967). In matters of kinship,
marriage and the family, early radicalism has given way to an archaic
strictness which is based on a dualistic vision of man as dominated by
his carnal nature until he is restored to the spiritual one. The history
of their views on marriage and the family reflects the continuing
polarity of freedom and restraint, of indulgence and asceticism, that
marks the history of reformist sects.

The Reformation itself raised the whole question of the relation of
Church to State in a very acute form. The prospect of a continuing
shift of property, and especially of land, from lay to ecclesiastical
hands was one which explicitly concerned the secular authorities,
whether royalty, nobility or commoner, especially those who had
rights to land. This concern was given prominence in the remarkable
statement of grievances formulated by the Imperial Diet in the City of
Worms in 1521 which gave birth to the Reformation. This first
meeting of Charles V with the German estates was also the occasion
of Martin Luther's appearance before the Emperor, who was force-
fully reminded of the 'oppressive burdens and abuses imposed . . . by
the Holy See in Rome'. But the protest also represented the continuation of a tradition dating from the middle decades of the fifteenth
century whereby successive Diets enumerated the grievances of the
nation (*gravamina nationis germanicae*) against the papacy (Dickens
1974: 7), which was itself part of a more general tradition of medieval
German 'anti-clericalism', indeed of reform, that went back at least
to the previous century. At the Diet of Worms, as with earlier
protests, many of the 102 *gravamina* dealt not so much with the
particular burdens imposed by Rome but with the nature of the
Church itself. Of special importance was no. 32, 'How Secular Property Comes into Ecclesiastical Hands':

> Seeing that the spiritual estate is under papal instructions never to
> sell or otherwise transfer the Church's real estate and immobilia
> to the laity, we think it advisable for His Roman Imperial Majesty
> to cause a corresponding law to be made for the secular estate, to
> wit, that no secular person be allowed to make over any part of
> his real property to any ecclesiastical person or institution, and
> that this proscription apply to inheritance as well. If such a law is
> not introduced without delay, it is possible that the secular estate

will, in the course of time, be altogether bought out by the Church
... and the secular estate of the Holy Roman Empire eventually
be entirely beholden to the Church. (Strauss 1971: 58)

The fear of an ecclesiastical take-over was precisely the fear that
was earlier embodied in the legislation on mortmain; it arose from
the extent of the lands that the Church had obtained and from the
fact that once acquired, they could not be released. Here again the
protests of the estates were directed to questions that had concerned
the laity as far back as the fourth century. The seventy-seventh of
the grievances complained that 'They Prevail upon the Old and the
Sick to Withhold Their Estate from Their Rightful Heirs'. 'Priests
and monks hover about a man in his final illness if they know him to
be rich in gold or land. They attempt to persuade him with cunning
words to leave his property to them, though more often than not the
estate should go to the man's heirs, offspring, or close friends'
(Strauss 1971: 62).

Lands were also, of course, purchased by the Church, and many
of the grievances relate to the problems arising from the Church's
quest for money, to be used for investment in land as well as for
maintenance. Money was raised by annates, pallium fees, by papal
dispensations and absolutions, indulgences, by payments for mis-
deeds, processions and prayers for the soul, by payments for grave
sites, tribute from artisans, and so on. Against all these forms of
revenue complaints were made which stressed the importance for
the community of the material cost of the spiritual benefits con-
ferred by the Church. 'Day after day (His Holiness) invents new
devices to enable him to squeeze money out of the German nation
...' (Strauss 1971: 56). Some of these concern the daily life of
individuals: 'money can buy tolerance of concubinage and usury',
bringing contempt upon the holy sacrament of marriage (p. 63).
'Popes and bishops reserve to themselves certain sins and offences
from which, they say, only they can absolve us. Whenever such a
"case" occurs and a man wishes absolution, he discovers that only
money can procure it for him' (p. 56). The 'very life blood is sucked
out of the poor, untutored laity, who are driven to distraction by
fear of the Church's ban ...' (p. 59).

The argument of these protests takes a stronger form than the one
I have put forward. The collection of money and land is a necessary
task of ecclesiastical organisations, but one that, pursued on a large
enough scale, was eventually bound to bring the Church into con-

flict with government, nobility and commoner alike. The raising of funds was not in itself a matter of abuse but a question of continuity, of maintaining an organisation that was at once religious, charitable, a patron of the arts, and devoted to its own interests. The German grievances suggest that those who were not in a position to marry, possibly through the ban on divorce or possibly because of the prohibited degrees, could live together providing an adequate payment was made to the Church (no. 91). Revenues from such sources were important (David 1981: 1053). But over the long term the collection of 'fines' was not the central issue in the Church's rulings on marriage. At times the 'toleration' of domestic sin may have been motivated by a desire to raise money but it is also evidence of the Church's insistence on penetrating the deeper recesses of daily life. Control was one aspect of the Church's early entry into the marriage arena. But the rules introduced or accepted by the Church were not simply a matter of control, nor yet of collecting fines from those who broke them. For we cannot set aside the specific character of those rules which provided a means of facilitating the transfer of property from secular to ecclesiastical hands. Such a project was not of course seen by the Church and its many supporters as a question of 'exploiting' the producers. For its members it was a means of saving souls, providing for the poor and of maintaining the Church of God on earth. Indeed, after the fourth century the accepted practice of the Church worked in a quasi-automatic way, as religiously sanctioned custom, as part of the concealed 'structure' of events, concealed because it was accepted rather than thought through by each generation. Luther's objections were to 'surface' elements, to the sale of indulgences, to deathbed donations. Nevertheless, part of the basis of the alienation of familial resources to the Church was indirectly undermined by the attempts of the Protestants to reinstate certain 'Mediterranean' elements of marriage and the family, enshrined in the Bible, for fundamentalist as well as for reformist reasons. After the Reformation, at least in Protestant areas, personal and family property was to be alienated in much smaller quantities to a simpler and more frugal ecclesiastical organisation. What was no longer taken by the Church could then be directed partly to the State and partly to the promotion of enterprises requiring the investment of capital; the dissolution of the monasteries was of critical importance for the early industrial development of England between 1540 and 1640 (Nef

1934: 4ff and 1937: 183); strategies of heirship could now be directed to the worldly interests of the family firm.

The situation in Germany was more acute than elsewhere. While the monarchs of countries like France and Spain had been able to set limits on the power of the Church, the absence of a central power in Germany meant that the papacy could impose heavy taxes both on clergy and on laity. German bishoprics provided salaries for Italians at the papal court. The sale of indulgences, to which Luther so strongly objected in the *Ninety-Five Theses* of 1517, was very widespread and it was the use of this method to raise funds for the rebuilding of St Peter's that set off the German reaction; the notion that 'everything might be done for money' was quite unacceptable to Luther, who went on to argue for the abolition of the special privileges of the clergy, the reform of the sacramental system of the Church (especially as it concerned marriage) and the liberation of Germany from foreign control.

The change in the notion of marriage was part of a wider process of secularisation, of the shift from ecclesiastical to civil jurisdiction. Marriage appears to have been widely recognised as a sacrament from the beginning of the thirteenth century when Innocent IV was concerned to refute the contrary view of the Waldensians, though it was not so declared until the sixteenth century. In fact, the word *sacramentum* was already being used for marriage in the eleventh century, both by Ivo of Chartres and by Hugh of Saint-Victor, for whom it was 'the greatest sacrament' (Duby 1978: 42,63). But such claims did not go unchallenged, even at this early date. The 'very cultured men of the highest spirituality' linked with the 'heresy of Orleans' were reticent about all sacramental gestures and disapproved of the Church's involvement in marriage, which was carnal, contemptible and a matter for the laity (Duby 1978: 51–2). Early reformers within the Church repeatedly took this contrary view. Later Calvin likened marriage to the cutting of hair, instituted by God, good and holy, but no sacrament (*Institution*, IV. xix. 34), while Luther (*Von dem Ehesachen*, 1530: 1) claimed that marriage was an external worldly thing, 'like clothing and food, house and property'. It was precisely these heretical doctrines the Council of Trent had in mind when it firmly included matrimony in the Seven Sacraments of the Evangelical Law, the New Law. While the Protestant Churches continued to be involved with marriage, they also contributed to its desacralisation.

The effort to liberate the Church and country from foreign control was vigorously supported not only on religious and nationalist grounds but by those who coveted the extensive property of the Church. The German princes soon began to confiscate its lands and income as well as abolishing Catholic worship. The effect of redistributing Church property was the same in Germany as the experience of other confiscations, with the exception of France at the time of the Revolution; those who gained most were 'the great landowners, whether they were noble or bourgeois, feudal or capitalist in origin', a result that tended 'to consolidate the aristocracy in the political sphere' (Bazant 1971: 4). Not unnaturally, the words of Luther and the acts of the princes also incited the peasants to action; in 1524 the Peasants' Revolt broke out, directed against temporal lords as well as against Catholic clergy. However their rebellion, which was crushed in the following year, received no support from Luther who attacked the uprising in his pamphlet, *Against the Robbing and Murdering Hordes of Peasants* (1525).

In England, the movement for reform existed at all levels of society, but it achieved its success, in confiscating the property of the monasteries, inhibiting bequests and changing the rules of marriage, in a very non-revolutionary way, from the top rather than the bottom. For the changes were initiated by the king himself, who was concerned with the way the rules of the Church impeded his ability to produce a 'natural' heir. In this case the rules affected the succession to high office, but the underlying problem was that of any family without a son.

Henry VIII's first marriage was to Catherine of Aragon, the widow of his dead brother Arthur. He was initially pressed to undertake this 'leviratic' marriage, a forbidden marriage to a brother's widow, for which a dispensation was obtained from the Pope. But his father, Henry VII, was persuaded to have second thoughts and decided that arrangements for the marriage should not be confirmed. Nonetheless, after the king's death, his son took the Spanish princess as his queen by public marriage. The ensuing union lasted for many years. Mary Tudor and other children were born, but no male issue survived and Henry decided that this failure to produce the heir so essential for the stability of the realm was a result of God's anger at his having neglected the injunctions of Leviticus. Henry was a good deal more literate than his father and his fear was based not only upon the rules of the Church but also upon a knowledge of the Biblical sources used to justify them.

The source in question was the statement made in Leviticus to the effect that it was unlawful to uncover the nakedness of one's kin and affines, which was interpreted as meaning that marriage to all such persons was prohibited. However, there was a more precise, and contrary, statement about leviratic marriage elsewhere in the Pentateuch where a man was enjoined by Moses to marry his brother's widow. The resolution of these two statements was not easy, given the initial assumptions about the meaning of Leviticus, and it was Leviticus and not Moses that Henry wanted to believe. To try and obtain a favourable decision about God's law, he engaged in a massive consultation of learned men all over Europe about the legitimacy of his first marriage, which devolved primarily into an enquiry into the meaning of the relevant Biblical statements. If the sources established the unlawfulness of marriage to 'affines' (even when the link was dead), then he was released from his earlier bond because it was generally considered, especially after Henry's declaration of independence from Rome in 1531, that while the Pope might have power to provide dispensations from the law of the Church, he could not do so from the law of God. This concession went against the general Catholic position of respect for the traditions of the Church, a position that had been essential to the establishment of Christian unity (Gager 1975: 34–40) and was equally essential to its maintenance.

The universities of Oxford and Cambridge, as might be expected, agreed with the king's case. In 1530 Oxford, the older institution, took the view that marriage to the brother's wife was contrary to God and to nature. So too did many other academies of learning, including the Sorbonne, whose decision, printed later that year, declared that the king's first marriage was unlawful and the Pope had no power to dispense him from those laws.[4]

Henry consulted not only the learned among the Catholics, but also the leading theologians among the Protestants in Germany and Switzerland. Some of these, including the Swiss reformer, Zwingli, were severe, agreeing essentially with Paris and stating that marriage within near degrees was hated even by the heathen nations (Burnet

---

[4] As Scarisbrick acutely remarks: 'It was the sort of competition in scriptural exegesis which the printing press and the recent renewal of Greek and Hebrew studies made easy and, to some, highly congenial . . .' (1968: 164).

1730: I,69). Others were more concerned with the discrepancy between Leviticus and Moses which they resolved by declaring that the Mosaic law on leviratic marriage was a special dispensation given by God to the Jews (p. 69), a doctrine which one of Henry's envoys, Crooke, found to be held by the Jews themselves. Crooke had been sent to Italy in order to copy out everything that he found in any manuscript of the Greek or Latin fathers 'relating to the Degrees of Marriage' (p. 65). The Jewish authorities consulted by Crooke recognised that Leviticus and Deuteronomy were opposed to one another and offered the following reconciliation: 'That the Law of marrying the Brother's Wife when he died without Children, did only bind in the land of Judaea, to preserve Families and maintain their Successions in the Land, as it had been divided by Lot. But that in all other places of the world, the Law of Leviticus, of not marrying the Brother's Wife was obligatory' (p. 66). On the other hand, the theologian Bucer, who later played an important part in the course of the Reformation in England, considered that if God had made such a dispensation for the purpose 'of raising up seed to his Brother', then others too were permitted to marry within these degrees (p. 69). Essentially the same position was taken by the Catholic cardinal, Cajetan, who held that the prohibitions of Leviticus were not part of the Moral Law since there were many instances of close marriage in the Bible. These rules were only Judiciary Precepts, the Law of the Church, from which the Pope could dispense. And in any case, the law in Leviticus against taking the brother's wife applied only during his lifetime (p. 77).

This self-evident truth was rejected by other Catholics and Protestants. Their position was justified by Pope Gregory's letter to St Augustine, which was still being used as a point of reference in the sixteenth century as it had been in the eighth. The rules against the levirate and against cousin marriage that entangled Henry's conjugal life were precisely those which formed the subject of the letter incorporated by Bede in his *History* eight centuries before. But at this juncture the rules affected succession to office rather than inheritance to property, although they also came to affect the property of the Church in a very radical way.

Henry's problems arose from the characteristics of what Duby (1978) has called the lay (or noble) model of marriage. That it was a general rather than a particular matter can be seen from the course of events in Russia at roughly the same period. While Russia had avoided the rise of heresy that dominated a large part of Catholic Europe, the accumulation of property by the Church presented severe difficulties for the authority of the State, especially as during the late fifteenth century some of the land owned by the boyars, the princely aristocracy, had been expropriated and turned into small holdings (*pomestya*). Towards the end of the reign of Ivan III (1440–1505), the Church's property around Novgorod was taken away and, inspired by the tsar, monastic possessions came close to being confiscated in their entirety. But the Orthodox Church succeeded in maintaining its position by being accommodating about this very problem of succession. When Tsar Ivan III was succeeded by his son, Basil, the continuity of the throne was placed in doubt. His first wife was barren and it was only with great difficulty that he persuaded the Church to annul the marriage.

Henry VIII was unable to get such agreement in the case of his marriage to Catherine of Aragon, partly because the papacy came under the effective control of her nephew, Charles V, the Holy Roman Emperor. Hence Henry's determination to reject the external control of the Church of Rome. But it was not until 1533 that he was able to resolve the issue and to settle the 'great Scruple' he had over his first marriage of twenty years' duration. With the assistance of Thomas Cromwell as Lord Privy Seal and Thomas Cranmer as Archbishop, the first marriage was declared void and Henry married Anne Boleyn. A series of statutes drafted by Cromwell altered the whole relationship between State, Church and people. The Church of England came into being; services were increasingly held in English and the king became owner of all monastic lands and wealth. In 1536 he began to sell off many of these new acquisitions, dissolving monasteries, increasing the wealth of the State as well as of the gentry to whom grants of land were made, and at the same time building up the central bureaucratic machinery to cope with this massive shift of resources. This confiscation of ecclesiastical property greatly benefited the aristocracy and gentry, and even Mary Tudor's attempt to restore Catholicism (on which her personal legitimacy depended) did not succeed in prising these lands away.

Catholic doctrine legitimised Mary because she relied upon the Pope's power to provide a dispensation for her father's 'leviratic' marriage to her mother. Elizabeth's legitimacy, on the other hand, depended upon the view that such a marriage was against God's law for which no dispensation was possible. When Elizabeth succeeded to the throne, Prince Philip of Spain, the widower of her sister and predecessor, Mary, made a secret proposal of marriage. One reason for Elizabeth's refusal was that her relation with Philip mirrored that of Henry VIII and Catherine of Aragon; if she approved the marriage of one man with two sisters, then she sanctioned the union of a woman to two brothers. And 'if that were a good Marriage, then she must be Illegitimate' (Burnet 1730: II,280).

Initially it was the marriage to the brother's widow rather than to a cousin that was at issue, and here the king supported the Church's rules, though he held different views on divorce (and hence on marriage as a sacrament). While reformers like Wycliff and Luther disapproved of the extended prohibitions on marriage to kin, and in any case regarded such rules as the law of the Church rather than of God, not all were in favour of marriage to close cousins. In England such marriages were permitted as the result of the strategy of heirship, essentially conjugal, pursued by Henry VIII. When this Catholic monarch divorced his foreign queen, Anne of Cleves, on the grounds of non-consummation, he wanted to marry Catherine Howard. Catherine was the first cousin of his second wife, Anne Boleyn, who had been executed on the grounds of adultery. Such a marriage was clearly forbidden under the rule of affinity, attributed to the same general prohibition in Leviticus as the levirate, that is, the prohibition on uncovering the nakedness of one's kin.

In order to marry Catherine Howard, Henry legalised marriage to all first cousins, not simply cousins of affines, under a statute of 1540.[5] The Act declared that when a marriage was consummated, it could not be annulled by reason of pre-contract, or of 'degree of kindred or alliance, but those mentioned in the Law of God' (Burnet 1730: II,212). Since pre-contract (that is, the virtual equation of the betrothal with marriage) was no longer to be considered grounds for annulment, the Act therefore set aside one of the reasons for dissolving the marriage of Anne Boleyn (who was said to have been 'pre-contracted') and therefore legitimised her daughter Elizabeth. But more immediately it legitimised the king's latest union. The comment of that royalist author and divine, Thomas Fuller (1608–61), on the affair was characteristic: 'The greatest good the land got by this match was a general leave to marry cousins-german, formerly

---

[5] 32 Henry VIII. cap. 38; *Statutes at Large* (London 1763), pp. 55–6. For a comprehensive treatment of the marriages of Henry VIII, see Scarisbrick 1968.

prohibited by the canon, and hereafter permitted by common law; a door of liberty left open by God in Scripture, shut by the Pope for his private profit, opened again by the king, first for his own admittance (this Catherine being cousin-german to Anne Boleyn, his former wife) and then for the service of such subjects as would follow him upon the like occasion' (Fuller 1952: 361; 1842: II,107).

This door to liberty was not widely accepted at the time, even by other Protestants. The Puritans of New England were worried about the laxity of the 'English nation' with regard to the prohibited degrees. Marriages to first cousins, by affinity as well as consanguinity, and to a deceased wife's sister were strongly opposed by their representatives. Judge Sewall regarded the fate of Catherine Howard as a warning to all. In rejecting the excessive strictness of the Roman Church, the English had gone 'beyond the golden mean towards the other Extream' (Howard 1904: II,213). New England preferred a different approach. As a result of pressure from ministers under Increase Mather in 1680, the law against incestuous marriages was passed (remaining in operation until 1785), forbidding marriage to the wife's sister or niece, though marriage to the husband's brother or nephew was not expressly prohibited. Once again the words of the Bible were used to justify a prohibition on what was expressly allowed in Ancient Israel (at least in the case of marriage to the deceased wife's sister). On the other hand, the Southern States of the U.S.A. followed the rules of the Church of England and only marriages within the 'levitical degrees prohibited by the laws of England' were forbidden (Howard 1904: II,234); as a consequence first-cousin marriage was allowed. Each group had their own version of what could be justified by Holy Writ.

The rules adopted by the Church of England derived partly from the changes introduced by Henry VIII and partly from the ideas of Protestant reformers. They were laid down by Matthew Parker, whom Elizabeth had appointed as head of her Church. As Archbishop, Parker became heavily involved in judging marital disputes. Norms in these matters had been much disturbed by the legislation of Henry VIII, by the shifts in the official religion wrought by his children, and finally by the uncertainty among Protestants about what was said in the Book, in the canons and by the theologians of various persuasions, all of whom were looked upon as possible sources of 'law'.

In one dispute, Barnaby Goge had become 'privily contracted' to

Mary Darrel without the knowledge of her parents, who claimed that she was contracted elsewhere 'to a certain Rich Man'. Parker came down in favour of the freedom of the choice of partner, though he recognised the dangers of this approach (Strype 1711: II,144). In another instance royal interests were involved. The Earl of Hertford had taken as 'his reputed wife', Lady Katherine Grey, the sister of Jane. 'Both He and She pretended a marriage, tho' at most it seems to have been but a Contract, consummated without the Ceremony of the Solemnization' (p. 118), for which presumption and clandestinity the queen committed them to the Tower. In the end both were sentenced by the Archbishop for fornication; their children were therefore illegitimate but the title was restored to a grandson by James I.

In 1560 prior to making a 'metropolitical visitation', Parker addressed all the bishops under his jurisdiction, asking them to enquire into people's shortcomings regarding marriage:

Item, Whether there be any in these Parties, that have maried within Degrees of Affinity or Consanguinity, by the Laws of God forbidden: Any Man that hath two Wives, or any Woman that hath two Husbands: Any maryed that have made Precontracts, and that have made privy and secret Contracts: Any that have maryed without Banes thrice solemnly asked: Any Couples maryed that live not together, but slanderously live apart: Any that have maryed in times by the Laws prohibited, or out of the Parish Church, where they ought to have the same solemnized. (Strype 1711: App. 20)

The general level of uncertainty can be gauged from the articles drafted in 1564 for the new Church of England. These statements were first formulated under Cranmer in 1553, revised early in Elizabeth's reign, and finally published in 1571. The 1564 draft stated 'That all such Mariages, as have been contracted within the *Levitical* Degrees, to be dissolved: And namelye, those who have maried two Sisters one after another, who are by common consent judged to be within the Case' (Strype 1711: App. 50). For there was to be no dispensation for marriages forbidden by God's law.

To reduce the uncertainty that surrounded marriage, Parker produced his Table of Kindred and Affinity in 1560 for the guidance of both the laity and the clergy. This table was part of a more general attempt to enforce *conformity* (hence the birth of the *non*-conformists) after a period of great dispute over normative behaviour. The pressure to conform was often linked to outward appearance rather than to inward doctrine. In 1568 there were great commotions in St John's College, Cambridge, which turned upon the question of whether or not surplices should be worn in chapel, failure to do so being accounted 'so foul a crime' in the Annals of the town. The 'hot dislikers of the ecclesiastical habits' were against the use of this papist clothing, but it was enforced and is still worn in chapel by many Fellows (Scott 1906–1913; Cooper 1843: 242–3).

The Table of Kindred and Affinity, originally known as 'An Admonicion', was first printed in 1560. It was clearly a provisional document since its subtitle reads '(for the necessitie of the presente tyme tyll a furder Consultation)'. Printed in the form of a broadsheet (the use of the new medium was important), it was intended to be set up in all churches (Strype 1711: II,88). The reason for the haste in its production – the second and final version appeared three years later – was that, according to Strype, Parker's biographer, 'incestuous and unnatural Contracts and Mariages ... were now very rife, to the great Scandal of the Nation ... That unnatural Filthiness was too much known and blazed there abroad, in that great liberty of Mariage, which was then used. A thing that made good Men lament, and the Adversaries Laugh' (III,p. 280). In London one Gerard Danet married his maternal half-sister and had two children; no amount of ecclesiastical persuasion would make them separate. In 1563 Bishop Jewell wrote to Archbishop Parker reporting the case of one Chafin who had married two sisters. 'I would they (the delegates) would decree it were lawful to marry two sisters, so should the world be out of doubt. As now it is past away in a mockery' (Bruce and Perowne 1853: 176–7). In the eyes of the clergy the country required guidance on these matters, which was what Parker's table was intended to give.[6] It set aside the multiple complexities of numerical reckoning of degrees produced by the civil law of the late Roman Empire and elaborated in a whole variety of ways by the canonists, especially by the medieval scholastics. In its place it offered a simple table, listing each forbidden relation by name, 25 male, 25 female, both in Latin and English, abandoning the *figura depicta* which had been for so long not only a ready reckoner for the

---

[6] The Table of Kindred and Affinity was first published in 1560 as a separate sheet. Its prohibitions were not formally made legal until Lord Lyndhurst's Act of 1835. In 1908 marriage to the dead wife's sister was legalised, although remaining a feature of the list printed in the Prayer Book until that was altered in 1946.

degrees but a representation of the genealogy of terms as a micro-cosm of the world.[7]

In producing the new English translation of the Bible (1572), Parker added a series of 'useful Tables', including 'A Table of Degrees of Kindred, which let Matrimony'; and another of 'Affinity and Alliance which let Matrimony', set at the 18th chapter of Leviticus. The Mosaic prohibitions are recognised as being very restricted in range. Those prohibited by kinship are mother, mother's sister, father's sister, sister, daughter and daughter's daughter; those prohibited by alliance are father's wife, uncle's wife, wife's sister, brother's wife, son's wife, wife's daughter, and the daughters of wife's son or daughter. Even this limited range slightly extends the levitical prohibitions (see *Kindred* 1940: 23). They had already been further extended for practical application in the Table of Kindred of 1560 which was a compromise between, first, the extensive prohibitions of the Catholic Church that had existed over the past twelve hundred years; second, the restricted range now attributed to the Bible as a result of the new-found literal interpretation (which was not unconnected with the invention of the printing press that had so widened the possibility of detailed textual examination); and third, the succession and marital problems of the monarchy.

In interpreting the Biblical degrees, the reformers regarded the Pope as having added prohibitions to those laid down by God, and as having made money by dispensing individuals from the wider range of degrees that he had established. But a further difference arose among the reformers about the interpretation of the reduced Levitical prohibitions. Like the Orthodox Jews, Luther thought that the Bible specified every prohibition that should be followed. On the other hand, Calvin considered that the prohibitions listed in the Old Testament were only illustrative; marriage should be forbidden between any two persons who were related as closely as those mentioned in the table. This principle, known as 'parity of reason', was then supplemented by deductions based on the interpretation of the sentence, 'the twain shall become one flesh'. By this latter principle the wife's relatives were to be regarded in the same way as a man's own; affinity (alliance) equalled consanguinity.

Henry VIII's legislation (25 Henry VIII. cap. 22; 28 cap. 7) had

[7] 'La notion scientifique et mystique du macrocosme et du microcosme faisait que l'on s'imaginait retrouver l'image même du corps humain le symbole des divers stades de la parenté et des âges du monde' (Champeaux 1933: 275).

been based upon Luther's view, though the king himself wished for further restrictions to be included on the grounds of 'parity of reason', as for centuries they had been by the Catholic Church. Luther's view on the range of prohibitions had been made clear as early as 1520 in 'The Babylonian Captivity of the Church'; 'those inflexible impediments derived from affinity, by spiritual or legal relationships, and from blood relationship must give way, so far as the Scriptures permit, in which the second degree of consanguinity alone is prohibited' (Lehmann 1959: 99). For a man, prohibitions are limited to the twelve persons listed in Leviticus 18, where only the first degree of affinity and the second of consanguinity are prohibited, and even here there are some exceptions since it was permissible to marry a niece (the oblique marriage). All this is repeated in 'The Estate of Marriage' (1539) where it is asserted that 'first cousins may contract a godly and Christian marriage' (Lehmann 1962: 23).

However, Archbishop Parker's table looked to Calvin's principles and embodied the prohibitions suggested by that reformer. From these impediments there was to be no dispensation at all since they represented the law of God not of man. The difference between the Lutheran (Levitical) and the Calvinist modes of calculation is seen very clearly in a letter from Jewell, the Bishop of Salisbury, to Archbishop Parker, dated November 1561, on the subject of 'the Lawfulness of Marrying Two Sisters Successively'. Following Leviticus Parker thought this not unlawful; Jewell disagreed, wishing 'ye had rather taken in hand some other matter to defend'. He goes on to acknowledge that Parker prefers 'Text' to 'Canons' but argues that certain prohibitions on 'Degrees of Consanguinity' which are not included in Leviticus must nevertheless have been present in Ancient Israel; for example, no mention is made of marriage to the grandmother, which, he claims, must have been prohibited (that is not the case in many human societies). So, too, the prohibition on marriage to the wife's sister is to be seen as a proper extension from that assumed to have existed on the brother's wife. These prohibitions, according to Jewell, were included in God's law and the Pope could neither give dispensation nor yet add to their number, except in the ways indicated, which were natural extensions of God's word in Leviticus (Strype 1711: App.,32–3). In a subsequent letter to Parker written on 16 June 1563, Jewell expressed the wish that the delegates would decree it lawful to marry two sisters 'so the world should be out of doubt' (Bruce and Perowne 1853: 176–7).

In fact the suggestions contained in Parker's letter of 1561 had already been incorporated in the Table published in 1560. The Table contained the interesting warning, from the standpoint of the desired 'conformity', that 'under the Degree of a Master of Art' it is forbidden to 'preach or expound the Scripture; but to read the Homilies: Nor to innovate or alter any thing, or use any Rite, but only what is set forth by Authority' (Strype 1711: II,88). However it was the new list that appeared in 1563 which became accepted as part of the canons of the Church of England, and which made several additions and a few deletions to the prohibitions, raising the total number of prohibited persons from 25 to 30. The deletions involved, first, substituting 'sister' for 'whole sister' and 'half sister', and second, deleting 'sister begot in fornication', a prohibition which was already part of a general footnote that equated 'unlawfull company' with 'laweful marriage' in this particular context. The extensions, on the other hand, were to affinal relations of quite a 'distant' kind (see Table 2).

The prohibitions themselves were endorsed in the Canon of 1603 (canon 99) which proposed that all such incestuous marriages should be dissolved. From 1681 the Table was printed at the end of the Book of Common Prayer, which had previously contained the whole of the canons of 1603, and it continued to be displayed publicly in every church 'at the charge of the Parish', as is still the case with the present Table (*Kindred* 1940: 15, *Canon Law* 1947: 127).

Despite the widespread availability of the printed lists of prohibited degrees at the time, as shown in the proceedings from the courts of Durham (e.g. Raine 1850: 25), there is some evidence to suggest that the public at first paid no great attention to 'unlawful' marriages, indeed even encouraged them. One Edward Ward, a husbandman of the county of Durham, married his uncle's widow and claimed not to know what was contained in the 'dyvers writing hanginge upon the pillers of ther church . . .', while his wife asserted that 'all the lordship and paroch of Gainford' knew of the relationship 'and yet never found fault with ther marriadg . . . but rather thinks good ther of, bicause she was his own uncle wyf' (Raine 1845: 59).[8]

---

[8] Keith Wrightson to whom I owe the above references also draws my attention to the incestuous union of John Crowe to the daughter of his dead wife. She had four children by him, at least one of whom was baptised, and claimed to have been married by the curate. Despite its attempts to enforce the degrees, the court had little coercive power against a union that seems to have been tolerated by the local community.

Table 2. *A comparison of the Tables of Kindred and Affinity of the Church of England* (1560–1940)

Relationship	Date of Table		
	1560	1563	1940
Grandmother	X	X	O
Father's mother	O	O	X
Mother's mother	O	O	X
Grandfather's wife	X	X	O
Father's father's wife	O	O	X
Mother's father's wife	O	O	X
Wife's grandmother	O	X	O
Wife's father's mother	O	O	X
Wife's mother's mother	O	O	X
Father's sister	X	X	X
Mother's sister	X	X	X
Father's brother's wife	X	X	O
Mother's brother's wife	X	X	O
Wife's father's sister	O	X	O
Wife's mother's sister	O	X	O
Mother	X	X	X
Stepmother	X	X	O
Father's wife	O	O	X
Wife's mother	X	X	X
Daughter	X	X	X
Wife's daughter	X	X	X
Son's wife	X	X	X
Sister	O	X	X
Father's daughter	O	O	X
Mother's daughter	O	O	X
Half-sister	X	O	O
Sister begot in fornication	X	O	O
Whole sister	X	O	O
Wife's sister	X	X	O
Brother's wife	X	X	O
Son's daughter	X	X	X
Daughter's daughter	X	X	X
Son's son's wife	O	X	X
Daughter's son's wife	O	X	X
Wife's son's daughter	X	X	X
Wife's daughter's daughter	X	X	X

Table 2. (*cont.*)

Relationship	Date of Table		
	1560	1563	1940
Brother's daughter	X	X	X
Sister's daughter	X	X	X
Brother's son's wife	O	X	O
Sister's son's wife	O	X	O
Wife's brother's daughter	X	X	O
Wife's sister's daughter	X	X	O
Total	25	30	25

X = present
O = absent

The 1563 Table of prohibited degrees continued as the ecclesiastical ruling until the present century, being changed only as the result of the proposals of the Commission reporting in 1940, which were confirmed by canon 38 of 1946 – the civil law had already changed in the nineteenth century. The present list reduces the number of prohibited relationships to 25 once again, including some division of the previous categories. For example, 'grandmother' is now split into 'father's mother' and 'mother's mother', the same differentiation being applied to the wife's ascendants. 'Half-sister' has now become 'father's daughter' and 'mother's daughter', while step-mother becomes 'father's wife'. These changes are in accord with the earlier lists which always specified the exact genealogical relationship (mother's sister) rather than the more general classifying terms of everyday discourse e.g. 'aunt' (see Table 2).

Given the widespread belief that in England, and indeed in the West as a whole, non-domestic ties of kinship mattered very little, the extraordinary fuss created by proposals to change these avoidances must occasion some surprise. The heat generated by the controversies of the nineteenth century, which continued into the twentieth, is enough in itself to cast doubt upon this view. But for many believers the prohibitions that were being reviewed represented the word of God. The Reformation denied that the wider set of prohibitions then practised by the Catholic Church (but much modified in more recent times) fell into this category. The preamble of statute 32 of Henry VIII (cap. 38) refused to accept that the existing prohibitions were 'God's law'; they were 'for their lucre by that court [the Pope's] invented, the dispensations whereof they always reserved to themselves . . . and all because they would get money by it'.

Henry's motives for changing the marriage rules were understandable. If my argument is correct, the strategy of heirship appropriate and advantageous to royalty and commoners alike was against the best interests of the Church, as well as being against the particular set and general ideology of marriage rules that had been elaborated by the Church in the fourth century. Henry would have been correct in interpreting these rules as inhibiting his ability to provide himself and his kingdom with an heir. However, in this preamble to statute 32 he attacked the marriage rules from another angle, that of the monetary interest of the clergy. This view was not elaborated merely in the context of his personal situation, but was widely held at the time. It had formed the substance of Luther's complaint about the prohibition on marriages of kin related in the fourth degree: 'Der Pabst aber hat sie verboten aus lauter Heucheley, und um Geldes willen dispensiet er, und Lässts zu.'[9]

The idea that money was at the root of all ecclesiastical evil was not confined to dissatisfied royalty or to high-minded reformers. The popular attitude towards dispensations comes out in Chaucer's *Pardoner's Tale*, and it is an attitude that persists today. A few years ago I visited a colleague working in the Abbruzzi region of central Italy. There was a marriage that week-end, the bride and groom being first (paternal) cousins whose farms were adjacent to one another, lying a little outside the town. Since the wedding took place in the church, the couple had of course obtained a dispensation to marry. Afterwards in the local café I asked how cousins could get married so easily. One of the men sitting around scraped his left palm with the right hand muttering, '*soldi, soldi*' – 'money, money'. There was no expression of moral stigma against such a marriage (though some other people may have had such qualms); it was simply a question of the tribute one had to pay to the priest.

Although this lay view of marriage appears to have been very widespread, many Protestant reformers discouraged marriages

[9] Cited Reich 1864: 135; Huth 1875: 79.

within the third degree. While Luther did not think they were positively harmful,[10] he considered them to be 'inexpedient on the ground that people would marry without love merely to keep property within the family, while poor women would be left spinsters' (Huth 1875: 152, following Reich 1864: 135). The argument is interesting, for it stresses one of the specific concerns that people had in making a close marriage. Why then should the Catholic Church have wished to prevent such unions? Because they were loveless? Or, as some have suggested, because they were so popular that money would pour in from dispensations? Or because the Church had some more general interest in seeing that property flowed to the glory of God and the maintenance of his Church? The position of the Church and its clergy was highly privileged in the village community as well as at other levels of society. There was no mystery to the villagers about how that position was sustained, at least for the daily upkeep of the priest. It came from their own pockets, being fed by their rents, their tithes, their bequests and their sins. Prominent among their sins was close marriage, and for this they paid. So the manifestations of resistance, of opposition to the ban on close marriage, which featured in the Protestant reforms, especially in England, were part of a more general reaction against Church prohibitions and all that these entailed. And they entailed not simply monetary payments, but much more importantly, they prevented the adoption of strategies by which men and women could provide themselves with heirs, arrange their holdings and incorporate their kin. The opposition between the interests and rules of the Church, and the interests and practices of the layman resulted in a kind of dual economy of kinship, one at the level of rules, one at the level of practice; one open, one hidden.

[10] Huth (1875: 152–3) regards Burton, the author of *The Anatomy of Melancholy* (1621) as the first person who maintained this idea, but as we have seen it is at least as old as the eighth century and the notion persisted, and still persists, in folk belief. For the eleventh century, Duby notes the 'persistent feeling that consanguineous unions were bound to produce monstrous offspring' (1978: 53). Burton in fact advises against marriages 'as are any whit allyed' but rather 'to make choice of those that are most differing in complexion from them' (1652: 62). The deleterious effects are physical rather than social.

8. *The hidden economy of kinship*

Earlier chapters have tried to show that, as well as being related to doctrinal and theological considerations, the norms and teaching of the Church were also linked, and sometimes more closely, with its economic and political interests, both of which were necessarily involved in the establishment of God's rule on earth. But this level is clearly not the only one on which we must examine European kinship, for resistance and opposition may be as important as control and imposition.

In dealing with historical materials, one is often restricted to data which relate to the more formal aspects of a society. The sources, too, tend to consist of works of theology rather than of expressions of popular belief, to be concerned with the written law rather than with oral custom, with the 'rules' rather than the guidelines of practice, let alone the unannounced or unpublicised breaches of either. Literate societies produce sets of norms formulated in writing which may be very far removed from practice. These written norms can have a reference group whose members take them seriously, but there may be other elements in the population, who may be defined by class, ethnicity, sex or literacy, who work by different sets of norms, lying outside the realm in which *le droit écrit* is dominant. These alternative beliefs and practices cannot simply be regarded as variants on a common, written theme, for they may represent different interests, different ideologies, and may thus stand in marked opposition to the other mode.

In his description of medieval French society, Duby emphasises that not only did laymen and clergy adhere to different mores, so too did the married and unmarried. For example, the policy of noble *lignages* in northern France was to entrust only one couple in each house with the task of procreation. The sons of the Lord of Ardres were unable to marry 'for the bed of the house was not yet vacant' (1978: 94); younger brothers were condemned to be bachelors, unless they 'humiliated' themselves by marrying an heiress and moving into her house, as was the case with Baldwin, future Count of Guines (pp. 89,101).

The policy of primogeniture that emerged in the middle of the eleventh century, when a stop was put to the extension of domains by the legalised pillage of Church estates, meant that only the eldest son could marry, for the others could no longer be provided with lands acquired by force. As a consequence the younger sons formed themselves into turbulent bands who were bound together by the chivalric ideal, by the impossibility of marriage, and by the practice of 'courtly love', the game of love that was 'the expression of profound hostility to marriage' (p. 14). This situation was generated by the existence of 'two separate and fundamentally hostile groups within high society'. However, their interests were partially reconciled at the end of the twelfth century when the re-orientation of marriage policies led to more sons of aristocratic families being able to take a legitimate wife. In this way the role of bachelor became a phase in the developmental cycle rather than a permanent way of life for younger sons.

The existence of such internal differences in the notions and practices of kinship, marriage and the family, even within a particular class, are too often neglected, particularly by those taking a cultural or holistic view of society. But since the family is linked to the economy, to religion, as well as to political life, we have to take into account differences related to class, sect, or to a written as opposed to an oral mode of communication. The existence of such partly submerged differences, of the lower as against the higher, the nonliterate as against the literate, requires a consideration of what might be called the hidden economy of kinship.

The argument runs as follows. If marriage and the family are pressed into the service of a specific group or organ of society – the State, a ruling class, the Church – there will tend to emerge a parallel set of practices which modifies the 'dominant' – the written – norms. In stratified societies these different practices are in many cases found to operate at different social levels. In pre-revolutionary China the masses, the poorer groups, did not follow the Confucian ideology; even the upper groups were unable entirely to conform to those elevated norms but nevertheless they differed systematically from the lower elements in their practice of widow remarriage and in their marital transfers (Wolf and Huang 1980). In traditional

India, too, there are systematic differences in the family patterns of higher and lower castes, arising in part out of the nature of their domestic economies, but also related to the rejection and modification of the dominant ideology by the subordinate groups.

In Europe the ideology of the Church and the practice of the people frequently diverged. Of course different classes or estates followed different practices. But the higher and lower orders were sometimes united in their resistance to the rules of the Church. This has led Duby (1978, 1981) to analyse the marriage patterns of northern France in the tenth and eleventh centuries as an opposition between noble and ecclesiastical concepts of marriage, an opposition which extended to royalty itself; rulers were after all only *primi inter pares*, and they had the same interests in their continuity as the nobility. The search of Henry VIII for other wives was not a demonstration of the lusty sexuality of an English hero; it was a quest for an heir, a male heir, to perpetuate the newly confirmed royal line. On the political level the conflict between the ecclesiastical and noble views of marriage represents an aspect of the struggle between 'Church' and 'State', between the interests of the two most powerful bodies in the land; in Henry VIII's case, marriages were political attempts to achieve continuity by using procedures forbidden in Church doctrine.

But this struggle was not only fought out in the arena of high politics. The rules of the Church gave rise to tensions throughout society since they prevented individuals from doing what they saw as being in the best interests, socially as well as personally, of themselves and their families. The written rules of the Church and State were internalised as norms only to a limited extent. Evidence for this, and for the fact that aspects of these European patterns of kinship and marriage were imposed from above and from outside, is provided by the continual resistance to them from below. The official schema forbade marriages between close kin, but such marriages continued to take place in significant numbers. Family interests led to arrangements in which the young age of the participants excluded the possibility of 'consent' of the parties in any meaningful sense (Turlan 1957: 481ff). Parents might enforce their wishes by the threat of disinheritance (p. 487). For their sons and daughters, clandestine marriages, which were valid but not licit under the Church's doctrine of consensual unions, offered a way round parental restrictions. The norms of the Church could be avoided by pre-emption, by establishing a union uncelebrated by the clergy (Sheehan 1971).

Even wrong marriages could be blessed with ecclesiastical approval by the simple expedient of the dispensation. Registers of such transactions provide a window on popular behaviour, and their scale shows that they were not 'deviant' (except in the lexicon of the Church) but an accepted alternative to the pattern of social action that the Church tried to enforce.

The evidence for such patterns is often fragmentary, coming from different times, different places, different sources. There are some accounts of the difficulties which the early Church encountered in its struggle to impose its rules upon its inhabitants of the newly Christian world. Throughout its history reformers pointed to the ease with which the congregation continued to fall into earlier ways. At the domestic level the Church's prohibitions and injunctions were frequently avoided, even disobeyed (Turlan 1957: 480). The actual extent of this disobedience is not known. Except for the registers of dispensations, which may themselves represent only the tip of the iceberg, the evidence for the practice of close marriage among the rural population is unlikely to achieve statistical reliability. But some accounts give a glimpse of the persistence of such forms of marriage. After the end of the eighteenth century the small isolated village of Pinon in the Auvergne gained fame as an example of 'communal' exploitation of the soil, with the different branches of one 'family' marrying among themselves. In 1787 the commune consisted of four such branches totalling 19 persons in all who married amongst themselves. Indeed, according to one source, the Pope had granted them a permanent dispensation against 'cousinage' (Dupin 1929: 47; Champeaux 1933: 248). They feared that out-marriage would 'enfeeble their customary ways', although one commentator, voicing an anxiety that runs as a continuing thread in Western European belief from the Dark Ages down to today, expressed the alternative view that the recent loss of population which they had experienced had been caused by this very practice of marrying kin.

More substantial evidence of close marriage is provided by Karnoouh's study of French peasants in Lorraine in the last two centuries, a part of the country that had a very strong Catholic tradition. Nevertheless, claims the author, 'they have always transgressed in very significant proportions, with or without the agreement of their bishops, the rules on the prohibited degrees of marriage laid down by the Church'. Between 1810 and 1910 as many as 50 per cent of marriages went against those rules. Many were between first cousins, while others were between uncle and niece. The majority were between individuals born and resident in the same village (1971: 41). The last point is critical, for it suggests that the parties and their families had overlapping interests in matters other than marriage itself.

The importance of cousin marriages in the recent past of the French village of Minot in Burgundy is noted by Verdier. 'Before', declared one mother, 'of course people used to marry cousins, the marriages would be arranged when people gathered in the evenings, they used to talk about them.' She hastened to add that today she would prefer her son to marry anyone other than a cousin and even a Black or Japanese for her daughter, but Verdier remarks that 'the proportion of in-marriage and out-marriage remains remarkably stable' (1979: 287–8).[1] In a general survey of rural France in the nineteenth century, Segalen claims that in-marriage, both within the community and between relatives, actually increased over that period (1980: 19). But unlike the figures from Lorraine, the recorded rates are not exceptionally high; the records consist of dispensations registered with the Church, which represent only a proportion of the actual total of such unions. In Loir-et-Cher, such marriages formed about 3.5 per cent of the total, rising at times to 5 and 6 per cent; in Finistère, the percentage was higher even at the beginning of the twentieth century.

Rates of in-marriage varied with the size of the village, the area in which it was located, and the freedom with which the dispensations were granted. Flandrin claims that in some mountain areas of France in the eighteenth century, the frequency was very high and 'almost all marriages had to take place with dispensations from the impediments on the grounds of kinship' (1979: 34). Such unions were often between cousins, some of whom had been brought up together because of the death of parents, a situation of which the registers of dispensations of marriage provide 'innumerable examples'. Some were oblique marriages between adjacent generations, as when, on the death of her husband, a sadler, Marie Varié, summoned her cousin to come and take over the shop and marry the eldest girl 'who was to inherit it in due course' (p. 44).

---

[1] On Minot, see also F. Zonabend, who describes how a mother would look for a spouse for an unmarried son or daughter: 'Généralement, elle commence par explorer sa propre parentèle, y cherchant un cousin proche ou éloigné, susceptible de convenir' (1980: 165).

The considerations that favoured in-marriage among kin were many and varied. Late marriage, servanthood, and other forms of lay celibacy (or postponement) increased worries about losing potential brides to outsiders. 'In many villages, if not in all', writes Flandrin of eighteenth-century France, 'the "big boys", grouped together as an institution, made efforts to establish their monopoly over the marriageable girls of the parish. Every girl married to an outsider represented, in fact, for the less fortunate among them, an increased probability of remaining a bachelor and a servant in the house of another. Thus it was that with cudgel-blows . . . they dissuaded outsiders from associating with the village girls. Furthermore, they proclaimed the dishonour of such girls as became interested in others than themselves. This attitude on the part of the village youths met with the approval of their parents, who were always perturbed if they saw a girl take away as her dowry a fraction of the patrimony of the village, to bestow it on a stranger who would not pay his share of the fiscal obligations of the parish. In short, the village community as such had all sorts of methods of preventing the marriages of girls with men from outside the village. This was the reason for the proportion of endogamous marriages, which was often startlingly high, and for the recourse to dispensations from the impediments on the grounds of kinship' (p. 47).

DIVORCE AND REMARRIAGE

The control the Church held over marital affairs meant that it could enforce its view of marriage as an indissoluble tie. Indeed that view was intrinsic to its appropriation of marriage to the religious domain, to the domain of God. If divorce was difficult, remarriage was impossible. Once again popular practice devised ways round ecclesiastical decree and the 'sale of wives' which existed in England over three centuries, has been described 'as an illegal form of divorce' – and remarriage (Menefee 1981).

Remarriage after the death of a spouse was another matter. The Church not only forbade marriage to the brothers and sisters of the dead spouse, as well as more distant affines, but frequently discouraged the remarriage of widows and widowers, although this was never absolutely prohibited as it was among the upper groups in Hindu India and in pre-revolutionary China where divorce was equally difficult. But while the disapproval had some effect on women of the aristocracy and the bourgeoisie, it had little among the peasantry or indeed among the ordinary inhabitants of towns.

The loss of a husband or a wife was common enough because of the high rates of mortality and the small differences in their ages at marriage ensured that both sexes were well represented in the bereaved. The late age of marriage for both meant a long generation, increasing the chances of orphanhood and of widow/widowerhood. Many bereaved parents were left with the sole responsibility of looking after the children, and remarriage was not only a great help domestically but also with looking after the farm or shop. Stepparenthood was therefore a common enough consequence of remarriage.[2] It is true that a local community might react by means of 'rough music' or similar forms of local protest against those remarriages made between partners unequal in wealth, age or status, just as it might so react against adultery (Davis 1975; Thompson 1972). But the reaction in both cases was to the incidence, the particular incident, not to the practice. One observer of French peasants in nineteenth-century Cantal describes how arrangements for remarriage followed straight on the funeral:

> When a husband loses his wife or a wife her husband, the surviving spouse at once invites everyone to a meal: this sometimes takes place in the house where the corpse is still lying, and the guests laugh, drink, sing and make arrangements for remarrying their host or hostess. The widower or widow receives proposals, and gives reasons for acceptance or rejection; it is only rarely that the party comes to an end before the arrangement has been concluded. (Hugo 1835, quoted by Flandrin 1979: 115)

While such an arrangement may not have been widespread, there were various regions of France in the seventeenth and eighteenth centuries in which the rapidity of remarriage was very marked. While only 6 per cent of widowers in Béarn remarried within six months, this figure rose to 55 per cent in the Vallage (Champagne) and 80 per cent in an urban parish in Lyons. For the sake of comparison Flandrin notes that in France as a whole in the 1950s, only 15 per cent of widowers remarried within the first year of the death of their spouse (pp. 115–16).

---

[2] I am making an implicit comparison with systems of early marriage for women and late marriage for men (E.F.L.M.) which are found with high rates of polygyny. In this case there will be many more children without a living male than a living female parent (on the concept of not having a father among the Tallensi, see Fortes 1949).

THE CONTROL OF SEXUALITY

The Church attempted to control the sexuality of the populace, both inside and outside marriage, in a variety of ways, many of which ran against lay interests and customs. Since intercourse was a *sine qua non* of marriage, and marriage in turn was a procreative union, it was surrounded with numerous restrictions. The sixth-century Penitential of Vinnian lays down a strict regime of sexual behaviour for the Irish of that period, making no concessions to a society accustomed to the practices of divorce, remarriage and concubinage. Not only do both partners in marriage have to be faithful, but in the case of transgression the innocent may suffer for the sins of the guilty. 'If either partner is unfaithful sexual union is to be suspended for a year as part of the penance.' Similarly, if the wife deserts her husband, he cannot remarry and must take her back if she returns. If an innocent woman is put away by her husband, she may take no other man. A further provision that must have been strongly resented by any man or woman wanting an heir, and one that ran against the whole Biblical tradition, was that 'if a man has a barren wife he may not turn her away, but both are to live together in continence.' 'Concubinage is completely rejected. Moreover married people are to abstain from each other by mutual consent on Saturday and Sunday, in the period between conception and birth, and during the three forty-day periods of abstinence in each year' (Hughes 1966: 53–4).[3]

Such abstinence, like clerical and lay celibacy, and like late marriage (whenever and wherever it appeared), no doubt contributed to controlling the long-term growth of the population. But other forms of birth control – coitus interruptus, abortion, contraception, and infanticide – were strongly condemned by the Church. Such condemnation was related to its view on the nature and beginning of human life. Most societies see the human personality as being composed of both spiritual and material elements, the former emanating from a supernatural source: in the words of T. S. Eliot's translation of Dante, 'Issues from the hand of God, the simple soul.' Hence the destruction of life has a religious as well as a secular dimension. But

[3] Even the regular prohibitions reduce the period in which intercourse is allowed to 175 days, less than half the year; in addition we need to include the many physiological and occasional prohibitions. The reasons for this requirement of continence among the lay folk was said to be so 'that they may be able to have time for prayer for the salvation of their souls'. If observed, such prohibitions would have acted as an effective restriction on the procreation of children.

the point at which life is believed to begin varies in different societies. The LoDagaa of northern Ghana do not see a child as fully
human until it can walk and talk; its earlier death is rarely treated
with overt regret, except by the parents themselves (Goody
1962a: 91–2). Christianity takes a more 'physiological' view, placing
the critical moment at the time of conception itself, and encouraging
birth control by avoiding intercourse rather than preventing pregnancy by mechanical or chemical means, or terminating it once it
has come to pass. Nevertheless there is plenty of evidence to show
that here too the teaching of the Church often ran contrary to lay
values, or at least to lay interests (Noonan 1965).

WET-NURSING AND FOSTERING

The control of sexuality was connected with the objection of churchmen to wet-nursing. To Bede the practice resulted from a couple's
desire to resume sexual relations following the early weaning of their
child by the mother; to some later churchmen the practice, while still
condemned, was found preferable to a husband seeking sex outside
of marriage. There were many other reasons for in-living nurses and
country 'baby-farms', but it is significant that despite the Church's
disapproval and despite the model of the Holy Family, it continued
to be so common a feature of life until the last century.

Adoption was easier to control being like marriage a legal act.
As a result it virtually disappeared from Christian Europe. But
fostering continued as part of the hidden structure of kinship. Indeed in the form of the in-living (or at least the in-working) servant
it was intrinsic to the domestic economy of much of Western
Europe.

LEGITIMACY IN BIRTH AND MARRIAGE

In many Eurasian societies concubinage constituted a legal form of
marriage, the children of which might well provide legitimate heirs.
In Christian Europe, however, concubinage was 'illegal' and its
offspring were illegitimate. Yet despite the constant admonitions
against it, the practice flourished among laity and clerics alike, and
was even encouraged by the Church's restrictions on divorce,
polygyny and the marriage of priests. The Church regarded such
forms of union as invalid as well as illicit, considering the off-

spring to be illegitimate, thus changing the whole concept of proper parenthood.

Illegitimate children are the result of not only unrecognised unions (and unrecognised offspring) but also of pre-marital intercourse. Despite the Church's views on these matters, the rates of 'illegitimate' births and pre-marital pregnancies in northern Europe could be very high, partly because of the late age of marriage for both men and women. The association between the late marriage of women and high rates of illegitimacy is not perfect but then perfect correlations are not characteristic of human affairs. What is obvious is that pre-marital pregnancies and births do not occur when the age of marriage for women is low enough, when pre-marital virginity is a function not so much of morality but of immaturity. Under such conditions, other forms of illegitimacy may be more common.

In southern Europe the control of sexuality was closer to 'Eastern' structures, or to 'Eurasian' patterns. The reasons lay partly in concepts of honour, partly in the pressures of a more extensive, or effective, network of kin, but also in the earlier age of marriage for women in many parts of the Mediterranean which inevitably meant that such control was more intensely felt and more easily maintained.

The initial definition of the nature of the conjugal union created the problems of illegitimate children so vividly portrayed in Shakespeare's *King Lear*. While God is called upon to stand up for bastards, their disabilities if not their creation were largely a matter of the ecclesiastical law. It was a problem that came to the fore in the sixteenth century when the Catholic reformers attempted to counter the growing threat of Protestantism. One means of doing this was to use the family, and specifically its women, as the instrument of Christianity. With this in mind the Church actively tried to eradicate concubinage among laymen as well as among the clergy (Flandrin 1979: 182), and to discourage those marriages that had not been solemnised by the Church. Those lay couples living in a state of concubinage were denounced from the pulpit and excommunicated. The result was a striking fall in the number of illegitimate children in France, a high proportion of whom were the offspring of such unions; in and around Nantes in the sixteenth century the children of 'concubines' formed 50 per cent of the total number of illegitimate births but this had fallen to 2.5 per cent by the end of the eighteenth century (p. 182). However, at the same time the fate of the unmarried mother worsened and the chances of her children's survival decreased. Their numbers were also reduced by the fact that the clergy often forced seducers to marry girls they had made pregnant, which led to an increase in the frequency of marriages preceded by conception.

CONSENT OF PARENTS, CONSENT OF SPOUSES

Another feature that distinguished clerical and lay models was notions of parental control of marriage. The Church encouraged consensus between the partners but considered that the consent of parents was in principle unnecessary. The individuals themselves were responsible for their acts in this respect as in matters of ownership and testament. But lay practice rejected such 'freedom', such lack of responsibility, and in this they were supported by the French State, by common practice and by Protestant reformers.

The differences between clerical and lay, between upper and lower, between literate and illiterate, overlap in some significant respects. They are of a kind to indicate that we are in the presence not simply of deviations or even variants, but in some respects of conflicting patterns of behaviour. Such differences exist even in that conservative, and to some extent unifying field, of kinship terminology. In an earlier study (1962b) I commented upon the recent use of the term *nanna* for 'grandmother' among lower groups in several regions of England, yet its complete absence from the dictionaries (as distinct from oral utterance), except in the form of *nanny*. I argued that among upper groups the child-caring functions of the grandmother, usually the mother's mother, were delegated to nannies. 'But the less affluent also have their proxy mothers, their nannas, although recruited by ties of kinship rather than on the labour market, and relieving the mothers from work rather than leisure.' Both the term and the role were foreign to the 'genteel' literary scholars who compile the dictionaries, but are none the less part of a submerged, non-literate pattern of terminology that itself represented the hidden economy of family life.

9. *The spiritual and the natural*

There is one feature particular to Europe which I have not discussed, partly because it is so significant that the issues it raises serve to summarise the central argument. For this striking feature was the distinctive, perhaps unique, way in which kin terms and practices were transferred to the religious domain. Such 'extensions' are not unknown in other societies especially in the sphere of politics where a king or chief may be perceived as the 'father' or 'grandfather' of his people. But in Christianity, kin terms were used not only for addressing the gods and the priesthood, but also for addressing all the fellow-members of the sect, and later those specially chosen as spiritual kin or godkin. God the Father is served by priests and helpers who are 'fathers' and 'brothers', 'mothers' and 'sisters'. The Head of the Church is *il Papa*, the Pope; the head of the monastery is called the Abbot, again a 'father', derived from the Aramaic *abbā*. Fellow members of the early Church were 'brothers' and 'sisters', while those chosen to be the godparents of one's children were *compatres* and *commatres*, the godchildren themselves being *filiolagium*, and the fellow godchildren forming a 'confraternity' of 'godsibs' or 'gossips'. And the changes in 'natural' kinship which occurred throughout Europe from Augustine's time on, were also embodied in the practices of spiritual kinship.

Blood-brotherhood and other forms of quasi-kinship are found in many societies – among the Scandinavian and German invaders of Western and Southern Europe, as well as among the Slavs of more recent times. Some authors have seen the origins of the Christian practice in these widespread customs. Others have called attention to the notion of sponsorship in the Eleusynian mysteries of the Greeks[1] and some to Roman legal terminology where *sponsio* in its

---

[1] Fairbanks (1910: 132) writes of the *mystagogus*, a director or confessor whose duty was to advise candidates for initiation as to necessary purifications, to instruct them as to the meaning of the ritual and to act as a guide during the whole ceremony.

wider sense originally signified a contract enforced by religious sanctions (Mintz and Wolf 1950: 343; Schultz 1951: 494). However this may be, the notion of spiritual kinship finds no warrant in the New Testament, and canon law refers to 'custom' as the basis on which it rests. Nevertheless, the practice became widespread throughout the Christian Church, although it was perhaps not so common in the west as in the south (Bennett 1979) or in the east (Patlagean 1978). According to Lynch, the separation of natural from spiritual kin began in the later fourth century, after the shift occurred from adult to infant baptism.

In the early Christian period sponsors for baptism were normally the parents. Certainly this seems to have been so during the time of St Augustine (A.D. 354–430). Bishop Boniface assumed that no-one else could act in this capacity, but Augustine pointed out to him that there were exceptional cases, such as slave-owners acting as sponsors for slave children, religious women for those who had been saved from exposure, and a few similar situations. The eventual change from parental to non-parental sponsorship meant that the sponsor participated in a spiritual birth and became a spiritual parent (Lynch 1980: 112). However, spiritual kinship had 'very concrete and unspiritual consequences' (p. 113), which is why monks and nuns were prohibited from taking on these roles. Lynch cites the revealing case reported by Gregory of Tours. A sixth-century Bishop of Rouen was accused of stealing some property that had been entrusted to him and he defended himself by claiming that the goods had been held for safe-keeping, but had been given out to help his godson: 'whatever belongs to my son Merovech, whom I received from the bath of regeneration, is seen to be mine as well' (p. 117; see Lynch for additional references).

Just as Christian baptism was held to replace the Jewish circumcision ('the circumcision made without hands', Colossians 2: 11), so too the later institution of godparenthood replaced the Roman adoption which had been rejected in many Christian circles. It was a form of quasi-kinship that substituted spiritual for material considerations; no longer were rights to property necessarily involved, although help and patronage might be. Baptism thus became a kind of adoption.

Such a view is expressed in the writings of the historian Procopius who refers to Christian baptism in his account of the 'scandals' in the family life of Belisarius (A.D. 505–565), the general of Emperor

Justinian. Before setting off for Libya in pursuit of the Vandal armies, Belisarius took a young man called Theodosius, whose ancestors had professed unorthodox views, and 'bathed this youth in the sacred bath, from which he lifted him with his own hands, thus making him the adopted child of himself and his wife, as is customary for Christians to make adoptions . . .' (*Anecdota* i. 14–19). What Procopius is describing is baptism, but he interprets it as a substitute for the adoption practised by the Roman nation. This being so, when Belisarius' wife, Antonina, fell in love with Theodosius and had intercourse with him, a secret which was betrayed to her husband by her servants, her 'child' was forced to flee to Ephesus.

Under the sixth-century legal reforms of the Emperor Justinian and under the influence of Christian doctrine, the practice of adoption was modified.[2] 'No longer', writes Biondi (1954: III,62), 'was it an act arranged between the two *patres* . . .' However, godparenthood took the form of just such an agreement between the 'fathers' and 'mothers' of the person concerned. 'Fictional' kinship both by adoption and by godparenthood could be established either between consanguineal kin or between non-kin; it could either intensify or extend family ties. However adoption lost its character as a 'strategy of heirship'; the legal sources are virtually silent on the subject of 'testamentary adoption' (Biondi 1954: III,63). But it did acquire an important metaphorical and supernatural dimension; the faithful were enjoined by St Augustine to make Christ a son (and heir); the faithful themselves are adopted through baptism; and the Church is adopted by the laity (Biondi 1954: III,62). Metaphor takes over the core meaning; 'symbol' becomes the dominant reality.

Just as adoption and fostering shared some of the characteristics of 'natural' kinship, so too did godparenthood. In Anglo-Saxon England the law of Ine, King of Wessex, read: 'If anyone kills the godson or godfather of another, the compensation for the (spiritual) relationship is to be the same as that to the lord' (Lancaster 1958: 369). Spiritual kinship tends to converge upon and duplicate its 'natural' counterpart, taking on rights and duties in vengeance

---

[2] On a possible form of godparenthood or adoption among early Celts and Germans, connected with the first cutting of a child's hair, see Faral 1929: I,107–8. In the particular case of the incident reported in the *Historia Britonum*, St Germain accepted the paternity of the son of the British chief, Vortigern, who had married his own daughter (Nennius 1838: 30).

and the feud, although in this particular instance, the level of compensation is linked to political rather than to kin relationships.

In other ways, too, the shift to spiritual parenthood was followed by a transfer of the norms applied to consanguineal and affinal kinship. The ban on marriage between those involved in baptismal sponsorship seems first to have been formulated by the Byzantine emperor, Justinian, who ruled from A.D. 527–65, in the context of the prohibition on marriage with a fictive child. He dismissed worries about marrying a freed slave of the household, providing there is mutual affection. But no-one, he argued would be so impious as to marry a girl who from the beginning had been brought up as his daughter, just as marriage between tutor (*tutor*) and pupil (*pupilla*) was forbidden (*Institutes* V. 6. 1). Then he went on to declare: 'We prohibit absolutely a marriage between godfather and god-daughter (*a sacrosancto suscepit baptismate*),[3] even when he has brought her up (as an alumna or foster child). For nothing demands so much paternal affection and impedes marriage as a tie of this kind, which through the mediation of God binds these two souls together' (*Institutes* V. 4. 26).

Prohibitions on marriage to spiritual kin, which emerged first of all in the Byzantine area, of which Italy was a part, were later extended. Godparenthood already existed among the Franks and in the Anglo-Saxon world but without any prohibitions on marriage; these were only imposed upon the West in the eighth century as a result of the growing influence of the papacy (Lynch 1980). This implication is drawn from the queries about the prohibition on marriage to the mother of the godchild, between *commater* and *compater*, raised in a letter of Saint Boniface (680–754) to Bishop Pehthelm of Whithorn in Scotland dated 735.[4] He wrote:

The priests throughout Gaul and Frankland maintain that for them a man who takes to wife a widow, to whose child he has acted as godfather, is guilty of a very serious crime. As to the nature of this sin, if it is a sin, I was entirely ignorant, nor have I ever seen it mentioned by the fathers, in the ancient canons, nor in

---

[3] The verb *suscipio* means 'to support' or 'to take up a new-born child from the ground and so to acknowledge it'.

[4] According to Niermeyer, the first use of *commater* occurs at the very end of the sixth century and *compater* about the same time, the latter also carrying the meaning of 'intimate friend' during the eighth century. The quality of *compaternitas* is reported during the same century.

the decrees of popes, nor by the Apostles in their catalogue of sins. (l. 32)

In a letter addressed to Archbishop Nothelm of Canterbury, Boniface asks for a copy of Pope Gregory's replies to Augustine because he is worried about the recognition given to marriages in the third degree. But he also raises the matter of the marriage to the widowed mother of the godchild, saying

> The Romans declare that this is a sin, even a capital sin, and say that in such cases a divorce should take place. They said that under Christian emperors, such a marriage was punishable by death or perpetual exile. If you find that this is accounted so great a sin in the decrees of catholic fathers or in the canons or even in Holy Writ, pray let me know it, that I may understand and know what is the authority for such an opinion. I cannot possibly understand how, on the one hand, spiritual relationship in the case of matrimonial intercourse can be so great a sin, while, on the other hand, it is well established that by holy baptism we all become sons and daughters, brothers and sisters of Christ and the Church. (l. 33, Emerton 1940: 61–3)

And Boniface returns to the subject in yet a third letter, one to his former pupil, Abbot Dudo, as of course did Luther, many centuries later, in much the same words. The sectarian brotherhood of the Church is opposed to the specificity of spiritual kinship.

Whatever the case in the West, the Eastern Church had ruled upon the subject in canon 53 of the Council *In Trullo* held in Constantinople in 692. The terms of the discussion are fascinating because they indicate the growing importance attached to the spiritual relationship and to the consequent devaluation of 'natural' ties, at least outside the families of birth and marriage. 'Whereas the spiritual relationship is greater than fleshly affinity; and since it has come to our knowledge that in some places certain persons who become sponsors to children in holy salvation-bearing baptism, afterwards contract matrimony with their mothers (being widows), we decree that for the future nothing of this sort is to be done. But if any, after the present canon, shall be observed to do this, they must, in the first place, desist from this unlawful marriage, and then be subjected to the penalties of fornicators' (Percival 1900).

Full acceptance of the two forms of parenthood, 'blood' and 'spiritual', separate but equal, together with the insistence that both fell within the same system of prohibited degrees, came about only gradually. But the two parallel systems were formally recognised in 813, when the Council of Mainz reasserted the decision that parents could not act as godparents to their own children.[5]

Godparenthood was not confined to a single set of relationships. Baptism and confirmation, which had originally been one rite, had become separate by the time of the Frankish kingdom of the eighth century, a development that was accompanied by the emergence of two sets of sponsors for the two acts.[6] For a long period it was also maintained that the sacrament of confession established a similar relationship of spiritual kinship between confessor and confessant, with the consequence that intercourse between them was incestuous; at the time priests were not necessarily celibate. The number of sponsors involved in baptism and confirmation increased with time and they too were included in the range of prohibitions. In 1298, when Pope Boniface VIII decreed that no ties of kinship arose from the confession, he also laid down that all the sponsors present at a given ceremony entered into a relationship of spiritual kinship with the person being sponsored. 'In extending Canon Law, and at the same time stressing dispensations from it', comment Mintz and Wolf (1950: 350), 'the Church added a source of income.' In doing so it increased its control over the domestic domain. But part of the problem of godparenthood seems to have been the exuberant development of the institution by the people themselves, possibly as a response to the diminishing importance of the wider ties of consanguinity, thus substituting a new series of supportive relationships both for the parents and for the children.

[5] Canon 55 of the Council of Moguntia (Mainz) read as follows: 'Nullus igitur proprium filium vel filiam de fonte baptismatis suscipiat: nec filiolam, nec commatrem ducat uxorem; nec illam cujas filium, aut filiam ad confirmationem duxerit. Ubi autem factum fuerit, separentur' (Mansi, *Concilia* XIV. col. 75).

[6] The evidence for this separation is contained in the Capitulary of King Pepin, King of the Franks, for 754–755. The discussion has to do with the prohibitions on marriage (*De incestis*), which include those on spiritual kin, and provides for financial penalties for disobedience: 'Si homo incestum commiserit de istis causis, de Deo sacrata, aut commatre sua, aut cum matrina sua spirituali de fonte et confirmatione episcopi, aut cum matre et filia, aut cum duabus sororibus, aut cum fratris filia aut sororis filia, aut nepta, aut cum consobrina atque subrina, aut cum amita vel matertera: de istis capitulis pecuniam suam perdat, si habet; et si emendare se noluerit, nullus eum recipiat nec cibum ei donet. Et si fecerit, LX solidos domno regi componat, usque dum se ipse homo correxerit. Et si pecuniam non habet, si liber est, mittatur in carcere usque ad satisfactionem. Si servus aut libertus est, vapuletur plagis multis; et si dominus suus permiserit eum amplius in tale scelus cadere, ipsos LX solidos domno rege componat (*Monumenta Germaniae Historica, Capitularia Regum Francorum* I. 31).

From the fourteenth to the sixteenth centuries attempts were made both by Church and State to limit the number of sponsors, which would have automatically reduced the range of prohibited marriages (Bossy 1973: 133). Eventually godparenthood, like close marriage and the celibacy of priests, became one of the subjects of the disputes leading up to the Reformation. In 1521 the German Estates petitioned the Pope to redress a series of wrongs; the objection to spiritual kinship arising from baptismal sponsorship heads the list of some sixty-odd complaints (Mintz and Wolf 1950: 350).[7]

It was mainly the restriction on marriage to spiritual kin rather than godparenthood itself that was condemned by the reformers. In 'The Babylonian Captivity of the Church' (1520) Luther protested against 'that nonsense about compaternities, commaternities, confraternities, consoroties, and confiliaties' which must be completely abolished as far as marriage is concerned (Lehmann 1959: 99). Later in 'The Estate of Marriage' (1539), an even stronger attack is made against 'these artificial, money-seeking impediments':

> The third impediment is spiritual relationship. If I sponsor a girl at baptism or confirmation, then neither I nor my son may marry her, or her mother, or her sister – unless an appropriate and substantial sum of money is forthcoming! This is nothing but pure farce and foolishness, concocted for the sake of money and to befuddle consciences. Just tell me this: isn't it a greater thing for me to be baptised myself than merely to act as sponsor to another? Then I must be forbidden to marry any Christian woman, since all baptised women are the spiritual sisters of all baptised men by the virtue of their common baptism, sacrament, faith, Spirit, Lord, God and eternal heritage (Eph. 4: 4–6). (Lehmann 1962: 24)

Luther was not against the spiritual relationship itself and godparenthood continued in the ceremonies and practices of the Church of England and similar bodies, although it necessarily disappeared from those Non-Conformist sects which did not acknowl-

---

[7] This at least is true of the Latin version of the final draft prepared by the Diet of Nuremberg in 1523, the first section of which (De dispensationibus aere redimendis) includes the following passage: 'Quod genus sunt: matrimoniorum tam innumera excogitata obstacula, ex affinitatis, publicae honestatis, cognatione spirituali legalique et consanguinitatis tam multis gradibus originem trahentia' (Münch 1830: 344). It is not so explicit in the German version which only mentions the money raised from marriage (Wrede 1901: 648).

edge the baptism of infants, or in some cases baptism in any form. One important feature that did persist was the naming of the children by the godparents, the senior of whom, in 90 per cent of the cases of the offspring of the nobility and gentry in fourteenth-century England, gave his or her own name. This practice still seems to have been the norm in most classes at the end of the seventeenth century, long after the Reformation (Bennett 1979: 8–9). Even today in the Anglican Church, it is godparents who give a child his name and the presence of parents is not essential at the Christening, although it is now encouraged. The Prayer Book lays down the following procedure:

> Then shall the Priest demand the Name of the Child; which being by the Godfathers and Godmothers pronounced, the Minister shall say, Dost thou, in the name of this Child, renounce the devil and all his works . . .

Finally, it is the godparents, not the parents, who become the sureties for the child's religious education, who have to ensure that he learn the Creed, the Lord's Prayer and the Ten Commandments 'in the vulgar tongue'. Indeed, similar formulae are used in the baptism of adults where godparents are also required. It is they who give a person his name, as the Confirmation Service later insists:

Question: What is your Name?

Answer: N. or M.

Question: Who gave you this Name?

Answer: My Godfathers and Godmothers in my Baptism; wherein I was made a member of Christ, the child of God, and an inheritor of the kingdom of heaven.

Question: What did your Godfathers and Godmothers then for you?

There seems to have been an important switch in the nature of naming practices in the eleventh and twelfth centuries (the period of the 'reforms'), at least among the aristocracy of France and Germany. In earlier times children had been named after grandparents, not by or after godparents (Bennett 1979: 9; Bloch 1961: I,45; Martindale 1977; Duby 1972). Subsequently the tendency was to take Christian names from and after godparents, an important indication of a shift of emphasis from kin to non-kin relationships, or rather from 'blood' to spiritual kinship. The effect, as Bennett has noted, was to diminish the actual stock of first names, especially the Germanic ones. With the increase in population and the decrease in names, the problem of homonyms became more acute, providing a stimulus to the development of surnames as a further card of identity (1979: 10). This innovation has been considered as an index of the growing strength of the *lignage*; but it could also be read as evidence for a move away from the kinship solidarities which are implied in those naming customs that identify persons belonging to alternate generations (i.e. grandchild and grandparent), and that for other parts of the world have been linked with lineage ties, with the worship of ancestors, and with beliefs in the transmission of spiritual elements of the human identity between the members of different generations (Radcliffe-Brown 1950).

Godparenthood continued after the Reformation but spiritual kinship was no longer a barrier to marriage. Nor, according to Luther, was adoption, since no such prohibitions were mentioned in Leviticus. Indeed godparenthood had no scriptural base at all. Some Protestants saw the institution as involving too radical a devaluation of 'blood-kinship' leading to a neglect of the parental role which the reformers were anxious to promote. It was one of the complaints of the Protestant Thomas Becon, Chaplain to Cranmer, that the Catholic Church 'will by no means suffer the fathers of the infants to be present at the baptism of their children' (1844: 228). Indeed, he appears to be querying the whole system of godparenthood on that account. Just as a mother should nurse her own child, so should a father be present at its baptism. Parental duties were supreme in religious as in other spheres.

The role of spiritual kinship has been seen as providing parents with an opportunity to extend, reinforce or sanctify their relations with other members of the community. In some regions and periods godkin were mainly consanguines while in others they formed a potential ladder for social advancement and were therefore chosen from prestigious outsiders or even friends. Unlike some of the other features of family life we have discussed, spiritual kinship was not accepted purely as an imposition but was vigorously embraced by the people themselves. It first developed in the late fourth century, at a time when wider bonds of kinship were under threat, partly because of large-scale socio-economic trends, partly because of the disruption of social life but partly too because the Church, for general and specific reasons, wanted to encourage its own forms of social relations. 'Given that spiritual kin relations involved no property rights', remarks Bennett (1979: 2), 'and positively impeded future matrimonial entanglements, such bonds were regarded as far less problematical than the regular ties of blood and marriage.' In addition, these links depended entirely on the Church for their definition and for their creation.

Godparenthood has served many functions since that time. Bennett sees it as a mechanism that encouraged the pagan invaders to come to terms with more complex forms of social organisation, 'with patronage as well as parentage, community as well as sibling solidarity' (p. 5). Others see it as a means which has enabled diverse groups and strata, for instance, Normans and English, Muslims and Christians, to enter into positive, interdependent relations one with another. In fourteenth-century England, for example, Bennett found extension (i.e. the choice of distant godparents) to be more important than intensification (i.e. the choice of related godparents); while kinsmen sometimes acted as godparents, there was little evidence to suggest that the institution was used to build up the *lignage* or to reinforce wider kinship ties (p. 6). The range of its functions are many, but what is critical for my argument is that spiritual kinship not merely supplemented but replaced aspects of the 'natural' variety. Not only in its sectarian phase but, for different reasons, in its ecclesiastical one, the Church actively encouraged quasi-kinship. Although the relation of godkinship to the strategies of heirship which I have discussed earlier is indirect rather than direct, the growth of spiritual kinship indicated the power which the Church had to substitute alternative institutions in the domestic domain. These new arrangements formed part of the more general shift of emphasis from consanguinity to conjugality and from kinship to quasi-kinship (with the various reservations I have made in the course of the discussion) that marked the development of European systems of kinship and marriage, developments which promoted the Church's doctrines and welfare but were also associated with changes in modes of production and of communication.

The history of the Eastern Church in matters of 'fictional' and 'spiritual' kinship was similar to that of its Western counterpart. Spiritual kinship became subject to the marriage prohibitions of 'natural' kinship; on the other hand adoption does not seem to have been set aside quite so firmly, and fictional 'brotherhood' (*affrèrement*) continued to be practised. Despite its condemnation as early as 285 by an imperial decree that declared adoption as a brother inconceivable and set aside any provisions for the inheritance of the patrimony, 'brotherhood' persisted until recent times (e.g. in Georgia, Dragadze 1980) and, like adoption, was subject to marriage prohibitions (Patlagean 1978).

Spiritual kinship epitomises the set of features that I have examined as characterising European patterns of family and marriage from the time of the later Roman Empire. I have argued that these features were developed from a 'Mediterranean' base, that is to say from a certain array of interrelated aspects of marriage and the family which are found in many of the major societies of the Middle East and Asia, which were earlier found in Europe and which are still found on the African and Asian shores of the Mediterranean. These features, which I earlier discussed in terms of the contrast between Africa and Eurasia, between broadly different types of social system, were looked at in the light of Guichard's distinction between oriental and occidental structures and of St Augustine's problems in converting the Anglo-Saxons to Christian ways,

THE AUGUSTINIAN FEATURES

The specific characteristics of the kinship practices of the early Christian period which I examined, included those mentioned by Bede in his version of Pope Gregory's letter to St Augustine, namely:
1. Close marriage
2. The levirate (and marriage to affines)
3. The sending out of children (when applied to wet-nursing; more generally it refers to adoption)
4. Concubinage
    These features are all interrelated and have in common their roles as 'strategies of heirship'. In the fourth century the Christian Church appears to have taken a definite line against the marriage of close kin (such as cousins) and of close affines (such as the brother's widow or husband's brother). At the same time the Roman practices of adoption and adrogation were dropped, while concubinage, in the form either of additional spouses or of irregular unions, was strongly condemned. Plural marriage was not a general feature of the Mediterranean world, certainly not of Rome; but in Rome, Greece and Israel a concubine could be taken as an additional spouse in order to provide an heir. This practice was no longer

condoned. Neither were the irregular unions into which priests and laymen alike continued to enter, despite the considerable attention which the subjects of clerical celibacy and lay monogamy received from the ecclesiastical authorities. However the most significant implication of these restrictions was that they redefined the notion of legitimacy, that is, of what constitutes a legitimate union and legitimate offspring. Legitimacy so defined was a precondition of the right to inherit, either as partner or as offspring; the Church, which largely controlled such matters, did not admit rights unless they derived from a 'valid' marriage.

In the course of my discussion I have touched on a number of other features that are sometimes assumed to distinguish European systems of marriage and the family, some of which have been discussed as part of the hidden economy of kinship. These various features, the ones to which I devoted most attention, were the insistence on the consensus of the partners to the marriage (often associated with a shift from consanguinity to conjugality as well as with the trend towards 'love' and 'partnership'), the virtual impossibility of divorce, the long-term change in marriage transactions from 'brideprice' to dowry and the emergence of a system of bilateral kin terms (sometimes associated with a move from 'patrilineal clans or lineages' or even 'patriarchy').

Some of these features were discussed because other writers had regarded them as basic to the development of family, kinship and marriage in Europe. The analytical problem here has been, first, to define these features in a manner sufficiently precise and relevant to allow the enquiry to be profitably pursued, and, second, to try and isolate those which have been seen as characteristic of advanced agricultural societies generally (though not necessarily appearing in every one), and those which are particular, either individually or in combination, to Europe, to Western Europe or even to England alone.

CONSENT, AFFECTION, LOVE

One of the features discussed was the requirement of the consent of the partners on the one hand and their affection and love in marriage on the other. In some form or other, the consent of the partners to marriage is required by most societies; indeed those with high divorce rates and polygynous marriage can hardly do without it even during the marriage. Agreement, even love, between the partners is not excluded from what are known as arranged, preferred or prescribed marriages. Certainly consent and 'conjugality' were widespread features of early Mediterranean societies – at least among the rich, from whom most of our evidence comes, whether in the form of literature, letters or the graphic arts. Love was not absent either within or outside marriage, though such affections were subject to structural constraints including the formal prohibitions of Church or State and the informal prohibitions of class and rank. In our modern sense, 'love' flourished when such constraints diminished, especially the requirement of parental consent as distinct from that of the partners.[8]

MARRIAGE TRANSFERS

The unity of husband and wife emerges from, and is encapsulated in, the dowry system which forms such an important part of kinship practice of the ancient Middle East. However, while there are variations in emphasis, I do not see the nature of marriage transactions as being either a major distinction between 'European' and 'Mediterranean' patterns nor yet a decisive element in the changes which have occurred in Europe over the past two thousand years, where the shift has been seen as being one of 'brideprice' to dowry. The advent of the German tribes entailed some change in the emphasis of marriage transactions away from the direct dowry of classical times. The gifts from the husband may have included an affinal payment to the bride's father as well as an indirect dowry, first of the paternal then of the bridal kind (*donatio*; morning gift). In the paternal kind, the gift goes to the bride but *through* the father (and sometimes to him as well). However, one payment does not exclude the other; in this case quite the contrary. Neither legal codes nor religious ceremonies by themselves provide sufficient evidence to enable us to reconstruct the system in its entirety. In England the formula, 'with all my worldly goods I thee endow' has continued to be used over the centuries despite all the various changes in marriage payments that have taken

---

[8] This dichotomy is perhaps unusual given the terms of the discussion. For example, of a tightly structured village in southeast India, Gough writes: 'Yet many women showed resilience and daring, and a surprisingly large number of married women carried on illicit affairs out of love rather than for money or from compulsion' (1982: 366).

place, and today even after their disappearance. Initially the explicit reference was to the indirect dowry, or rather the dower, to which a woman was entitled on her husband's death, and to which she acquired a claim at marriage, partly as the result of bringing wealth into the union as part of her own (direct) dowry. In such a direct dowry the difference between a cash payment and land is clearly important, partly because of the implications of transferring immovables when these are the means of primary production, and partly because the first is more straightforwardly a form of paying off the departing daughter (Appendix 2).

There is one other relevant point raised by the dowry. I have treated these marriage transactions as part of the devolution of property to the heirs over the lifetime of the holder. Direct dowry is a woman's portion in a system where property is passed down from the conjugal pair (either separately or together) to children of both sexes. It is her 'lot'. But just as such marriage settlements are not inconsistent with an indirect dowry being provided by the husband either at the marriage or later at his death (i.e. a dower), so they are not incompatible with a woman receiving a further part (or even the main part) of her portion as an inheritance from her parents at their death. In the well-known case of Islamic law a woman receives only half the inheritance of a man, but then she has already been endowed, indirectly at least, at marriage.

DEVOLUTION AND DEMOGRAPHIC VARIABLES

It is clear that the earlier property is handed on, for example, at the offspring's marriage rather than at the parent's death, through dowry rather than through inheritance, the earlier is pressure exerted on reorganising the family's holding. This pressure is even greater when younger sons as well as daughters are entitled to take out their endowment, which happened in fourteenth-century Halesowen (Razi 1981: 7). Such early transmisson may depend upon funds being raised by mortgaging the main estate. The handing over of that estate itself involves the early 'retirement' of the senior generation once the control of the property has been passed down, in the way that Fulani fathers pass on their herds at the marriages of their sons, leaving themselves in the end with but a few cattle and 'one foot in the grave' (Stenning 1958). Transfer at marriage, as practised in Ireland in the 1930s (Arensberg and Kimball 1940), would appear to encourage a later age of marriage because of the reluctance of the present holders either to divide or hand on the estate in its entirety, although the desire of the betrothed pair to accumulate property by other means before marriage may also be a contributory reason. Of course, in considering the process of transmission, it is important to take into account the content of the transfer, which immediately raises questions of class and the nature of the relations of men and women to property widely conceived. The transmission of property which one 'owns' and exploits (as among many African cultivators) has different implications than the transmission of land that one 'owns' but does not exploit (as often with the lands of Church, royalty or nobles) or of land to which one has some kind of tenancy right whether this depends upon the 'voluntary' payment of rent, in money, services or a share of the crop, or upon a more general arrangement of a hierarchical kind. Tenancy of the first kind is likely to encourage greater mobility between holdings (as is an abundance of land and a shortage of labour); the concentration of money rents and the absence of rights of ownership in productive resources is likely to produce less emphasis on the continuity of the farm (as distinct from the family), indeed on the process of transmission as a whole. Moreover the absence of any except minimal property rights will lead to differences in marriage transactions and in domestic relationships.

One of the consequences of a later age of marriage for women is the lengthening of the generation gap. Children are more likely to be looked after by older and even widowed mothers, whose control and management of property are greater even when they remarry. A later age of marriage for both sexes seems to be associated with significant rates of celibacy (that is, the percentage who never marry), and this in turn is linked with the promotion of clerical celibacy (e.g. Smith 1981) that marks the temple-building religions. The reasons for these associations are many and complex. They include the ascetic rejection of gratification that often constitutes one element of stratified societies (Goody 1982), as well as the requisites of a perpetual corporation so clearly understood by the ecclesiastical reformers of the eleventh century. Such abnegation may also comprise more widespread components that derive from a generalised opposition between the sexes. For 'nuptuality', seen by Wrigley and Schofield (1981) as the critical element in the growth of the population of England after the Reformation, is a highly complex variable associated with ideological factors, the structure of domestic groups, the devolution of property and access to economic resources.

Where the bulk of the property is handed on later, either at death, or by the type of indirect dowry that does not take effect until widowhood (the dower), early 'retirement' is not at issue and there would seem to be less pressure to delay marriage for this reason, though other factors may of course militate in favour of later unions. With delayed transfer, an individual has either to work under his father's management or else to go off into service or into some other occupation.

While the laws arising from the Germanic invasions brought a greater emphasis on the indirect dowry, there appears to have been a move towards the direct dowry around the eleventh century (Hughes 1978; App. 2). Direct and indirect dowry are often associated with high and low strata respectively, since they relate to access to valued resources. An increase in those resources, a shift in productive relations, these could bring about a greater emphasis on the direct dowry. In any case, this change must be seen in the light of the Church's interest in the endowment and independence of women, for a direct share in paternal wealth enables a daughter more easily to hand over the 'dowry' for religious and charitable purposes.

The way in which property is passed on may therefore be associated with some of those features which Hajnal and other demographic historians have seen as being typical of European marriage patterns. Some of these are in fact found more widely distributed than in Europe (or Western Europe) alone; high proportions of never-married occur among the peoples of the Indo-Tibetan frontiers (Carrasco 1959: 69; Chen 1949); late marriage for men and women is found in Roman Egypt (Hopkins 1980). The factors behind these forms of domestic life are many, and not necessarily 'functional' in a simple sense. Once established as a trend a particular age of marriage may be difficult to vary; a late or early age may have to continue as a norm in situations very different from that in which it had its functional origins, not as a survival but because people are locked into a particular system. In my own experience the very high differential age of marriage found among the Konkomba of northern Ghana (late for men, early for women) has proved very resistant to modification, despite the wishes of many young men and women, and the pressures from outsiders (Tait 1961; Goody fieldnotes); the brides are simply not there to enable a sudden change to take place. When variations in an already established 'norm' do occur, they may arise from a number of factors which are specific to an individual case; it has been suggested that, at Colyton, Devon, in the later seventeenth century such changes were due to a desire to adjust the number of children to a favourable or disastrous sequence of events, so that the age of marriage reacted to local changes in the economy or the demography (Wrigley 1969: 35).

KIN GROUPINGS

The bilateral organisation of the European family is often contrasted with the system of patrilineal clans (and patriarchal authority) that obtained along the Muslim shores of the Mediterranean – and possibly in parts of Europe itself at an earlier time. I have argued, first, that bilateral kinship and patrilineal descent groups (clans) are not necessarily incompatible, especially where men and women inherit from each other, devolving property in both directions; and that terms like patrilineal are often too vaguely defined to make discussion fruitful. Nonetheless, a contrast does exist between Europe and North Africa, at least with the rural pastoral areas of that region. Moreover, in Europe, changes in the social system, especially in the means of gaining a livelihood, have certainly increased the bilateral reckoning and bilateral balance. Over the last hundred years the system of dowry and inheritance has tended to give way to an investment in upbringing and education, accompanied by the abandonment of direct support for the parental generation who either have to make their own provision for retirement or else to rely upon the government or employer. Not absolutely; differences between countries are related to the methods of financing education, health, housing and pensions; even in England, some middle-class parents still make provision for housing their children, while children offer some support, especially to widowed parents.

This stripping away of all except the minimal ties and duties of kinship had already begun with the Church's dependence on the 'voluntary' alienation of the goods and services which was promoted by its advocacy of the independence of its individual members, or at least of its married couples. The elaborate counting of degrees might seem to stress the weight given to wider bilateral links but the purpose of such computation was to announce the negative rather than the positive obligations of kinsfolk. The emphasis came firmly to be placed on the interlocking elementary families of birth and marriage, though the laity did not always follow subserviently in the Church's footsteps.

Already before the Christian era, the societies of the Ancient Mediterranean and Near East placed some stress on the cognatic calculation of kinship, on 'bilateral' usages of kin terms, on conjugality. But these tendencies developed more strongly under the sectarian pressures of the Christian Church, which insistently played down the role of kinship, a trend that was further bolstered by an advancing economy and a proliferating administration. As we have noted, some resistance to this attempt to switch from the family was offered at all levels but particularly by the richer elements on the one hand, the large landowners, and the semi-independent tribes on the other.

DIVORCE

The doctrines of the Church not only emphasised the bonds of conjugality but they also stressed the importance of consensus, of the initial agreement between the partners in a sacramental union, which could not be dissolved by formal divorce as distinct from informal separation, except by setting aside the marriage because it breached the prohibited degrees or had not been consummated. Here again the emphasis was on the sexual act itself, and only adultery provided sufficient grounds for dissolving an established marriage. But the disapproval of divorce was not peculiar to the Christian Church; marriage was not easily dissolved in Ancient Israel, nor among the upper groups in traditional India and China. Such impediments to divorce were a widespread but not universal feature of what Talcott Parsons has called 'advanced oriental societies', for in Egypt, ancient and modern, divorce rates are 'high'. Nevertheless, low rates of divorce was positively associated (not of course in any absolute way) with the early establishment of a conjugal fund. Once established, a marriage and its fund were difficult to dissolve[9], being brought into being by a 'match', and certainly difficult to reduplicate. Polygyny was of course forbidden, under the

---

[9] It is possibly the case that for marriage, all 'large' transfers, including bridewealth, have a similar effect. Evans-Pritchard's contention that the stability of marriage permits high bridewealth does not affect the correlation itself, although it constitutes an alternative explanatory hypothesis, one which is in my view less satisfactory.

name of bigamy. No second marriage was permitted, unless the first had ended in death. The remarriage of widows was not encouraged though difficult to prevent. The difficulty of divorce and the restrictions placed on remarriage, the absence of plural marriage or even of concubinage, meant that parents who were childless, either through infertility or misfortune, could not seek to provide themselves with heirs by replacing their partners. In other words, they were unable to pursue a strategy of heirship common in the Ancient Middle East and in Eurasia generally. They were denied, by the rules of the Church, the ability to introduce a new partner or 'fictional' children in order to continue their line. Of course the Church's control over divorce and marriage varied over time. While it was concerned about these matters from the fourth century, the enforcement of Church rules increased from the twelfth century onwards, partly through the pressure from rural chapters. In the same period English liturgies encourage marriage at the church door and early in the following century the calling of banns is introduced.

One of the implications of the Church's control over marriage, particularly the termination of marriage, was its concern with the separation of property as well as the separation of persons leading to 'a partial statement and defence of the property rights of women during and after their marriage' (Sheehan 1963a: 109). The interest in marriage was also linked to disposition in wills, and both affected the position of women in important ways, at least in the context of the ecclesiastical mode.

VIRGINITY AND HONOUR

A long-standing feature of Mediterranean societies was the importance placed on the virginity of the bride at her first marriage, a requirement that has both social and religious roots. The prohibition on pre-marital intercourse is found widely throughout Eurasia, but around the Mediterranean the idea was especially strong and linked to concepts of honour and shame. Guichard has observed that these notions appear to be connected more with women in the Mediterranean region and in Southern Europe, and more with property in the North. The difference is doubtless related to the earlier age of female marriage in the South. Where women marry young, the code of honour can be more easily sustained, the breaches being both less frequent and more serious. Moreover the courtship of adolescents is restricted, possibly pre-empted, by parental choice. On the other hand, later marriage for women makes pre-marital chastity more difficult to maintain; choices are freer, courtships are longer and delays in marriage lead if not always to 'illegitimacy', at least to bridal pregnancies and to the acceptance of mantle-children, those 'covered' by the subsequent marriage of their parents.

The timing of marriage is linked to virginity in another way. Formal marriage in front of the church door may be only a second and less important phase of a marriage that was effectively begun either at a public betrothal or at a private 'handfasting', followed by sexual intercourse. The first breaching of a woman's maidenhood seems to have received greater emphasis in the South, though it was everywhere significant. Some have regarded the passage of the morning-gift from husband to wife on the day after the wedding as being, even in the northern half of Europe, a proof of the virginity of the bride which had now been finally destroyed by her husband, once and for all time. If so the disappearance of this particular form of payment may be related to a postponement of the age of marriage combined with the greater emphasis on the validity of the betrothal as a *de facto* marriage, providing a pledge was followed by a sexual act. Indeed Christian marriage was only finally completed when it was consummated by intercourse between husband and wife. One flesh made them one fund. In the custom of Beauvaisis the allocation of a dower (*douaire*) depended upon having kept '*compaignie charnelle*', while that of Ecloo in Flanders stated: 'Le mari et la femme après la consommation du mariage sont communs tant de leur biens que de leur corps' – 'in their goods as in their bodies' (Lotthé 1909, cited Turlan 1957: 486).

The Mediterranean stress on virginity has also to be seen in the context of the control of marriages by kin, who are more concerned with contracting a union which is 'honourable' than one which is based on the agreement, choice or 'love' of the partners. From one point of view, this difference forms part of the opposition between the ecclesiastical stress on consent, and the lay emphasis on honour. But there is a more general factor involved. 'Love' is often associated with choices that run contrary to parental consent or which fall outside the obligations of marriage. It was the very difficulties placed in the way of Romeo and the young Juliet by the hostility of their kin that were in a sense a condition of their love, or of the dominant role it played in their lives. However, the opposition between duty and choice does not imply the total absence of love in those cases where marriage is subject to parental constraints or societal preferences. 'Love' in a conjugal rather than a courting context is not incompatible with arranged unions, whether between kin or not. A strong affectionate component entered into the brother-sister marriages of Roman Egypt as revealed by the letters of the participants in this extreme situation, and such sentiments are found just as often in less extreme situations. But where a greater emphasis is placed on the consensus of the partners than on the wishes of the parents, kin or the wider society, there is possibly more scope for affection. That certainly was the view of the Church, who encouraged personal choice in marriage as strongly as they did in testament. But parents might take the view that such self-regarding unions could more easily end in hate even if they more frequently began in love. It was a situation in which neither the Church nor the parents was a disinterested party.

The influence of the Church can be gauged by looking outside Europe at other regions that have accepted Christianity. There is one important example, that of Ethiopia, to whose special position in Africa I have elsewhere drawn attention. The similarities with Europe are significant, some appearing to derive from the socio-economic system and some from Christianity. There was a large build-up of Church property and lands. At the same time Crummey (1981b) confirms the active role of women in the transmission and sometimes management of landed property. The kinship system of Christian Ethiopia is organised in a bilateral fashion; the norms of the Ethiopian Orthodox Church include: 'the sanctity and indissolubility of (monogamous) marriage, an institution ordained for the procreation of children' (Crummey 1981a: 1). But priests, who are allowed to marry, cannot divorce, while monks and nuns remain celibate. Lay patterns differ considerably, permitting frequent divorce and early marriage with property-conferring contracts. While ecclesiastical law insisted on a wide range of prohibited degrees, the desire of nobles to consolidate their property nevertheless gave rise to close marriages (p. 13).

The suggestion that the Church's rules on marriage and the family were connected not only with ethical and doctrinal considerations, but also with strategies of heirship, may strike some readers as fanciful, objectionable, or both. Let me say, first, that all kinship systems are bolstered or promoted by such moral doctrines, so that these have to be viewed in their social contexts rather than as ethical absolutes; just as close marriage was condemned by the Christian Church for a variety of moral reasons, so close marriage in south India was associated with the purity of a family (Trautmann 1981: 408). Second, in positing a connection between rules of marriage, attitudes to family and kin, and the transfer of property, it may seem that I have allocated the Church a rather calculating role in the development of kinship. But when I refer to the Church acting in its own interest, I do not necessarily mean that the whole Church was monolithically engaged in consciously promoting those interests. The very use of the term 'Church' involves the kind of shorthand that is inevitable in any attempt to cover so extensive a geographical and temporal span. Clearly, the interests of the Church were differentiated, variable over time, ambiguous, and sometimes contradictory. Rules laid down more or less consciously may lose any intentional thrust; ways of action may be adopted through the strength of forces that are never consciously understood; the explicit intentions of an action may be less important than the implicit connotations. Moreover, I do not necessarily imply by 'interests' that the concerns of a particular individual or corporation are purely self-oriented, for such a body may direct its charitable and other efforts towards the outside world. I am talking about the means by which ends are achieved, whether or not those means are aspects of the actor's intention. In such a traditional body most decisions are made on the basis of precedents which need have no very direct relation with present interests or alternative ways of acting. Moreover, decision-making was often very dispersed or diffuse. But in the long run, I do assume some kind of a relationship between actions and interests, especially when a new set of norms emerges to replace the old.

The emphasis on interest is also part of an expository mode, and I am certainly aware that in developing one line of argument, I may have tended to set aside other factors of importance. The attempt to sketch out certain long-term trends in the domestic organisation of societies in relation to their modes of livelihood has been called 'historical materialist' and I do not wish in any way to set aside the influences that the phrase implies. I take such an approach as a point of departure and one that generates useful and interesting hypotheses; but if it promotes the economy to a position unjustified by the data, then I am at fault. It is not my aim to 'explain' religious systems in economic terms, but to draw out some of the implications, particularly in the realm of kinship, marriage and the family, of the rapid growth of the major organisation in society – other than the State (or government) itself – which required massive support for the continuity of its operations. Such support came from income and endowments. But endowments had to be built up and once accumulated were always liable to depredation; hence accumulation had to be a continuous process.

The extent to which these practices were introduced in order to encourage this process is arguable, though there is much evidence to suggest that such was their effect. But certainly, the Church's control over marriage was subsequently used for this purpose. I conclude with one striking example from the very north of Scotland in the sixteenth century, which was one of the areas where the Church, this time in cahoots with the State, used its influence in order to gain political and economic control in the domestic domain over regions that could be seen as both 'tribal' and 'pagan'.

The extraordinary accumulation of property by the Christian Church in Western Europe, achieved, as we have seen, through the donation and purchase of land, was made possible by the development of a system of 'advanced agriculture', helped on its way by the introduction of the plough by the Celts and the Romans (possibly earlier), which could be exploited by ecclesiastical landlords on an extensive scale. We have tried to understand the mechanisms behind this accumulation, to see how it was accomplished in the first centuries of the Church's life through changes wrought upon the existing patterns of marriage and the family, of kinship and affinity. But on the northernmost Gaelic periphery of Europe, the full impact of the Church was felt only at a much later date, and in the sixteenth century it is still possible to observe some of the actual processes of change at work, at least in the upper levels of society. For here we meet a situation similar to that described by Bede, where Christianity was in the throes of becoming a dominant ideology and the Church was establishing its organisation in an area where its influences had hitherto been small or non-existent.

The province of Strathnaver in the extreme north-west of Scotland, known as Duthaich 'Ic Aoidh, the Land of the Mackays, constituted the northern outpost of Gaeldom after the Germanic-speaking peoples of the Viking Age had conquered the Islands of Scotland, as well as much of the land of Caithness and Sutherland. The earliest administrative link between Strathnaver and its neighbours was provided by its inclusion in the bishopric of Caithness established under the new religious organisation promoted initially by Queen Margaret, but more particularly by her son, David I (1124–1153), during whose reign both the feudal order and monasticism were strongly developed (Duncan 1975: 134; Mitchison 1970: 19).

The social organisation of the Highlands appears to have been based upon what has been called the 'conical clan', with a firm structure of authority and ownership under a hereditary chieftain. This was very different from the unilineal descent groups (the clans and lineages) of societies which are found today in Africa or in the rural Middle East. The clans were internally stratified into chief and subject, though held together by common bonds in which putative descent and dependence were inextricably mixed. 'Whether his clansmen considered themselves to be Mackays in the sense of a common descent from a heroic ancestor called Aodh, or in the sense of being Mackay's vassals, is beyond surmise' (Grimble 1965: 14). Their fictions of descent are 'antiquarian speculation' rather than 'tribal folk memories'.

This structure was threatened by the development of the Scottish kingdom and the advance of Christendom, whose eventual domination was secured, at least in part, by applying or manipulating new rules of legitimacy, both for spouses and for children. Up to the seventeenth century every known marriage of a Chief of Mackay had been made outside the clan, although, since 'until the sixteenth century the Chiefs invariably chose their wives from the principal houses of Scottish Gaelic society' (p. 14), these marriages were within the same social group. However, 'even exogamy' (that is, out-marriage), writes Grimble, 'could not protect the Chiefs of Mackay, living in a world of limited choice ... from marriage within the uncanonical degrees that required a church dispensation. Nor could a marriage of the most solemn dynastic kind necessarily be celebrated with sufficient formality in the eyes of a church that maintained no ministry in the province' (p. 15).[10] Whatever they did, they could not prevent the approaching powers from regarding the marriages as illegitimate.

[10] See Anton (1958: 89–102).

Once it had defined the 'legitimate' rules and form of marriage, the dominant power, whether the Scottish State or the Catholic Church, could then bastardise claimants whose parents were married by local custom. The Mackays made every effort to prevent such accusations, since 'the succession of legitimate heirs to their chieftainship was at stake' (p. 15). Aodh, Chief of Mackay, who secured recognition from James IV of his title to Strathnaver in 1496, also obtained formal legitimation of his two sons under the Privy Seal in 1511.

Behind Mackay's efforts lay the crumbling of ancient power and the northward extension of Norman feudalism. The former kingdom of Earl Thorfinn the Mighty was split into three to form Orkney, Caithness and Sutherland in 1201. William the Lion established the earldom of Sutherland which later fell into the hands of the Gordons. In the early sixteenth century the Gordons acquired it first by obtaining a 'brieve of idiocy' against the incumbent Sinclair, Earl John, then later by declaring his son by his first marriage an idiot, and his son by his second marriage a bastard, despite the fact that the mother, the Countess, was drawing her widow's terce. Finally, in the name of his wife, Elizabeth, daughter of Earl John by his first wife, Adam Gordon claimed the earldom. Against a background of intrigue and manipulation of this kind, the ruling Mackays clearly wanted to establish their claims as securely as possible *vis à vis* the king, which they did by performing services for James V of Scotland, including giving him assistance in suppressing the very Gaelic population from whom they came.

Their efforts were set at nought by the death of James V after the battle of Solway Moss against the English in 1542. The king was succeeded by his week-old daughter, Mary Queen of Scots. Hamilton of Arran became regent on behalf of the Catholic party, while his rival, Stewart of Lennox, committed himself to the Protestants, who looked in turn to the English. Lennox's brother was Robert, Bishop of Caithness, an unconsecrated youth who tried to keep in favour with both parties by marrying his sister, Helen (a widow who had already had an illegitimate son by her cousin, James V) to the Catholic Earl of Sutherland, to whom he conveyed the greater part of his episcopal properties for safe-keeping.

Mackay's son had been captured by the English at Solway Moss and apparently committed himself to support the Protestant cause in Scotland. In 1544, two years after that battle, he took part in an unsuccessful attack upon the regent in Glasgow. In 1550 he succeeded his father, at a time when the Catholic party of the queen was in the ascendant. Moreover, when the new Earl of Sutherland was in France, Sinclair, the son of the former heir to that earldom who had first been bastardised and then murdered, was murdered in his turn. He was cousin to the new Chief Mackay who thereupon proceeded to march into Sutherland only to be chased out by the Gordons. Mackay expected to lose all his titles when Sutherland, who was the northern Lieutenant, returned. However, the latter was anticipated by the Bishop of Orkney, employing the same legal devices that Adam Gordon had used in Sutherland. 'In October 1551, the Bishop registered a precept, showing that Aodh's grandparents had not been properly married, that Aodh's father was consequently illegitimate and that Aodh was therefore incapable of inheriting from him' (Grimble 1965: 29).

The Bishop of Orkney, Robert Reid, then made an agreement with the ex-chief which stated that although the Mackay lands were now in the hands of the queen, Aodh could have them back for 4,000 merks Scots, apparently paid to the Bishop; he obtained the overlordship of Strathnaver in 1553 and then bestowed the heritable use on Mackay.

In the story of the Mackays, the power to recognise 'marriages' and hence to bastardise the children of 'non-marriages', was used by Church and State to gain control over a quasi-independent chiefdom and then to confiscate the lands of its ruler. 'Kinship' mechanisms were employed to achieve political, religious and economic domination. The 'ideology' was provided by the Church, the 'force' by the State.

The interests of the Church and State in the accumulation of territory and property did not always go so conveniently hand in hand. Not only were there constant local problems, but the extent and rapidity of the accumulation of property by the Church, combined with its limited capacity to defend its gains except by religious sanctions (that is, by doctrine or ideology, together with the more specific tools of the curse, the blessing and excommunication), made it open to the kind of depredation that was successfully practised by Charlemagne and Henry VIII on the Catholic Church of France and England, by Lenin on the Orthodox Church of Russia and by Muhammad Ali on Muslim possessions in Egypt. The appeal was obvious. During the Reformation in Germany, 'some of the Catholic princes were scarcely more scrupulous than the Lutherans in seizing the property of the religious Orders' (Lea 1900: 10); at the Reichstag in Augsburg in 1524 both parties seriously proposed the secularisation of all of the Church's property in Germany. In nineteenth-century Mexico the confiscation of Church lands appealed to both conservatives and liberals (Bazant 1971: 5); in Spain the conservative landowners soon learned to defend the practice. Nevertheless, the Church continued in its attempts to accumulate property, 'heedless of the temptations which it was offering and of the risk which it might run whenever circumstances should weaken its awful authority over the minds of princes and peoples. It did not anticipate that the time would come when those who might shrink from spoliation would reconcile their consciences to the euphemism of "secularization" ' (Lea 1900: 10).

The process of secularisation has been considered by many authors in relation to such ideological and economic developments as the rise of capitalism, the growth of industrial society and the demystification of the world. But it must also be seen as directly linked, not only to patterns of ownership and occupation, of accumulation and investment, of 'rational' authority and bureaucracy, but also to domestic life. The reduction in the range of the prohibited degrees of marriage, the freedom to marry the dead wife's sister, the legalisation of adoption, the increasing ease of divorce, the acceptability of weddings in the registry office, has to be seen as linked to the weakening of the Church's power to accumulate property, and a concomitant weakening in its wealth, position and influence.

This essay has attempted to cover so vast a span of time and space that it must appear superficial in its treatment to many specialist scholars. Such an approach was inevitable since my concern was with broad problems of change in the patterns of family and marriage in Western Europe, looked at against the wider background of comparative sociology (or 'social anthropology'). These problems are ones which have long puzzled me in thinking about the country in which I live compared to those I have studied in Africa, India and the Mediterranean. What I have presented is an attempt to sketch out an explanation. It suggests in very general terms why certain major changes in the patterns of kinship in Britain and Western Europe took place in conjunction with the expansion of the Christian Church and its doctrines. It was these changes that set aside some of the earlier practices of the indigenous peoples as well as those of the Roman legal codes and of the Old and New Testaments themselves, leading to an opposition between the new 'European' and the older 'Mediterranean' orders, the 'occidental' and the 'oriental' structures, the Christian and the non-Christian modes.

For the Church to grow and survive it had to accumulate property, which meant acquiring control over the way it was passed from one generation to the next. Since the distribution of property between generations is related to patterns of marriage and the legitimisation of children, the Church had to gain authority over these so that it could influence the strategies of heirship. This essay has attempted to show how this came about and what it brought about.

Appendix 1. Kin groups: clans, lineages and lignages

In drawing his contrast between Eastern and Western structures, Guichard expresses a common view when he describes the Eastern mode of descent as 'strictly patrilineal (only kinship in the paternal line is reckoned)', the Western as 'clearly bilineal' (i.e. cognatic), great importance being attached to the maternal family and to affinity. On the other hand the medievalist, Duby, analyses the growth of the agnatic *lignage* in the eleventh century, while Stone, the English historian of the early modern period, writes approvingly of the changes in England from 1560 to 1640 as a 'shift from a "lineage society" characterized by bounded horizons and particularized modes of thought, to the more universalistic standard of values of a "civil society" ' (1977: 134). The disagreement as to the structure of European kin groups goes back to earliest times, for while writers like Philpotts (1913) and Lancaster (1958) have emphasised the bilateral nature of Anglo-Saxon kinship, Charles-Edwards has insisted upon the presence of agnatic lineages (1972).

The discussion is confusing firstly because of the way in which the terms are used and secondly because of the hidden assumptions about the nature of the opposition between, say, agnatic and cognatic or between extended and conjugal families. In many cases the arguments can be resolved by a sharper definition of terms and by appreciating that a system of agnatic clans or lineages does not exclude the active presence of bilateral kinship.

Kin groups, groupings, ranges and reckoning
Let us begin by trying to clarify the terms of the argument, since words like patrilineal and bilateral, lineage and clan, agnatic and cognatic, are used by various authors with considerable variations in meaning.

In medieval times the Latin terms *agnatio* and *cognatio* sometimes meant paternal and maternal kin but more usually the classical

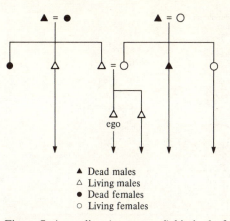

▲ Dead males
△ Living males
● Dead females
○ Living females

Figure 7. Ascending (or personal) kindred of ego to two ascending generations

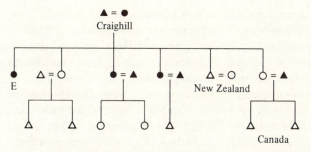

Figure 8. Descending kindred of Craighill family involved at death of E

usage applied by which *cognatio* referred to the whole bilateral range of kin on both sides, one's ego-oriented or personal kindred, that is, the range of kin traced through father and mother (Figure 7). Bilateral networks of this kind, sometimes forming (overlapping) groupings, exist in virtually all human societies, as is the case with the descending kindred, the offspring of a conjugal pair through males and females over 'n' generations (Figure 8). For both these types of kin range or grouping are based upon the bilateral character of the conjugal family, with children tracing filiation through both mother and father.

On the other hand, unilineal modes of reckoning trace ties through only one sex, male in the case of patrilineal (sometimes

224   *Appendix 1*

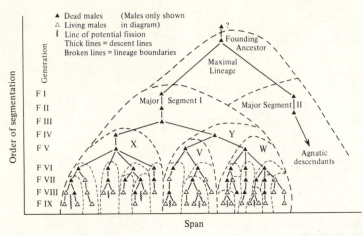

Figure 9. The paradigm of a lineage system (from Fortes 1945: 34)

'agnatic') systems, female in the case of matrilineal (sometimes 'uterine') ones. Such modes of reckoning are used to create exclusive, that is, non-overlapping descent groups (UDGs, unilineal descent groups), clans or lineages of either the patrilineal or matrilineal variety. By 'clan' we mean the largest such unit, the members of which acknowledge common descent (e.g. from the eponymous Donald of MacDonald) but are unable to specify the exact ties. Within the more restricted lineage, specific genealogical ties are recognised (Figure 9). Unlike kindreds such unilineal groups usually have particular names (e.g. MacDonald) as well as technical terms (e.g. *clann*, *sept*) so that membership is more or less unambiguous, though in some cases shifts do occur and in others proximity plays as much importance as filiation.

I have touched here upon the membership and organisation of descent groups. But links of filiation to one or both parents may be used in a variety of other contexts, for the inheritance of property or for succession to office. These modes of reckoning have different implications depending upon the context. Succession to office often has different rules, since office is (virtually) indivisible and exclusive, whereas membership of a kin group is available, indeed a necessity, for all. Hence the fact that the Anglo-Saxon genealogies of the segments of royal dynasties, which are mainly concerned with succession to high office, are agnatic does not mean that we are in the presence of a system of patrilineal clans or lineages that operate more widely through society. Secondly, the existence of bilateral inheritance or devolution is perfectly compatible with a certain type of patrilineal clan. We have an example of the first in the Gonja kingdom of West Africa (Goody 1967), and of the second in the clans of Ancient Israel or of early twentieth-century China.

Apart from contextual differentiation of this kind, there is no contradiction in the co-presence of patrilineal and matrilineal clans in the same society; of these double descent systems, there are a number of examples from West Africa (Goody 1956, 1969). And because of the essentially bilateral nature of kinship (or the family) as distinct from descent, a member of any patrilineal descent group will inevitably have an important tie with the patrilineal descent group of his mother (the members of which are his mother's brothers). In a system of double descent (i.e. with coexisting patrilineal and matrilineal descent groups) he will also have an important tie with his father's matrilineal clan; these ties are what Fortes has called 'complementary filiation' (1953).

In a condensed fashion I have tried to sketch out some of the main morphological possibilities. But the interpersonal relationships and collectivities involved clearly have different behavioural contents and in very general terms these are sometimes classified as stronger or weaker. For example Guichard regards Arab lineages as stronger than Roman because women do not change their affiliation at marriage (though the same appears to have been true of Rome from the second century B.C.). Gluckman (1950, 1971) and Leach (1957) have taken precisely the opposite line, assuming that the strength of a lineage can be measured by its ability to absorb incoming wives. Both these perspectives require some modification since at every marriage some rights in women (as in men, children and property) are transferred, but never, except in the case of slaves and possibly concubines, the total quantum of rights that her kin have in her or that she has in them. The error arises partly from the adoption of exchangist views concerning the transfer of women at marriage, which appear to confuse physical movement (which most conjugal activity requires) with the acquisition of rights. Individuals (in this case, women) are treated as objects rather than as 'bundles of rights' which can be re-allocated in various ways.

There are problems to do not only with the 'strength' of descent groups but even more so with the exclusivity (i.e. strictness) of reckoning relations in one line or another. For example, Guichard looks upon oriental structures as strictly patrilineal, that is, where only kinship in the paternal line is reckoned. While exclusivity may apply to the membership of unilineal descent groups, it does not necessarily apply to other spheres of the social system and cannot apply to the kinship system as a whole. As I have argued, we have first to specify the context in which the reckoning takes place, whether it has to do with membership of a kin group (e.g. 'descent'), succession to office, the inheritance of property, or some more general context of filiation (kinship). As far as the latter is concerned, virtually no system excludes a recognition of the kin both of the father and of the mother. As far as the former goes, even patrilineal clans may sometimes recruit through females, just as they never exclude recognition of maternal kin, whether these relatives are found within or outside the clan.

Let me discuss the latter point first. I make the qualification because the Scottish clan, like the Arab counterpart, was never exogamous; that is, in-marriage was allowed, though I do not know that it was ever encouraged as in the Arab case. When in-marriage of this kind occurs, then both parents belong to the same clan, and the mother's sub-group of that clan is obviously important to the off-spring. When a marriage took place outside the clan, then a child of such a union was sometimes chosen to serve as an intermediary in a dispute between the two groups, as has been reported for many parts of the world. On a rather trivial level the continuing importance of the mother's clan is illustrated by the fact that it is a recognised feature of Scottish custom – though presumably of no greater antiquity than the linking of tartan to clan (Grimble 1980: 215ff) – that a man can wear the kilt of his mother's clan as well as his own.

It is therefore mistaken to take the part played by the maternal lineage (or maternal family, or maternal uncle) as an indication of the weakness of agnatic relationships, much less of the earlier existence of matriliny. The mother's brother (and the mother's patrilineage) has an intrinsic role to play for the members of a patrilineal descent group, a role that is no way incompatible with the system itself (Radcliffe-Brown 1924, 1940; Goody 1969: 39ff).[1]

The recruitment through females to a patrilineal clan is described

[1] On the importance of the mother's brother, see Homans 1941: 131,191–374, and Martindale 1977.

for many parts of the world, though variations occur in the ease and method by which it is done. Firstly, there is the loose attachment associated with the residence of non-agnates among the dominant patrilineal group. Where clans are localised, i.e. where they have specific territories, there will almost certainly be some members of other clans living in the same area. In the first place there are wives (and mothers) from those clans. Then sisters who have married out may return with their young children following the break-up of their conjugal family through widowhood, divorce or separation. In Ireland, for example, it was possible for a man to become attached to his maternal kin group as if it was his paternal one (Charles-Edwards 1972: 28). Grown men and women may arrive as refugees, slaves or as supporters. In the eyes of outsiders, such individuals may be confused with clansmen proper, if only because the name of the clan and the territory it occupies are often the same. But certainly in Africa, residence alone rarely carries with it full membership of a unilineal descent group.

However the attachment of non-agnates to a clan may be a more deliberate matter. Among the LoDagaa of northern Ghana, the children of an unmarried girl became members of the mother's patrilineal clan, though some distinction between the children of women and of men is initially retained. While we can speak here of maternal filiation, this mode of recruitment is concealed by a jural fiction as far as the descent group is concerned, for this unit remains resolutely patrilineal in ideology as well as in organisation.

The lineage and the lignage

A related problem of definition that requires some clarification, not only for general comparative purposes but mainly for elucidating the development of European kinship, is the nature of the 'lineage'. I have already spoken of the 'segmentary lineage' in reference to Africa and Guichard includes the *lignage* among the characteristic features of oriental structures. Both he and I are using the terms for the kind of branching, segmentary group analysed by Evans-Pritchard among the Nuer, following a usage of some earlier anthropologists though the concept was developed by writers such as Ibn Khaldun and Durkheim. However misunderstandings inevitably arise because the original term, more current in French than in English, was derived from medieval usage and has been employed in a variety of ways. Some use the word to denote a specific line (or lines) of ascendants, usually traced through men but sometimes through women, as in the phrase 'a man of noble *lignage*'. Others take it to mean an aristocratic 'house' (*maison*) whose identity over time is assured by a landed estate, claims to office, titles or other relatively exclusive rights. It is the second usage that Duby (1977: 10) adopts when he talks of the appearance of *lignages*, agnatic in character and practising primogeniture, at the time of the establishment of a feudal, chivalric aristocracy in the latter half of the tenth century or the beginning of the eleventh.[2] These are the '" maisons" nobles, carrying a name that is handed down from generation to generation and from male to male, and endowed with a sense of genealogy (*conscience généalogique*)' (Guichard 1977: 88).[3]

There is some evidence for this process of agnatic consolidation at a yet earlier date. Following Vinogradoff, Bullough draws attention to the emphasis that substantial landowners gave, already in ninth-century Germany, to 'agnatic kin at the expense of cognatic' (1969: 17). After a period lasting until the eleventh century, during which the process was possibly slowed down, there was further consolidation. While small landowners, whether peasants or gentry, wanted to maximise their cognatic kin ties, what mattered to the magnates was unchallenged possession of lands and office: 'in this context the important relationships were those of descendance or "lineage", and cousinly relationships were more often a source of tension and dissension than the reverse' (p. 17). Here the *lignage* is a narrow agnatic line of filiation rather than a branching lineage (descent group) of the African or Chinese kind.

When Duby also writes of the 'tightening of lineage structures' in northern France in the latter part of the eleventh century, it is this same process to which he refers. The emerging stability arising from a decrease in war and pillage involved a shift to a hereditary system. For now the aristocratic patrimony had to be preserved not by force

---

[2] 'En réalité, dans l'aristocratie de la région mâconnaise, à partir de la fin du Xe siècle, un mouvement devient nettement perceptible, qui conduit de structures de parenté relativement lâches, à des structures beaucoup plus rigides. Le lignage se constitue, avec les progrès de l'indivision et de la primauté des mâles. Le nom de la famille apparaît alors, puis les armoiries' (Duby 1977: 10). See also Génicot 1962.

[3] Guichard does point to the differences (p. 89) between these Western and the Eastern lineages, the former being marked by 'bilateral' features, e.g. by the bilateral prohibitions on marriage, insisted upon by the Church, and the bilateral claims involved in blood-guilt, insisted upon by the civil authorities.

but by adopting a system of devolution based on primogeniture, where a younger son only took a legitimate wife if she was an heiress (1978: 11). As a result, he claims, marriageable women were available as brides to those of lower rank, so that, as in any hypogamous system, the mother's brother often ranked higher than the father, a point made for Germany as well. In the case of the unmarried males, the bachelors formed turbulent bands of young men dedicated to chivalric adventure and to courtly love.

Duby's view on the 'solidarity of the aristocratic *lignage*' is related to changes in tenurial practice, namely the increasing tendency to treat family land as impartible (Duby 1972; Martindale 1977: 28). Such consolidation can also be seen as the denial of the wider lineage ties (based on sibling solidarity) in favour of a noble line of filiation that placed a great emphasis on marriage and the 'quest for rich heiresses'.[4]

In the course of this interesting argument, Duby appears to use the term *lignage* (translated as 'lineage') as generally synonymous with house (*domus*) and 'race', which, according to Flandrin, was also the case in French dictionaries of the seventeenth and eighteenth centuries when it had ceased to be a current term (1979: 11,15). Flandrin himself is mainly concerned with the family in a later period but he does refer to the earlier process whereby the *lignage* became 'more narrowly based under the influence of the patrilinear tendencies which preceded the introduction of patronymic surnames' (p. 25). However the introduction of such names has been attributed to another quite different factor, namely, the diminution of the stock of first names through the practice of naming children after godparents rather than grandparents (Bennett 1979). Subsequently 'the ties of lineal solidarity became weaker', a process he associates with the reduction of the impediments on marriage to kin. Lineal solidarity was at its strongest between the tenth and twelfth centuries when the ban on cousin marriage was at its most extensive; Flandrin even suggests that canonical legislation may have been responding to changes in lineal solidarity.

Flandrin's thesis runs somewhat counter to that of Duby (1978) who insists upon the opposition between ecclesiastical and lay (or at least noble) patterns of kinship and marriage. The period during which he sees a weakening of lineage solidarity appears to corre-

---

[4] On the 'quest for rich heiresses' in twelfth-century literature, see Duby 1973.

spond to that of Duby's tightening of lineage structures, one which Hughes also regards as the time when lineages were strengthened by the adoption of a direct dowry in cash (1978: 289). The reason behind this apparent divergence lies partly in Flandrin's identification of the *lignage* of the tenth and eleventh centuries (which he distinguishes from 'race', 'house' and 'household') with what is often called in English a kindred, or more technically 'a descending kindred' (and by some a 'bilateral descent group'), that is to say, 'an assemblage of individuals who descended or claimed to descend from a common ancestor'. To this specification Flandrin adds 'either in the male or the female line', though the kindred would best be described as recruited 'both in the male and female lines' (or better, 'both through males and females'). It is the individuals so defined that exercise rights over one another, as for example, in the 'lineal repurchase right' (*le retrait lignager*, the right of first refusal of lands belonging to kin).[5] The phrase '*either* in the male *or* the female line' characterises eligibility to what Freeman has called 'utrolateral' groupings (1961; Firth 1963) where there is the alternative of attaching oneself (or of being attached) either to the father's or to the mother's side. This type of linkage is activated in Europe as elsewhere, when an estate (or title or office) passes through sons and daughters rather than going to more distant males. But both these types of grouping need to be further distinguished from the kind of 'personal kindred' so important in Anglo-Saxon England in the context of the feud. The same grouping is apparently referred to in the sixteenth-century account of Corsican feuds in which all a man's kinsfolk to the third degree of relationship were involved (Flandrin 1979: 16). This grouping is certainly not unilineal, and it is ego-oriented rather than ancestor-oriented, consisting (unlike the descending kindred) of a grouping unique to each individual, the members of which he can call upon for assistance in feud.

These different usages of *lignage* may represent a set of multiple meanings borne by the term at one point in time; again they may reflect changes over time; and finally they may arise out of the conceptual difficulties of the interpreter. In any case the multiplicity

[5] The definition of *retrait lignager* needs expanding. It appears relatively late in French law (first mentioned in Picardy in 1210) and is clearly a successor to the earlier custom known as *laudatio parentum* of the Franks (found as early as 820) whereby kinsfolk (heirs) had to agree in writing to the alienation of property (Olivier-Martin 1929: 273).

of usages itself brings out the problem involved in using actor concepts as analytic terms, especially when that analysis covers a large span in time and space. Sufficient has been said to show that these *lignages* have little to do with the lineages of the Bedouin of North Africa, the Nuer of the southern Sudan and the Tallensi of northern Ghana. For this reason it would perhaps be better to speak of them as 'houses' or alternatively to preserve the French form. They are organised around a 'pedigree' of the kind by which the House of Windsor sometimes traces its fanciful descent from Brut of Troy; contrast the 'genealogy' that organises a branching lineage, of the kind analysed prototypically by Evans-Pritchard for the Nuer (1940). In this African context, the lineage is a type of unilineal descent group, large in scale and internally segmented, in which the relations between the members are calculated in precise genealogical terms, not necessarily biological for they may of course be putative, invented. In principle, the span of the lineage is closely related to the order of segmentation, or less technically and less precisely, the spread to the depth, the numbers to the genealogy. Clearly there are points in common (e.g. 'agnaticism') between the two usages. But the differences are very marked and arise from differences in the social systems, especially in the modes of livelihood and the type of polity.

The question of the definition of lineage or clan is not merely an academic matter; it influences what is to be explained and the kind of explanation to be offered. In his recent review of studies relating to the origins of the 'European marriage pattern' in England, which takes Hajnal's variables and argument as its starting point, R. M. Smith draws attention to the widely held assumption that fertility is generally higher in societies with 'corporate' kin groups, because children are especially favoured; by contrast 'bi-lateral kinship societies usually have a cognatic descent system with a low emphasis placed on fertility' (1979: 99). I know of no evidence that, holding constant other variables such as the productive system, would appear to support this statement; Africa is a test case. But that is not the immediate point. The author links these observations with the presence of unilineal descent groups ('lineages') in fifteenth-century Tuscany and their absence in England, with its cognatic system, that is, with the opposition that Macfarlane sees between ancestor-focused descent systems and the ego-oriented ones that are said to characterise the English.

The *lignages* of Tuscany were certainly very different from the corporate unilineal descent groups to which the theoretical assumption refers. While I do not suppose that Italian kinship was precisely the same as the English, *lignages* were also to be found in England (Martindale 1977). While effective bonds of kinship may have spread more widely in Italy, the terminology shows them to be equally cognatic or bilateral (Appendix 3). The form of English medieval terminology was not basically different from that which obtained in the rest of Europe including Tuscany. Indeed the change from Roman (and Anglo-Saxon) usage seems to have originated in Italy itself.

With regard to social groupings, England appears to have had from an early period an organisation of social groupings based upon the personal kindred (i.e. ego-oriented). But the existence of such groupings is not incompatible with those of an ancestor-oriented kind, not only at the dynastic level but also on a more informal one. For example, on the death of my Scottish grandmother, her property was divided out among her many children and grandchildren on the basis not of individuals (*per capita*) but of stocks (*per stirpes*). This grouping, a descending, 'ancestor-oriented' kindred, was partly held together (or apart) by the interest in the property, and there is evidence of similar considerations being at work from the earliest period of English and Scottish history.

Such a grouping is not altogether dissimilar from the so-called *lignages* or houses of medieval Tuscany (and of propertied families in England), though their extent and the degree of agnatic emphasis varied from time to time and from society to society, especially where office was concerned (for this is necessarily less divisible than property). But in any case these *lignages* (which Flandrin sees as 'cognatic' rather than agnatic) are very different from the type of corporate descent group characteristic of, say, African lineage systems and referred to in the suggested correlation with low fertility.

Patrilineal or bilateral?

Having made some necessary distinctions we can perhaps look again at the opposition between the patrilineal or agnatic structures of the Orient and the bilateral or cognatic ones of the Occident. At the same time we can reconsider the general view that the development of European patterns of kinship consists in the substitution of bilateral for patrilineal reckoning (with the periodic strengthening of the agnatic *lignage*). These views raise the same kind of difficulty as the contention that extended kinship (family, household) gave way to a conjugal (elementary, nuclear) unit. It is not a matter of replacement. The shifts involve the disappearance of patrilineal descent groups, leaving the bilateral core of kinship as the dominant form; or of stripping away the more distant ties in a bilateral system. The bilaterality was always there; even where unilineal descent groups existed in the major societies of Europe and Asia, they were often given a bilateral 'twist' by the existence of 'diverging devolution', the transmission of parental property to women as well as to men by endowment or by inheritance, which meant that joint holdings were constantly being partially dissolved and reconstituted. And the dowry, which continued to be important in many English marriages till the First World War – and in France up to more recent times (*Code Civil* art. 1387ff) – was present in early Mediterranean civilisations, sometimes in a largely indirect form but often in a mainly direct one, a pre-mortem inheritance.

The clan systems of the Ancient Mediterranean, the *genos* of Greece, the 'tribes' of Israel, the agnatic groups of Rome, which were characterised by these 'bilateral' features, gradually disappeared. But there were areas of Europe in which groups of this kind did continue to function. In the early medieval period, the system obtaining in Ireland, and hence in Scotland after the Dalriadic settlement in the mid sixth century, was clearly patrilineal in one sense, as we see from existing clan and personal names. Like the suffix 'son' in Scandinavia, the prefix 'O' (or Uí) in Ireland (e.g. O'Neill) or Mac in Scotland (e.g. MacDonald) were indications of agnatic filiation. In early Ireland and Scotland these names were also used to designate large-scale descent groups, the members of which traced links to a putative ancestor (e.g. Donald) and were divided into sub-groups or septs. These clans were associated with rights to office as well as to estates. The High Kingship of Ireland was vested in a specific clan (or clans) and the territory of the realm was seen as divided into districts associated with each clan, though these arrangements were by no means immutable.

According to Charles-Edwards, before the changes of the seventh century, Irish society 'had a kinship system based upon a lineage consisting of the agnatic descendants of the great-grandfather or the youngest generation of the lineage' (1972: 15). Above this was a further level, for ego had more relatives who themselves belonged to 'lineages' of their own. 'His whole kindred was a group of related lineages comprising all those descended from ego's great-great-great-grandfather' (p. 16). Since the words used for kinsmen in Irish, Welsh and Breton were the same, he argues that they had the same kinship system as recorded in the Old Irish Laws and brought across by the invading Celtic tribes in the first millennium B.C. Holding that similarities in the concepts of the hide – the basic holding of one freeman cultivating with a plough – must be derived from a common European past, he proposes that the kinship systems themselves were also similar.

The description that is offered could as well be of a descending kindred as of an agnatic lineage. The question is not to define patrilineal as against bilateral societies or kinship systems but to discover whether groups or groupings of such and such a kind were recognised or utilised by the actors. Some authors have insisted upon the agnatic character of Irish kinship, and Bullough, drawing a comparison with Rome, regards it as the only such example in early medieval Europe (1969: 13). Some have commented on its bilateral character, especially in the context of the feud as distinct from succession to office among the aristocracy. In fact we know very little of the organisation of commoners (Ó Corráin 1972, 1978). In any case the reciprocal obligations of Irish kin were clearly very different from those of Rome, not least because of the need for 'mutual self-help and protection, vendetta and settlement by composition for which the kin-group had collective responsibilities' (Bullough 1969: 13).

Among the Germanic peoples who established themselves in the Roman Empire between the late fourth and late sixth centuries, the law codes laid down similar vengeance responsibilities for kin. These were often traced in a bilateral manner. Despite this widely held view that Anglo-Saxon 'kindreds' were bilateral in character, anyhow for the purposes of compensation and vengeance, Charles-Edwards argues that the kinship system was agnatic, basing his discussion partly on Welsh laws and partly on the nature of royal genealogies. Certainly there was some emphasis given to the patriline, especially in the context of succession to high office, but it is far from clear that there were patrilineages in the sense that the author seems to be implying by his references to the Nuer and the Chinese. For in both these societies individuals are specifically allocated to *named* patrilineal descent groups, which are important in a range of social contexts although different in significant ways that are related to the political, economic and religious systems.

Unlike the Celts, the Germanic tribes appear to have lacked such named groups and the agnatic character of the kinship system has been denied by many writers. Martindale claims that there is no reason to think that 'the upper ranks of society were organised into lineages which were, for all significant purposes, patrilineal' (1977: 39–40). She supports her argument by referring to the significance of the maternal line among aristocrats of the early Middle Ages (Bullough 1969; Leyser 1979)[6] and draws attention to the need to distinguish patrilineal lineages from the lines of agnatic filiation (*lignages* or *lignées*), especially in relation to the position of women. If we set aside dynastic reckoning, the conclusion seems acceptable, although not because of the importance of maternal kinship which is perfectly compatible with patrilineal clanship.

In Scotland groupings of kin were also very important, again partly because of the nature of the political system. 'Traditionally it is the country where kings are weak and kindreds strong, and feuds raged endlessly and bloodily' (Wormald 1980: 57). Certainly the feud continued in a quasi-legal form under the monarchy until the beginning of the seventeenth century. Significantly it was in the Highlands, a marginal area difficult to control, that such struggles went on for another two hundred years, part of the contrast that developed between the 'civilisation' of the lowlands and the 'barbarism' of the high (p. 79).[7]

The feud continued, in a modified form, in many other parts of upland Europe until quite late. In Piedmont, visitations of the late sixteenth century showed parishes where people had not gone to Church for their Easter communion because of the hostility between groups of people. In mid-sixteenth-century Northumberland a preacher reports on the impossibility of getting families in dispute to hear his sermons, and the same problem existed, Bossy suggests, in 'any upland region of Europe' (1970: 55). The Counter-Reformation made strong efforts to suppress feud and to limit the strength of

---

[6] In Germany in the early Middle Ages, writers were more anxious to mention the maternal than the paternal ancestry of a great personage (Leyser 1968: 34–5). 'Maternal kin mattered as much as paternal and even more if it was deemed to be nobler' (p. 33).

[7] Even in early and mid-sixteenth-century England, the highland zone of the north and west was an area where royal writ and royal courts were less important for the enforcement of law than the blood feud and the vendetta, which depended upon the responsibilities of kin as instruments and objects of vengeance (Stone 1977: 127).

kin groups in its attempt to impose a system of 'parochial conformity'. In this it was often more successful than the Church of England; for example, English women of the late seventeenth century conceived 'illegitimate' children at three times the rate of the French among whom local supervision was stronger (Bossy 1970: 54).

The composition of groupings involved in feuding and compensation is a matter of great significance for the social structure. In Scotland much fighting was between the clans (Macgregor 1907). But what kind of groupings conducted the feud? Wormald describes the kin group as agnatic, which gave it a continuing strength (1980: 67); 'it was relatives on the father's side who recognised kinship' and the cohesion of the group was further strengthened by the territorial proximity of its members.

However, for other purposes bilateral kinship seems to have played a role that was not simply one of 'complementary filiation' in a unilineal system (Fortes 1959). For it was the victim's 'four branches of kin', two on the father's, two on the mother's side (presumably the 'descending kindreds' of the four grandparents) who had to give the 'letter of slains', stating that the offender and his kin had made full and acceptable compensation (assythment). Only they could release him, although for the period when documentary evidence is available it appears that only a smaller group of kin, virtually the family of birth, were directly involved (Wormald 1980: 62,66,68).

Of the patrilineal clans of the western Highlands we know little before the Norse invasions of the ninth century, when the newcomers destroyed the religious houses and took over their lands (Wainwright 1962). The Celtic inhabitants, whose language they adopted, were clearly neither annihilated nor absorbed, though many of the later clans trace their ancestry to Norsemen. The famed founder of the MacDonalds was Somerled; MacLeod is a Norse name, as is MacCaskill, MacIvor, Macaulay, Gunn, Tolmie and MacCrault. Since these clans are not by origin Celtic, at least as far as their eponymous ancestors are concerned, they may represent not so much a continuation of an ancient Indo-European system but rather the specific creation of the particular situation in Scotland, especially in the Highland area.

For the Lowlands in the late Middle Ages we have fuller information on the nature of clanship ties (Smout 1969: 35). One important feature was the way that 'magnates', lords of the land, accumulated clansmen around them. 'When a great family rose in power . . . his surname rose with him. "None durst strive against a Douglas, nor yet a Douglas man" ' (pp. 38–9). It was 'the combination of feudal and family loyalties that made the followings of the magnates cohesive and almost indestructible units. Forfeiture of estates by the crown could destroy a feudal tie in its legal sense, but it was quite useless in eradicating a family loyalty' (p. 39).

In both the Highlands and the Lowlands, landowners were surrounded by 'clansmen', whose affiliation was certainly not always by 'descent' and who included members of other clans. In other words while clanship could be acquired by other means, it was not defined by political or economic relations alone: it existed in its own right, independently, and to this it owed something of its continuing strength.

Patrilineal clans, then, were characteristic of these Celtic peoples on the periphery of Europe and their significance varied over time (Byrne 1971). But their organisation was very different from the clans and lineages described for Black Africa or even for the tribal peoples of North Africa and the Middle East. In the first place, they were not characterised by a segmentary structure in which the constituent units were broadly homologous; they resembled rather those 'conical clans' described by Wolf (1959: 136; Adams 1966: 88) in which one section of the clan dominated the rest. The clan was internally stratified, especially with regard to rights over property and office. The leader lived in a castle, handed down to his heir; the clansman lived in a black house acquired from his own kin.

The existence of forms of patrilineal clanship in these areas did not mean that maternal kin were not given great recognition, nor that bilateral groupings were unimportant in matters to do with 'law' (the feud) and inheritance. And those areas that lacked such clans tended to put more emphasis on other forms of social grouping and other ways of reckoning relationships.

Bilaterality in kinship and in transmission
An appreciation of these distinctions affects theoretical arguments in another way. In rejecting the association of dowry with bilateral institutions, Hughes (1978) is using the terms bilateral, patrilineal and lineage in a different way than I have suggested above, the divergence in usage being as much a problem for the comparative sociologist as it is for those primarily interested in Western societies. As I pointed out in the first chapter, the term 'lineage', adopted for a

particular purpose by writers like Fustel de Coulanges, Gifford, Radcliffe-Brown and more especially by Firth, Evans-Pritchard and Fortes, had its origin in the European social system. So too did words like patrilineal. Their subsequent use in a wider context and in a more specific manner inevitably raises problems.

Looking at the wider context, there is little or no evidence for patrilineal descent groups (patrilineal UDGs) on the continent of Europe in the post-Roman period, with the exception of some peripheral mountain areas. The importance of 'houses' (*albergi, familia, lignage*) based on patrifiliation and linked to property and office, is undeniable, especially among the aristocracy. That is another matter. The significance of such 'house' groups varied from time to time in ways that may have been linked to changes in marriage transactions. But all such transactions were perfectly compatible with the presence of bilateral inheritance or with what I have called diverging devolution, which includes the endowment at marriage of both sons and daughters. A system that allocates parental property to daughters as well as to sons, whether by dowry or by inheritance, is already 'bilateral' from the standpoint of the transmission of wealth. The setting aside of collateral kin (the 'avaricious kinsmen') can hardly make it less so. Only by defining dowry as disinheritance and taking the inheritance as constituting the whole process of devolution can the point be sustained.

Certainly there was a patrifilial bias to the European system. But the maintenance of property and office in male hands is not best carried out by the allocation of a share to women, which is what dowry does. One may keep critical property, such as land, out of their hands, as Salic law insisted in a different context, or one may attach property to them as wives (by *morgengabe* or dower) rather than as daughters (by *dot* or dowry). But it is surely the former (the indirect dowry) rather than the latter that maintains the paternal 'house', for the woman is then endowed by the house into which she normally moves. In any case, both in France and in England, the 'house' or *maison* was a feature of the aristocracy rather than of the bourgeoisie, where as Flandrin has pointed out, the notion of *famille* was more important. In the eighteenth century Abbé Girard declared that *famille* 'is more properly used of the bourgeoisie, and *Maison* of people of quality' (Flandrin 1979: 6). Equally the 'concept of *lignage* was more deeply rooted among the elites than among the people' (p. 9).

To conclude, I have tried to make it clear that the terms 'patrilineal', 'matrilineal' and 'bilateral' mean different things depending upon the context one is considering, whether membership of a kin group, succession to office, inheritance of property and so on. Bilateral societies can be defined as those without unilineal descent groups, but even when the latter are present, virtually all reckoning of kinship ties is bilateral in the sense that for many purposes relationships are traced through both mothers and fathers, through daughters as well as sons. Even where lineages (as distinct of *lignages* or *lignées*) existed in Europe, their structure was modified by the presence of 'bilateral inheritance', that is, diverging devolution.

Appendix 2. From brideprice to dowry?

Many discussions about the nature of marriage and its associated transactions assume a long-term shift from bridewealth to dowry. The nineteenth century adopted the notion of a progression from promiscuity to marriage, first in the form of capture, then by purchase, later by dowry. In this century, too, many scholars dealing with the early history of European and Asian societies have attempted to see, in their fragmentary records, a movement from purchase (bride*price*), or at least exchange (bride*wealth*), to dowry. In a useful summary of the evidence for Western Europe, the American historian, Howard, saw marriage in England as developing from 'capture', to 'purchase' (a payment to the father), to a payment to the bride by the groom (indirect dowry) and eventually to a payment made to her by *her* own parents (direct dowry).[1] Even today many discussions are phrased in similar terms. The progression is sometimes linked, explicitly or implicitly, to supposed changes in the position of women (since ideas of 'purchase' tend to equate the members of that sex with chattels) as well as to the emergence of conjugal and affectionate families, based on love and individual choice rather than compulsion and sale. Typically these features are seen as contrasting the occidental structures of Europe with the oriental structures of North Africa and the Middle East.

These assumptions bear upon the general thesis of this essay in various ways which need to be examined. There has certainly been some long-term shift in the nature of marriage transactions. In hunting and gathering societies, little property changes hands on these occasions, either by exchange or for endowment. What we find are direct or generalised forms of exchanging conjugal rights over men and women, that is, the 'elementary forms' of Lévi-Strauss (1949). A

---

[1] Howard's scheme of development of English marriage runs: (a) marriage by capture; (b) marriage by purchase, 'real contract' (immediate exchange) (pre-historic); (c) purchase paid, nuptials postponed (Tacitus); (d) token (*arrha*) paid, *weotuma* postponed to nuptials and given to bride (dcwer) (no longer 'sale'); (e) promise (betrothal), nuptials (tenth century); (f) self-bewedding and self-gifta (where the father has only a veto), with nothing in the case of a widow (thirteenth century).

spouse is acquired by direct (e.g. sister) exchange or as the result of accepting a promise, pledge or prospect of future return (that is, by delayed reciprocity). In societies practising pastoralism and simple agriculture, found in Africa until recently (and even today), marriage is usually marked by substantial transfers of material objects between the kin of the groom and the kin of the bride. These transfers are referred to as bridewealth rather than brideprice in order to set aside some of the word's misleading implications (Radcliffe-Brown 1950). For in these 'complex systems', as Lévi-Strauss called them, the transaction is not one of purchase but rather a pledge of future unions. In advanced agricultural societies, the transfers of property tend to go to the wife herself rather than to her kin, whether directly from the parents or indirectly from the groom (and often from both).[2] Whereas bridewealth payments are relatively standardised, dowry varies in kind and quantity according to the wealth and status of the bride and her family, the very poor making only very limited transfers, perhaps none at all; in Asia it is the lower groups that tend to give an indirect dowry, while the upper groups provide a direct one. In industrial societies, payments of this kind tend to disappear. In nineteenth-century England, the process began with the urban working classes who married without any such transfers; the middle and the upper classes only abandoned the dowry around the end of the century; though other forms of endowing children remain, devolution tends to get put off until death itself.

Marriage transfers in dotal systems

The evidence for this developmental sequence is comparative and analytic rather than historical, as in the case of the earlier schemas elaborated by various scholars in the last century and implicitly assumed by many in this. It allows no room for either marriage by capture or by purchase, at least in any literal sense. Marriage is more often a matter of an exchange in which notions of seizure and price generally seem out of place. It is true that the early codes of the German peoples, which, except for the Anglo-Saxon laws, are all written in Latin, use the term *pretium* for one of the main payments made at marriage, apparently going from the groom's kin to the bride's father. However the literal notion of 'price' seems out of place and initially I will adopt the neutral term 'parental fee' (the

---

[2] See my *Production and Reproduction* (1977) for a further discussion on this point. By advanced agriculture I mean essentially the use of the plough or of complex irrigation.

wife-giver's fee). One reason for such a usage is that the payments to the father may often be a form of endowment of the bride, and hence be linked to the devolution of property (by dowry or inheritance) not to a daughter, but at least to women in general and a daughter-in-law in particular. In this situation the transfer should be viewed as going *through* rather than *to* the father.

The close interrelation between ways of allocating property to a woman, whether by the husband or by the father, whether at marriage or at the death of the spouse, is brought out in the English terminology for these transactions. The *O.E.D.* gives three main meanings for 'dowry'. The first (obsolete) is the same as the first meaning given for another term, 'dower', which is usually a counterpart of the dowry itself and is defined as:

Dower: The portion of a deceased husband's estate which the law allows to his widow for her life.

The second meaning is the main one we associate with the present use of the word, the direct dowry:

Dowry: The money or property the wife brings her husband; the portion given with the wife; tocher; dot; cf. Dower 2 (for exactly the same meaning is given under that head; tocher is the Scots form, derived from the Gaelic).

The third (again precisely the same as the third meaning of dower) is what I have called 'indirect dowry':

a present or gift by a man to or for his bride.

Note that there are two forms of indirect dowry indicated by the words 'to' or 'for' the bride: the first is the husband's gift to the wife, which in Teutonic societies took the form of a donation *propter nuptias* or of the morning-gift (O.E. *morgengifu*), formerly 'morwyn-gift' or 'moryeve', defined as 'the gift made by the husband to the wife on the morning after the consummation of the marriage. Also sometimes misused for dowry.' A constant misuse is nevertheless a kind of use which indicates the close relationship between the transactions. This link is shown again in Skene's definition of 'morning-gift' in 1597: 'It is given to the woman, to the effect, that after the decease of her husband, she may sustaine and nourish hir selfe, induring all the daies of her life-time. Therefore it is called *Vitalitia Morganaticum* from the Dutch word *Morgengab*, morning gift, is ane kinde of dowry, in the second signification.' This indirect dowry made to the bride could include land as well as movables and was variable in quantity and in kind depending on the status of the partners. Interestingly a 'morganatic marriage' was so called because the wife and children of such a union were entitled only to the morning-gift and not to other payments; the union was also known as a left-handed marriage since the groom gives the bride his left hand instead of his right. Things were not right without direct dowry as well.

The second is the gift to the wife's father (often, as we have seen, 'for' the wife) and it is this transaction that the late nineteenth century often called by the term 'brideprice'. One concrete example of this transfer is the Arabic payment *mahr* (sometimes the Hebrew *mohar*) which has to be distinguished from bridewealth proper, although it may have the same direction and even the same recipients as bridewealth. Indeed, at least in upper strata, this payment always appears to be part of a more inclusive system of transfers that includes ones to the bride herself, either from the groom or from her parents. Not all of such affinal gifts may go straight to the bride; some of what does, goes in equipment. Writing of what he calls 'brideprice' in the Middle East, Patai remarks that part, and occasionally all of it, is 'spent by the father of the girl on her trousseau. Silver and gold jewelry – earrings, nose rings, bracelets, anklets – form an important part of the outfit received in this manner by a girl from her father' (1959: 57). Such an endowment is an index of a status as well as a reserve of wealth. Hence the property transmitted to the bride is functionally related to dowry payments, whether or not the particular transaction was historically developed from an earlier system of bridewealth.

Dowry and inheritance

At least in the form of dowry and dower, dotal systems in their turn are closely associated with 'bilateral inheritance'. The use of the terms 'portion' or 'lot' in English provides one indication of this link, of the view that dowry is a share of or claim upon the family holding, not necessarily an equal one. The view emerges from the interesting passage in Roger Manning's versified version of *The Story of England* of 1338, where King Conant, a relative (*cosyn*) of the previous King of Britain but himself King of Brittany, sent back to his earlier homeland for wives for his men: 'ffrensche wymen wolde (th)ey non take ... To have cleym (th)orow heritage, Ne dowarye (th)orow mariage' (lines 6535–8).

Some societies treat the giving of a dowry or of inheritance to a woman as alternatives. Others allow both. In Anglo-Saxon England a woman could inherit as well as acquire property at marriage; a man could leave property to his wife as a dower (at least for her lifetime) and a wife, less commonly, to her husband. She could also bequeath property to children of both sexes. The wills made by women show little preference for sons as against daughters. Wulfwaru left her property, land and chattels to be divided more or less equally between her two sons and two daughters (Whitelock 1930: 62–5). Death transactions were closely tied to marriage transactions; both are facets of the inclusive process of devolution, in this case of what I have called 'diverging devolution' since parental property is transmitted to both males and females.

The dower and other forms of indirect dowry (transfers from the husband to the wife) are also related to the process of inheritance. The will of Thurstan granted to his wife Aethelgyd 'everything which I have in Norfolk, as I gave to her before as a marriage payment and in accordance with our contract'. The testament reaffirms the marriage contract. The Anglo-Saxon reads: 'ic an mine wife Ailgiðe al þe þing þe ic have on Norfolke so ic it her hire gaf tō mund and tō máldage]', the last phrase being a Scandinavian expression where *mundr* refers to the transfer to the bride before the marriage ('originally to the bride's guardian', claims the editor, speculatively), and *máldaga*, the agreement about succession to property (Whitelock 1930: 82–3, 195). In this text the transfer is not specifically called a morning-gift (*morgengifu*), which may have been an additional prestation. But mention of such payments under this name was made in wills; for example, Aelfhelm confirms the allocation of property (including land) to his wife at their marriage (pp. 31–2). In post-conquest documents, the word *morgengifu* disappears in favour of *dos* (p. 144), a change which is of more than terminological significance.

This link between dowry and inheritance is not simply a matter of definition, as we see from the history of marriage transactions in early Spain. The freedom of Visigothic wives to dispose of their *dotes* and other gifts stemming from their husbands has been ascribed to the interests of the Arian Church who profited from female generosity.[3] But the effect of later legislation was to restrict this

---

[3] King describes this view as 'seductive' and refers to T. Melicher, *Der Kampf zwischen Gesetzes- und Gewohnheitsrecht im Westgotenreiche* (Weimar, 1930), pp. 221, 258, and to E. F. Bruck, *Kirchenväter und soziales Erbrecht* (Berlin–Göttingen–Heidelberg, 1956), pp. 147–9.

freedom and to guarantee the children of the union a share in paternal (*bona paterna*) and maternal (*bona materna*) property. They received four-fifths of all those goods, excepting the dowry given by
one spouse to the other, and they got the same proportion of the
family inheritance held by, or due to, each parent. Of the *dos*, three-
quarters had to be reserved for the children, to be shared equally, no
grounds for disinheritance being given in the laws (King
1972: 246–7). The Roman woman also had her freedom, comments
King, because she had to preserve all the property coming from her
husband, including the *donatio ante nuptias*, for her children. The
difference in freedoms lay in the Visigothic woman's ability, under
their strongly Christian code, to alienate a proportion of her land
from her children to the Church.

Marriage transfers in early German tribes

The evidence for the marriage practices of the Germanic tribes
derives from a variety of sources. In the earlier period, it could come
only from their literate neighbours, the Romans, and here the most
important commentator is Tacitus. Second, there is the evidence of
the German laws and third, that from documents and literature. The
account in the *Germania* of Tacitus contains a statement about the
difference between German and Roman forms of marriage. The
dowry (*dos*), he wrote, 'is brought by husband to wife, not by wife to
husband' (*Germania* XVIII), a transfer that was of considerable
economic importance, consisting of 'oxen, horse with reins, shield,
spear and sword'. Howard regards this commentary as providing
part of the 'abundant' evidence for 'wife-purchase' in early Europe,
which later (as expressed in the title of a major section of his own
work) 'yields to marriage'. Although the Roman historian represents this gift as being paid to the bride, Howard suggests that 'it is
probable that in this particular he is mistaken, and that, in accordance with the early practice, it was really paid to the guardian, for
it is very unlikely that the stage of the dower had already been
reached' (1904: I,252). His contention that the indirect dowry had
changed from a parental to a bridal one might receive some limited
support from the content of the transaction,[4] were it not that Taci-

---

[4] There is perhaps an analogous custom reported from Burgundy in recent times
where the wife is presented with some tools of her husband's trade which she then
has to use, an initiation into the future conjugal partnership (Segalen 1980: 37).

tus, who uses the term *dos*, explains the nature of these gifts in his subsequent remarks. The young bride receives the oxen and other gifts. She presents her husband with arms. By this interchange of gifts, she is reminded that 'she is coming to share a man's toils and dangers'. But the gifts are for her and not for her kinsfolk. 'She is receiving something that she must hand over unspoilt and treasured to her children, for her son's wives to receive in their turn and pass on to the grandchildren'. In other words the gifts she receives are used to endow her son's wife; there is continuity in the line of female filiation but no question of purchase or price or even (as Pollock and Maitland saw) the 'sale' of the *mund* or protectorship. Nevertheless the term *weotuma* (Burgundian, *wittimon*), used to refer to the major marriage transaction in Anglo-Saxon sources, has been constantly construed in this way, as have the alternative terms, *gyft* and *feoh*, or, in the Latin Germanic codes, *pretium* and *pecunia pro puella data*. In the Latin *leges barbarorum* the root, *emo*, to buy, is a common expression (e.g. in *Lex Saxonum*); however before we can understand this usage the whole semantic field of the word in this kind of socio-economic system has to be examined in detail and alternative explanations for such a usage have to be reckoned with, especially given the circumstances and the language in which the codes were composed. Even in early Rome there is little evidence that *coemptio* had anything to do with sale, price or purchase as we usually understand the terms.

The interpretation that most closely fits the transactions described by Tacitus is that both parties bring property into the marriage, and that the bride is endowed by the groom (what I call an indirect dowry) as well as by her parents, the arms constituting a kind of direct dowry. This set of transactions, according to Caesar's account, also obtained among the Celtic peoples of Roman Gaul. 'The men, after making due reckoning, take from their own goods a sum of money equal to the dowry they have received from their wives and place it with the dowry. Of each such sum account is kept between them and the profits saved: whichever of the two survives receives the portion of both together with the profits of past years' (*Gallic War* VI. 19).

The second set of sources are the Germanic laws, *leges barbarorum*, which were written under the influence of Roman law and the Christian religion. This caveat applies even to the earliest (that is, the Visigothic) codes, at the beginning of the second half of the fifth century, to the Burgundian and Salic (Frankish) laws of the beginning of the sixth century, to the Lombard code of northern Italy in the mid seventh century (sometimes said to represent the 'purest' Germanic law) and to the Saxon laws which date from the beginning of the ninth century at the time of the conquest and conversion of Saxony by the forces of Charlemagne.[5] These collections are partial statements of 'customary laws' with portions copied from other codes, strongly influenced by Rome and Christianity, the remnants of jural systems that were in the process of being modified by religious and political factors. They suffer from the major defects of many early codes resulting from the advent of literacy, indeed of much written law altogether, for they try to reduce complex transactions to simple sentences, turning the intricate rites and processes of marriage or death into a terse and partial statement of a limited range of legal rights and duties. The anthropologist would happily exchange a detailed description of a marriage, particularly of a trouble case, for the sketchy formulations of enquiring scribes. For they inevitably choose different aspects of a jural system to write down and may well produce a show of difference when we should perhaps be looking for variations on a common theme.

Of the special laws issued by Saxon kings Seebohm remarked that they should be regarded as 'modifications of custom' made necessary at different periods by new circumstances. Hence 'no one of the sets of laws can be expected to give a general view of custom as a whole' (1911: 337). With these warnings in mind we can look at the Germanic system of marriage payments, not necessarily all identical, as they are laid out in the Lombardic Laws. There are three kinds of marital prestation which are dealt with explicitly under the section (cap. 182) on the rights of the widow.

If a widow remarries, the second husband should give to the heir of the first husband half the *meta* that was offered when she was betrothed. If the heir does not accept the *meta*, then it goes to the widow together with her *morgengab* which is an indirect (bridal) dowry given to her by her husband on the morning after her wedding night and possibly connected with ideas of virginity, or at least

---

[5] The Anglo-Saxon is the only Germanic code written in the vernacular. But the works were not, of course, composed until after the conversion to Christianity. According to Bede, even in England we are left with 'judicial decrees after the example of the Romans' (Bede, II. 5), derived from ecclesiastical scribes (Whitelock 1979: 357).

of first marriage. In addition she takes 'that which she brought with her from her own relatives', that is, her father's gift (*faderfio*). If she returns to her father's house, she keeps the first (here *metfyo*) and the second for herself, but the father's gift she returns to the common pool of her family's property, from which is deducted the amount given to her late husband's kin to release her *mundium* (legal control); the total amount is then divided out equally. In other words her direct dowry is returned to the pool before the inheritance is shared out (cap. 199). It would appear that if a woman was still married to her husband at the time of the parent's death, she would receive an amount additional to her dowry, to make up her 'share' (e.g. cap. 158).

The *meta* has been translated both as ' "purchase price", the sum paid by a man to the father of his affianced bride' (Drew 1973: 260) and as a 'marriage portion' which, in certain circumstances, comes under the control of the bride (cap. 178, Drew 1973: 84). The translator comments that part or all may have been included in the *faderfio* (or direct dowry) 'which became part of her personal property and which seems to have taken the place of what would have been her share of the division of the family estate on the death of her father if she had remarried in her father's house' (p. 247). In other words 'dowry', direct and indirect, is closely linked to the inheritance by females of parental property.

There is little doubt that we have to look at these payments as a system rather than simply as a transition from one form of payment, bridewealth (or price), to another, dowry. For a well-to-do bride is endowed by her parents as well as by the groom, and the parental endowment at least is closely linked to inheritance; indeed inheritance and endowment must, I have argued, be looked at as a joint process of 'diverging devolution' (Goody 1976a; Le Roy Ladurie 1972). Of course the timing of this devolution is important; whether it comes at the marriage of an offspring or on the death of a parent may have important implications which we will examine later. Meanwhile the main features of the system can be represented in the manner shown in Figure 10.

The problematic transfer is the first, referred to as *meta* in the Lombardic Laws, for this is the one often referred to as brideprice or bridewealth. I have argued that the first term is misleading not only because of the implications of price and purchase, but because, as in the case of bridewealth, it appears to refer to a distinct regime

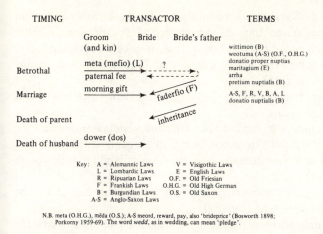

Figure 10. Early European marriage transactions

or system of payments; hence the use of the term as descriptive of one component of a complex system (a system that entitled women to a share in the parental estate) automatically gives rise to the notion that this payment represents a survival from an earlier dispensation.

Even if we reject this notion, the terms in which it is cast, the evidence used and the methods adopted, we still have to recognise that gifts from the groom have some similarities with bridewealth itself for they are sometimes made not to the bride (in what I have called an indirect, bridal dowry) but to her father, or rather, her *parentes*. This is the case in the Saxon laws where it is stated: 'Uxorem ducturus 300 solidi parentibus eius' (cap. 40). 'For taking a woman (in marriage) 300 solidi are (to be given) to her *parentes*', more if she goes without their consent. Such a payment is elsewhere called *pretium emptionis*. The same body of laws refers to the *dos* a woman receives at the death of her husband (cap. 47). This proportional payment, which differed in the different districts, was a 'dower' rather than a direct or indirect dowry (Seebohm 1911: 216–217), though at other times the word *dos* refers to another set of gifts; for example, in Tacitus *dos* is given by groom to bride at marriage rather than death.

None of the laws provide evidence of a bridewealth system as such, but only of transactions between the groom and the bride's *parentes*. Aethelbert's law includes mention of such a payment by which the groom is said to 'buy' (*gebigeð*) his wife. These are the earliest Anglo-Saxon laws, promulgated by the Kentish king who was reigning at the time of the arrival of St Augustine in 597, although in fact our only text dates from four centuries later.

The position of the wife is interesting. There is reference at one and the same time to:

(a) a payment made (*gebigeð*, 'buys') for a maiden, which is returned if she leaves (cap. 77).

(b) the 'morning-gift' made to her after the wedding and which she retains even if she does not bear a child (cap. 81). This indirect (bridal) dowry sometimes took the form of land (Attenborough 1922: 178).

(c) her own goods (direct dowry) that return with her under the same circumstances (cap. 81).

(d) a conditional dower: if she bears a child she is entitled to half the goods left by her husband, even if she departs with the children (cap. 78–9).

(e) fines for elopement: in such a case a man pays 50 shillings to the 'owner' for his consent, and 20 shillings to her fiancé if she is already betrothed.

The other Germanic codes allow for the husband's gifts to go to the wife rather than to the father. Among the Franks it has been claimed that the *arrha* was a survival of brideprice but it appears to mean 'earnest-money'. According to Galy (1901), who espouses the notion of a shift in Germanic custom from the *pretium nuptiale* to the *dos*, the betrothal always included the handing over of a pledge (*arrhes*) to the bride's parents as part of the contract. The wedding itself followed after quite a long interval (p. 80) by which time the *pretium nuptiale* was transferred to the bride's father who at first 'probably' passed on some to his daughter, and later gave her the lot (p. 77). However, formulary evidence shows that by the sixth century the payment to the bride's father was (or 'had become') a standardised prestation of a solidum and a denarium, a 'shilling' and a 'penny', which has been described as 'the vestigial remains of a brideprice' (Hughes 1978: 267). At that time the *dos*, dot or dowry was given direct to the bride; without this gift there was no marriage. Indeed the phrase *nullum sine dote fiat conjugium* (no marriage without 'dowry'), referring to the husband's gift to the wife, was widely used in later documents.

Some authors have discerned faint traces of 'bridepurchase' or 'brideprice' in other German codes; Howard mentions the Alammanic, the Bavarian, Visigothic, Burgundian and Lombardic (1904: I,264–6). Even if we were to accept this nomenclature and the implied developmental schema, the situation was quite different at the time when the laws were composed. 'Brideprice', remarks Hughes, 'had generally disappeared' (1978: 267), a position that had been recognised by earlier authorities. 'In the time of the folk-laws – from the sixth to the ninth century – we see among all the German tribes a change take place: the withrum, that is the purchase price, is no longer paid to the guardian, that is the seller, but to the bride herself; so that the right of the guardian was practically limited to the receipt of the handgeld, that is to a merely formal fulfillment' (Sohm 1875: 33; Howard 1904: I,266).

One of the most fully documented systems of marriage and kinship that emerged out of the early conjunction of the Germanic tribes with Roman law and Christian religion is that of the Visigothic kingdom of Spain that flourished for the three hundred and fifty years between the decline of the Western Empire in 376 and the Muslim invasion of 711. Of these documents the most important is the great legal compilation reissued by King Ervig in 681 from the code of Reccaswinth (or Chindaswinth) in the mid seventh century.

By 376, according to King (1972: 223), the kindred had already become a less significant feature of social organisation without being simply replaced by Roman models: 'Kinsmen as a body had very little power . . . It was the monogamous family which now constituted the basic social group', possibly because of the growth of a strong centralised monarchy that usurped the political and legal powers of the kindred. At the same time, the position of women with regard to inheritance was improved, for 'the old Roman preference for agnates and the Germanic refusal to allow women the inheritance of immovables disappeared' (p. 223).[6]

---

[6] While I follow King's discussion of the historical situation, I hesitate to accept his account of the wider changes that are supposed to have occurred, for the reasons I elaborated in the first chapter. For example, the conjugal family was certainly important before, within the framework of wider kin groups. And the Roman preference for agnation has to be seen in the context of the fact that it was a dotal regime, that is to say, women took property (including land) with them at marriage and by so doing clearly pre-empted their right to inheritance from the agnatic fund. Of course there are two kinds of 'agnatic fund', one that limits access to the resources to males alone and another that allows those resources to be transmitted, often in a differential way, to both men and women members. Here we are dealing with the latter kind, which is in this sense bilateral, and hence more homologous with the kindred than with the patrilineal clan.

We have noted for other areas that inheritance cannot be considered separately from marriage transactions, which were organised in the following manner. When the arrangements for a marriage had been agreed, the first step was the betrothal. This preliminary stage took the form of an undertaking before witnesses that the marriage would take place, as a pledge of which a ring was handed over or, alternatively, the pledge was given in writing. At the same time the transfer (or promise of transfer) of the 'dowry' from the groom's side to the bride was made. In the text this indirect dowry appears as *pretium* (hence the translation, 'brideprice'), *mercatio* (hence the translation, 'bridepurchase') or *dos*. It is clearly akin both to the *morgengabe* of German custom (but handed over before marriage) and the *donatio propter nuptias* of late Roman law, the usual Roman *dos* being something different, namely *ex parte sponsae*, a transfer from the side of the bride. Subject to certain conditions, the property handed over was at the free use and disposal of the woman. Moreover it was of high economic significance and 'negotiations about its size were doubtless the major concern of the two sides before the betrothal' (King 1972: 225–6). Ervig's code prescribed a limit to this transfer, one-tenth of all a man owned or stood to inherit, but this maximum might be exceeded in the case of nobility and if the surplus was matched by an equivalent gift *ex sponsa*.[7] One authority argued for the essential equality of *dos* and *donatio*,[8] the matched contributions of the bride and groom, but matching took various forms, not all of them involving a balance of gifts. However the question of equality of contribution is inevitably difficult to assess even in concrete situations.

One gets a fuller picture of marriage when turning to the third source, the wills and charters of the Anglo-Saxons, the great histories of Gregory of Tours and Bede of Northumbria, by which the summary statements of the codes can be tested and judged.

These documents show that whatever the German tribes may have given to their wives, there is no question that the rich at least also provided a substantial dowry for their daughters or sisters. When on the death of Clovis in A.D. 511 his sons divided his kingdom into four equal parts, they agreed to the marriage of their sister

---

[7] There is an earlier reference to half a man's goods being handed over (King 1972: 226, fn. 2).

[8] King 1972: 226, fn. 3).

to Amalaric, son of the Gothic king of Spain. So, according to Gregory of Tours, they sent her into Spain 'with a store of rich ornaments' (Dalton 1927: II,86). His grandson Chilperic (d. 584) sent Rigunth, his daughter by Queen Fredegund, to the Goths with a large number of slaves and 'large treasures'; in addition her mother presented her with a great quantity of gold and silver and garments (all taken from 'my own possessions' and nothing from the 'public treasure'), plus an endowment of fifty wagons that was further augmented by booty plundered on the way (pp. 277–8). In the end the death of her father meant the treasure was taken from her control before she reached the Gothic boundary.

The transmission of property to daughters at marriage did not prevent them receiving wealth at their parents' death. 'Beretrude on her death bed named her daughter as her heir, but left some property to the nunneries which she had founded, and to the cathedrals and churches of the holy confessors' (p. 406). The daughter appears to have had a claim on her mother's property as well as a duty to pay her debts; in Beretrude's case, a certain official tried unsuccessfully to claim one of the estates on the grounds that her son-in-law had taken some of his horses.

The agreement that Gregory of Tours helped to negotiate between King Guntram, King Childebert and his mother, Queen Brunhild, declared that whatever Guntram has given, or will give, to his daughter Clodetild 'in all kinds of property, or in men, in cities, lands or revenues, shall remain under her power and control' (p. 390), for her to dispose of as she wishes. No distinction is made in the timing of the gifts; the kings agree to protect the property of their sons and daughters as it exists at the death of their father. As for Brunhild, she had come from Spain with great treasures to marry Sigibert and her older sister Galswinth was married to his brother, Chilperic, also bringing great treasures, though she threatened to leave these behind and return to her own country. But she also received 'as dowry or *morgengabe*, which is to say, morning gift' from her husband the cities of Bordeaux, Limoges, Cahors, Lescar and Cieutat, which Brunhild acquired at her death. The agreement stipulated that the Queen should retain the first of these cities but that the others should be held by Guntram while he lived, after which they would go to Brunhild and her heirs (p. 391).

We find a similar set of prestations in Anglo-Saxon England. One text, dated by Liebermann as 975–1030, provides instructions on

'How a man shall betroth a maiden, and what agreement there ought to be' (Whitelock 1979: 467). It is clear that the woman herself had to accept the husband and he had first to announce how he will maintain her. He then offers 'a remuneration for rearing her' (which does not necessarily go to the father) and finally states what he will give her for accepting his suit (that is, as a *donatio propter nuptias* or morning-gift, the formal difference between them being mainly one of timing) and what she will get at his death i.e. the dower amounting to half his goods.

The instructions are directed to the groom, so that there is no mention of a direct dowry from the father. There is a rearing fee together with an indirect (bridal) dowry in the shape of the groom's donation or morning-gift as well as the promise of a dower. Two Old English marriage agreements published by Whitelock, which fall within the period ascribed to the betrothal instructions, also stress the endowment of the bride by the groom. In the first, Wulfric promises Archbishop Wufstan that when he takes his sister as wife, she will have various lands, some for her lifetime, some for her disposal, together with gold, men and horses (i.e. an indirect bridal dowry). In the second agreement, from Kent, the bride received gold on acceptance of the bridegroom's suit, then lands, livestock and slaves. In neither case is any specific mention made of payment to the father, nor yet of a direct dowry; the property goes directly to the wife from the husband.

However it is clear from King Alfred's will (probably of 879–888) that daughters received houses and land at the death of their fathers or mothers, and hence possibly as direct dowry at their marriage. This will asks that booklands be not alienated from the kindred and that they return to the testator's nearest kin if the recipients have no children. An attempt is also made to preserve property within the line from which it derived, whether the male line (the spear side) or the female line (the spindle side). The principles behind these latter dispositions seem very similar to those operating among the LoDagaa of northern Ghana (Goody 1962a) and again in later English law.

The use of the term 'remuneration for rearing' ('rearing fees') takes us to the heart of the problem about the husband's gift. We have seen that some authors draw a radical distinction between gifts which go to the father (or *parentes*) and those which go to the bride. From one point of view that is correct. A fee for rearing is some kind of 'compensation' for or recognition of the role a parent or pro-parent has played. But in many cases this gift is received by the father only to be passed on to the daughter; in other instances part is kept by the father. Even where the father keeps the entire payment (and this situation would fall outside my definition of indirect dowry), the gift from the groom to '*parentes*' can be seen as a compensation not so much for the past (the rearing of the bride) as for the present or the future, that is, for the wealth that was to devolve either at the bride's marriage in direct dowry or at her father's death by inheritance. However, so often, as in the Saxon laws or in the case of the Islamic *mahr*, one does not know whether the father has retained the payment (legitimately or not), perhaps keeping it as a future resource for his daughter, or whether he has passed it on, in other words, whether it is an indirect (paternal) dowry or an affinal payment (or what is often called 'brideprice').

Changes in medieval Europe
In her valuable article entitled 'From brideprice to dowry in Mediterranean Europe' (1978), Hughes analyses the changes that took place in Southern Europe from the early to the late Middle Ages. She describes this process as a reversion to the dotal system of Greece and Rome and a move away from the 'brideprice' of the invading Germanic peoples. The husband's gift and the *morgengabe* is seen as resting on 'bilateral and conjugal principles', whereas the dowry was 'the symbol of patrilineal status' (pp. 290–1). For 'dowry formed part of a status, rather than an inheritance system' (p. 290) and emerged as a mode of *disinheritance*, 'consolation for an exclusion from succession that was increasingly secured in Mediterranean Europe by entail fortified by female renunciations' (p. 288). In this way 'dowry flourished to drive out other marital assigns where men used their rights over the women of their lineage, particularly their daughters, as a way of asserting status or competing for it' (p. 290). She goes on to claim that, 'far from being a daughter's simple or natural claim in a system of bilateral descent, as Goody has suggested, the medieval Mediterranean dowry rose to prominence as a form of disinheritance within a social group whose organization had become significantly *less* bilateral' (p. 290); it was perhaps these heightened dowries that may have won for women 'more extensive inheritance rights in their patrilineage'.

The difference of view depends partly upon the use of concepts.

The question of the term 'brideprice' has already been discussed; so too have the distinction between *lignage* and lineage (Appendix 1), the notion of patrilineal and bilateral, and the relationships between dowry and inheritance. Leaving aside the question of definitions, the complementary relations between these latter come out in the events which Hughes herself analyses. In northern Italy in the tenth century the daughter received her direct dowry (*faderfio*) at marriage, whereas men inherited at the death of the father, recalling the structure revealed in the Lombardic Laws (Violante 1977). As a widow she kept a *tertia* or *quarta*, the right to which she received with the *donatio propter nuptias* or with the *morghincap* (the morning-gift); she usually stayed in the husband's house after his death and, 'dans un engagement de succession', was sometimes designated *domina* or administrator of the estate.

The part of the estate assigned to the widow usually remained 'ideal', but she had to be consulted before the real division took place – for 'la communion familiale des biens' was always breaking up and being reconstituted, only lasting in effect until the death of the husband or marriage of a daughter. A widow might obtain more freedom, especially in Lombardy, by declaring herself *ancilla Dei*, even though she continued to stay in her husband's house. By this legal subterfuge she became a servant of God and could dispose freely of a third of her goods. As was clear in the Visigothic case, the ability of a widow to dispose of property, the control a woman had over the marital assigns, was good for the Church but bad for the family estate. The tension was apparent. In the following century, around Milan, women were excluded from their father's heritage in order to limit the dispersal of property; instead the cash dowry (paid in money) was developed, 'en guise de compensation'. Landed property went to males and at the same time the *donatio propter nuptias* and the *morghincap* ceased to be offered (Violante 1977: 114). This process is the very kind analysed by Hughes and again brings out the links between the different phases of a system of devolution that allocates property both to men and women at marriage, at bereavement or on both occasions. The changes indicated may have involved a shift from inheritance to dowry, from indirect to direct transfers and from land to movables, but they did not exclude women from a share in the conjugal estate of their parents.

The allocation of property to women, whether as cash or land, must threaten the notional unity of the patrimony. But such an allocation was also the condition of the preservation and possible extension of family interests, as well as of the status system itself. It is a paradox that requires further elaboration.

At one level it is impossible to maintain the patrimony intact when one practises diverging devolution. The 'family estate' or 'conjugal fund' is constituted and dispersed with each marriage, with each death, with each transaction between generations. But it is possible to 'protect' the most significant segment, namely land, the basic productive resource, by providing all the siblings except one with other items of wealth. Essentially this is the function of primogeniture, entail, or ultimogeniture, of all forms of single-heir devolution; one heir takes over the critical part of the estate, the other siblings being endowed in different ways. For the estate is always subject to the claims of other siblings, even if in the extreme case of younger sons in hard-up families, their rights stop at maintenance as bachelors (Homans 1942: 135–9; see also Duby 1972). Frequently these alternative endowments will not be 'equal' to that received by the main heir, whatever the sex of the junior siblings; and daughters may be excluded altogether from taking any land, either as dowry or as an inheritance, especially if they are marrying out.[9] In this way some link is maintained between estate and patriline (*lignage* or *lignée*). But such a link is always temporary if limited to the direct line of males, for in roughly some 20 per cent of cases there will be no heirs and in another 20 per cent there will be only daughters.

Indirect dowry, especially of the bridal kind, would seem to work in favour of maintaining the unity of a particular estate, since women receive wealth from their husbands (with whom they reside) rather than from their parents (whom they have left), establishing a temporary conjugal fund out of the contributions made by the groom's kin. Even if these include land, it is still not dispersed. If it is comprised of wealth, the wealth does not leave the house unless the marriage comes to an end, even though it changes hands, or at least title, within that house. Women are tied more closely to their hus-

---

[9] The problem of deciding what is an equal share is particularly difficult when the share is allocated before the estate is finally divided, because an early division will obviously tend to be conservative and cannot take account of any later increase or decrease in value. Hence the problem of 'option' under the customary law of some areas of France (Yver 1966; Le Roy Ladurie 1972; Goody 1976c). Option meant that a son or daughter who had left home and had received an endowment (in France both sexes were *doté*), could hand back the share when the fund was finally divided so that they could partake equally with their other siblings.

band's families but they do not split up their own natal estates, which is one reason why these forms of marital assign are found in poorer, low-status families, where ethnographers have tended to call them brideprice, contrasting them with the dowry of the upper status groups. On the other hand direct dowry carries higher status because it demonstrates publicly that a man has the capacity to ensure the maintenance of his daughter. Dowry, especially direct dowry, is always an instrument and product of stratification. In the English village of Halesowen in the fourteenth century, the daughters of rich villagers were endowed with good dowries, were more carefully guarded, married earlier, and produced fewer illegitimate children (Razi 1980: 68). Meanwhile the daughters of the poorer villagers had to postpone marriage, some never marrying, others leaving home for work. These poorer girls were the ones who were fined for *leyrwyte* (incontinence); 26 per cent of the daughters of poor families conceived out of wedlock, only 5 per cent of the rich families did so (p. 66); earlier marriage meant greater chastity.

The early transfer of property through the direct dowry can be regarded as providing a woman with her 'lot'. But it may also mean that her natal kin are more heavily involved in the marriage and its offspring than where the dowry comes from the kin of the groom. Hughes argues that the direct dowry protects the lineage (i.e. *lignage*) and encourages 'the full integration of daughters' (1978: 289). For if her fund is provided directly rather than indirectly, the result is to draw attention away from the conjugal bond and focus it instead on the relation between the couple and the wife's kin, whose rights towards the children of the marriage are guaranteed by the dowry. 'In Siena, for instance, the presence of a dowry allowed the wife's family formally to participate in the upbringing of her children . . .' (p. 284). The right of the brother-in-law to interfere if there was any mismanagement of the dotal fund may have promoted 'that association between brothers-in-law that is characteristic of business life with the patriciates of some late medieval cities', where the wife's brother almost invariably assumed the dominant role. At the same time the separation of goods is seen as being 'implicit in the dotal marriage' (p. 282), since the marriage is funded from two distinct sources, not one as with the indirect dowry.

One of the important contributions of Hughes' article is to point to the shift in emphasis in the nature of marital transactions over this period, a different question from that of the overall change from 'brideprice' to 'dowry', to answer which we need to survey a much longer time-span. The change in emphasis of the marital transactions is away from husband's gifts, whether bridal (or conjugal, to the wife) or parental (or affinal, to her father), and towards the assignment of a direct dowry to the wife. The corollary is the move away from the inheritance by a married woman from her parents (she takes that at marriage rather than bereavement) and towards the inheritance from her husband (the wedding gift is postponed to the dower at his death). Shift one set and almost automatically the other shifts. In other words she receives her direct endowment at an earlier point in time and her support from her husband at a later one.[10] This is the change that Whitelock noted in the terminology of English wills, that Violante saw as occurring in north Italy in the twelfth century and that Hughes observes in a wider range of Western European societies, linking the change to Duby's notion of the strengthening of agnatic *lignages* at that period. Before commenting on this last thesis, let us ask what would be the likely effects of such a change.

There are two elements to be examined. On the one hand there is the shift from indirect to direct dowry, and on the other is the question of the earlier devolution of property to the bride as distinct from the groom. How does earlier devolution affect intra-familial relations? If a woman receives her portion as a dowry at marriage, with no entitlement to inherit at a later stage, even if the initial assign did not represent an equal share, then she has been set up once and for all, and the support she can expect from her kin is in protecting what she has already received. But the dowry may also take the form of instalment payments or a promissory note, in which case the marriage transaction will merge with inheritance; the wife, indeed the conjugal pair as a whole, will have less 'freedom', becoming more dependent upon the continued goodwill of the parents.

The extreme instance of this dependency is the female heiress, the epiklerate, where the father's productive property is handed over to

---

[10] The general interpretation of marriage payments offered here is in line with Walters' analysis of the comparative legal context of the early Welsh law of matrimonial property (1980), which I read only after making my comments. A common characteristic of the dower, he writes, is that 'it corresponds to or is a substitute for a right of succession' ('inheritance', in my terminology). He goes on to point out that 'the exact nature of the wife's title to dower, upon, during and after marriage depends upon the state of the contemporary law concerning joint and separate property, and whether some kind of community of movables was recognised . . .' (pp. 129–30).

the daughter and managed (sometimes appropriated) by an incoming husband. In a hypogamous marriage, as this is likely to be, an indirect dowry makes little or no sense.

A very clear illustration of such a filiacentric union, of what I have called the Zelophehad situation (1962a: 319) after a judicial decision given by Moses (Numbers 27: 4, 36: 8–9), occurred in the history of the princely house of Monaco, revealing some of the social implications of the marriage of an heiress. The fifteenth-century ruler, Giovanni Grimaldi, provided in his will that if his son should die without a male heir, the estate was to descend to his son's daughter 'on condition that she marry a member of the *albergo* Grimaldi', which was not altogether a descent line (*lignage*), much less a segmentary lineage, but 'a formal union of (related and unrelated) aristocratic families who shared the same urban space' (Hughes 1978: 289). The rulers of Monaco were one of four branches of the Grimaldi *albergo* originating in Genoa where this type of union developed from the thirteenth century onwards, possibly avoiding the ban on kinship marriage. At other times an outside husband marrying an heiress had to become a member of the *albergo* by taking the Grimaldi name, a common enough stipulation of filiacentric unions or other forms of property settlement, although the allegiance and naming of the children of the marriage is usually the central issue. In this situation there would be no endowment of the wife by the husband and her father would doubtless attempt to keep control of the property as long as possible, although the promise of future access to the bride's estate is clearly a major component in the marriage.

On the other hand the transmission of parental property to outmarrying women in the shape of a direct dowry encourages the early break-up or mortgaging of the family estate and the same fate arises from the endowment of 'non-inheriting' sons. Some protection can be gained by reserving the land itself for a single heir, especially a son who can contract a standard (i.e. virilocal) marriage. Hughes notes that urban society in Southern Europe tended increasingly to reserve real property for males. Husbands often preferred cash dowries which could be more easily merged with their own estates, although these amounts had to be restored on the dissolution of the marriage unless wives were to be provided with a living from the husband's property. She argues that a direct dowry in cash increased the degree of control possible to the husband, for land is easier to account for and easier to protect. On the other hand, the broad contrast with an indirect dowry suggests that the directly endowed wife, unless she was an 'heiress', would tend to be more independent of both husband and father.

In listing the characteristic features of Eastern and Western structures, Guichard did not specifically include the nature of marriage transactions though it would have been in keeping with the general trend of his analysis. Patrilineal systems are often associated with bridewealth, bilateral ones with dowry. I have suggested that some of the terms of this contrast need to be qualified. Unless one is comparing the nomadic pastoralists of the Fezzan with the city dwellers of Florence, the contrast needs to be more subtle, more shaded. In particular the evidence for a shift from a bridewealth (or brideprice) *system* to a dowry *system* seems weak, almost entirely dependent upon the identification of single transfers that are embedded in different sets of transactions, with the result that there is a drastic foreshortening of the historical perspective. However, the shift in emphasis to which Hughes and others have pointed is a significant fact which requires an explanation. The link with the growth of agnatic *lignages* seems too specific. Even if we accept that description of what was happening, it is difficult to see how this growth, which was limited to the upper echelons of society, was better promoted by these particular changes in marriage transactions, rather than, say, by the total exclusion of daughters (from movables as well as land), or by the complete reliance on the husband's gifts. The shift has taken place over a long term, over a wide area and among different strata; it requires a more general explanation.

The change of emphasis to direct dowry was a change in tune with Roman law, although there too a husband made a 'donation' at marriage. Should the move to direct dowry, which is a move to earlier and increased control by married women, be examined in the context of the Church's emphasis on women as independent owners of alienable property? It is surely one aspect of the Church's increasing interest in marriage and inheritance from the beginning of the fourth century, which was later rekindled by the reforms of the eleventh.

Appendix 3. 'Bilaterality' and the development of English kin terminology

We have seen that many features thought to be characteristic of modern European kinship have a long history which is not confined to that continent alone. 'Bilaterality' was one such feature in question. There has, of course, been some change in Europe over the centuries. Patrilineal clans, where they existed, have mostly disappeared. Bilateral reckoning dominates more exclusively the computation of kin and the type of terminology, though its range of application has certainly narrowed. If we look at the recorded changes in kin terms over time these developments cannot be regarded as initiated by the growth of feudalism, by industrialisation, nor yet by specific ethnic or cultural factors. For when they first come to our attention the kinship systems of the major Eurasian societies already had a strong bilateral component about them, linked to the presence of dowry and to a number of related factors (Goody 1976a). But subsequently Europe saw some significant changes from the types of terminology that were widespread in Eurasia. The critical shifts that led to our present system began long ago and were pan-European. They were introduced at roughly the same time and place as other features of the kinship system we have examined, that is to say, before Vulgar Latin had split into the ancestors of the Romance languages.

In technical terms, the shift in the European kinship terminology has been from a bifurcate-collateral system to a lineal one. The former splits (forks, bifurcates) the paternal and maternal lines, providing individual terms for six roles in the parental generation, that is, for father, father's brother, father's sister, as well as for mother, mother's brother, mother's sister. The lineal system on the other hand provides a single term for the male siblings of the parents (e.g. 'uncle'), which differs from the 'father' term; the same applies to females of that generation, giving four terms in all. It is not therefore a 'classificatory system' in Morgan's restricted sense and does not emphasise the unity of parents' siblings of the same sex (e.g. 'father' = 'father's brother'), as might be expected in a society where clans or lineages played an important role. It has been suggested by Anderson that the factors involved in the emergence of the distinction between 'father' and 'father's brother' may have included 'the greater strength of the nuclear family within the extended family, or, perhaps in the inheritance of property, in addition to jointly owned property, which is inherited only by lineal and not by collateral descendants' (1963: 6). Those terminological distinctions were already present in many classical Mediterranean societies. Moreover the distinctions between the 'nuclear' and 'extended' family, and between 'personal' and 'family' property were certainly not inventions of the Indo-Europeans; both are firmly established in much simpler societies in northern Ghana and elsewhere (Fortes 1945: 178; Goody 1956).

The shift that occurred was from an 'individualising' terminology for the senior generation (separate terms for all) to one that distinguishes the parental pair by grouping paternal and maternal siblings of the same sex together under one term – 'uncle' or 'aunt'. For European languages this move from bifurcate-collateral to lineal appears to have begun in Vulgar Latin at the end of the Roman period. Today lineal terms are found in modern French, Spanish, Sephardic-Spanish, Portuguese, Italian, Catalan, Provencal, Rhaetian and Rumanian. Anderson sees this change as connected with the development of the Roman Empire, and specifically with the processes of colonisation and commercialisation, which led to the displacement of the extended by the conjugal family, to the breakdown of the earlier concept of family property, to the introduction of testamentary inheritance and to bilateral prohibitions on marriage. But, as we have seen, these changes in terminology (and the bilateral prohibitions on marriage) belong to the decline rather than the zenith of that empire: the author himself recognises that the change in terminology happened later than the social changes themselves but before 'the isolation of these peoples from each other following the breakdown of the Roman military organization and school system around 700 A.D.' (Anderson 1963: 6–7; Grandgent 1908: 3–4).

Among the Mediterranean peoples, only the Greeks give any indication of an earlier use of lineal terminology, although that set of terms was certainly an alternative to the dominant, bifurcate-collateral set. Alternate terminologies pose a problem for analysis, because we are only likely to know about them when the evidence is abundant. The Greek terminology may possibly have influenced the Latin, for the terms for uncle (Gk. *theios*) and aunt are clearly related to the words in Italian (*zio*), Spanish and Portuguese. However this may be, we have to recognise that while the type to which our present terminology belongs was not a dominant feature of the Ancient Mediterranean, it certainly gained wide currency among the Romance languages in the post-Roman period. The classical Latin term for mother's brother (*avunculus*) gave birth to 'uncle' which was then used bilaterally for the brothers of both parents. In parallel fashion the term for the father's cross-sex sibling (*amita*) becomes 'aunt' and is applied to both sides. In this way bifurcate-collateral gave way to lineal. It was only at a later date that the Germanic languages adopted this type of terminology, in England through the invasions of the Norman French, in Germany in the seventeenth century, while in Scandinavia these southern influences have not yet gained the ascendency even today. As with classical civilisation, Christianity and the Renaissance, the flow has been from south to north.

In the case of the Germanic languages the earliest modification in the terminology first appears around A.D. 1100 and has been attributed to the weakening of kinship obligations and ties under pressure from feudal institutions (Anderson 1963: 17), a hypothesis that is consistent with one interpretation of the increased emphasis on the *lignage*. But in Germany the shift to a lineal terminology took place only in the seventeenth century under the same influence, that of France, which had led to the earlier change in the Anglo-Saxon vocabulary.

The original Anglo-Saxon terms were of course cognate with Old High German (O.H.G.); so too was the structure. In Old High German the words for parental siblings differentiated each genealogical position, in bifurcate-collateral fashion:

fetiro (*fatureo*)	=	father's brother
oheim	=	mother's brother
basa	=	father's sister
muoma	=	mother's sister

The terms *nevo/nefo* and *nift* were used for child's son (grandson) and child's daughter (grand-daughter) respectively. In the Middle High German period after A.D. 1100, the last two terms took on their present meanings (sibling's child) as well as being used for cousin (parent's sibling's child). A study of six thirteenth-century genealogies showed that the term was twice used for a nephew (sister's son), twice for a first cousin (MBS, FZS), once for a first cousin once removed (FZDS) and once for a first cousin twice removed (MZSSS) (Szemerényi 1977: 182). In addition, right down to Luther, father of the New German, the word still carried the significance of grandson. Moreover *neve* came to be employed reciprocally for 'uncle' and *nift* for 'aunt', just as the nephew could be called *oheim*. This usage introduced a lineal system, though the earlier bifurcate-collateral terms were also current.

The use of these two terms, *nevo* and *nift*, 'nephew' and 'niece', continued over a long period; only in the late eighteenth century did *nefo*, *neffe*, cease to be used for grandchild, by which time the alternative form, *enenkel* (a diminutive of *ano*, grandfather), had already appeared in Middle High German (Szemerényi 1977: 52) with the gradual restriction of *neffe* and *nichte* to 'nephew' and 'niece'.

At the same time as this change was taking place, the term *vetter*, derived from O.H.G. *fetiro* for father's brother, took on the additional meanings of 'cousin', 'brother's son' and, in the plural, 'relations' in general. Today the usual meaning is 'cousin' (Szemerényi 1977: 182). In a parallel fashion the term *basa* (from O.H.G. for father's sister) became used for women of these same generations. The downward shift of these two terms for paternal siblings to ego's own and junior generation seems to have resulted from the adoption of the words for the mother's siblings *oheim* and *muhme*, for 'uncle' and 'aunt' in a lineal system, making redundant the two other terms for parents' siblings. Note that it was the terms for maternal rather than paternal siblings that became generalised in this 'lineal' way.

The reinterpretation of the earlier set of terms brought German into line with the older lineal system of the Romance languages, from which the Germans themselves later borrowed *onkel* and *tante*. Whereas it was the force of Norman arms that had been the immediate cause of the change in Anglo-Saxon terminology, it was the high prestige of French culture in the seventeenth century that led the Germans to adopt the same extra-familial terms as the English had done some six centuries earlier, namely *onkel* and *tante*, *cousin* and *cousine*.

In Anglo-Saxon, *nefa* appears to have had a similar range of meanings as in Old High German, namely, 'nephew', 'grandson', 'male cousin', and for *nift*, 'niece', 'grand-daughter', 'female cousin'.[1] After the Norman invasion the French 'cousin' came partially to replace *nefa*/*nift*, being used to denote 'a collateral relative more distant than a brother or sister; a kinsman or kinswoman, a relative; formerly very frequently applied to a nephew or niece' (*N.E.D.*, *cousin*) and this wide usage continued right down to the nineteenth century; even today the term 'cousin' crosses the generations. Meanwhile the terms nephew/niece were used not only in their present sense but, until the seventeenth century, for grandchild as well. It was the sixteenth century that saw the use of the term grandson;[2] for ascendants, *grand* had earlier been borrowed from the French; the same *grand* was now adopted for descendants whereas the French equivalent more logically emphasised the opposite attribute, *petit*. The usage, however curious from an etymological standpoint, identifies the alternate generations in a way similar to later German terminology, providing a modified example of a reciprocal usage not uncommon in the world of kinship systems.

The identification between grandson, nephew and cousin is found in other Indo-European languages (Szemerényi 1977: 50). The Latin *nepos*, the Old High German *nefo*, the Old English *nefa*, all carry the meaning of nephew as well as grandson. The Greek *aneptios*, derived from grandson, stands for 'cousin' and in Modern Greek, 'nephew'. In Latin the meaning 'nephew' appears to have emerged only after the fourth century A.D. In Old French the word still carried the meaning of 'grandson', though it later shifted to 'nephew' in both French and Italian,[3] while in the Hispanic peninsula the Spanish *neto*(*a*) and Portuguese *neto*(*a*) continue to refer only to the 'grandson' down to the present day. This distribution of usages in the Romance languages suggests to Szemerényi 'that the original meaning was "grandson", which shifted to "nephew", "cousin", etc. in various areas', often in historical times (p. 156,168). The terms came to refer to a constellation of relations of different generations but subsequently became limited to 'nephew' or 'cousin' rather than 'grandchild' in most languages, with the result that other terms had to be invented or adapted for the latter relationship.

---

[1]   Lancaster (1958) gives *swor* (or *swear*, p. 237) for cousin, especially on the mother's side. The terminology seems variable. She reports *nefa* as also meaning stepson.

[2]   The earliest recorded use is 1586. I am indebted to Malcolm Ruel for his comments.

[3]   In Italian, grandson/grand-daughter and nephew/niece continue to be covered by the single term, *nepote*.

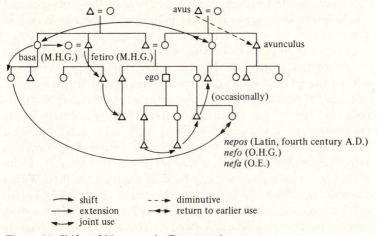

Figure 11. Shifts of kin terms in European languages

As we have seen, a similar change took place in German, though in a downward rather than an upward direction; *fetiro/vetter* shifted from 'father's brother' to 'cousin', while the parallel term for 'father's sister', *base/basa* in O.H.G. and M.G.H., were later used for 'mother's sister' and 'father's brother's wife', before dropping down the generations to be applied even to 'niece' and 'cousin'. Today the normal meaning is 'female cousin', and only in Switzerland does it mean 'aunt' (Szemerényi 1977: 192).

There was a similar development in Celtic where we find terms of the *awos* family giving rise to 'grandfather' and 'uncle' (Charles-Edwards 1971: 106),[4] and of the *nepōts* class producing 'grandson', 'nephew' (sometimes 'sister's son'), 'cousin'. Here as in Latin, the 'grandson' and 'grandfather' usages seem to have provided the starting point, at least for the second set (Charles-Edwards 1971: 121). But in Brythonic, the ancestor of the southern dialects, *awos* was lost, leaving *awintros* and *neīs* (from *nepōts*) as a pair, their influence on each other producing a correlative pair, *neīs* becoming 'nephew in general' and *awintros*, 'uncle in general'. Once again the

---

[4] There seems little theoretical or empirical justification for the equation of *awos* with '*paternal* grandfather'. The translation is in line with a general emphasis on the agnatic element in Celtic kinship (Charles-Edwards 1972) but not with other discussions of Indo-European terminologies, much less with the usual pattern of kin terms for alternate generations.

result was a lineal system, parallel to those of the Romance and Anglo-Saxon languages which had influenced Welsh and Breton in this direction.

In Norman England this change was not only one of structure but of differential borrowing. The particular loan words taken from French to replace Anglo-Saxon roots stressed not only the bilateral character of kinship (which was also a feature of the earlier bifurcate-collateral system) but the distinct nature of the elementary family (which was now given greater stress by the lineal system). Of course the recognition of more extended kinship links and residence in larger households is perfectly consistent with the presence of smaller units known as elementary (conjugal or nuclear) families. Within the wider set of kinship usages, the elementary family is often given specific recognition by means of distinct terms, especially in societies marked by diverging devolution and its associated features (Goody 1976b).

Even in the Anglo-Saxon period, the terminology tended to isolate the elementary family as in other Indo-European systems. It was not classificatory but descriptive (or individualising), to take up Morgan's usage; that is to say, lineal kin are differentiated from collaterals. *Broðer* (full sibling) is set aside terminologically from cousin. A similar separation is made at the first ascending generation. *Eam* (mother's brother) is distinguished from *faeder* (father), and the latter term is very close to but distinguished from, *faedera* (father's brother). Similar distinctions hold true of the terms for mother, mother's sister and father's sister.

In discussing the extent to which the terms for more distant kin were actually applied, Lancaster maintains that there is little in the cousin terminology to suggest that usage was not restricted 'to a relatively small set of kin centred upon Ego' (1958: 237). Indeed, her conclusions suggest not only the absence of unilineal descent groups but the presence of a much smaller circle of effective kin than is often supposed. This conclusion has not gone unchallenged (Charles-Edwards 1972); certainly the reckoning of kinship ties differs in range in different contexts (Bullough 1969: 15; Leyser 1968: 36) and to this flexibility the terminology alone is not a very sensitive guide. However the elementary family itself, or rather the families of birth and of marriage, of orientation and procreation, is very clearly set aside in the terminology, a fact that is strikingly brought out by the changes resulting from the Norman Conquest.

Generation

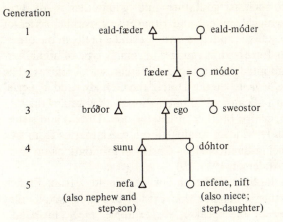

Figure 12. Anglo-Saxon terms for lineal kin

With some small modifications the Anglo-Saxon terms for members of the elementary family (as well as those for husband and wife) are the same as in modern English (Figure 12). On the other hand, those for collaterals changed radically with the invasion of the Norman French. In the first ascending (parent's) generation, 'aunt' (Latin, *amita*) replaced both *modrige* (mother's sister) and *faðu* (father's sister), while 'uncle' (Latin, *avunculus*) replaced *faedera* (father's brother) and *eam* (mother's brother).

The 'core' terms for affines also stayed the same, 'husband' (from *bonda*) and 'wife' (*wyf*). All other affinal terms underwent a change by taking the Anglo-Saxon word for the parallel consanguine, e.g. 'brother', and adding to it that curious suffix 'in-law' (brother-in-law, aunt-in-law) which was also used for step-relations until well into the nineteenth century. With the affinal terms for ego's own generation, the same kind of 'bilateral' simplification occurs as with those for parents' siblings (i.e uncle, aunt). That is to say, brother-in-law can mean either sister's husband or wife's brother.

The English affinal terms are clearly linked to the introduction of Christian rules of marriage. The way in which the nuclear terms, 'father', 'mother', etc., are modified by the phrase 'in-law' acknowledges the fact that, from the standpoint of marriage, these relatives are kin in the eyes of the Church. Canon law places them in the prohibited range of marriage partners, just as it does those linked by

spiritual kinship, such as 'godfather' and 'godmother'.[5] All three
systems, consanguineal, affinal and ritual, use a parallel series of
terms to which a suffix is added in one case and a prefix in the other.

In other major European languages, a similar type of affinal terminology was adopted but using a different set of affixes. The
French add *beau/belle*, as do the Dutch; the Germans add a special
morpheme as an indicator of affinity, though they retain the Old
High German terms for brother-in-law (as does Dutch) and sister-
in-law. Significantly Yiddish retains all the special terms from Old
High German, being unaffected by Christian prohibitions on marriage to affines (Anderson 1963: 29).

The English adoption of the 'in-law' terminology from French
eliminated a further difference that existed in Anglo-Saxon, that
based on the sex of the speaker, for example, *tacor*, husband's
brother, *aetum*, sister's husband (Lancaster 1958: 248). For Classical
Latin Anderson lists seven terms for affines of ego's own generation,
including *levir*, husband's brother, and *cognatus*, wife's brother. In
Vulgar Latin *cognatus* came to mean 'brother-in-law', foreshadow-
ing the developments in the Romance languages, among which the
French system of affinal terms is unusual (Anderson 1963: 28), bearing more resemblance in pattern to those of German and English.

The change in Latin usage occurred by the fourth century when
the word *cognatus* took on meanings other than (roughly) 'cognate',
and came to mean not only 'brother-in-law' and 'sister-in-law' but
exceptionally other affinal relations as well. At the same time the
Roman term *adfinis* (*aff*-), relation by marriage, disappeared. In this
way 'affines' became kin ('cognates'), a terminological change that
was in keeping with the prohibition on marrying the relative of a
spouse; affines were effectively incorporated, at least legally, as 'in-
laws', into the range of an individual's kin. The usage appears to
have been a well established one in spoken (Vulgar) Latin, for deriv-
atives of *cognatus* are found in almost all the Romance languages,
including Rumanian (*cumnat*) (Bullough 1969: 10). Its use was
linked to the efforts of churchmen from the sixth century onwards
'to get the Christianized Germanic peoples, whose own traditional

---

[5] The specific form of the English affinal terms is presumably derived from the
distinction in later Roman law between, for example, *pater ex natura* and *pater ex
lege*, the father in nature and the father in law, the latter referring to an adopter
(Biondi 1954: 61); it is a distinction lying at the heart of the objection of Salvian and
others to 'fictonal kinship' as a strategy of heirship.

attitudes were under certain circumstances often very different – among them the Burgundians, the Anglo-Saxons, and later the Lombards – to accept the incestuous nature of marriage or adultery with a sister-in-law' (Bullough 1969: 11). Chapter 9 of the Roman synod of 721 declared that 'If anyone shall have taken a wife from his own *cognatio* or whose *cognatus* (that is affine, in-law) he already is, let him be anathema' (pp. 11–12).

While the Norman conquest resulted in the substitution of French terms for Anglo-Saxon ones outside the elementary family, leaving untouched the Germanic roots within, this substitution did not happen all at once, at least according to the exiguous documentary records. According to the *New English Dictionary*, the first written use of 'uncle' was *c.*1290 (South English Legendary, I. 205, lines 31–2). The term 'aunt' made its appearance in writing about 1300; Mountfort . . .' his aunte sone' (Robert of Gloucester, para. 571, lines 12045–46) while that of 'cousin' ('cosin') is recorded in *Cursor Mundi* (IV. iii,p. 1390, line 24312) in 1300, about the time when we come across the in-law suffixes for affinal relations (e.g. 'brother-in-lawe').

As I have mentioned, the term 'cousin' was initially used in a much wider sense since it could also include 'nephew' and 'niece', indeed virtually any 'relative' outside the nuclear kin, or rather 'line of filiation'. However we find *nece* and *newewe* with their present-day meanings in wills of the early fifteenth century (Furnivall 1882: 50, referring to a will of 1422, which also gives us 'god doutghter'). 'Cousin' in the sense of 'brother's son' turns up in Shakespeare's *Much Ado About Nothing* (I. ii. 2) and much later in Richardson's *Clarissa Harlowe* (1748, I. vi. 36), 'Cousin Harlowe, said my aunt Hervey, allow me to say that my cousin Clary's prudence may be confided in'; she was speaking to her nephew about her niece. In other words the term could signify any kinsman outside the elementary family, of the same or junior generation, although it was also employed in the stricter modern sense.

The adoption of French terms did not mean the complete abandonment of the Anglo-Saxon ones. A fourteenth-century text (*c.* 1330) gives us '(th)y sister sonne am I, (th)ou eam & I cosyn' (Hearne 1810: IIII,189), a redundancy that occurs again in Trevisa (1872): Higden Rolls IV. 235): '(th)at was Aristobolus, his eme and unkel'. It is perhaps significant that the distinction between the males of the parental generation was kept up after it had been dropped for females, presumably because of the greater importance of the males and their substantially different roles that continued into the period of the medieval romances. One interesting use appears in a deposition about a will made in the parish of Huyton, near Liverpool, in 1563, in which Richard Pendleton had left a 'tacte' of ground to the children of his daughter Emma, though another claimant asserted he had also bequeathed it to his sisters. On the afternoon of the testator's death, he was asked, 'Eame Richard, will you have any thinge alterid in your will.' And he replied, 'No, neiboures.' On the use of this term of address, Furnivall comments, 'Uncle, tho he was Grandfather' (1897: 132), a usage that appears similar to the association in Latin between grandfather and uncle. The relationship is not explicitly mentioned in the text, and the internal evidence seems to stress 'kithship' rather than 'kinship'; in which case 'eame' would be used as a term of respect for a senior member of the community.

The word 'eam' continued to be employed in a number of regions of England, being part of the vocabulary of eastern Scotland until quite recently. It was used by Walter Scott in *The Heart of Mid-Lothian* (1818) and a century earlier the term makes its appearance in a highly pregnant proverb: 'Many aunts, many emms, many kinsfolk, few friends' (Kelly 1721). Its more recent use is recorded in *The English Dialect Dictionary* (1900) for Yorkshire and for Shropshire, where it was declared to be 'all but extinct'. In these regions of England and Scotland the word clearly formed part of a 'submerged' kinship terminology, of which *nanna* for grandmother, especially mother's mother, was another example (Goody 1962b), and which perhaps became submerged through the domination of the written language that at once represented a regional (southern), a class (upper and middle) and an urban constituency.

Standard and local terminologies existed side by side. In addition we find a third set of kinship terms used by the Church in order to calculate the degrees of consanguinity that determined the range of prohibited marriages. This range was usually represented in the form of the tree of consanguinity.

The juridical sources for these trees were twofold: in the West the *Sententiae Pauli* (IV. 11), and in the East, the *Institutes of Justinian* (III. 6) of A.D. 533. Both of these texts were primarily concerned with degrees of consanguinity from the standpoint of inheritance, a concern that derived from earlier Roman law. 'It is the originality of the early Middle Ages', claimed Patlagean, 'to have turned them towards new ends that had taken on an importance hitherto unknown' (1966: 65), that is, the negative end of prohibiting marriage superseded the positive one of regulating inheritance; the practice of collateral inheritance being now condemned, or at least restricted, by some churchmen, the system was remodelled for regulating marriage.

The principle behind the section of Justinian concerned with calculating the degrees of relationship (*de gradibus cognationis*) in the context of inheritance is that 'every new person born adds a degree'. By this calculus it is 'easier to tell in what degree of relationship someone is than to identify him by the term proper to the nature of his relationship' (Justinian III. 6; Thomas 1975: 180). The bias introduced into a system of kinship nomenclature by a method designed to provide a calculus of proximity for the purpose of inheritance is clear. There will be a strong tendency to provide specific labels for each kinship position genealogically defined, a trend that is reinforced by the reduction of oral speech to a written format. 'Since the truth imprints itself more on the minds of men when it is seen than when it is heard, we held it necessary after expounding the degrees of kindred, to record them in the present book so that the young, by both seeing and hearing, might completely comprehend the doctrine thereof' (p. 180). The importance of this representation by means of a visual matrix emerges in the statement that 'some relationship is ascendant (*supra*) some descendant (*infra*) and some collateral (*transverso*) which gets its name from "side" (*latus*)'. The same system, with its visual, genealogical format, is employed in the West by Paulus who also accepts the seventh such degree as the limit for the reckoning of inheritance and hence the limit of kinship.[6]

The visual forms of these genealogical schemas are of great interest. Beginning in the eighth century with the oldest manuscript of Isidore of Seville we find the degrees of consanguinity being represented in the form of a crucifix. Later on other documents display the same information in the shape of a tree (*arbor iuris*) or of a man. The connections between the three forms were developed by subsequent artists, for the man comes to be represented as Christ (Patla-

---

[6] 'Successionis idcirco gradus septem constituti sunt, quia utterius per rerum naturam nec nomina inveniri, nec vita succedentibus prorogari potest' (*Sententiae Pauli* IV. 11. 8).

gean 1966: 67), attesting to the celestial origin of the marriage prohibitions. In this type of representation of kinship by the human (or
divine) figure, a link has been seen with the ancient Germanic mode
of computation based on the articulations of the human body
(Chapter 6). Was the Christ figure a translation of the Germanic
mode of reckoning? A number of authors (e.g. Patlagean 1966: 68;
Lancaster 1958: 231; Bullough 1969: 15) have claimed that the evidence for the systematic calculation of kinship by reference to the
human body is from a much later period. Even though Damian
refers to the human body in the treatise defending the Germanico-
canonical system,[7] the first full account appears in the collection of
laws known as *Sachsenspiegel* (1220–1235); earlier references to
'knee' (or *genu*, *genucula*) have apparently to be taken in the general
sense of 'articulation', joint (*Edict. Rotar.* 153; *Lex Salica*
XLIV. 9,10; *Lex Ribuaria* LVI. 3),[8] though of course a general
connection between body and kin is thereby established and the
possibility of a more precise link does not lie far below the surface of
many human cultures.

In these figures, the central trunk (*truncus*) consists of two lines,
one paternal, one maternal, which are divided into six generational
segments running upwards from the father/mother, and six running
downwards from the mother/daughter (Figure 13). In the same horizontal axis as the father are a number of boxes each containing
one relationship term, 'brother', then 'brother's son' and so on.
Thus the horizontal axes cut across generations in a way that is
similar to some of the terminological usages we have just looked at.
In reckoning the steps from the common ancestor, the Roman law
adds a degree (*gradus*) for each of the first six generations in the
trunk, starting with the top and continuing to the generation of

---

[7] 'Quod instar humani corporis sex gradibus consanguinitas terminetur' (Damian, *De
   Parentelae Gradibus* chap. II, col. 183; Migne, *Patrologiae* tom. 145, p. 193).
[8] See also Bullough (1969: 15), but Charles-Edwards (1972: 23) insists on 'knee'
   apparently in the general sense. It should be added that a further terminology of
   cousinhood differs once again from the two ecclesiastical systems; it is the one that
   many nations of Western Europe use in everyday speech. In this system a first cousin
   (2nd degree Germanic, 4th degree Roman) is a child of the parent's siblings, a
   second cousin (3rd/6th degrees) a child of the siblings of grandparents; the sequence
   is ordered on a lateral (i.e. horizontal) count of genealogical boxes beginning with
   ego. Kin related to these cousins in a lineal (i.e. vertical) way are described, e.g. as a
   second cousin once removed, the specification of distance again referring to a visual
   representation of a matrix of boxes. An analysis of this system would require much
   more time and research.

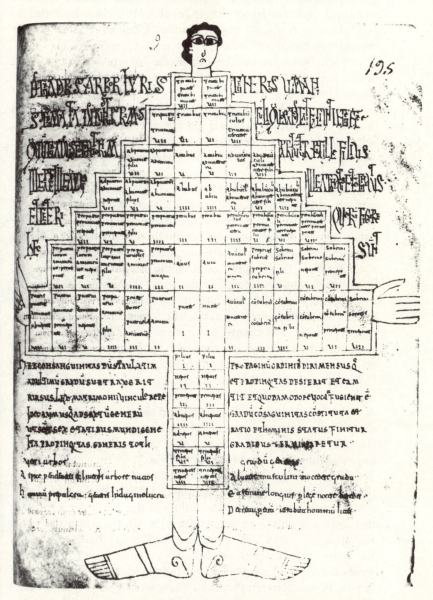

Figure 13. The Cross, the Tree, the Man. A table of consanguinity from an eleventh-century manuscript of Isidore of Seville (Patlagean 1966: 67)

ego's parents. A variation occurs in the later western tradition stemming from Isidore of Seville (*c.* 560–636) which is related to legal changes. A seventh degree is added, placing 'uncle' instead of 'brother' at the side of 'father'.

The common feature of these three types of representation, which are all concerned with degrees of kinship (genealogical distance between kinship positions) rather than the recording of individual genealogies, much less terms of address, is that each of the forms chosen, the cross, the man and the tree, is essentially bilateral. One side of the two dimensional figure balances the other, not only in the number of roles recognised but to a large extent in the structure of the terminology as well.

This cruciform table of kindred, which involves an equal elaboration on both sides, emerged in the context of the calculation of prohibited degrees of marriage; inheritance, with which earlier calculations were concerned, would certainly have required a different representation, because it sets up priorities (e.g. brothers before sisters) rather than simply establishing ranges. In transmission, males were counted before females, even though in 543 a law of Justinian suppressed the special features of *adgnatio* thus leaving the system of 'consanguinity' (i.e. bilateral kinship) on its own (Patlagean 1966: 79). The change was symptomatic. By the fourth century, according to Bullough, the legal significance of the agnatic tie had greatly diminished, especially in the sphere of inheritance. In the following century, a claim to inherit from one's *agnatus proximus* would have been difficult to sustain (1969: 8). However the *arbor juris* itself continued to preserve some difference in terminology for the two sides, paternal and maternal, because it maintained intact the bifurcate terms of Classical Latin, differentiating parental siblings individually, and putting on one side the vernacular words of Vulgar Latin which had long since developed a lineal form. Each position in the figure needed a distinctive label. On the other hand, ever since the sixth century the editors of the *Institutiones* in Latin had drawn attention to the tendency in Greek to use the terms *thios/thia* for 'uncles' and 'aunts', a 'lineal' usage that is reflected in the figures themselves (Patlagean 1966: Table 1). But in most respects the terminology used in calculations of this kind, which were imposed from above rather than rising from below, was not only conservative but was removed from the usages current in other contexts of social life. For instance, the terminology used in the tree tended to become more elaborate as the prohibitions were extended by the Church (p. 78); in other words, the nomenclature responded to the need to represent the new injunctions in a visual form.

In concluding these comments on the development of English kinship terminology, the first point to note is that the merger of French and Anglo-Saxon terms increased the 'nominal' independence of the elementary family (or line of filiation) and increased the bilateral balance. Since the Norman conquest, there have been other changes in terminology, and more particularly in usage, as in the case of 'cousin' and 'nephew/niece'. There were undoubtedly important regional and class variations of the kind pointed out in the use of the term 'nanna'. But, as a system or structure (in Piaget's sense) capable of being analysed in its own right (for example, as a set by the methods of componential or other type of formal analysis), the terminology has remained much the same since the Norman conquest.

There are two additional points I want to draw out of these facts. Firstly, the kin terms themselves appear to have been relatively little influenced by the enormous changes in culture and society that have taken place in Western Europe from the eleventh century to this day. No one doubts that patterns of marriage, inheritance and family behaviour have undergone very important changes over this period but the terminology itself is not a very sensitive indicator of what was taking place. We still use the same terms in roughly the same genealogical ways as our distant ancestors, despite the changes in the quality and structure of relations. The linguistic correlates of fundamental changes could only be discerned by examining the interactive process at a subtler level. The major shift in terminology happened as the immediate result not of a process of internal adjustment to these major socio-economic changes but through the military and cultural domination arising from the Norman conquest.

At first sight the second point appears to run counter to the first. The change to terms of French origin for collaterals was not simply one of vocabulary but also of structure. Though this change came about through external pressure, it was nevertheless in tune with a more general movement towards the elimination of lateral differences in the kinship terminologies of Western Europe which was undoubtedly in line with certain broad features of the changes in kinship systems that were taking place. Anderson has remarked that 'where historical data are available it was found that contemporary

Indo-European systems of the lineal type were in every instance preceded by terminologies of either the bifurcate-collateral or of the mixed type. Specifically, this was found to be true among certain societies speaking Germanic, Romance, Greek, Celtic, Slavic and Baltic languages' (1963: 9). This shift he attributes to 'the replacement of the patrilineal extended family by the conjugal family as the basic unit of social organization', that is, to the change that other writers have seen as linked to Byzantium, the late Roman Empire, early Anglo-Saxon England, the Black Death of the fourteenth century (Razi 1981: 3) or that either facilitated or followed the development of industrial society. Domestic life certainly reacted to the major changes in the economy both before and after industrialisation. Some features of the existing system may have helped to stimulate the accumulation of the necessary capital and the work ethic. However, as with other major features examined in this essay, changes in the form and content of the kinship terminology, gradual as these were, owe their origin to much earlier influences which mark Western Europe as a whole – bifurcate-collateral systems are already 'bilateral'. The development of a lineal set of terms we see as linked to the economy of religious and state institutions rather than to the economy of production itself. Anderson himself remarks that in most of Western Europe 'Christianity is associated with the use of lineal terms' (1963: 7). This type of nomenclature does seem to have followed the adoption of Christianity, very slowly in some cases. But once again, the development had little to do with the Roman background or the Jewish scriptures. It was an original feature of early medieval Christianity, to be associated with the shift from sect to Church and with the great build-up of the latter as a major feature of society, indeed as its Second Estate.

References and bibliography

Abrams, P. and McCulloch, A. 1976, *Communes, Sociology and Society*, Cambridge

Acta Conciliorum et Epistolae Decretales ac Constitutiones summorum Pontificum (ed. J. Hardouin), 1714, Paris

Adams, R. M. 1966, *The Evolution of Urban Society: Early Mesopotamia and Prehispanic Mexico*, London

Anderson, R. T. 1963, Changing kinship in Europe, *Kroeber Anthrop. Soc.* 28: 1–47

Angenendt, A. 1972, *Monachi Peregrini*, Munich

Anton, A. E. 1958, Handfasting in Scotland, *Scott. Hist. Review* 37: 89–102

Arensberg, C. and Kimball, S. T. 1940, *Family and Community in Ireland*, Cambridge, Mass.

Argyle, M. 1958, *Religious Behaviour*, London

Attenborough, F. L. 1922, *The Laws of the Earliest English Kings*, Cambridge

Barlow, F. 1963, *The English Church 1000–1066: a constitutional history*, London

Barnes, J. A. 1957, Land rights and kinship in two Bremnes hamlets, *J. R. Anthrop. Inst.* 87: 31–56

Bazant, J. 1971, *Alienation of Church Wealth in Mexico: social and economic aspects of the Liberal Revolution 1856–1875*, Cambridge

Becon, T. 1844, *The Catechism of Thomas Becon, S.T.P.* (ed. J. Ayre), Parker Society, Cambridge

Bede 1969, *Ecclesiastical History of the English People* (ed. B. Colgrave and R.A.B. Mynors), Oxford

Bennett, M. 1979, Spiritual kinship and the baptismal name in traditional European society. In L. O. Frappell (ed.), *Principalities, Powers and Estates: studies in medieval and early modern government and society*, Adelaide

Biddle, M. (ed.) 1976, *Winchester Studies I. Winchester in the Early Middle Ages: an edition and discussion of the Winton Domesday*, Oxford

Bieler, L. (ed.) 1963, *The Irish Penitentials*, Dublin

Billar, P. P. A. 1982, Birth control in the medieval West, *Past and Present* 94: 3–26

Biondi, B. 1952–4, *Il Diritto Romano Christiano*, 3 vols., Milan

Black-Michaud, J. 1975, *Cohesive Force*, Oxford

Bloch, M. 1961, *Feudal Society*, 2 vols., London (1st Fr. ed. 1939–40)

Blok, A. 1974, *The Mafia of a Sicilian Village, 1860–1960*, Oxford

Boehmer, H. 1921, Das Eigenkirchentum in England. In *Texte und Forschungen zur Englischen Kulturgeschichte: Festgabe für Felix Liebermann zum 20, Juli 1921*, Halle

Bossy, J. 1970, The Counter-Reformation and the people of Catholic Europe, *Past and Present* 47: 51–70

1973, Blood and baptism: kinship, community and Christianity in Western Europe from the fourteenth to the seventeenth centuries. In D. Baker (ed.), *Sanctity and Secularity: the Church and the World*, Cambridge

1975, The social history of confession in the age of the Reformation, *R. Hist. Soc.* 5th ser., 25: 21–38

Bosworth, J. 1898, *An Anglo-Saxon Dictionary*, London

Bouchard C. B. 1981, Consanguinity and noble marriages in the tenth and eleventh centuries, *Speculum* 56: 268–87

Bourdieu, P. 1977, *Outline of a Theory of Practice*, Cambridge (Engl. ed. of *Esquisse d'une théorie de la practique, précedée de trois études d'ethnologie kabyle*, 1972, Geneva)

Braudel, F. 1972 (1966), *The Mediterranean and the Mediterranean World in the Age of Philip II*, vol. I, London (transl. of revised Fr. ed.: 1st ed. 1949)

Brehaut, E. (transl.) 1916, *History of the Franks by Gregory Bishop of Tours*, New York

Brett, M. 1975, *The English Church under Henry I*, London

Brooke, C. N. L. 1964, *Europe in the Central Middle Ages 962–1154*, London

1969, *The Twelfth Century Renaissance*, London

1978, *Marriage in Christian History*, Cambridge

Brown, P. 1972, *Religion and Society in the Age of Saint Augustine*, London

Bruce, J. and Perowne, T. T. (eds.) 1853, *Correspondence of Mathew Parker, D. D., Archbishop of Canterbury*, Parker Society, Cambridge

Bruck, E. F. 1956, *Kirchenväter und soziales erbrecht*, Berlin

Bruns, H. T. 1839, *Canones Apostolorum et Conciliorum saec. IV–VII*, Berlin

Bullough, D. A. 1969, Early medieval social groupings: the terminology of kinship, *Past and Present* 45: 3–18

Burnet, G. 1730, *The History of the Reformation of the Church of England*, 3 vols., Dublin (1st ed., London, 1715)

Burton, R. 1652, *The Anatomy of Melancholy*, London

Byrne, F. J. 1971, Tribes and tribalism in early Ireland, *Eriu* 22: 128–66, Dublin

Caesar, Julius 1917, *Caesar, The Gallic War*, with an English translation by H. J. Edwards, London

Caldwell, J. C. 1976, Toward a restatement of demographic transition theory, *Population and Development Review* 2: 321–66

Calvin, John 1611, *The Institution of Christian Religion* (transl. Thomas Norton), London

Canon Law (S.P.C.K.) 1947, *The Canon Law of the Church of England Being the Report of the Archbishop's Commission on Canon Law, together with Proposals for a Revised Body of Canons*, London

Carrasco, P. 1959, *Land and Polity in Tibet*, Seattle, Washington

Catholicisme: hier, aujourd'hui, demain, Paris, 1948

Champeaux, E. 1933, Jus Sanguinis, *Rev. hist. de droit français et étranger*, 4e sér.12: 241–90

Charles-Edwards, T. M. 1971, Some Celtic kinship terms, *Bull. Celtic Studies* 24: 105–22

1972, Kinship, status and the origins of the hide, *Past and Present* 56: 3–33

Chen, Han-seng 1949, *Frontier Land Systems in Southernmost China: a comparative study of agrarian problems and social organisation among the Pai Yi people of Yunnan and the Kamba people of Sinkang*, New York (Inst. of Pacific Relations)

Clunies Ross, M. 'Concubinage' in Anglo-Saxon England, M.S.

Cooper, C. H. 1843, *Annals of Cambridge*, 2 vols., Cambridge

Cooper, J. P. 1967, The social distribution of land and men in England, 1436–1700, *Econ. Hist. Rev.* 20: 419–40

1977, Patterns of inheritance and settlement by great landowners from the fifteenth to the eighteenth centuries. In J. Goody, J. Thirsk, and E. P. Thompson (eds.), *Family and Inheritance: rural society in Western Europe, 1200–1800*, Cambridge

Corbett, P. E. 1930, *The Roman Law of Marriage*, Oxford

Corbett, W. J. 1926, The development of the Duchy of Normandy and the Norman Conquest of England. In *The Cambridge Medieval History*, vol. 5, Cambridge

Coulton, G. C. 1937, *Sectarian History*, Taunton

Coverdale, Michael 1575, *The Christian State of Matrimonye* (transl. of H. Bullinger, *Der christliche Ehestand*, Antwerp, 1541), London

Crummey, D. 1981a, Family and property among the Amhara nobility, M.S.

1981b, Women and landed property in Gondarine Ethiopia, *Int. J. of African Historical Studies* 14: 443–65

Dalton, O. M. (ed.) 1927, *The History of the Franks, by Gregory of Tours*, Oxford

Damian, P. (*c.* 1063) 1663, *Beati Petri Damiani, Cardinalis, Episcopi Ostensis, ordinis sancti, Opera Omnia* (ed. C. Caetani), Paris

Daudet, P. 1933, *Études sur l'histoire de la jurisdiction matrimoniale de l'église*, Paris

Dauvillier, J. 1933, *Le Mariage dans le droit classique de l'Église dépuis le Decret de Gratien, 1140, jusqu'à la mort de Clement V, 1314*, Paris

1970, *Les Temps apostoliques: Ier siècle* (Histoire de Droit et des Institutions de l'Église en Occident, vol. II), Paris

Dauvillier, J. and Clercq, C. de 1936, *Le Mariage en droit canonique oriental*, Paris

David, M. 1981, Le mariage dans la société féodale, *Annales E.S.C.* 36: 1050–55

Davis, N. Z. 1975, *Society and Culture in Early Modern France*, Stanford, Calif.

Davis, J. 1973, *Land and Family in Pisticci*, London

D'Evelyn, C. and Mill, A. J. (eds.) 1956, *The South English Legendary*, Early English Text Society, vol. 235, London

Dickens, A. G. 1974, *The German Nation and Martin Luther*, London

Donahue, C. 1976, The policy of Alexander the Third's consent theory of marriage, *Proceedings of the Fourth International Congress of Medieval Canon Law, Toronto, 1972*, Vatican City, pp. 251–81

Dragadze, T. 1980, Blood brotherhood in Georgia. Paper presented at the Department of Social Anthropology, University of Cambridge

Drew, K. F. (transl.) 1973, *The Lombard Laws*, Philadelphia

Donati Commentum Hecyrae, B. G. Teubner, 1905, Leipzig

Duby, G. 1972, Lignage, noblesse et chevalerie au XIIe siècle dans la région mâconnaise: une révision, *Annales E.S.C.* 27: 803–23

1973, Remarques sur la littérature généalogique en France. In *Hommes et structures du moyen âge: recueil d'articles*, Paris and The Hague

1977, Présentation de l'enquête sur 'famille et sexualité au moyen âge'. In G. Duby, and J. Le Goff (eds.), *Famille et parenté dans l'occident médiéval*, Rome

1978, *Medieval Marriage: Two Models from Twelfth-Century France*, Baltimore

1974, *The Early Growth of the European Economy*, London

1981, *Le Chevalier, la femme et le prêtre: le mariage dans la France féodale*, Paris

Dumont, L. 1981, La genèse chrétienne de l'individualisme: une vue modifiée de nos origines, *Le Débat* 15: 124–46

Dumville, D. N. 1977, Kingship, genealogies and regnal lists. In P. H. Sawyer and I. N. Wood (eds.), *Early Medieval Kingship*, University of Leeds

Duncan, A. A. M. 1975, *Scotland: the making of the kingdom*, Edinburgh

Dupin, C.-R. 1929, Une communauté familiale en Auvergne, *L'Auvergne Littéraire, Artistique et Historique* 48: 41–52

Durham, M. E. 1928, *Some Tribal Origins, Laws and Customs of the Balkans*, London

Dyer, C. 1980, *Lords and Peasants in a Changing Society: the estates of the Bishopric of Worcester 680–1540*, Cambridge

Emerton, E. (transl.) 1940, *The Letters of Saint Boniface*, New York

Esmein, A. (1891) 1919–34, *Le Mariage en droit canonique*, 2nd ed., 2 vols., Paris

Evans, J. 1969, *Life in Medieval France*, 3rd ed., London (1st ed. 1925)

Evans-Pritchard, E. E. 1940, *The Nuer: a description of the modes of livelihood and political institutions of a Nilotic people*, Oxford

Fairbanks, A. 1910, *A Handbook of Greek Religion*, New York

Faith, R. 1983, Seigneurial control of women's marriage, *Past and Present* 99: 133–48

Falletti, L. 1923, *Retrait lignager*, Paris

Faral, E. 1929, *La Légende arthurienne*, vol. I, Paris

Firth, R. 1963, Bilateral descent groups: an operational viewpoint. In I. Schapera (ed.), *Studies in Kinship and Marriage*, London

Flandrin, J.-L., 1975, *Les Amours paysannes (XVIe–XIXe siècle)*, Paris
1979 (1976), *Families in Former Times*, Cambridge

Foley, W. M. 1915, Marriage (Christian). In J. Hastings (ed.), *Encyclopaedia of Religion and Ethics*, London, 8: 433–43

Foote, P. G. and Wilson, D. M. 1980 (1970), *The Viking Achievement*, London

Fortes, M. 1945, *The Dynamics of Clanship among the Tallensi*, London
  1949, *The Web of Kinship among the Tallensi; the second part of an analysis of the social structure of a Trans-Volta tribe*, London
  1953, The structure of unilineal descent groups, *Am. Anthrop.* 55: 17–41
  1959, Descent, filiation and affinity: a rejoinder to Dr. Leach, *Man* 59: 193–7, 206–12
Fransen, G. 1970, La formation du lien matrimonial au moyen âge. In R. Metz and J. Schlick (eds.), *Le Lien matrimonial*, Strasbourg
Freeman, J. D. 1961, On the concept of the kindred, *J. R. Anthrop. Inst.* 91: 192–220
Fuller, T. 1842 (1655), *The Church History of Britain*, 3 vols., London
  1952 (1662), *The Worthies of England*, London
Furneaux, H. (ed.) 1841, *The Annals of Tacitus*, 2 vols., Oxford
Furnivall, F. J. (ed.) 1882, *The Fifty Earliest English Wills in the Court of Probate, London, A.D. 1387–1439*, Early English Text Society, vol. 78, London
  (ed.) 1897, *Child Marriages, Divorces, and Ratifications, etc. in the Diocese of Chester, A.D. 1561–6*, Early English Text Society, vol. 108, London
Gager, J. G. 1975, *Kingdom and Community: the social world of early Christianity*, Englewood Cliffs, N.J.
Galy, C. 1901, *La famille à l'époque mérovingienne*, Paris
Gaudemet, J. 1957a, *La Formation du droit séculier et du droit de l'Église aux IVe et Ve siècles*, Paris
  1957b, *L'Église dans l'Empire romain, IV–V siècles*, Paris
  1962, Les transformations de la vie familiale au Bas-Empire et l'influence du Christianisme, *Romanitas* 4: 58–85
  1980, *Sociètés et mariage*, Strasbourg
Génicot, L. 1962, La noblesse au Moyen Âge dans l'ancienne 'Francie', *Annales E.S.C.* 17: 1–22
Gerber, H. 1980, Social and economic position of women in an Ottoman city, Bursa, 1600–1700, *Int. J. Middle East Stud.* 12: 231–44
Gibbon, E. 1880 (1776), *The History of the Decline and Fall of the Roman Empire* (ed. W. Smith), 7 vols., New York
  1896–1900 (1776), *The History of the Decline and Fall of the Roman Empire* (ed. J. B. Bury), 7 vols., London
Gilby, T. (ed.) 1964, *Summa theologiae*: Latin text and English translation, introduction, notes, appendices and glossaries, 60 vols., London
Glick, T. F. 1979, *Islamic and Christian Spain in the Early Middle Ages: comparative perspectives on social and cultural formation*, Princeton
Gluckman, M. 1950, Kinship and marriage among the Lozi of Northern Rhodesia and the Zulu of Natal. In A. R. Radcliffe-Brown and D. Forde (eds.), *African Systems of Kinship and Marriage*, London
  1955, *Custom and Conflict in Africa*, Oxford
  1971, Postscript 1971 to Marriage payments and social structure among the Lozi and Zulu (1950). In J. Goody (ed.), *Kinship*, London
Godefroy, L. 1927, Le mariage au temps des Pères, art., *Dictionnaire de Théologie Catholique*, Paris, 2078–123

Goffin, R. J. 1901, *The Testamentary Executor in England and Elsewhere*, Cambridge

Goitein, S. D. 1978, *A Mediterranean Society: the Jewish communities of the Arab world as portrayed in the documents of the Cairo Geniza*, vol. III, *The Family*, Berkeley, Calif.

Goody, E. N. 1974, *Contexts of Kinship*, Cambridge
1982, *Parenthood and Social Reproduction*, Cambridge

Goody, E. N. and Goody, J. 1969, Cross-cousin marriage in northern Ghana. In J. Goody, *Comparative Studies in Kinship*, Stanford

Goody, J. 1956, *The Social Organisation of the LoWiili*, London
1957, Fields of social control among the LoDagaa, *J. R. Anthrop. Inst.* 87: 75–104
1962a, *Death, Property and the Ancestors*, Stanford
1962b, On nannas and nannies, *Man* 288
1967, The over-kingdom of Gonja. In D. Forde and P. Kaberry (eds.), *West African Kingdoms*, London
1968, Introduction to *Succession to High Office* (ed. J. Goody), Cambridge
1969, *Comparative Studies in Kinship*, Stanford
1972, The evolution of the family. In P. Laslett (ed.), *Household and Family in Past Time*, Cambridge
1973, Polygyny, economy and the role of women. In J. Goody (ed.), *The Character of Kinship*, Cambridge
1976a, Introduction to J. Goody, J. Thirsk and E. P. Thompson (eds.), *Family and Inheritance: rural society in Western Europe 1200–1800*, Cambridge
1976b, *Production and Reproduction*, Cambridge
1976c, Inheritance, property and women: some comparative considerations. In J. Goody, J. Thirsk and E. P. Thompson (eds.), *Family and Inheritance*, Cambridge
1982, *Cooking, Cuisine and Class*, Cambridge

Goody, J. and Harrison, G. A. 1976, The probability of family distributions. In J. Goody, *Production and Reproduction* (Appendix 2), Cambridge

Gough, K. 1982, *Rural Society in Southeast India*, Cambridge

Grandgent, C. H. 1908, *An Introduction to Vulgar Latin*, Boston

Gratian, 1879, Decreti Secunda pars. In *Corpus Iuris Canonici*, A. Friedberg (ed.) after Richter, A. L., Leipzig

Grimble, I. 1965, *Chief of Mackay*, London
1980, *Clans and Chiefs*, London

Guerreau-Jalabert, A. 1981, Les structures de parenté dans l'Europe médiévale, *Annales E.S.C.* 36: 1028–49

Guichard, P. 1977, *Structures sociales 'orientales' et 'occidentales' dans l'Espagne musulmane*, Paris

Habakkuk, H. J. 1955, Family structure and economic change in nineteenth-century Europe, *J. Economic Hist.* 14: 1–12

Hair, P. E. H. 1966, Bridal pregnancy in England in earlier centuries, *Population Studies* 20: 233–43
1970, Bridal pregnancy in earlier centuries further examined, *Population Studies* 24: 59–70

Hajnal, J. 1965, European marriage patterns in perspective. In D. V. Glass and D. E. C. Eversley (eds.), *Population in History*, London

Hallam, H. 1868, *View of the State of Europe during the Middle Ages*, London

Hammel, E. A. 1968, *Alternative Social Structures and Ritual Relations in the Balkans*, Englewood Cliffs, N.J.

Harnack, A. von, 1908, *The Mission and Expansion of Christianity in the First Three Centuries*, 2 vols., New York

Hartley, S. H. 1975, *Illegitimacy*, Berkeley, Calif.

Hay, W. 1967 (*c.* 1534), *William Hay's Lectures on Marriage* (transcribed, transl. and ed. by J. C. Barry), Edinburgh

Hazeltine, H. D. 1930, General Preface to D. Whitelock (ed.), *Anglo-Saxon Wills*, Cambridge

Hearne, T. 1810 (1725), *The Works of Thomas Hearne M.A. Peter Langtoft's Chronicle (as illustrated and improv'd by Robert of Brunne) from the death of Cadwalader to the end of K. Edward the First's Reign, Vol III Containing the First volume of Peter Langtoft's Chronicle*, 4 vols., London

Helmholz, R. M. 1974, *Marriage Litigation in Medieval England*, Cambridge

Henderson, E. F. (transl. and ed.) 1925, *Select Historical Documents of the Middle Ages*, London

Herbermann, C. G. *et al.*, 1907, *The Catholic Encyclopedia*, 15 vols., New York

Herlihy, D. 1961, Church property on the European continent 701–1200, *Speculum* 36: 81–105

1962, Land, family and women in Continental Europe, 701–1200, *Traditio* 18: 89–120

Herlihy, D. and Klapisch-Zuber, C. 1978, *Les Toscans et leurs familles: une étude du catasto florentin de 1427*, Paris

Hess, A. C. 1978, *The Forgotten Frontier: a history of the sixteenth-century Ibero-African frontier*, Chicago

Holles, G. 1937, *Memorials of the Holles Family, 1493–1656* (ed. A. C. Wood), Camden Soc., 3rd ser., 55, London

Holdsworth, W. S. 1903–9, *A History of English Law*, 3 vols., London

Holt, J. C. 1972, Politics and property in early medieval England, *Past and Present* 57: 3–52

Homans, G. C. 1941, *English Villagers of the Thirteenth Century*, Cambridge, Mass.

Hopkins, K. 1980, Brother/sister marriage in Roman Egypt, *Comparative Studies in Society and History* 22: 303–54, reprinted K. Hopkins, *Sociological Studies in Roman History*, vol. 3, Cambridge, forthcoming

Hoskins, W. G. 1976, *The Age of Plunder*, London

Hostetler, J. A. 1963, *Amish Society*, Baltimore

Hostetler, J. A. and Huntington, G. E. 1967, *The Hutterites in North America*, New York

Howard, G. E. 1904, *A History of Matrimonial Institutions*, 3 vols., Chicago

Howard, H. F. 1935, *An Account of the Finances of the College of St. John the Evangelist . . . Camb., 1511–1926*, Cambridge

Hughes, D. O. 1978, From brideprice to dowry in Mediterranean Europe, *Journal of Family History* 3: 262–96

Hughes, K. 1966, *The Church in Early Irish Society*, London

Hugo, A. 1835, *La France pittoresque*, 3 vols., Paris

Hurstfield, J. 1958, *The Queen's Wards: wardship and marriage under Elizabeth I*, London

Huth, A. H. 1875, *The Marriage of Near Kin*, London

Isidore 1911, *Etymologiarum Sive Originum* (ed. W. M. Lindsay), Oxford

Jenkins, D. and Owen, M. E. 1980, *The Welsh Law of Women, studies presented to Professor Daniel A. Binchy on his eightieth birthday, 3rd June, 1980*, Cardiff

Jennings, R. C. 1975, Women in early 17th-century Ottoman judicial records: the Sharia court of Anatolian Kayseri, *J. Econ. and Soc. Hist. of the Orient* 18: 53–114

John, E. 1960, *Land Tenure in Early England*, Leicester
1966, Folkland revisited, *Orbis Brittannia and Other Studies*, Leicester

Jones, A. H. M. 1963, The social background of the struggle between paganism and Christianity. In A. Momigliano (ed.), *The Conflict between Paganism and Christianity in the Fourth Century*, Oxford
1964, *The Later Roman Empire 284–602*, Oxford

Justinian 1806, *Code et novelles de Justinien; novelles de l'empéreur Leon; fragmens de Gaius, d'Ulpien et de Paul; avec le texte Latin à côté*, (transl. D. Godefroy and M. Hulot), Paris

Karnoouh, C. 1971, L'oncle et le cousin, *Études rurales* 42: 7–51

Kelly, J. 1721 *A Complete Collection of Scottish Proverbs, Explained and made Intelligible to the English Reader*, London

Kharve, I. 1953, *Kinship Organization in India* (Deccan College Monograph Series, no. II), Poona

Kindred and Affinity as Impediments to Marriage: being the report of a commission appointed by His Grace the Archbishop of Canterbury, London 1940

King, P. D. 1972, *Law and Society in the Visigothic Kingdom*, Cambridge

Knowles, D. 1940, *The Monastic Order in England*, Cambridge
1970, *Thomas Becket*, London

Kosminsky, E. A. 1956, *Studies in the Agrarian History of England in the Thirteenth Century*, Oxford

Lafont, R. 1971, *Clefs pour l'Occitanie*, Paris

Lambert, W. (ed.) 1868, *The Canons of the First Four General Councils of the Church, and those of the Early Local Greek Synods, in Greek, with Latin and Revised English Translations . . .*, London

Lancaster, L. 1958, Kinship in Anglo-Saxon society, *Brit. J. Soc.* 9: 230–50, 359–77

Larner, J. 1971, *Culture and Society in Italy 1290–1420*, London

Laslett, P. 1977, *Family Life and Illicit Love in Earlier Generations: essays in historical sociology*, Cambridge

Lea, H. C. 1867, *An Historical Sketch of Sacerdotal Celibacy in the Christian Church*, Philadelphia
1900, *The Dead Hand: a brief sketch of the relations between Church and*

State with regard to ecclesiastical property and the religious orders, Philadelphia

Leach, E. R. 1957, Aspects of bridewealth and marriage stability among the Kachin and Lakher, *Man* 57: 50–5

Le Bras, G. 1927, Mariage: la doctrine du mariage chez les théologiens et les canonistes depuis l'an mille, *Dictionnaire de Théologie Catholique* IX. ii (1927), 2123–223

Le Bras, G. 1968, Le mariage dans la théologie et le droit de l'Église du XIe au XIIIe siècle, *Cahiers de civilisation médiévale* 11: 191–202

Leclerq, J. 1979, *Monks and Love in Twelfth-Century France*, Oxford

Leeds, E. T. 1936, *Early Anglo-Saxon Art and Archaeology*, Oxford

Lehmann, H. T. (ed.) 1959, *Luther's Works*, vol. 36, *Word and Sacrament*, II, A. R.Wentz (ed.), Philadelphia

(ed.) 1962, *Luther's Works*, vol. 45 *The Christian in Society*, II, W. I. Brandt (ed.), Philadelphia

Lemaire, A. 1929, Origine de la règle 'Nullum sine dote fiat conjugium', *Mélanges Paul Fournier*, Paris

Le Roy Ladurie, E. 1972, Systême de la coutume; structures familiales et coutumes d'héritage en France au XIVe siècle, *Annales E.S.C.* 27: 825–46 (English transl. 1976, Family structures and inheritance customs in sixteenth-century France, in J. Goody, J. Thirsk and E. P. Thompson, (eds.), *Family and Inheritance: Rural Society in Western Europe 1200–1800*, Cambridge

1976, *Montaillou, village occitan de 1294 à 1324*, Paris (London, 1978)

1980, Le carré d'amour occitan, *Le Débat* 3: 62–87

Lesne, E. 1910, *Histoire de la propriété ecclésiastique en France*, vol. 1, *Epoques romaine et mérovingienne*, Lille

1922, *Histoire de la propriété ecclésiastique en France*, vol. 2, *La Propriété ecclésiastique et les droits régaliens à l'époque carolingienne* fasc. 1. *Les Étapes de la sécularisation des biens d'église du VIIIe au Xe siècle*, Lille

Lévi-Strauss, C. 1949, *Les structures élémentaires de la parenté*, Paris

Leyser, K. J. 1968, The German aristocracy from the ninth to the early twelfth century, *Past and Present* 41: 25–53

1970, Maternal kin in early medieval Germany: a reply, *Past and Present* 49: 126 34

1979, *Rule and Conflict in Early Medieval Society*, London

Lindemann, M. 1981, The regulation of wet-nursing in eighteenth-century Hamburg, *J. Family History* 6: 379–95

Lindsay, J. 1976, *The Troubadours and their World of the Twelfth and Thirteenth Centuries*, London

Lotthé, L. 1909, *Le Droit des gens mariés dans la Coutume de Flandre*, Paris

Lowie, R. H. 1928, A note on relationship terminologies, *Am. Anthrop.* 30: 265–6

Luther, Martin 1521, *De votis monasticis judicium*, Wittembergae

1896, *Luther's Primary Works* (transl. H. Wace and C. A. Buchheim), London

1967, *Works*, R. C. Schultz (ed.), Philadelphia

Lynch, J. 1980, Spiritual kinship and sexual prohibitions in early Medieval

Europe, M.S. paper presented to the Congress of Medieval Canon Law, Berkeley, Calif.

Macfarlane, A. 1970, *Witchcraft in Tudor and Stuart England*, London
1978, *The Origins of English Individualism: the family, property and social transition*, Oxford

Macgregor, A. 1907, *The Feud of the Clans, together with the history of the feuds and conflicts among the clans in the northern parts of Scotland and in the Western Isles, from the year MXXXI unto MDCXIX*, Stirling

Manning, R. (of Brunne) (1338) 1887, *The Story of England*, F. J. Furnivall (ed.), Rolls series, London

Mansi, G. D. 1759–1927, *Sacrorum Conciliorum Nova et amplissima collectio*, 56 vols., Florence, Venice, Paris, Arnheim

Margulies, C. S. 1962, The marriages and the wealth of the Wife of Bath, *Med. Studies* 24: 210–16

Martindale, J. 1977, The French aristocracy in the Early Middle Ages: a reappraisal, *Past and Present* 75: 5–45

Mattingley, H. (ed.) 1948, *Tacitus on Britain and Germany*, London

McLaren, D. 1978, Fertility, infant mortality, and breast feeding in the seventeenth century, *Medical History* 22: 378–96
1979, Nature's contraceptive. Wet-nursing and prolonged lactation; the case of Chesham, Buckingham, 1578–1601, *Medical History* 23: 426–41

Menefee, S. P. 1981, *Wives for Sale: an ethnographic study of British popular divorce*, Oxford

Meyrick, F. 1880, Prohibited degrees, art., W. Smith and S. Cheetham (eds.), *A Dictionary of Christian Antiquities*, vol. 2, London

Meyvaert, P. 1971, Bede's text of the *Libellus Responsionum* of Gregory the Great to Augustine of Canterbury. In P. Clemoes and K. Hughes (eds.), *England Before the Conquest: studies in primary sources presented to Dorothy Whitelock*, Cambridge

Middleton, R. 1962, Brother-sister and father-daughter marriage in Ancient Egypt, *Am. Soc. Rev.* 27: 603–11

Miller, E. 1951, *The Abbey and Bishopric of Ely*, Cambridge
1952, The state and landed interests in thirteenth-century France and England, *Transactions of the Royal Historical Society*, 5th Ser., 2: 109–29

Mintz, S. W. and Wolf, E. R. 1950, An analysis of ritual co-parenthood (compadrazgo), *Southwestern J. Anthropology* 6: 341–65

Mitchison, R. 1970, *A History of Scotland*, London

Mitterauer, M. and Sieder, R. 1982, *The European Family: patriarchy to partnership, 1400 to the present*, Oxford (1st German ed., 1977)

Molin, J-B. and Mutembe P. 1973, *Le Rituel du mariage en France du XIIe au XVIe siècles*, Paris

Momigliano, A. D. (ed.) 1963, *Conflict between Paganism and Christianity in the Fourth Century*, Oxford

Montagne, R. 1930, *Les Berbères et le Makhzen dans le sud du Maroc*, Paris

Monumenta Germaniae Historica, Legum Sectio II, 1883; *Capitularia Regum Francorum*, A. Boretius (ed.), 2 vols., Hannover

Moore, R. I. 1977, *The Origins of European Dissent*, London

Morris, C. 1967, William I and the Church courts, *Engl. Hist. Rev.* 82: 449–63

Morris, R. (ed.) 1874 (*c.* 1300), *Cursor Mundi (The Cursor of the World): A Northumbrian Poem of the XIVth Century*, Early English Text Society, London

Mortimer, R. C. 1940, Prohibited degrees in the Western Church. In *Kindred and Affinity as Impediments to Marriage*, London

Munch, E. (ed.) 1830, *Vollständige Sammlung aller ältern und neuern Konkordate, nebst einer Geschichte ihres Entstehens und ihrer Schicksale*, vol. 1, Leipzig

Mundy, M. W. 1979, Women's inheritance of land in highland Yemen, *Arabian Studies* 5: 161–87

Murdock, G. P. 1949, *Social Structure*, New York

Murphy, R. and Kasdan, L. 1959, The structure of parallel cousin marriage, *Am. Anthrop.* 61: 17–29

Murray, A. 1978, *Reason and Society in the Middle Ages*, Oxford

Nef, J. U. 1934, The progress of technology and the growth of larger scale industry in Great Britain, 1540–1640, *Economic History Review* 5: 3–24

1937, Prices and industrial capitalism in France and England, 1540–1640, *Economic History Review* 7: 155–85

Nelli, R. 1969, *La Vie quotidienne des Cathares du Languedoc au XIIIe siècle*, Paris

Nennius 1838, *Historia Britonum ad fidem codicum manuscriptorum recensuit Josephus Stevenson*, London

Niermeyer, J. F. (ed.), 1976, *Mediae Latinitatis Lexicon Minus*, Leiden

Noonan, J. T. 1965, *Contraception: a history of its treatment by the Catholic theologians and canonists*, Cambridge, Mass.

1972, *Power to Dissolve: lawyers and marriages in the courts of the Roman Curia*, Cambridge, Mass.

1973, The power to choose, *Viator* 4: 419–34

1977, Who was Rolandus? In K. Pennington and R. Somerville (eds.), *Law, Church and Society: essays in honour of Stephan Kuttner*, University of Pennsylvania

Ó Corráin, D. 1972, *Ireland before the Normans*, Dublin

1978, Nationality and kingship in pre-Norman Ireland. In T. W. Moody (ed.), *Nationality and the Pursuit of National Independence, Historical Studies* 11: 1–35, Belfast

Olivier-Martin, F. (ed.) 1929, *Histoire générale du droit français public et privé des origines à 1815*, Paris

Oesterlé, G. 1949, Consanguinité, art., *Dictionnaire du droit canonique*, vol. 4, Paris

O'Sullivan, J. F. 1947, *The Writings of Salvian, the Presbyter*, Washington

Pagels, E. 1980, *The Gnostic Gospels*, London

Painter, S. 1960, The family and the feudal system in twelfth-century England, *Speculum* 35: 1–16

Parker, M. 1560, *An admonicion (for the necessitie of the presente tyme tyll a furder Consultation) to all suche as shall intende hereafter to enter the state of Matrimonye godly and agreablye to lawes*, London

Patai, R. 1959, *Sex and marriage in the Bible and the Middle East*, New York
    1981, *The Vanished Worlds of Jewry*, London
Patlagean, E. 1966, Une réprésentation byzantine de la parenté et ses origines
    occidentales, *L'Homme* 6: 59–81
    1977, *Pauvreté économique et pauvreté sociale à Byzance 4e–7e siècles*, Paris
    1978, Christianisation et parentés rituelles: le domaine de Byzance, *Annales E.S.C.* 33: 625–36
Patterson, N. T. 1981, *Kinship and Law in Pre-Norman Ireland*, Ph.D. thesis,
    Harvard University
Pauli, Iulii, 1880, *Sententiarum ad Filium, Libri Quinque*. In *Institutionum et
    Regularum Iuris Romani Syntagma* (ed. R. Gneist), Leipzig
Percival, H. R. (ed.) 1900, *A Select Library of Nicene and post-Nicene Fathers
    of the Christian Church*, vol. 14, *The Seven Ecumenical Councils of the
    Undivided Church*, Oxford
Peters, E. L. 1976, Aspects of affinity in a Lebanese Maronite village. In J. G.
    Peristiany (ed.), *Mediterranean Family Structures*, Cambridge
Peters, V. 1965, *All Things in Common: the Hutterian Way of Life*, Minneapolis
Philpotts, B. S. 1913, *Kindred and Clan*, Cambridge
Pickering, D. 1763, *Statutes at Large from the thirty-second year of King
    Henry VIII to the seventh year of King Edward VI inclusive*, Cambridge
Pokorny, J. 1959–69, *Indogermanisches Etymologisches Wörterbuch*, 2 vols.,
    Bern
Pollock, F. and Maitland, F. W. 1895, *The History of English Law before the
    time of Edward I*, Cambridge
Procopius 1935, *The Anecdota or Secret History* (transl. H. B. Dewing),
    London
Raban, S. 1974, Mortmain in medieval England, *Past and Present* 62: 3–26
Radcliffe-Brown, A. R. 1924, The mother's brother in South Africa, *S. Afr. J.
    Sci.* 21: 542–55 (reprinted in *Structure and Function in Primitive Societies: essays and addresses by A. R. Radcliffe-Brown*, London, 1952)
    1940, On joking relationships, *Africa* 13: 195–210 (reprinted in *Structure
    and Function in Primitive Societies: essays and addresses by A. R. Radcliffe-Brown*, London, 1952)
    1950, Introduction to A. R. Radcliffe-Brown and C. D. Forde (eds.),
    African Systems of Kinship and Marriage, London
Raine, J. (ed.) 1845, *Depositions and other Ecclesiastical Proceedings from the
    Courts of Durham, extending from 1311 to the reign of Elizabeth*, Surtees
    Soc. Publ. vol. 21, London
    (ed.) 1850, *The Injunctions and other Ecclesiastical Proceedings of Richard
    Barnes, Bishop of Durham, from 1575 to 1587*, Surtees Soc. Publ.
    vol. 22, Durham
Razi, Z. 1980, *Life, Marriage and Death in a Medieval Parish: economy,
    society and demography in Halesowen 1270–1400*, Cambridge
    1981, Family, land and the village community in later medieval England,
    Past and Present 93: 3–36
Reich, E. 1864, *Geschichte, Natur-und Gesundheitslehre des ehelichen Lebens*,
    Cassel

Robert of Gloucester, 1887 (*c.* 1300), *The Metrical Chronicle of Robert of Gloucester* (ed. W. A. Wright), London

Robertson, A. J. 1939, *Anglo-Saxon Charters*, Cambridge

Robinson, J. (1807) 1827, *Archaeologia Graeca or the Antiquities of Greece*, London

Rosambert, A. 1923, *La Veuve en droit canonique jusqu'au XIVe siècle*, Paris

Rose, H. J. 1924, *The Roman Questions of Plutarch*, Oxford

Ruel, M. 1982, Christians as believers. In J. Davis (ed.), *Religious Organisations – Religious Experience*, London

Runciman, S. 1947, *The Medieval Manichee*, Cambridge

Russell, J. B. 1965, *Dissent and Reform in the Early Middle Ages*, Berkeley, Calif.

Sacrorum Concilium, Venice, 1773

Saint-Marty, L. 1930, *Histoire populaire du Quercy; des origines à 1800*, Cahors

Salvien de Marseille, 1971–5, *Oeuvres*, G. Lagarrigue (ed.), Paris

Scammell, J. 1974, Freedom and marriage in medieval England, *Economic History Review* 27: 523–37

Scarisbrick, J. J. 1968, *Henry VIII*, London

Schultz, F. 1951, *Classical Roman Law*, Oxford

Schaps, D. M. 1979, *Economic Rights of Women in Ancient Greece*, Edinburgh

Scott, R. F. 1906–1913, *Notes from the Records of St. John's College, Cambridge*, 3rd series, privately printed

Searle, E. 1979, Seigneurial control of women's marriage: the antecedents and function of merchet in England, *Past and Present* 82: 3–43

    1981, Women and the legitimisation of succession at the Norman Conquest. In R. A. Brown (ed.), *Proceedings of the Battle Conference on Anglo-Norman Studies*, III, 1980

Seebohm, F. 1911, *Tribal Custom in Anglo-Saxon Law*, London

Segalen, M. 1980, *Mari et femme dans la société paysanne*, Paris

Sheehan, M. M. 1963a, The influence of Canon Law on the property rights of married women in England, *Medieval Studies* 25: 109–24

    1963b, *The Will in Medieval England from the Conversion of the Anglo-Saxons to the End of the Thirteenth Century*, Toronto

    1971, The formation and stability of marriage in fourteenth century England: evidence of an Ely register, *Medieval Studies* 33: 228–63

    1974, Marriage and family in English conciliar and synodal legislation. In J. R. O'Donnell (ed.), *Essays in Honour of Anto Charles Pegis*, Toronto

    1978a, Choice of marriage partner in the middle ages: development and mode of application of a theory of marriage, *Studies in Medieval and Renaissance History* 1: 1–34

    1978b, Marriage theory and practice in the conciliar legislation and diocesan statutes of medieval England, *Medieval Studies* 40: 408–60

Sheehy, M. P. 1962, *Pontifica Hibernica: Medieval Papal Chancery Documents concerning Ireland, 640–1261*, vol. I, Dublin

Shepher, J. 1971, Mate selection among second generation Kibbutz adolescents and adults: incest avoidance and negative imprinting, *Arch. Sex. Beh.* 1: 293–307

Shorter, E. 1975, *The Making of the Modern Family*, New York

Sisam, K. 1953, Anglo-Saxon royal genealogies, *Proc. Brit. Acad.* 39: 287–348

Skene, J. 1597, *De Verborum significatione: The Exposition of The Termes And Difficill Wordes, Contained in the Foure Buikes of Regiam Majestatem*, Edinburgh

Smith, R. M. 1979, Some reflections on the evidence for the origins of the 'European marriage pattern' in England. In C. Harris (ed.), *Sociology of the Family* (Sociological Review Monograph, 28), Keele

  1981, The peoples of Tuscany and their families in the fifteenth century: medieval or Mediterranean? *J. Family History* 6: 107–28

Smout, T. C. 1969, *A History of the Scottish People, 1560–1830*, London

Snodgrass, A. M. 1974, An historical Homeric society, *J. Hellenic Studies* 94: 114–25

Sohm, R. 1875, *Das Recht der Eheschliessung*, Weimar

Solinas, P. 1977, La Famille. In F. Braudel (ed.), *La Mediterranée*, vol. 2, Paris

Stenning, D. J. 1958, Household viability among the Pastoral Fulani. In J. Goody (ed.), *The Developmental Cycle in Domestic Groups*, Cambridge

Stenton, F. M. 1947, *The English Woman in History*, London

  1971, *Anglo-Saxon England*, 3rd ed., Oxford

Stone, L. 1977, *The Family, Sex and Marriage in England 1500–1800* (abridged ed. 1979), London

Strauss, G. 1971, *Manifestations of Discontent in Germany on the Eve of the Reformation: a Collection of Documents . . .*, Bloomington, Indiana

Strype, J. 1711, *The Life and Acts of Matthew Parker, The First Archibishop of Canterbury in the Reign of Queen Elizabeth*, 4 books, London

Stubbes, P. 1877 *Anatomie of the Abuses in England in Shakespeare's Youth*, (ed. F. J. Furnivall), New Shakespeare Soc. Ser. VI, no. 4, London

Sussman, G. 1975, The wet-nursing business in nineteenth-century France, *French Historical Studies* 9: 304–28

  1977a, Parisian infants and Norman wet-nurses in the early nineteenth century, *J. Interdisciplinary History* 7: 637–53

  1977b, The end of the wet-nursing business in France, *J. Family History* 2: 237–58

Szemerényi, O. 1977, *Studies in the Kinship Terminology of the Indo-European Languages, with special reference to Indian, Iranian, Greek, and Latin, Acta Iranica, Textes et Mémoires*, vol. 7, *Varia 1977*, Teheran-Liège

Tacitus 1913, *The Annals* (transl. J. Jackson, Loeb Classical Library), Cambridge, Mass.

Tait, D. 1961, *The Konkomba of Northern Ghana*, London

Tangl, M. (ed.), 1916, *Die Briefe des Heiligen Bonifatius und Lullus*, (*Monumenta Germaniae Historica*), Berlin

Tanner, N. P. (ed.), 1977, *Reports of the Norwich Heresy Trials of Sixty Men and Women between the years 1428 and 1431,* Camden Society, London 1979, *Heresy Trials in the Diocese of Norwich 1428–1431,* Royal Historical Society, London

Tate, W. E. 1969, *The Parish Chest: a study of the records of parochial administration in England,* 3rd ed., Cambridge (1st ed. 1946)

Taviani, H. 1977, Le mariage dans l'hérésie de l'an Mil, *Annales E.S.C.* 32: 1074–89

Thomas, J. A. C. 1975, *The Institutes of Justinian: text, translation and commentary,* Cape Town

Thomas, K. 1971, *Religion and the Decline of Magic: Studies in Popular Beliefs in Sixteenth and Seventeenth Century England,* London

Thompson, E. P. 1972, 'Rough music': le Charivari anglais, *Annales E.S.C.* 27: 285–312

Thompson, F. 1973, *Lark Rise to Candleford,* London (first published 1939–43)

Thorpe, B. 1865, *Diplomatarium Anglicum Aevi Saxonici,* London

Tillion, G. 1966, *Le Harem et les cousins,* Paris

Todd, J. H. 1842, *An Apology for Lollard Doctrines,* Camden Society, London

Trevisa, J. 1872, *Polychronicon Ranulph Higden Monachi Cestrensis together with the English Translations of John Trevisa and of an unknown writer of the Fifteenth Century* (ed. Rev. J. R. Lumby), London

Turlan, J. M. 1957, Recherches sur le mariage dans la practique coutumière (XIIe–XVIe), *Rev. historique de droit français et étranger* 35: 477–528

Tylor, E. B. 1889, On a method of investigating the development of institutions; applied to laws of marriage and descent, *J. Anthrop. Inst.* 18: 245–69

Ullmann, W. 1969, *The Carolingian Renaissance and the Idea of Kingship,* London

Verriest, L. 1959, *Questions d'histoire des institutions médiévales. Noblesse, chevalerie, lignages. Conditions des biens et des personnes. Seigneurie, ministèrialités, bourgeoisie, échevinage,* Brussels

Verdier, Y. 1979, *Façons de dire, façons de faire,* Paris

Vieillard, G. 1931, Récits peuls du Macina et du Koumari, *Bull. Com. d'Ét. hist. scient. d'Afrique occidental française* 14: 137–56

Violante, C. 1977, Quelques caracteristiques des structures familiales en Lombardie, Émilie et Toscane aux XIe et XIIe siècles. In G. Duby and J. le Goff (eds.), *Famille et parenté,* pp. 87–151

Vogel, C. 1976, Les rites de la célébration du mariage: leur signification dans la formation de lien durant le haut moyen âge. In *Il matrimonio nella societa altomedievale* (Settimani di studio del centro italiano di studi sull'alto medioevo, Spoleto, 24), pp. 397–465

Vogt, J. 1963, Pagans and Christians in the family of Constantine the Great. In A. Momigliano (ed.), *The Conflict between Paganism and Christianity in the Fourth Century,* Oxford

Wace, H. and Schaff, P. (eds.) 1893, *Nicene and Post Nicene Fathers of the Christian Church,* vol. 6, *St. Jerome: Letters and Selected Works,* Oxford

Wainwright, F. T. (ed.) 1962, *The Northern Isles*, Edinburgh
Walters, D. B. 1980, The European legal context of the Welsh law of matrimonial property. In D. Jenkins and M. E. Owen (eds.), *The Welsh Law of Women*, Cardiff
Whitelock, D. (ed.) 1930, *Anglo-Saxon Wills*, Cambridge
1979, *English Historical Documents, c. 500–1042*, 2nd ed., London (1st ed. 1955)
Whitelock, D., Brett, M. and Brooke, C. N. L., (eds.) 1981, *Councils and Synods with other documents relating to the English Church*, 2 vols., vol. 1, A.D. 871–1204, part ii, 1066–1204, Oxford
Wolf, A. P. and Chieh-Shan Huang 1980, *Marriage and Adoption in China, 1845–1945*, Stanford
Wolf, E. R. 1959, *Sons of the Shaking Earth*, Chicago
Wormald, J. 1980, Bloodfeud, kindred and government in early modern Scotland, *Past and Present* 87: 54–97
Wormald, P. 1978, Bede, 'Beowulf' and the conversion of the Anglo-Saxon aristocracy. In R. T. Farrell (ed.), *Bede and Anglo-Saxon England* (British Archaeological Reports, 46), Oxford
Wrede, A. (ed.) 1901, *Deutsche Reichstagsakten: Jügere Reihe*, III, Gotha
Wrightson, K. 1982, *English Society 1580–1680*, London
Wrigley, E. A. 1969, *Population and History*, London
1978, Fertility strategy for the individual and the group. In C. Tilly (ed.), *Historical Studies of Changing Fertility*, Princeton
Wrigley, E. A. and Schofield, R. S. 1981, *The Population History of England 1541–1871: a reconstruction*, London
Wyclif, J. 1842, *An Apology for Lollard Doctrine* (ed. J. H. Todd), Camden Society, London
Wynne-Tyson, E. 1965, *Porphyry on Abstinence from Animal Food*, London
Yver, J. 1966, *Egalité entre héritiers et exclusion des enfants dotés: essai de géographie coutumière*, Paris
Zonabend, F. 1980, *La mémoire longue: temps et histoire au village*, Paris

Glossary

adrogation	the adoption of adults
affine	one related through marriage
agnate	one related through male links only
brideprice	a loose term referring to any transaction between groom and/or kin and bride and/or kin
bridewealth	the marriage payments made by the kin of the groom to the kin of the bride
clan	a unilineal descent group of widest extent, in which the most inclusive relationships are not reckoned through a genealogy
cognate	one related through either male or female links
compradrazgo	a form of 'spiritual' or ritual kinship (i.e. fictional'), uniting the parents of god-children
concubine	a second-class wife, either the junior partner to the main wife/wives or the unique partner in a secondary union (e.g. of priests)
cross-cousin	father's sister's children, mother's brother's children
endogamy	the rule of in-marriage
exogamy	the rule of out-marriage
levirate	the obligation to marry one's brother's widow (dead husband's brother) and to produce children to the dead man's name
lignage	an agnatically based group of lineal kinsfolk
lineage	a branching unilineal descent group in which ties are traced genealogically
parallel cousin	father's brother's children, mother's sister's children
polyandry	the legitimate current marriage of one woman to two or more men
polygyny	the legitimate current marriage of one man to two or more women (bigamy is the illegitimate version)
sororate	the obligation to marry the dead sister's husband (dead wife's sister)
widow inheritance	the obligation to inherit widows of close kin

Index

marriage, 185ff, 229–30; in Ethiopia, 214; *see also* Duby, G.
Lea, H. C., 80–1, 130–2, 220
Leach, E. R., 225
legacies, 89, 93, 101; restrictions on, 94
legal fictions, 47, 72, 75, 77, 100, 101
legitimacy, of bride-children, 152; of children, 76, 191ff, 205, 213, 236, 258; of children of Henry VIII, 171ff; and fornication, 174; and incest, adultery, 135; and inheritance, 205; and publicity, 151; in Scotland, 217–19; of wife, 76, 134, 169ff, 191ff, 205, 229
Leo VII, Pope (963–5), 135
Lesne, E., 100
Le Roy Ladurie, E., 15, 70, 114, 120n, 123, 248, 257
levir, 270
levirate, 36, 39, 40, 60, 63, 80, 95, 204ff; and adoption, 72; and Henry VIII, 168ff, 172; Puritans, 173; and St Basil, 40
Leviticus, 48, 50, 53, 48, 152, 168ff, 172, 174, 176ff
Lévi-Strauss, C., 43, 240
Leyser, K. J., 64, 65ff, 112n, 116, 118, 121–3, 134, 235, 268
Lex Saxonum, 65, 246–7, 249; *see also* Saxons
Libellus Responsionum, 35
lignage, 11, 16, 22, 29, 121, 222ff, 227ff, 235, 255ff; Cadolingi, 109; contracting, 145; *des frères*, 141; in northern France, 183; strengthening of, 202–3, 229, 259, 261, 264
lignée, 11, 235; lineal continuity and Church, 133
lineage, 16, 109, 202, 222ff, 227ff, 237, 255ff; agnatic, 11, 13, 233–4; segmentary, 227; strength of, 225; and terms, 263
lineal terminology, 262ff, 268, 276, 278
literate/illiterate, 193
Livy (59B.C.–A.D.17), and cousin marriage, 52
LoDagaa, 191, 225, 227, 254, 263
Lollards, 157, 162ff
Lombard code, 67n, 247, 256, 271
Lorraine, 30, 186ff
love, 9, 24, 153, 205ff, 213–14, 240; Cathars, 159; courtly, 184, 229; marriage without, 182; poetry, 28;

songs of the Troubadours, 28, 159
lust, and marriage to close kin, 57
Luther, Martin (1483–1546), on abuses, 164; on cousin marriage, 172; on dispensations, 146, 166, 181–2; on godparenthood, 198, 200; on marriage, 167, 176ff, 202; on monastic vows, 79; and the New German, 265; on parental consent, 152; on peasants, 168
Lynch, J. H., 195, 197

Macfarlane, A., 9n, 12, 27, 231
Mackays, the, 216–19
magnates, 237
mahr, 243, 255
Manichaeism, 78, 79, 85, 158–9
mantle-children, 77, 213
marriage, age at, 128, 151, 185; in Ancient Greece, 38; arranged, 206, 214 (and love); ceremony 146, 159, 174; Christian prohibition of, 55; civil, 152; close, 6, 42 (Irish), 186, 204ff; to close affines, 39; to close kin, 39, 80, 84, 182, 185, 215; companionate, 129; control of, 42, 45; delayed, 8, 47, 113, 128, 149n, 188, 189, 190, 192, 208–9; differential ages at, 128, 189; in Ethiopia, 214; indissolubility of, 134; and land, 121; licit, 147, 149, 185; of priests, 133; renunciation of, 118, 158; transactions, 23, 184, 206ff, 204ff; valid, 147, 149, 174, 185, 205; *see also* brideprice, bridewealth, dowry
marriage, 'elementary' systems of, 240; complex systems of, 241
marriage prohibitions, 48ff; to affines, 56, 80; extension of, 118; and inheritance, 56; rejection of, 158, 161–2, 163, 184; second degree, 144; within four degrees, 35, 44, 144; within seven degrees, 44, 52, 56; within seven canonical degrees, 56, 133, 135
marriage as sacrament, 59, 146, 147, 151, 165; not among Cathars, 159; Henry VIII, 172; not among Lollards, 163; Protestant view, 167
Martindale, J., 201, 229, 232, 235
mass, nuptial, 146–7

matriachal authority, 21; *see also* domestic authority
matrilineality, 13, 16, 17; and patrilineality, 27
Matthew, Gospel according to, 40, 41, 60–1, 85, 87, 92, 97
Mediterranean marriage, 166, 192, 204, 212ff, 221
Mediterranean, the two sides, 6ff, 31, 204, 210; unity of, 6, 9, 12
Mesopotamia, 15
meta, 248
microcosm/macrocosm, 175–6
military service, 120, 129ff
Miller, E., 109n, 110, 111, 119, 120n, 131
Minot (Burgundy), 187
missions, 34, 91
mistresses, 77, 134
Monaco, princely house of, 260
monasteries, conduct of, 112; dissolution of, 166, 171; endowment of, 107, 110, 113, 122; in Ethiopia, 214; income of, 127; new orders, 133
monasticism, 47; and asceticism, 78, 96–7; reaction to, 110; in Scotland, 217
monogamy, 4, 5, 11, 37, 85, 205; and concubinage, 76; in Ethiopia, 214; and marriage age, 129; and polygyny, 27
Montaigne, M. de. (1533–92), 57, 59
morganatic marriage, 243
morning gift, 110, 152n, 213, 238, 242, 247, 249, 252, 253, 254, 256
mortmain, 95, 123, 129ff, 164ff
Moses, Book of, 169ff, 176, 260
mother, unmarried, 192
mother and daughter, marriage to, in Ireland, 45
'mother's brother', 226, 229, 264
mundium, 246, 248
Mundy, M., 13

naming of children, 201, 229, 260; of husbands of heiresses, 260
nanna, 193, 272
nannying, 69, 193
nationalism and anti-clericalism, 167–8
natural, heir, 168; kin, 101; and legal, 270n; marriages, 175; milk, 69; and spiritual, 194ff, 202ff

Nelli, R., 25n, 71, 92n, 159–60
'nephew'/'neice', 265ff, 271
Nicholas II, Pope (1058–61), 135
noble and ecclesiastical models of marriage, 185; *see also* Duby, G.
nomadic tribes, 7, 17, 23, 210, 261
Norman Conquest, 22, 44, 74n, 77n, 115, 116, 125, 133, 150; and kin terms, 264ff, 277
Nuer, 21, 231, 234
nunneries, 65, 95, 97, 253; income of, 127; and land, 66
nuns, and land, 121
nuptuality, 208

oblique marriage, 49, 50 (brother's daughter), 51, 53, 55, 177, 187
one-bed households, 183
optative transmission, 123, 257
orphans, 64, 85, 95, 189
Orthodox Church, and cousin marriage, 33; and marriage of priests, 79; in Russia, 170ff
Otto I, Emperor (919–73), 109n
out-marriage, 4, 17, 20, 31ff, 57, 138, 186; and Church, 149; and dispersal, 59; and feudalism, 144; in Scotland, 217; and solidarity, 145

paintings, of Madonna and child, 153–4
Palestine, kinship, 53, 61, 63, 64, 84, 88, 155
parental agreement, 24, 25, 86, 151ff, 185, 193, 212; parental fee, 241
parents and children, 8, 13, 25, 85, 98; authority, 164; childless, 212; consent, 148, 150, 151ff, 206; and degrees, 139; and delayed marriage, 208–9; fictional, 197; and the priesthood, 81; and Protestants, 202; and retirement, 210; and sects, 90
parents' siblings, 276; unity of, 263
parity of reason, 176ff
Parker, Matthew, Archbishop (1504–75), 173ff
partibility, 118ff
pastoralists, 16, 17
Patlagean, E., 25, 39, 51, 155, 273, 274–5, 276
patria potestas, 72, 86

patriarchal authority, 21, 28, 86;
   family, 84, 88; *see also* domestic
   authority
Patrick, Saint (d. 463), 44, 62
patrifiliation, 238
patrilineality, 11, 12, 13, 17, 18, 21,
   222ff, 229, 237, 238, 267; and
   marriage, 261; patrilineal clans, 20,
   31, 210ff, 233, 262; and recruitment,
   227; terms, 265
patrimony, notional unity of, 256
patronage, of the arts, 157; of
   churches, 133; and godparenthood,
   195, 202–3; *see also* advowson, royal
patronymics, 15, 145, 202, 228, 229
Patterson, N., 29, 30n, 81
Pauline views, 46, 78, 85, 90
peasants, 189; charters, 131;
   independent, 15, 114; Luther and,
   168
pedigree, 231
Peters, E. L., 13
Plutarch (*c.* 46A.D.–*c.* 120A.D.), 51–2
polygyny, 4, 6, 11, 13, 24, 27, 41, 95,
   211–12; and adoption, 72;
   Anabaptist, 163; and concubinage,
   76, 191; and consent, 205; and
   divorce, 25; Irish, 80; and Judaism,
   80; and marriage age, 129, 189n;
   sororal, 62;
population growth, 190; and
   inheritance, 119
Porphyry (*c.* 233–304), 78n
Portugal, mortmain in, 131; terms, 266
post-partum sex taboo, 37
premier lit, 86
pre-marital cohabitation, 152; sex, 192,
   212, 258
pretium, 241, 246, 252
priests, care of, 64; class of, 78, 80; and
   inheritance, 125, 132, 165; marriage
   of, 191 (*see also* concubinage)
primogeniture, 118ff, 184, 228–9, 257
printing, 175, 176, 178 (of Table of
   Kindred and Affinity)
Procopius (*c.* 499–565), on baptism,
   195
production, modes of, 4, 203, 209, 210,
   215, 231
property, transmission of, 13, 19, 76,
   208ff, 212, 215
Production and Reproduction, 4, 7, 129,
   241, 262

Protestantism, 3, 9, 157ff; and cousin
   marriage, 33; and donations, 125,
   166; and parental agreement, 25,
   148; and prohibited degrees, 48, 152
proximity, and clanship, 224, 227; and
   degrees, 273; and kinship, 260
Puritans, and close marriage, 173
purity of family, 215

'race', 229, 230
Razi, Z., 9n, 207, 258, 278
rearing fee, 254
reforms, of eleventh century, 48, 80ff,
   107, 108, 113, 118ff, 125, 133, 135,
   152, 155, 261
registers, 152, 186, 187
'regular life', the, 133
religious belief, and the developmental
   cycle, 124
remarriage, ban on, 62, 188ff; enforced,
   66 (Saxony); restriction on, 110
rents, cash, 120
residence, post-marital, 19; and clans,
   227; and family, 26; virilocal, 19, 63
retirement, 207–9, 210
retrait lignager, 123–4, 141, 230
Robert the Pious, marriage of (996),
   135
Romance kin terms, 263, 270
Roman law, 36; adoption, 72; bequests,
   96; concubinage, 76; cousin
   marriage, 55ff; degrees, 272; divorce,
   41; incest, 39; inheritance, 272;
   marriage payments, 261; oblique
   marriage, 50; widow marriage, 60
Rome, 17, 18, 33; *campagna*, 15;
   Christian, 34; clans, 234; end of
   empire, 6, 9, 22; and Germany, 245;
   and kin terms, 263, 270; language,
   22, 34; women, 245
'rough music', 189
royal patronage, 105, 108, 110, 112;
   revenues, 111, 112, 117
rules and practice, 182, 183ff; resistance
   to rules, 183ff

Sachsenspiegel, and degrees, 136, 274
salvation, 134; and Cathars, 159–60;
   and donations, 124; and marriage,
   158
Salvian (fifth century), v, 40, 99ff, 270